CRISIS AND SURVIVAL IN LATE
MEDIEVAL IRELAND

Crisis and Survival in Late Medieval Ireland

The English of Louth and Their Neighbours, 1330–1450

BRENDAN SMITH

OXFORD
UNIVERSITY PRESS

Great Clarendon Street, Oxford, OX2 6DP,
United Kingdom

Oxford University Press is a department of the University of Oxford.
It furthers the University's objective of excellence in research, scholarship,
and education by publishing worldwide. Oxford is a registered trade mark of
Oxford University Press in the UK and in certain other countries

© Brendan Smith 2013

The moral rights of the author have been asserted

First Edition published in 2013

Impression: 1

All rights reserved. No part of this publication may be reproduced, stored in
a retrieval system, or transmitted, in any form or by any means, without the
prior permission in writing of Oxford University Press, or as expressly permitted
by law, by licence, or under terms agreed with the appropriate reprographics
rights organization. Enquiries concerning reproduction outside the scope of the
above should be sent to the Rights Department, Oxford University Press, at the
address above

You must not circulate this work in any other form
and you must impose this same condition on any acquirer

British Library Cataloguing in Publication Data
Data available

ISBN 978–0–19–959475–7

Printed and bound by
CPI Group (UK) Ltd, Croydon, CR0 4YY

Links to third party websites are provided by Oxford in good faith and
for information only. Oxford disclaims any responsibility for the materials
contained in any third party website referenced in this work.

For Annabel, Finnian, Leo, and Andrew,
and in memory of Seamus Smith (1926–2011)

Preface

My father died while I was writing this book. In the last few years of his life we would drive occasionally through north county Dublin and Meath, avoiding the motorway, to cross the Boyne into Louth at Oldbridge and King William's Glen. Wending our way over the Sliabh Beagh hills, with their remarkable views of the plains of Meath to the west and the Irish Sea to the east, we would criss-cross the county before finishing with a fine meal at the Monasterboice Inn. If the weather was good, reminders of our trip would await us on our return to Howth, since from its summit we could see to the north the heights of the Cooley peninsula, and behind them again the mountains of Mourne. The Louth–Meath connection started a long time ago: to afford my mother occasional respite from child-rearing, my father would bundle his offspring into the car and we would be shown the glories of the Boyne valley. Often such trips would end with a visit to the relics of St (then Blessed) Oliver Plunkett, archbishop of Armagh, at St Peter's church in Drogheda. That more than forty years later I should be writing about Drogheda, Louth, Plunkets, and archbishops of Armagh amused my father to the end.

I am grateful to past and present commissioning editors at Oxford University Press for inviting me to write this book and seeing it through the publication process. Rupert Cousens, Stephanie Ireland, Cathryn Steele, Emma Barber, and Christopher Wheeler deserve my special thanks, as do the proofing team. Dr Paul Glennie of the Department of Geography at the University of Bristol put me in contact with Mr Simon Powell who demonstrated not only skill but great patience in constructing the maps. My thanks to them both, and to Dr Evan Jones who helped with the design of the tables. The permission of the Director of the National Museum of Ireland to reproduce the cover image is gratefully acknowledged.

My thanks are due to the anonymous readers of the initial book proposal and then the draft itself for their very helpful comments and advice. I would like to thank the staff at the various libraries and archives at which the research for this book was carried out. Mr Robert Yorke, archivist at the College of Arms, now retired, remembered Professor Otway-Ruthven consulting material in the College, which was a reassuring link with the past. Dr James Ross at The National Archives (Kew), Dr Aideen Ireland of the National Archives of Ireland, and Dr Julian Harrison of the British Library all helped me track down material which I would otherwise have missed. It was a special privilege to be shown around the Venerable English College in Rome, which occupies the site of medieval pilgrim hospital of St Thomas of Canterbury, by its Rector, Mgr Nicholas Hudson.

The friendship and advice of two colleagues at Bristol, Dr Ian Wei and Dr Kieran Flanagan, are recorded with special gratitude. The University of Bristol awarded me a Research Fellowship to allow for the completion of the book, and I am particularly grateful to Professor Ronald Hutton and Professor Roger Middleton for their support. Encouraging words at various times from Professor Jim Lydon,

Professor Robin Frame, Professor Steven Ellis, and Professor Seymour Phillips helped greatly in finishing this project. Dr Chiara Buldorini, Dr Sparky Booker, and Dr Peter Crooks gave me access to their unpublished Ph.D. theses, and Dr Crooks also allowed me early sight of the wonderful 'Calendar of Irish Chancery Letters [CIRCLE]' website which he worked so hard to complete. Dr Elizabeth Matthew, Professor Chris Given-Wilson, and Dr Colmán Ó Clabaigh OSB read drafts of the proposal and individual chapters and saved me from many errors. My greatest debt in this regard is to Dr Katharine Simms, who in a typically generous manner read the entire book in draft.

My greatest personal debt is to my wife, Annabel, for support in so many ways. As a journalist she even offered to sprinkle her 'fairy dust' over my prose—an offer which the reader may conclude I was foolish to decline.

Bristol
Summer 2012

Contents

List of Maps   x
List of Tables   xi
List of Abbreviations   xii

Introduction   1

I. CRISIS AND SURVIVAL

1. False Dawn: 1330–1369   25
2. Friends Like These: William Windsor and Edmund Mortimer, 1369–1381   51
3. Richard II and his Legacy, 1382–1405   76
4. 'The Poor Commons', 1405–1450   107

II. SETTLER SOCIETY

5. The Church   135
6. The Towns   159
7. The Marches   183

Conclusion   211

Bibliography   221
Index   243

List of Maps

1. Louth and adjacent parts   xviii
2. Louth and Ireland   24
3. Louth connections beyond Ireland   75
4. Religious houses in Louth   134
5. The Irish in Louth   193
6. The marches of Louth and Meath and neighbouring Irish lordships   210

List of Tables

1. Sheriffs and keepers of the peace to 1450 — 15
2. The Verdon family in Louth and Meath — 19
3. Parish church dedications in late medieval Louth — 198
4. Succession to Irish lordships adjacent to Louth — 217

List of Abbreviations

AC	*The Annals of Connacht*, ed. A. M. Freeman (Dublin, 1944)
Account Roll of Holy Trinity, Dublin	*Account Roll of the Priory of the Holy Trinity, Dublin, 1337–1346*, ed. J. Mills (Dublin, 1891)
A. Clon.	*The Annals of Clonmacnoise*, ed. D. Murphy (Dublin, 1896; repr. Llanerch, 1983)
Acts of Colton	*Acts of Archbishop Colton in his Metropolitical Visitation of the Diocese of Derry*, ed. William Reeves. Irish Archaeological Society (Dublin, 1850)
Admin. Ire.	H. G. Richardson and G. O. Sayles, *The Administration of Ireland, 1172–1377*. Irish Manuscripts Commission (Dublin, 1963)
AFM	*Annála Ríoghachta Éireann: Annals of the Kingdom of Ireland by the Four Masters from the Earliest Period to the Year 1616*, ed. and tr. John O'Donovan, 7 vols (Dublin, 1851; 3rd edn, 1990)
Aithdioghluim Dána	*Aithdioghluim Dána: A Miscellany of Irish Bardic Poetry, Historical and Religious, including the Historical Poems of the Duanaire in the Yellow Book of Lecan*, ed. and tr. Lambert McKenna SJ, 2 vols. Irish Texts Society (Dublin, 1939–40)
Alen's Reg.	*Calendar of Archbishop Alen's Register, c.1172–1534*, ed. Charles Mac Neill. Royal Society of Antiquaries of Ireland (Dublin, 1950)
Anal. Hib.	*Analecta Hibernica, Including the Reports of the Irish Manuscripts Commission* (Dublin, 1930–)
'Ancient Deeds'	'Calendar of Documents Relating to Medieval Ireland in the Series of Ancient Deeds in the National Archives of theUnited Kingdom', ed. Paul Dryburgh and Brendan Smith, *Anal. Hib.* 39 (2006), 1–61
AU	*Annála Uladh, Annals of Ulster*, ed. W. M. Hennessy and B. Mac Carthy, 4 vols (Dublin 1887–1901; 2nd edn, 1998)
bar.	Barony
Betham, *Origin and History*	William Betham, *The Origin and History of the Constitution of England and of the Early Parliaments of Ireland* (Dublin, 1834)
BL	British Library
Cal. Carew Mss.	*Calendar of the Carew Manuscripts Preserved in the Archiepiscopal Library at Lambeth, 1515–74*, ed. J. S. Brewer and W. Bullen, 6 vols (London, 1867–73)

CCR	*Calendar of Close Rolls* (London, 1892–)
CDI	*Calendar of Documents Relating to Ireland*, ed. H. S. Sweetman, 5 vols (London, 1875–86)
CFR	*Calendar of Fine Rolls* (London, 1911–)
Chartul. St Mary's, Dublin	*Chartularies of St Mary's Abbey, Dublin ... and Annals of Ireland, 1162–1370*, ed. J. T. Gilbert. 2 vols. Rolls Series (London, 1884–6)
Christ Church Deeds	*Christ Church Deeds*, ed. M. J. McEnery and Raymond Refaussé (Dublin, 2001)
CJR	*Calendar of Justiciary Rolls*, 3 vols (Dublin, 1905–)
CLAJ	*Journal of the County Louth Archaeological and Historical Society*
Clarke, 'William of Windsor in Ireland'	Maude V. Clarke, 'William of Windsor in Ireland, 1369–1376', *PRIA* 41 (1932–4), C, 55–130
Clyn	*The Annals of Ireland by Friar John Clyn*, ed. Bernadette Williams (Dublin, 2007)
COA	College of Arms, London
COA Rep. Records of the Exchequer, 42–51 Edward III	Betham. Repertory to Records of the Exchequer, i. 42 Edward III—51 Edward III
COA Rep. Records of the Exchequer, 1–10 Richard II	Betham. Repertory to Records of the Exchequer, ii. 1 Richard II to 10 Richard II
COA Rep. Records of the Exchequer, 10–22 Richard II	Betham. Reportory to Records of the Exchequer, iii. 10 Richard II to 22 Richard II
COA Rep. Records of the Exchequer, Henry IV	Betham. Repertory to Records of the Exchequer, iv. Henry IV
COA Rep. Records of the Exchequer, 1 Henry V–39 Henry VI	Betham. Repertory to Records of the Exchequer, v. I Henry V–39 Henry VI
COD	*Calendar of Ormond Deeds, 1172–1603*, ed. Edmund Curtis, 6 vols. Irish Manuscripts Commission (Dublin, 1932–43)
Connolly, 'Ancient Petitions'	'Irish Materials in the Class of Ancient Petitions (SC 8) in the Public Record Office, London', ed. Philomena Connolly, *Anal. Hib.* 34 (1987), 1–106
Connolly, 'List of Irish Material ... (C. 260)'	'List of Irish Material in the Class of Chancery Files (Recorda) (C. 260) Public Record Office, London', ed. Philomena Connolly, *Anal. Hib.* 31 (1984), 3–18
CPI	*Chartae, Privilegia, et Immunitates* (London, 1889)
CPL	*Calendar of Entries in the Papal Registers Relating to Great Britain and Ireland: Papal Letters* (London, 1893–)
CPR	*Calendar of Patent Rolls* (London, 1891–)
Curtis, *Richard II in Ireland*	Edmund Curtis, *Richard II in Ireland, 1394–5, and the Submissions of the Irish Chiefs* (Oxford, 1927)

Davies, *Lords and Lordship*	R. R. Davies, *Lords and Lordship in the British Isles in the Late Middle Ages*, ed. Brendan Smith (Oxford, 2009)
De Annatis Hiberniae	*De Annatis Hiberniae: A Calendar of the First Fruits' Fees Levied on Papal Appointments to Benefices in Ireland ad 1400 to 1535*, ed. M. A. Costello OP (Dundalk, 1909)
Dowdall Deeds	*Dowdall Deeds*, ed. C. McNeill and A. J. Otway-Ruthven. Irish Manuscripts Commission (Dublin, 1960)
Dowling	*The Annals of Ireland by Friar John Clyn and Thady Dowling*, ed. Richard Butler (Dublin, 1849)
EHR	*English Historical Review*
Facs. Nat. MSS Ire.	*Facsimiles of the National Manuscripts of Ireland*, ed. J. T. Gilbert, 4 vols (Dublin, 1874–84)
Frame, *English Lordship in Ireland*	Robin Frame, *English Lordship in Ireland, 1318–1361* (Oxford, 1982)
Frame, *Ireland and Britain*	Robin Frame, *Ireland and Britain, 1170–1450* (London, 1998)
Frame, 'Commissions of the Peace'	Robin Frame, 'Commissions of the Peace in Ireland, 1302–1461', *Anal. Hib.* 35 (1992), 3–43
Gormanston Reg.	*Calendar of the Gormanston Register*, ed. James Mills and M. J. McEnery (Dublin, 1916)
Griffith, 'Talbot–Ormond Struggle'	Margaret C. Griffith, 'The Talbot–Ormond Struggle for Control of the Anglo-Irish Government, 1414–47', *IHS* 2 (1941), 376–97
Gwynn and Hadcock, *Medieval Religious Houses Ireland*	Aubrey Gwynn and R. Neville Hadcock, *Medieval Religious Houses Ireland* (London, 1970; repr. Dublin, 1988)
Handbook and Select Calendar … Ireland	*Handbook and Select Calendar of Sources for Medieval Ireland in the National Archives of the United Kingdom*, ed. Paul Dryburgh and Brendan Smith. The National Archives (Dublin, 2005)
'Henry Marleburrough's Chronicle of Ireland'	'Henry Marleburrough's Chronicle of Ireland', in *The Historie of Ireland*, ed. Meredith Hanmer, Edmund Campion, and Edmund Spencer (Dublin, 1633)
Hogan, *Priory of Llanthony*	Arlene Hogan, *The Priory of Llanthony Prima and Secunda in Ireland, 1172–1541: Lands, Patronage and Politics* (Dublin, 2008)

IEP	*Irish Exchequer Payments, 1270–1446*, ed. Philomena Connolly. Irish Manuscripts Commission (Dublin, 1998)
Inquisitions and Extents	*Inquisitions and Extents of Medieval Ireland*, ed. Paul Dryburgh and Brendan Smith. List and Index Society, 320 (Kew, 2007)
'Lord Chancellor Gerrard's Notes on his Report on Ireland'	'Lord Chancellor Gerrard's Notes on his Report on Ireland', ed. C. McNeill, *Anal. Hib.* 2 (1931), 93–291
Lynch, *View of the Legal Institutions*	William Lynch, *A View of the Legal Institutions, Honorary Hereditary Offices, and Feudal Baronies, Established in Ireland during the Reign of Henry the Second* (London, 1830)
Mac Firbis, *Annals*	'Annals of Ireland from the Year 1443 to 1468 Translated from the Irish by Dudley Firbissse, or as he is More Usually Called, Duald Mac Firbis, for Sir James Ware, in the Year 1666', ed. John O'Donovan, in *Miscellany of the Irish Archaeological Society*, i (Dublin, 1846), 198–302
MacLysaght, *Irish Families*	Edward MacLysaght, *Irish Families: Their Names, Arms and Origins* (Dublin, 1957)
Misc. Ir. Annals	*Miscellaneous Irish Annals (ad 1114–1447)*, ed. Séamus Ó hInnse (Dublin, 1947)
NAI	National Archives of Ireland
NHI i	*A New History of Ireland*, i. *Prehistoric and Early Ireland*, ed. Dáibhí Ó Cróinín (Oxford, 2008)
NHI ii	*A New History of Ireland*, ii. *Medieval Ireland 1169–1534*, ed. Art Cosgrove (Oxford, 1987)
NHI ix	*A New History of Ireland*, ix. *Maps, Genealogies, Lists*, ed. T. W. Moody, F. X. Martin, and F. J. Byrne (Oxford, 1989)
NLI	National Library of Ireland
Ó Clabaigh, *Friars in Ireland*	Colmán Ó Clabaigh, OSB, *The Friars in Ireland, 1224–1540* (Dublin, 2012)
Original Letters	*Original Letters Illustrative of English History, Including Numerous Royal Letters*, ed. H. Ellis, 2nd ser., 4 vols (London, 1827)
Otway-Ruthven, 'Partition of the de Verdon Lands'	A. J. Otway-Ruthven, 'The Partition of the de Verdon Lands in Ireland in 1332', *PRIA* 66 (1968), C, 401–55
Oxford Dictionary of National Biography (Oxford, 2004)	H. D. G. Matthew and Brian Harrison (eds), *Oxford Dictionary of National Biography* (Oxford, 2004); online version at <http://www.oxforddnb.com/>

Parls. & Councils	*Parliaments and Councils of Mediaeval Ireland*, i, ed. H. G. Richardson and G. O. Sayles. Irish Manuscripts Commission (Dublin, 1947)
PICHC	*Proceedings of the Irish Catholic Historical Committee*
PKCI	*A Roll of the Proceedings of the King's Council in Ireland for a Portion of the Sixteenth Year of the Reign of Richard the Second, AD 1392–93*, ed. James Greaves (London, 1877)
PRIA	*Proceedings of the Royal Irish Academy*
Proceedings and Ordinances	*Proceedings and Ordinances of the Privy Council of England*, ed. N. H. Nicolas, 7 vols (London, 1834–7)
PROME	*The Parliament Rolls of Medieval England, 1275–1504*, ed. Chris Given-Wilson (gen. ed.) *et al.*, 16 vols (Woodbridge, 2005)
RCH	*Rotulorum Patentium et Clausorum Cancellariae Hiberniae Calendarium*, ed. E. Tresham (Dublin, 1828)
Rec. Comm. Ire. Rep., 1811–15	*Reports of the Commissioners Appointed by His Majesty to Execute the Measures Recommended in an Address of the House of Commons Respecting the Public Records of Ireland; with Supplement and Appendixes*, 3 vols (London, 1815–25), i, rep. 1–5 (1811–15)
Reg. Fleming	*The Register of Nicholas Fleming, Archbishop of Armagh 1404–1416*, ed. Brendan Smith. Irish Manuscripts Commission (Dublin, 2003)
Reg. Kilmainham	*Registrum de Kilmainham*, ed. C. McNeill. Irish Manuscripts Commission (Dublin, 1932)
Reg. Mey	*Registrum Johannis Mey: The Register of John Mey Archbishop of Armagh, 1443–1456*, ed. W. G. H. Quigley and E. F. D. Roberts (Belfast, 1972)
Reg. Octaviani	*Registrum Octaviani, alias Liber Niger: The Register of Octavian de Palatio, Archbishop of Armagh 1478–1513*, ed. Mario Alberto Sughi, 2 vols. Irish Manuscripts Commission (Dublin, 1999)
Reg. St John, Dublin	*Register of the Hospital of St John the Baptist Without the Newgate, Dublin*, ed. E. St John Brooks. Irish Manuscripts Commission (Dublin, 1936)
Reg. Swayne	*The Register of John Swayne, Archbishop of Armagh and Primate of Ireland 1418–1439*, ed. D. A. Chart (Belfast, 1935)
Reg. Sweteman	*The Register of Milo Sweteman, Archbishop of Armagh 1361–1380*, ed. Brendan Smith. Irish Manuscripts Commission (Dublin, 1996)
Rep.	Repertory to
Rep. DKI	*Reports of the Deputy Keeper of the Public Records of Ireland* (Dublin, 1869–)
RIA	Royal Irish Academy
Richardson and Sayles, Irish Parliament	H. G. Richardson and G. O. Sayles, *The Irish Parliament in the Middle Ages* (Philadelphia, 1964)

Rotuli Selecti	*Rotuli Selecti ad Res Anglicas et Hibernicas Spectantes, ex Archivis in Domo Capitulari Westmonasteriensi, Deprompti*, ed. Joseph Hunter (London, 1834)
Rymer, *Foedera*	*Foedera, Conventiones, Litterae et cuiuscunque Generis Acta Publica*, ed. Thomas Rymer, 20 vols (London, 1704–35)
Sayles, *Affairs*	*Documents on the Affairs of Ireland before the King's Council*, ed. G. O. Sayles. Irish Manuscripts Commission (Dublin, 1979)
SHR	*Scottish Historical Review*
Smith, *Colonisation and Conquest*	Brendan Smith, *Colonisation and Conquest in Medieval Ireland: The English in Louth, 1170–1330* (Cambridge, 1999)
Stat. Ire., Hen. VI	*Statute Rolls of the Parliament of Ireland, Reign of King Henry VI*, ed. Henry F. Berry (Dublin, 1910)
Stat. Ire., John–Hen. V	*Statutes and Ordinances and Acts of the Parliament of Ireland, King John to Henry V*, ed. Henry F. Berry (Dublin, 1907)
Statutes of the Realm	*Statutes of the Realm*, ed. A. Luders, T. E. Tomlins, and J. Raithby, 11 vols (London, 1810–28)
TNA	The National Archives: Public Record Office, London
TRHS	*Transactions of the Royal Historical Society*
Vetera Monumenta	*Vetera Monumenta Hibernorum et Scotorum Historiam Illustrantia*, ed. A. Theiner (Rome, 1864)

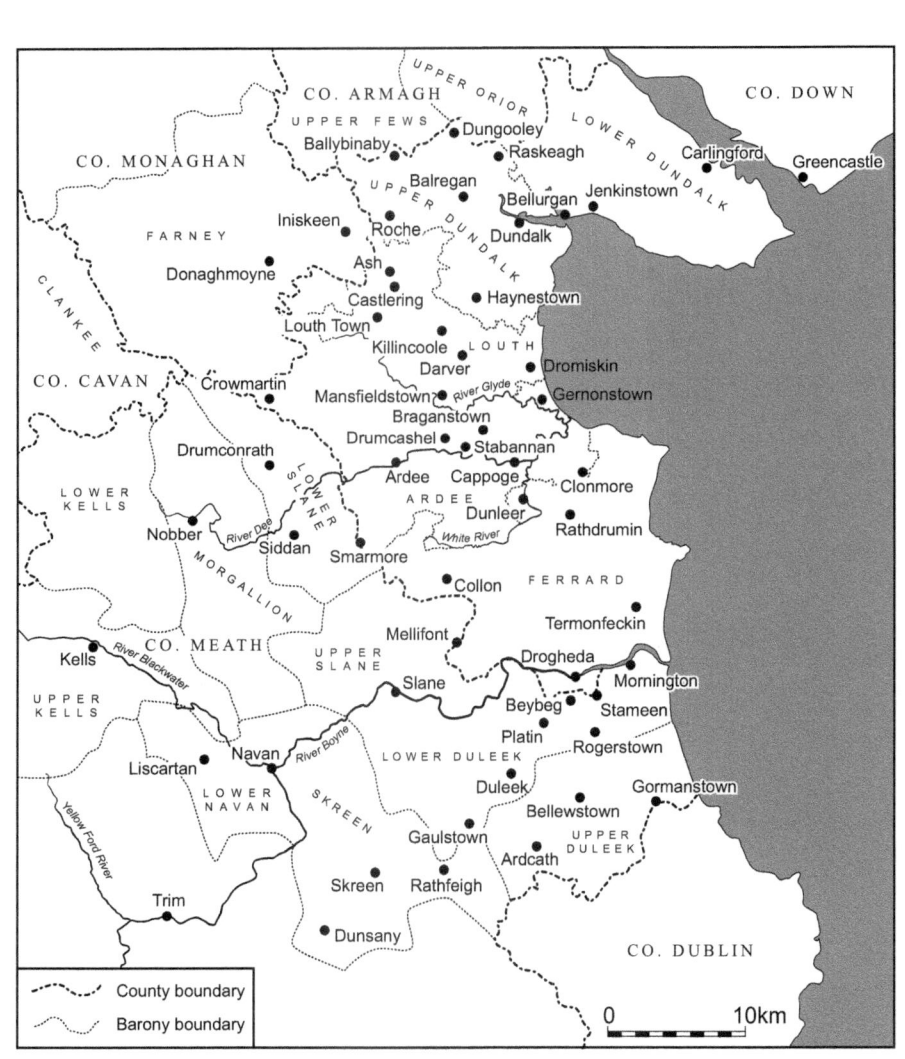

Map 1. Louth and adjacent parts

Introduction

> There is not a place of splendour or a dark corner of the earth that does not deserve, if only a passing glance of wonder and pity.
>
> (Joseph Conrad, preface to *The Nigger of the 'Narcissus'*, 1897)

Local studies have long been recognized by historians as providing rich opportunities to engage with the medieval past. Ireland is particularly well placed to benefit from this approach, since in the late Middle Ages its politics was highly regionalized and it lacked a central authority that came close to exerting authority throughout the entire island. A significant moment in modern scholarship on north-west Europe in the Middle Ages was the publication in 1953 of Georges Duby's *La société aux XIe et XIIe siècles dans la région mâconnaise*, which advocated new approaches to the study of historical communities and inspired many subsequent investigations into regional society in France and beyond.[1] For the study of English political society in the late Middle Ages, 1953 was also a momentous year, since it witnessed the delivery by K. B. MacFarlane of the Ford lectures at Oxford that were eventually to be published in 1973 as *The Nobility of Later Medieval England*.[2] Although concerned with different periods of time and different countries, Duby and McFarlane had in common a willingness to incorporate previously unused or underused original source material in their work, and to subject well-known historical material to vigorous and fruitful re-examination. The study offered here of how society developed in one small part of late medieval Ireland has been shaped by the scholarship inspired by these insights.

McFarlane's new approach to the nobility led to reconsideration of the nature of the local societies in which the magnates exercised their power and from which they drew their wealth and political support.[3] His doctoral student, Rees Davies, demonstrated just how fruitful such an approach could be in his pioneering study

---

[1] For 'the wave of Duby-inspired medieval social history, regionally defined and rurally focused, that followed' publication of the book: Frederic L. Cheyette, 'Georges Duby's *Mâconnais* After Fifty Years: Reading it Then and Now', *Journal of Medieval History*, 28 (2002), 291–317.

[2] The impact of McFarlane's work is discussed in R. H. Britnell and A. J. Pollard (eds), *The McFarlane Legacy: Studies in Late Medieval Politics and Society* (Stroud, 1995).

[3] An important work from the 1960s that addresses the issues raised by both Duby and McFarlane is Rodney H. Hilton, *A Medieval Society: The West Midlands at the End of the Thirteenth Century* (Cambridge, 1966, 2nd edn 1983). See also Christopher Dyer, Peter Coss, and Chris Wickham (eds), *Rodney Hilton's Middle Ages: An Exploration of Historical Themes* (Oxford, 2007).

of the society of the Welsh March in the late thirteenth and fourteenth centuries.[4] Davies's book, published in 1978, marked the beginning of a period of roughly fifteen years in which a series of studies of particular localities transformed understanding of the nature of politics and society in late medieval England. Whereas the focus of Davies's study had been a number of contiguous lordships held by great men with possessions elsewhere in England, the unit of investigation favoured by most scholars at this time was the county. Monographs by Nigel Saul on Gloucestershire and Sussex, and by Paul Booth and Philip Morgan on Cheshire, concentrated on the fourteenth century, while Michael Bennett's study of Cheshire and Lancashire was concerned with the half-century between 1375 and 1425.[5] The fifteenth-century Midlands drew particular attention: Derbyshire was the subject of a 1983 monograph by Susan Wright, while the early 1990s witnessed the publication of exhaustive treatments of Leicestershire by Eric Acheson, Nottinghamshire by Simon Payling, and Warwickshire by Christine Carpenter.[6] More recently, the continuing value of county-based studies with a medieval focus has been demonstrated in a superb monograph on Suffolk and a valuable collection of essays on Kent.[7]

The county, however, did not enjoy a monopoly of scholarly interest in the re-examination of how political society operated in late medieval England. Parts of the country such as East Anglia and the far North were seen to have a natural, regional, unity that transcended the county boundaries contained within them.[8]

---

[4] R. R. Davies, *Lordship and Society in the March of Wales, 1282–1400* (Oxford, 1978). For the development of Davies's doctoral thesis into this book and other works: Huw Pryce, 'Robert Rees Davies, 1938–2005', *Proceedings of the British Academy*, 161 (2009), 135–55, esp. 142–3.

[5] Nigel Saul, *Knights and Esquires: The Gloucestershire Gentry in the Fourteenth Century* (Oxford, 1981); Nigel Saul, *Scenes from Provincial Life: Knightly Families in Sussex, 1280–1400* (Oxford, 1986); Paul H. W. Booth, *The Financial Administration of the Lordship and County of Chester, 1272–1377* (Manchester, 1981); Philip Morgan, *War and Society in Medieval Cheshire, 1277–1403* (Manchester, 1987); Michael J. Bennett, *Community, Class and Careerism: Cheshire and Lancashire Society in the Age of Sir Gawain and the Green Knight* (Cambridge, 1983).

[6] Susan M. Wright, *The Derbyshire Gentry in the Fifteenth Century* (Chesterfield, 1983); Eric Acheson, *A Gentry Community: Leicestershire in the Fifteenth Century, c.1422–c.1485* (Cambridge, 1992); Simon Payling, *Political Society in Lancastrian England: The Greater Gentry in Nottinghamshire* (Oxford, 1991); Christine Carpenter, *Locality and Polity: A Study of Warwickshire Landed Society, 1401–1499* (Cambridge, 1992). Staffordshire and Shropshire provided the geographical focus for an important study of relations between crown and locality in the early 15th cent.: Edward Powell, *Kingship, Law and Society: Criminal Justice in the Reign of Henry V* (Oxford, 1989).

[7] Mark Bailey, *Medieval Suffolk: An Economic and Social History 1200–1500* (Woodbridge, 2007); Sheila Sweetinburgh (ed.), *Later Medieval Kent, 1220–1540* (Woodbridge, 2010).

[8] Philippa C. Maddern, *Violence and Social Order: East Anglia 1422–1442* (Oxford, 1992); Christopher Harper-Bill (ed.), *Medieval East Anglia* (Woodbridge, 2005); Anthony Goodman and Anthony Tuck (eds), *War and Border Societies in the Middle Ages* (London, 1992); John C. Appleby and Paul Dalton (eds), *Government, Religion and Society in Northern England 1000–1700* (Stroud, 1997); Cynthia J. Neville, *Violence, Custom and Law: The Anglo-Scottish Border Lands in the Later Middle Ages* (Edinburgh, 1998); Christian D. Liddy and Richard H. Britnell (eds), *North-East England in the Later Middle Ages* (Woodbridge, 2005); M. L. Holford and K. J. Stringer (eds), *Border Liberties and Loyalties: North-East England, c.1200–c.1400* (Edinburgh, 2010). Given its links to Ireland, it is unfortunate that south-west England has not been subjected to similar examination. Some relevant work is cited in Brendan Smith, 'Late Medieval Ireland and the English Connection: Waterford and Bristol, ca. 1360–1460', *Journal of British Studies*, 50 (2011), 546–65.

Furthermore, the study of individual magnates and magnate families, which proceeded in parallel with the growth of interest in county studies, afforded insights into the nature of late medieval English political society that at times sat awkwardly with the picture presented in some county-based analyses.[9] The need to combine examinations of how political authority was exercised in particular localities with an appreciation that the power and influence of particular noble families knew no county boundaries and might be exercised in several different parts of late medieval England at the same time was argued in important essays by Christine Carpenter in 1994 and by Gerald Harriss in 1993 and 1995.[10] Already, in 1990, Simon Walker—a doctoral student of Harriss's—had pointed the way forward in a study that examined the relationship of the dukes of Lancaster in the late fourteenth century with the political elites of the counties of Lancashire, Sussex, and the north Midlands from which they drew their most important supporters.[11] One of Carpenter's doctoral students, Helen Castor, subsequently picked up this baton and produced an intriguing study of how these and other counties fared after 1399 when their Lancastrian lords also sat on the throne of England.[12] It is on the basis of work of this sort that sophisticated and convincing accounts have been put forward in recent years by Harriss, Carpenter, and others that explain the nature of late medieval English political society in terms of the relationship—often mutually supportive but occasionally competitive and violent—between royal government, the nobility, and the local 'gentry' elites.[13] Just as such insights should help to shape the approach of historians to late medieval Ireland, so the Irish experience can enrich understanding of how political society operated in the several parts of north-west Europe dominated by English ways and English laws.

In Ireland, a strong tradition of interest in local history has borne fruit in the publications of county and diocesan history societies, and the quantity of fine scholarship contained therein on the medieval history of particular localities has been supplemented since 1975 by chapters on the Middle Ages in the county

---

[9] For the period covered by this book: Kenneth A. Fowler, *The King's Lieutenant: Henry of Grosmont, First Duke of Lancaster 1310–1361* (London, 1969); Carole Rawcliffe, *The Staffords: Earls of Stafford and Dukes of Buckingham 1394–1521* (Cambridge, 1978); Barry Coward, *The Stanleys, Lords Stanley and Earls of Derby 1385–1672* (Manchester, 1983); Anthony Goodman, *John of Gaunt: The Exercise of Princely Power in Fourteenth-Century Europe* (Harlow, 1992). The nature of magnate power in the localities is explored in Chris Given-Wilson, *The English Nobility in the Late Middle Ages* (London, 1996).

[10] Christine Carpenter, 'Gentry and Community in Medieval England', *Journal of British Studies*, 33 (1994), 340–80; Gerald Harriss, 'Political Society and the Growth of Government in Late Medieval England', *Past and Present*, 138 (1993), 28–57; G. L. Harriss, 'The Dimensions of Politics', in Britnell and Pollard, *McFarlane Legacy*, 1–20.

[11] Simon Walker, *The Lancastrian Affinity 1361–1399* (Oxford, 1990).

[12] Helen Castor, *The King, the Crown, and the Duchy of Lancaster: Public Authority and Private Power, 1399–1461* (Oxford, 2000).

[13] Philip Morgan, 'The Ranks of Society', and Anthony Goodman, 'Kingship and Government', both in Ralph Griffiths (ed.), *The Fourteenth and Fifteenth Centuries* (Oxford, 2003), 59–85 and 183–215; Christine Carpenter, 'England: The Nobility and the Gentry', in S. H. Rigby (ed.), *A Companion to Britain in the Later Middle Ages* (Oxford, 2003), 261–82; Gerald Harriss, *Shaping the Nation: England 1360–1461* (Oxford, 2005), part I: Political Society.

'History and Society' volumes produced by Geography Publications.¹⁴ The nineteenth and early twentieth centuries were a rich period for the publication of local history monographs in Ireland, and parts of Louth and surrounding areas were the subjects of full-length studies that continue to be of value to the medievalist.¹⁵ Several recent monographs covering a slightly later period of Irish history than that with which this book is concerned demonstrate a new vitality in the scholarly examination of local societies and suggest approaches that can be profitably followed by medieval historians.¹⁶ The fourteenth and fifteenth centuries are included in recent studies of the Gaelic lordships of Leinster and west Cork by Emmett O'Byrne and Colin Breen respectively, while understanding of the economic and social structures of parts of Ireland heavily settled by the English has been advanced in the last ten years by impressive studies of Trim and the Dublin region.¹⁷ In a scholarly career spanning four decades, Robin Frame has reshaped our perception of the nature of English rule and English society in late medieval Ireland. While his analysis acknowledges the highly regionalized nature of the country and its politics, it also stresses that power in the Lordship was shared and exercised by officers of the crown, the nobility, and local elites in an arrangement which in general outline, if not in detail, should appear familiar to students of late medieval political society in England itself.¹⁸ Frame's insight, that Ireland was part of a larger 'English world' that at times in the late Middle Ages encompassed the entire British Isles and large parts of France, is beginning to bear fruit in studies that recognize that 'Englishness' and English political culture did not end at the borders of England.¹⁹

It is hoped that the examination of the politics of an Irish county and the territories that adjoined it presented here will add to understanding both of Ireland and

---

¹⁴ The twenty-first History and Society vol., concerned with Co. Longford, was publ. in 2010.

¹⁵ John Dalton, *The History of Drogheda with its Environs; and an Introductory Memoir of the Dublin and Drogheda Railway*, 2 vols (Dublin, 1844); E. P. Shirley, *The History of the County of Monaghan* (London, 1879); James B. Leslie, *History of Kilsaran* (Dundalk, 1908).

¹⁶ David Edwards, *The Ormond Lordship in County Kilkenny, 1515–1642: The Rise and Fall of Butler Feudal Power* (Dublin, 2003); Christopher Maginn, *'Civilizing' Gaelic Leinster: The Extension of Tudor Rule in the O'Byrne and O'Toole Lordships* (Dublin, 2005); Anthony M. McCormack, *The Earldom of Desmond, 1463–1583: The Decline and Crisis of a Feudal Lordship* (Dublin, 2005); Mary Ann Lyons, *Church and Society in County Kildare, c.1470–1547* (Dublin, 2000).

¹⁷ Emmett O'Byrne, *War, Politics and the Irish of Leinster, 1156–1606* (Dublin, 2003); Colin Breen, *The Gaelic Lordship of the O'Sullivan Beare* (Dublin, 2005); Michael Potterton, *Medieval Trim: History and Archaeology* (Dublin, 2005); Margaret Murphy and Michael Potterton, *The Dublin Region in the Middle Ages: Settlement, Land-Use and Economy* (Dublin, 2010).

¹⁸ Brendan Smith, 'Introduction', in Brendan Smith (ed.), *Ireland and the English World in the Late Middle Ages: Essays in Honour of Robin Frame*, (Basingstoke, 2009), 1–6.

¹⁹ Robin Frame, *The Political Development of the British Isles 1100–1400* (Oxford, 1990; 2nd edn 1995); Robin Frame, 'The Wider World', in Rosemary Horrox and W. Mark Ormrod (eds), *A Social History of England 1200–1500* (Cambridge, 2006), 435–53. It is significant that one of Christine Carpenter's doctoral students is to the fore in advancing the 'English world' approach: Andrea C. Ruddick, 'Ethnic Identity and Political Language in the King of England's Dominions: A Fourteenth Century Perspective', in Linda Clark (ed.), *The Fifteenth Century VI: Identity and Insurgency in the Late Middle Ages* (Woodbridge, 2006), 15–31; Andrea C. Ruddick, 'Gascony and the Limits of Medieval British Isles History', in Smith, *Ireland and the English World*, 68–88. Also very important is David Green, 'Lordship and Principality: Colonial Policy in Ireland and Aquitaine in the 1360s', *Journal of British Studies*, 47 (2008), 3–29.

the larger 'English world' in the late Middle Ages. Before considering the character of Louth, it is necessary to discuss briefly the nature of the sources on which this study is based, and the ways in which they shape its structure and findings. In comparison with much of the rest of Ireland, the county is fortunate in the range and quantity of material relating to it that still survives. The charter collections of the families of Dowdall and Preston, for instance, are unmatched in Ireland in recording the activities in the land market of families below the level of magnate, while the episcopal registers of the archdiocese of Armagh—of which Louth was a part— which survive in incomplete form from the 1360s to the sixteenth century, have no equivalent elsewhere on the island.[20] It is also fortunate that the cartularies of some of the important religious houses in Dublin and in Britain that held land in Louth have survived, with the records of the Augustinian houses of Llanthony in Wales and Gloucester containing information of particular value.[21] The county features prominently in the records relating to or emanating from medieval Ireland that formed part of the archives of the English crown and now reside for the most part in The National Archives (TNA) at Kew.[22] Predictably, its concerns take up even more space in the records of the Irish chancery, which in their original form were destroyed in 1922 but which have been reconstituted and made accessible by Peter Crooks.[23] Finally, the native Irish annalistic tradition was particularly strong in Ulster, and the fortunes of the lordships that bordered Louth, and the dealings of their rulers with the settlers there, can be followed in their pages in some detail.[24]

On the other hand, it is also the case that some of the records upon which historians of localities in England rely most heavily in their investigations are not available for Louth.[25] The sole local chronicle source produced in the county—a set of annals drawn up in one of the churches in Drogheda dedicated to the Blessed Virgin—survived into the seventeenth century, but only the very brief extracts copied from it then by Sir James Ware now exist to be consulted.[26] In general, the

---

[20] An accessible introduction to the sources available to the historian interested in English Ireland is Philomena Connolly, *Medieval Record Sources* (Dublin, 2002). The best account of the Armagh registers is the introduction to *Reg. Mey*. Transcripts of unpubl. charters dating from the 13th to the 15th century relating to property transactions centred on Braganstown (bar. Ardee), and concerning the families of Repenteny and Clinton, are at NAI MS 1121, Bellew Deeds. The originals are in the possession of Lord Bellew at Barmeath Castle.

[21] The Welsh house of Llanthony, dedicated to St John, was founded on the lands of Hugh de Lacy near Abergavenny at the beginning of the 12th century. In the mid-1130s the majority of its canons moved to a new foundation, also called Llanthony, dedicated to the Virgin, at Gloucester: Hogan, *Priory of Llanthony*.

[22] For Irish material in TNA, including a list of published documents: *Handbook and Select Calendar...Ireland*. For Louth records now in the British Library see the bibliography at the end of this book. The issue rolls of the Irish exchequer, which were sent to Westminster for purposes of audit, have been edited by Connolly: *IEP*.

[23] <http://chancery.tcd.ie> A printed version of the Irish chancery rolls will be published in 2013. In the notes containing Irish chancery material that follow I have referred not to the website, but to the sources upon which it relies.

[24] Indispensable in using the range of material available is Katharine Simms, *Medieval Gaelic Sources* (Dublin, 2009).

[25] Consider the manuscript sources listed in the works on English localities discussed above.

[26] 'Two Old Drogheda Chronicles', ed. Diarmuid Mac Iomhair, *CLAJ* 15 (1961), 88–95.

survival rate of chronicles produced in the parts of Ireland under English control in the Middle Ages is poor, although the affairs of Louth, and more especially Meath, are touched upon in what still exists.[27] Almost entirely absent for Louth are the numerous types of records associated with the manorial economy and aristocratic household—both lay and religious—that historians of English localities have used to construct accounts of their subject areas. Beyond our reach are the '[m]anorial accounts and surveys, household accounts, receivers' accounts and valors, court rolls, registers of correspondence, indentures of personal service, and muster lists' that Davies notes as being available for the historian of lordship at the local level in England.[28] The fact that the Church was a large landowner in Louth makes the absence of surviving estate records from important houses such as the Cistercian abbey of Mellifont or the Augustinian house of St Mary's, Louth, particularly unfortunate.[29] Nor does much of the medieval fabric of churches in Louth survive, limiting the use that can be made of monuments such as brasses and stained glass to explore the self-image of the local elite.[30] The family deeds of the Dowdalls and Prestons, moreover, contain very few of the private letters that have been the basis for much stimulating work on late medieval English local society.[31] Finally, only a small fraction of the records relating to late medieval Louth produced as a result of the judicial and financial activities of the king's ministers in Ireland now survives. Brief, edited versions of the Irish pipe rolls—annual exchequer accounts of royal revenue arranged by county—were published from 1869 onwards, but had reached only the middle of the fourteenth century when the originals were vaporized in the Four Courts fire of 1922. The records of the central courts based at Dublin, and the courts of

---

[27] A. B. Scott, 'Latin Learning and Literature in Ireland, 1169–1500', *NHI* i. 988–93.

[28] Davies, *Lords and Lordship*, 8–9, 36–9. For surviving Irish inquisition material: *Inquisitions and Extents*. This does not include relevant material still residing in the Chancery Miscellanea files at Kew. For discussion of these: J. Hogan, 'Miscellanea of the Chancery, London', *Anal. Hib.* 1 (1934), 179–219.

[29] The registers of the archbishops of Armagh do contain some relevant material. Some examples of studies of localities in England where the Church was a significant landowner are: F. R. H. Du Boulay, *The Lordship of Canterbury: An Essay on Medieval Society* (London, 1966); Barbara Harvey, *Westminster Abbey and its Estates in the Middle Ages* (Oxford, 1977); Margaret Bonney, *Lordship and the Urban Community: Durham and its Overlords, 1250–1540* (Cambridge, 1990); Richard Britnell (ed.), *The Winchester Pipe Rolls and Medieval English Society* (Woodbridge, 2003); P. L. Larson, *Conflict and Compromise in the Late Medieval Countryside: Lords and Peasants in Durham, 1349–1400* (London, 2006).

[30] A superb study of local political society in late medieval Kent and east Surrey based on brasses is Nigel Saul, *Death, Art and Memory in Medieval England: The Cobham Family and their Monuments 1300–1500* (Oxford, 2001).

[31] Imaginative use of family archives has illuminated political society in Lincolnshire, the Thames Valley, East Anglia, the West Midlands and the far North: Peter Coss, *The Foundations of Gentry Life: The Multons of Frampton and their World, 1270–1370* (Oxford, 2010); Colin Richmond, *The Paston Family in the Fifteenth Century: The First Phase* (Cambridge, 1990); Colin Richmond, *The Paston Family in the Fifteenth Century: Fastolf's Will* (Cambridge, 1996); Colin Richmond, *The Paston Family in the Fifteenth Century: Endings* (Manchester, 2000). See also the introductions to *Kingsford's Stonor Letters and Papers, 1290–1483*, ed. Christine Carpenter (Cambridge, 1996); *The Plumpton Letters and Papers*, ed. Joan Kirby (Cambridge, 1996); *The Armburgh Papers*, ed. Christine Carpenter (Woodbridge, 1998).

the itinerant justices, which visited Louth frequently, suffered the same fate. Only three of the 448 medieval plea rolls then preserved in the Public Record Office of Ireland survived the inferno of 1922, by which time only a small number had been edited and published.[32]

In short, the range and quantity of original sources available for the study of a local society in late medieval Ireland are deficient in important respects. It remains the case, however, that much of value survives, and that it has yet to be fully exploited. 'That the history of medieval Ireland is imperfectly known', Richardson and Sayles remarked fifty years ago, 'arises not so much from lack of material as from imperfect exploration of what is available'.[33] It is by recognizing the limitations of the evidence available to us that we avoid excessive speculation while still addressing issues that merit attention. The absence of manorial accounts for Louth, for instance, makes it difficult to assess the wealth of the county, yet to fail to attempt to do so would be remiss. The records of the Irish exchequer give the impression that Louth was a poor place, but must be used with caution. Of the £2,671 received at the exchequer between Michaelmas 1331 and Trinity 1332, only £37 came from Louth, while between Easter 1353 and Hilary 1354 the county proffered £60 of the £2,241 received.[34] Between February 1365 and July 1366, over £4,250 flowed into the exchequer, of which the contribution from Louth was £78, and half a century later the county proffered £20 of the £1,831 collected by the exchequer between January and October 1427.[35] The picture was similar in relation to parliamentary subsidies. The subsidy of 1346 raised a little over £461, of which £12 came from Louth, while of the more than £950 granted in subsidies to the lieutenant, James Butler, earl of Ormond, in parliament in 1420–1, Louth provided slightly less than £66.[36]

To these contributions of the lay community of the county, however, need to be added the sums raised from the townsmen of Drogheda (in both Louth and Meath) and from the clergy of that part of the diocese of Armagh in which Louth lay. Drogheda contributed £213 to exchequer receipts in 1331–2, and £165 in 1427, while the clergy of Armagh provided a subsidy of £10 to the lieutenant, Thomas of Lancaster, at the Kilkenny parliament of 1409, and almost £12 to his deputy,

---

[32] *Rep. DKI* 55, 17–24. Connolly, *Medieval Record Sources*, 18–26. Court records as a source for the history of localities are explored in Robert C. Palmer, *The County Courts of Medieval England, 1150–1350* (Princeton, 1982).

[33] H. G. Richardson and G. O. Sayles, 'Irish Revenue, 1278–1384', *PRIA* 62 (1961–3), C, 87–100, quote at 99. One of Louth's finest local historians, Fr Lawrence Murray, in considering the medieval history of chantries in the county in 1939, summed up a more general situation nicely: 'In our study of the chantry system we found little to guide us on the Irish side—apart, of course, from plenty of documentary evidence': L. P. Murray, 'The Ancient Chantries of Co. Louth', *CLAJ* 9 (1939), 181–208, quote at 181.

[34] Frame, *English Lordship in Ireland*, 82.

[35] TNA E 101/244/9; TNA E 101/248/1; Steven G. Ellis, 'Ioncam na hÉireann, 1384–1534', *Studia Hibernica*, 22–3 (1982–3), 39–49.

[36] Frame, *English Lordship in Ireland*, 83; *Parls. & Councils*, xxiv–xxvii, 131–82; Elizabeth Matthew, 'The Financing of the Lordship of Ireland under Henry V and Henry VI', in Tony Pollard (ed.), *Property and Politics: Essays in Later Medieval English History* (Gloucester, 1984), 97–115.

Thomas Butler, in the following year.[37] Not all subsidies were granted in parliament, it should also be remembered, and the settlers in Louth proved willing on occasion to agree to local subsidies to resist their Irish enemies. In 1400, in order to repulse the attacks of O'Neill, the community of the county agreed to a subsidy of 10s from each carucate of land and 40d from each pound's-worth of chattels possessed by tenants who held more than ten acres of land in Louth.[38] Finally, it is necessary to bear in mind that not all of the money raised in Louth in the service of the crown reached the Irish exchequer.[39] The £20 subsidy granted to Brian MacMahon by the commons and clergy of Louth in 1441, for instance, did not pass through the hands of the treasurer.[40]

If the absence of much of the material that would illustrate the extent and value of the property held by the settler families of Louth can lead to an underestimation of the economic well-being of the county, it also hampers an appreciation of the importance of landlordship as a signifier and guarantee of status in local society.[41] Contemporaries certainly understood its worth, as is suggested by the charter issued in French at Dundalk in August 1366 by John Bellew, who had recently acquired a substantial portion of the Verdon inheritance in Louth. Describing himself as 'lord of Dundalke and le Roche', he announces that he 'has appointed John Douedale to be his seneschal and his attorney of his courts in the lordships of the aforesaid manors, and to let to farm lands and tenements and to do all that pertains to the office of seneschalcy; the lord taking for firm and stable whatever John does in his name for his profit during pleasure'.[42] The registrars of the archbishops of Armagh were in general careful to employ the correct titles of the individuals whose names they recorded, and it is in the episcopal registers that most instances of the use of the word 'lord' to describe some of the important settlers in Louth are found. It was as 'dominus de Beulu' (Beaulieu, bar. Ferrard), that Nicholas Howth witnessed an agreement drawn up by Archbishop Milo Sweteman with the Irish of Ulster in 1373, and Sweteman referred to John Clinton as 'lord of Drumcashel' in 1366, 1368, and 1369, and to Roger Gernon as 'lord of Gernonstown' in 1375.[43] In 1449, Archbishop John Mey condemned an attack on the palace of the bishop of Down conducted 'by Lord James White, knight' (*domini Jacobi White, militis*), a substantial Louth landowner, and others.[44] Obscure individuals who have left virtually no impression on our surviving records were careful

---

[37] *Reg. Fleming*, 89, 101–2. For subsidies from 1436, 1442, 1446, 1447, 1449, and 1450 see *Reg. Swayne*, 164, 188, 193, 194, 195, 196. Drogheda contributed £9 to the subsidy of 1420–1, and the clergy of Louth £19: *Parls. & Councils*, 131–82.

[38] *RCH*, 158 no. 119; 159 no. 7. For the issue of local subsidies: Richardson and Sayles, *Irish Parliament*, 154–9.

[39] Richardson and Sayles, 'Irish Revenue', 87–100. 'To put the position in another way, the revenue figures do not fully represent the financial burden upon the taxpayer' (p. 92). Robin Frame, 'Military Service in the Lordship of Ireland, 1290–1360: Institutions and Society on the Anglo-Gaelic Frontier', in his *Ireland and Britain*, 279–99.

[40] NLI MS 2689, ff. 143–4.

[41] Davies, *Lords and Lordship*, 140–57.

[42] *Dowdall Deeds*, 96–7. A hundred court operated at Roche in 1332: Otway-Ruthven, 'Partition of the de Verdon Lands', 421. (A hundred was a subdivision of a county.)

[43] *Reg. Sweteman*, 15, 37, 41, 113, 154.   [44] *Reg. Mey*, 170–4.

to apply the term *dominus* to themselves when the occasion arose. In 1364, one of those who witnessed a grant by John Stanley, burgess of Drogheda, of his rights in lands north of the town was 'Richard Stanley, lord of Berlystoun [Marlay, bar. Ferrard]', of whom no further mention can be found, while the 'Peter Parys, lord of [*the unidentified*] Aghyre', who granted land at Termonfeckin in 1372 to Walter Dowdall is equally elusive.[45] Scarcely more significant in local affairs was John Serle, 'lord of Gilbertstown and Stormanstown [bar. Ardee]', whose claim to have the right of presentation to the vicarage of Clonkeen (bar. Ardee), was questioned by Archbishop Nicholas Fleming in 1411.[46]

Having one's legitimate authority acknowledged by one's tenants was integral to the institution of lordship. In 1407, Roger Gernon declared that he held Gernonstown of Thomas Faunt, lord of the manor of Ardee, 'by service of a rose'.[47] In the 1360s, the archbishop of Armagh demanded that John Plunket, lord of Beaulieu, and others, deliver to him the annual payments of three pounds of wax and three pounds of pepper by which they held their lands.[48] An expression of lordship closely linked to the possession of land that was defended with great care in Louth was the right to present clergy to the parochial churches situated on seigniorial manors.[49] The Faunts, lords of Ardee, succeeded in protecting their right to appoint to the vicarage of Ardee from the competing claims of the hospital of St John the Baptist of Ardee, in the 1430s.[50] Less fortunate was John Bellew, 'lord of Dundalk', who struggled unsuccessfully for much of the first quarter of the fifteenth century to have acknowledged his right to present the vicar to the parish church of St Nicholas, Dundalk, while the claim of John Repenteny (now Pentony), 'lord of Drumcar', to be patron of the parish church of that manor in 1428 was superseded by that of the abbot of St Mary's, Dublin.[51] John Serle's claim to have the right to present to the church of Clonkeen appears not to have been upheld, since in 1433 it was said to lie with 'John Taaf, *armiger*, patron'.[52] That the issue was a sensitive one is suggested by an incident from 1373 in which one of the most prominent lords in Louth, Thomas Verdon, confronted and verbally abused Milo Sweteman, archbishop of Armagh, in the chapel of the episcopal manor at Termonfeckin for challenging his right of presentation to the church of Feld (now Haynestown, bar. Upper Dundalk).[53]

The archbishops of Armagh were conscientious in attempting to identify the true patrons of parish churches in Louth, but were content to support the rights of local lords once they had been established. In December 1408, Archbishop Nicholas Fleming ordered that an inquisition be held to determine with whom the right

---

[45] *Dowdall Deeds*, 94–5, 101.

[46] *Reg. Fleming*, 161–2. This was perhaps the same John Serle who with his wife, Cecelia, petitioned the Irish parliament in 1385 for return of land in Louth seized by the sheriff: COA Rep. Records of the Exchequer, 1–10 Richard II, 486.

[47] COA Rep. Records of the Exchequer, Henry IV, 190.

[48] *Reg. Sweteman*, 13.

[49] For the lord of the manor and his church in 14th-cent. Sussex, see Saul, *Scenes from Provincial Life*, 140–60, and in Lincolnshire, Coss, *Foundations of Gentry Life*, 176–82.

[50] *Reg. Octaviani*, ii. 57, 59–61, 89.   [51] See below, p. 166; *Reg. Swayne*, 93–4, 133–4.

[52] *Reg. Octaviani*, ii. 97.   [53] *Reg. Fleming*, 247–9.

of presentation to the rectory of the church of Carrickbaggot (bar. Ferrard) lay. The verdict was unequivocal: 'Richard Bagot of Carryk, as the jurors perceive by ancient writings and by the said Richard's oath and other evidences, is the true patron and to him the presentation belongs, and he is in possession of the right to present.'[54] In similar fashion, inquisitions conducted on behalf of Archbishop Swayne in 1435 and 1436 decided that the right of presentation to the churches of Barronstown (bar. Upper Dundalk) and Mansfieldstown (bar. Louth) lay respectively with Sir John Bellew and Sir Nicholas Taaf.[55] In the early fourteenth century, John Plunket had been permitted to found and construct a new parish church to serve his manor of Beaulieu, and the right of his descendant, Walter Plunket, lord of Beaulieu, to present to the rectory of the church went unchallenged a century later.[56] The right of John Babe (now Babb) the elder, 'lord of Darver', to present to the vicarage of Darver was confirmed by the pope in 1427.[57] It was unusual for churchmen below the rank of bishop or prior to also be secular lords, yet in 1426 Archbishop Swayne acknowledged that the right of presentation to the rectory of Killincoole (bar. Louth) lay with 'Lord Henry Saundyr, chaplain, lord of Killincoole'.[58]

Another indication of the importance the settlers in late medieval Louth placed on the ownership and transmission of land is to be found in the popularity among them of the entail and the enfeoffment to use. These were devices by which a property-owner altered the legal status of his land in order to gain the power to determine its descent.[59] 'The bias of these settlements', Rees Davies observed with regard to their operation in England, 'was in favour of male heirs', and the same was true in Louth.[60] The families of Bocombe, Dowdall, Gernon, Hadsor (now Hodger), Keppok, Plunket, and Verdon employed entails at various times between the 1330s and 1400s to ensure that female relatives did not inherit their lands.[61] Families were also careful to preserve the legal documents that guaranteed their property-owning rights. In 1397, John Dowdall was able to produce before the Irish exchequer a charter from 1332 proving that the manner in which he held land inherited from his father, Walter, did not make him liable for Walter's debts.[62]

---

[54] *Dowdall Deeds*, 151–2.

[55] *Reg. Swayne*, 155; *Reg. Octaviani*, ii. 70. In 1347, Richard Taaf was pardoned upon payment of ½m for having 'succeeded his father Nicholas and grandfather, Nicholas, in illegal possession of the advowson of the church of St Mary, Maundevileston [Mansfieldstown]': *CPR 1345–8*, 360.

[56] *Reg. Fleming*, 109–10, 126–7; Paul Brand, 'The Formation of a Parish Church: The Case of Beaulieu, County Louth', in John Bradley (ed.), *Settlement and Society in Medieval Ireland: Studies Presented to F. X. Martin O.S.A.* (Kilkenny, 1988), 261–75.

[57] *CPL 1417–31*, 498 (where 'Babe' appears as 'Bake'); *Reg. Octaviani*, ii. 53–4.

[58] *Reg. Swayne*, 47.

[59] Joseph Biancalana, *The Fee Tail and the Common Recovery in Medieval England, 1176–1502* (Cambridge, 2001), 141–87.

[60] Davies, *Lords and Lordship*, 144–8, quote at 147.

[61] *Dowdall Deeds*, 139–40, 164; COA Rep. Records of the Exchequer, 10–22 Richard II, 265; COA Rep. Records of the Exchequer, Henry IV, 274, 277; *RCH* 75 no. 109; 110 no. 13; 155 no. 10; 173 no. 63; BL Add MS 4790, ff. 27b–28; *PKCI* 196–9; *CPR 1367–70*, 33; *Reg. Sweteman*, 32–3. For the use of such devices in contemporary Warwickshire: Carpenter, *Locality and Polity*, 96–152.

[62] COA Rep. Records of the Exchequer, 10–22 Richard II, 265.

In 1426, John White, burgess of Drogheda, and his wife and sons, petitioned Archbishop John Swayne 'to admonish unknown persons to restore the letters, charters, obligations, indentures and muniments they had taken' from them.[63]

Landlordship is under-represented in the surviving evidence at our disposal in comparison to the material that illuminates the relationship of the elite in Louth to the crown and its representatives in Ireland. This has the potential to lead to an overestimation of the importance of office-holding, and of the county as a focus of loyalty, in the structuring of local society, and a downplaying of the significance of ties of lordship and tenure that transcended county boundaries. The county was certainly an important institution in the lives of those who wielded power in late medieval Louth, but so also was the patronage of the lords of Trim, in whose neighbouring liberty many of them held significant estates.

This preliminary excursion into the topics of the wealth of Louth and the nature and exercise of lordship in the county, prompted by a consideration of the nature of the evidence available to us, has brought to light the names of many of the settler families that will feature repeatedly in what follows. Bellew, Gernon, Clinton, White, Dowdall, Plunket, Taaf, Verdon, Bagot, Babe, Bocombe, Hadsor, and Keppok—it is with the fortunes of members of these families, settled in Louth and adjacent parts of Meath since the decades around 1200, that this book is primarily concerned.[64] Much of what we would like to know about their lives and ambitions is hidden from us, but the surviving records do afford us an insight into some important aspects of how political society operated in a late medieval Irish county. In particular, much can be gleaned from the abundant information that records the interactions of these families with the crown and its Irish administration. Receipt of an individual summons to fight alongside the king, for instance, was an unambiguous indicator of political worth and at the beginning of our period such summonses were issued to a number of settlers in Louth. The occasion was Edward III's 1335 campaign against the Scots, in which the town of Drogheda was to play an important role. The leading resident lords in the county, Nicholas and Milo Verdon, were called upon to join their king, as were the *armigeri* (esquires) Mahon Cruys, Luke Netterville, John Clinton, Roger Gernon, Richard Taaf of Liscartan, John Hadsor, John Gernon of Killincoole, Richard Taaf of Castlelumny, Gerald Clinton, and Peter Cusack.[65]

It is unsurprising that the surnames of the recipients of individual military summonses in 1335 should also feature prominently among the ranks of those who held the highest posts in local government in late medieval Louth, since officeholding was a reliable indicator of social status. The office of sheriff was an elected position and in the period 1330–1450 was usually held by members of settler families that had arrived in the county in the decades of original conquest.[66] Walter

---

[63] *Reg. Swayne*, 43. In the previous year the charters and muniments of the priory of St Mary d'Urso, Drogheda, had been carried off by enemies of the house: *Reg. Swayne*, 42.

[64] For their earlier history see Smith, *Colonisation and Conquest*.

[65] NLI MS 2, 61–2.

[66] A description of the election process from 1355 is to be found at *RCH* 64 no. 146. For the earlier history of the families mentioned below see Smith, *Colonisation and Conquest*.

Exeter and James Audley in the late 1340s and early 1350s, Peter Repenteny in the mid 1360s, and David Napton in 1377 are examples of such individuals from the reign of Edward III.[67] To their number can be added from later reigns Peter Pipard in 1380, John Babe before 1396 and in 1404, John Cusack in 1407–8, and Walter Plunket in 1409–10. A select group of families provided several holders of the office in the same period, with the surnames Gernon, Clinton, Taaf, Hadsor, and Dowdall recurring in the list of sheriffs. Of this group, the Dowdalls were unusual in being town-based, rather than hailing from the countryside. They had close dealings with another Dundalk family, the Tanners, that provided two sheriffs to the county, both named Matthew, in 1381–2 and 1419–20. The rise of local families to prominence in Louth also left its mark on the list of sheriffs of the county. John Bellew became the first member of his family to serve as sheriff of Louth when appointed to the post in 1402, and his son and namesake served in the same capacity in the late 1420s.

The heads of the greatest of the settler families in Louth, the Verdons, considered the office of sheriff beneath them, perhaps on account of the process of election involved in appointment to the post, but were content to serve as keepers of the peace in Louth.[68] Nicholas and Milo Verdon had done so in 1312, and Milo's son, Richard, acted in this capacity in 1373–4 and 1382, as did Richard's son, Bartholomew, in 1400, 1415, 1420, 1421, and 1425. The most obvious difference in terms of the backgrounds of those appointed as keepers of the peace compared with those elected as sheriffs was that the former group included churchmen. Priors of the Augustinian house of St Mary's, Louth, served as keepers or justices of the peace in 1385, 1409, 1420, 1425, while another of those appointed in the latter year was the abbot of the Cistercian house of Mellifont. Archbishops of Armagh were appointed to the post in 1409, 1420, 1425, and 1449, while the bishop of Meath, William Hadsor, acted in the same capacity in 1431. With the exception of ecclesiastics, there was a considerable degree of overlap between those who served as keepers of the peace and those who served as sheriffs, with the families of Gernon, Clinton, Taaf, Hadsor, Dowdall, Repenteny, Tanner, Plunket, Babe, Bellew, Cruys, White, Teeling, Talbot, and Bagot providing men to both offices between 1360 and 1430. One responsibility of the keepers of the peace was to oversee the election of the sheriff, a responsibility that they shared with the county coroner. In most cases coroners in Louth did not advance to higher office, but Geoffrey Rushbury, who was coroner in 1347 and again in 1355, was elected sheriff in the latter year.[69]

Men from the same small number of prominent local families that held the most important posts in local government in Louth also received temporary

---

[67] For what follows, see Table 1.

[68] Nicholas Verdon did serve as seneschal of Trim in 1339–42 while the liberty was in the hands of the crown: *Rep. DKI 47*, 47. For the history of the office of keeper in Ireland, see Robin Frame, 'The Judicial Powers of the Medieval Irish Keepers of the Peace', in his *Ireland and Britain, 1170–1450* (London, 1998), 301–17. For what follows see Table 1.

[69] Connolly, 'List of Irish Material… (C. 260)', 12–13; TNA E 101/243/4, 11.

appointments to serve as justices on the various assizes established by the crown in the county as the need arose.[70] The justices appointed to more general commissions to hear and determine (oyer et terminer) a range of issues including charges of sedition came from the highest stratum of local society, and might have previous experience of service as justices of the benches in Dublin. Sir Robert Preston and John Cruys were appointed to such a commission in December 1384, while Richard Verdon and John Heyne, *narrator* (pleader or lawyer), received similar appointments in 1406.[71] More specific assizes were also staffed by men of local importance. John Dowdall and Geoffrey White served as justices of gaol delivery in the barony of Dundalk in 1374, and before June 1377 Dowdall also served as a justice of labourers, alongside Simon Woodman.[72] Reginald Hadsor, Robert Heyroun, Walter Cusack, and Thomas Goodman were among the other members of important settler families in Louth who served as justices of labourers in Louth in the 1370s.[73]

The most sensitive of the assizes were those of novel disseisin, since they concerned the property rights of the neighbours of those appointed to serve on these judicial panels.[74] In the early 1380s, justices were asked to decide in cases of novel disseisin taken by John Crophull and John Bellew, who had come into ownership of parts of the Verdon inheritance, against, among others, Richard Verdon, Geoffrey White, and Walter Dowdall. It was probably in recognition of the sensitive nature of these cases that a former justiciar (chief governor) of Ireland, John Bromwich, was appointed to head the panel of justices.[75] That he was joined on the bench by two men of substance from the town of Drogheda, Richard Mole and John Ashwell, rather than from the county, might also reflect a desire to avoid accusations of partiality from the contending parties.[76] The surnames of other prominent Louth families appearing in the lists of those who served as justices on assizes of novel disseisin in the 1380s include Plunket, Babe, Keppok, Napton, Kinton, Cusack, and Gernon, while John Dowdall served in the same capacity in 1384 in a case concerning a tenement in Ardee taken by Roger Gernon against Adam Gernon and David Kinton.[77] Accusations of novel disseisin against leading churchmen or serving sheriffs of Louth usually led to the appointment of men of particular local importance to serve on the assize. Richard and James Verdon and Roger Gernon acted in this capacity in a case taken against the prior of Ardee in June

---

[70] Assize: '(i) Legislation; (ii) procedures arising from such legislation; (iii) the body carrying out such procedures; (iv) the trial itself'. John Hudson, *The Formation of the English Common Law: Law and Society in England from the Norman Conquest to Magna Carta* (Harlow, 1996), 241.

[71] *RCH* 121 no. 85; 184 no. 151; *Dowdall Deeds*, 144.

[72] COA Rep. Records of the Exchequer, 42–51 Edward III, 142, 429.

[73] *Parls. & Councils*, 53–4; COA Rep. Records of the Exchequer, 42–51 Edward III, 279, 364.

[74] 'An action for novel disseisin was a means of recovering land from which the occupier had been ejected (disseised) without due process of law, or as part of a genuine disagreement about ownership or the right to occupy': Anthony Musson and W. Mark Ormrod, *The Evolution of English Justice: Law, Politics and Society in the Fourteenth Century* (Basingstoke, 1999), 122.

[75] Bromwich was appointed in Sept. 1379 and served from Dec. of that year until the following May: *NHI* ix. 474.

[76] *RCH* 106 no. 16; TNA E 101/246/5; COA Rep. Records of the Exchequer, 1–10 Richard II, 342–3.

[77] COA Rep. Records of the Exchequer, 1–10 Richard II, 372, 376, 378; *RCH* 121 nos. 79 and 82.

1410, and in the same month Sir John Bellew did the same in an action concerning the sheriff, Walter Plunket.[78]

County and crown interacted not only in the local courts, but also in the highest court in the land, parliament. To receive an individual summons to attend parliament was a mark of prestige for the recipient, and it is no surprise that those thus summoned from Louth were from the same families that staffed local government in the county. In 1372 the sheriff of Louth was ordered to deliver summonses to attend a great council to be held at Dublin to Richard Taaf of Braganstown, John Clinton, John Hadsor, Roger Gernon of Rathbrist, Geoffrey White, Matthew Tanner, Walter Dowdall, John Taaf, John Stanley, John Napton, John Kinton, Robert Babe, Thomas Clinton, and James Audley. Those summoned individually to a council at Dublin in January 1375 included from Louth Richard Verdon, Roger Gernon, Richard Taaf, and John Taaf.[79] Of these fifteen individuals seven had already served as either sheriff of Louth or keeper of the peace there (John Clinton, Richard Taaf, James Audley, Roger Gernon, John Taaf, John Hadsor, and Roger Gernon), while two more—Geoffrey White and Matthew Tanner—would proceed to hold one or both of these offices before the end of 1381.[80] Seventy years later, members of the same families were still receiving individual summonses to parliament. Among those thus summoned by the lieutenant, James Butler, earl of Ormond, to attend a great council at Drogheda in 1444 were Sir Nicholas Taaf, John Gernon, Roger Gernon, Thomas Babe, John Clinton, Robert Clinton, Richard Verdon, and John Hadsor ('Hodsone').[81]

Prominent individuals from Louth might also attend parliament as the elected representatives of the county. Roger Gernon and Richard Vernon were elected to the parliament convened by William Windsor at Dublin in April 1370, and were imprisoned by him for refusing to agree to a subsidy he demanded.[82] Bartholomew Verdon and Richard Bagot were elected to the Dublin parliament of June and December 1420 that granted a large subsidy to the lieutenant, James Butler, earl of Ormond, and went on to serve as assessors of the subsidy on the county alongside Roger Gernon, Nicholas Taaf, John Clinton of Cappoge, and Walter Plunket.[83]

The value of their estates, and their role in governing the county on behalf of the crown distinguished the most important settlers in Louth from their neighbours, and it is no surprise that marriage alliances among them were common.[84] The survival of the medieval records of the Dowdall family affords an insight into some of these alliances.[85] In the late fourteenth and early fifteenth centuries,

---

[78] *RCH* 196 nos. 76, 91.
[79] Betham, *Origin and History*, 311–14; Lynch, *View of the Legal Institutions*, 321.
[80] I am assuming that the Roger Gernon of Rathbrist summoned in 1372 was the same individual as the Roger Gernon summoned in 1375.
[81] *PKCI* 307.   [82] Clarke, 'William of Windsor in Ireland', 115.
[83] *Parls. & Councils*, 134–5, 151–2.
[84] For marriage as a means of improving one's status in contemporary England: Simon J. Payling, 'Social Mobility, Demographic Change, and Landed Society in Late Medieval England', *Economic History Review*, 45 (1992), 51–73.
[85] *Dowdall Deeds*, xv–xxi. I cite only references to Dowdall marriages not found in the *Deeds* in what follows.

Table 1. Sheriffs and keepers of the peace to 1450

SHERIFFS OF LOUTH, 1234–1450		
Ralph Pichford	1234–5	*Rep. DKI 34*, 35
William Talon	1260–2	*Rep. DKI 35*, 39, 42
William Bakepuz	1265–6	*Rep. DKI 35*, 46
John Fyshyde	1266–7	*Rep. DKI 35*, 46
John Pichford	1270–2	TNA E 101/230/2
William Talon	1272–5	NLI MS 761, 12–13; *Rep. DKI 36*, 24, 26
Thomas Mymmes	1275–9	*Rep. DKI 36*, 38, 49
Roger Crumba	1279–80 (?)	*COD* i. 79–80
Nicholas Netterville	1281–2	TNA E 101/230/16
Thomas Mymmes	1282–3	NAI RC 11/6
Nicholas Netterville	1283–5	*Rep. DKI 37*, 70, 75
William Spineto	1285–91	*Rep. DKI 37*, 28, 38, 44
Thomas Stanley	1291–4	TNA E 101/231/6; *Rep. DKI 37*, 53
Richard Taaf	1294–5	*Rep. DKI 37*, 53; NAI RC 7/3, 223
William Hatch	1296–9	TNA E 101/232/24; *CDI iii*, no. 587
Roger Gernon	1299–1300	*Rep. DKI 38*, 52; *CDI iii*, no. 705
Hugh Clinton	1300–1	*Rep. DKI 38*, 52
Roger Roth	1301–5	*Rep. DKI 38*, 52, 71; *CJR* ii. 31–2
Hugh Clinton	1305–7	*Rep. DKI 39*, 25; NAI Ex 2/2, 255
Benedict Hauberge	1307–9	*Rep. DKI 39*, 32; NAI Ex 2/2, 255
Walter Dowdall	1309–10	*Rep. DKI 39*, 32; NAI Ex 1/1, m. 49d
Richard Gernon	1310–11	*Rep. DKI 39*, 36; *CJR* ii. 169–70[1]
Benedict Hauberge	1311–15	*Rep. DKI 39*, 36, 48, 52[2]
John Cusack	1315–18	*Rep. DKI 39*, 52, 67; NAI RC 8/10, 160
Walter de la Pulle	1318–20	*Rep. DKI 42*, 64; TNA E 101/237/7
John Cusack	1328–9	*CPR 1327–30*, 532
Geoff. Brendewode	1329–31	*Rep. DKI 43*, 40; TNA E 101/239/26
John Gernon	1331–2	*Rep. DKI 43*, 52; TNA E 101/239/26, 27
John Clinton	1332–3	TNA E 101/239/27
Richard Taaf	1334–5	*Rep. DKI 45*, 29
John Clinton (?)	1335–6	*Rep. DKI 45*, 29
Peter Hadsor	1336–7	NAI RC 8/15, 300
Richard Taaf	1337–9	*Rep. DKI 45*, 31
John Clinton	1339–41	*Rep. DKI 47, 23*, and *53*, 24
Richard Taaf	1341–2	*Rep. DKI 53*, 25
James Audley	1345–6	TNA E 101/241/14
Walter Exeter	1346–7	TNA E 101/241/14
Peter Hadsor	1347–8	TNA E 101/241/14
Gerald Clinton	1348–50	TNA E 101/241/18
William Lowys	1350–2	TNA E 101/241/20
Robert Tancard	1352–3	TNA E 101/242/13
James Audley	1353–4	TNA E 101/243/1
Geoffrey Rushbury	1354–5	TNA E 101/243/11
John Clinton	1355–6	TNA E 101/243/11; *RCH* 57 no. 109
William Dowdall	1358–63	TNA E 101/244/4; *Dowdall Deeds*, 89, 92–3
Richard Taaf	1364–5	TNA E 101/244/9
Peter Repenteny	1365–6	*Reg. Sweteman*, 30–1
John Dowdall	1373–5	*Dowdall Deeds*, 103
John Taaf	1375–6	COA Rep. Records of the Exchequer, 42–51 Ed. III, 279

(continued)

Table 1. Sheriffs and keepers of the peace to 1450 (*continued*)

John Taaf	1377–8	COA Rep. Records of the Exchequer, 1–10 Ric. II, 1
David Napton	1378–9 (?)	COA Rep. Records of the Exchequer, 1–10 Ric. II, 11
Matthew Tanner	1379–80	COA Rep. Records of the Exchequer, 1–10 Ric. II, 92
Peter Pipard	1380–1	COA Rep. Records of the Exchequer, 1–10 Ric. II, 188
John Dowdall	1381–2 (?)	*Dowdall Deeds*, 113–14
Milo Hadsor	1382–3	*Dowdall Deeds*, 115–16
John Cruys	1383	COA Rep. Records of the Exchequer, 1–10 Ric. II, 383
Milo Hadsor	1383–4	COA Rep. Records of the Exchequer, 1–10 Ric. II, 388
George Teeling	1385–6	*RCH* 124 nos. 70, 71
Robert Clinton	1386–7	*RCH* 136 nos. 205, 206
John Dowdall	1388–9	COA Rep. Records of the Exchequer, 10–22 Ric. II, 252
John Dowdall	1389–90	COA Rep. Records of the Exchequer, 10–22 Ric. II, 54
Milo Hadsor	1391–2	*Dowdall Deeds*, 130
John Babe	1395–6 (?)	COA Rep. Records of the Exchequer, 10–22 Ric. II, 265
John Clinton	1396–7 (?)	COA Rep. Records of the Exchequer, 10–22 Ric. II, 265
Thomas Talbot	1400–1	*RCH* 160 no. 11
John Dowdall	1401–2	'Henry Marleburrough's Chronicle of Ireland', 215
John Clinton	1402	*RCH* 162 no. 215
John Bellew	1402–3	*RCH* 172 no. 1
John Babe	1403–4	TNA C 260/118/31
Richard Fitz Richard	1405–6	COA Rep. Records of the Exchequer, Henry IV, 182
John More	1406–7	*RCH* 183 nos. 106, 107
John Cusack	1407–8	*RCH* 188 no. 11(b)
Richard Fitz Richard	1408–9	*RCH* 193 no. 176
Walter Plunket	1409–10	*RCH* 196 no. 91
Walter Uriel	1415–16	COA Rep. Records of Exchequer, 1 Hen. V–39 Hen. VI, 489
John Gernon	1415–16	COA Rep. Records of Exchequer, 1 Hen. V–39 Hen. VI, 512
Nicholas Taaf	1416–17	NAI, RC 8/36, 36–7
John Bradeston	1419–20	*Rotuli Selecti*, 59
Matthew Tanner	1420–1	TNA E 101/247/8
Nicholas Taaf	1421–2	TNA E 101/247/15; *RCH* 240 no. 56
James White	1424–5	E 30/1558
John Bellew	1425–7	TNA E 101/248/1; *RCH* 236 no. 55
Nicholas Taaf	1431–6 (?)	*IEP* 574
Henry Gernon	1445–6	E 30/1567

KEEPERS/JUSTICES OF THE PEACE IN LOUTH 1312–1450
(All references may be found in Frame, 'Commissions of the Peace')

Before 16 April 1312	Milo Verdon; Nicholas Verdon
1362	Gerald Clinton; John Clinton; Henry Cruys
12 January 1365	Richard Taaf 'and others'
6 November 1372	Roger Gernon; John Taaf; Nicholas (*recte* Richard?) Verdon
20 October 1373	John Dowdall; Roger Gernon; John Hadsor of Cappoge; John Taaf of Castlelumney; Richard Verdon
September 1375	William Brown; Peter Repenteny
4 May 1380	John Taaf; Geoffrey White of Dundalk
8 March 1382	John Brisbon; Roger Gernon; Milo Hadsor; Walter Plunket; Matthew Tanner; Richard Verdon; Geoffrey White
7 October 1385	Prior of Louth; John Brisbon; Robert Clinton; John Dowdall; Matthew Fleming; Robert Gernon; Stephen Gernon; Reginald Hadsor; Matthew Tanner; John White
7 December 1385	Prior of Louth; John Brisbon; John Dowdall; Matthew Fleming; Robert Gernon, jun.; Matthew Tanner; George Teeling; John White
17 December 1386	John Brisbon; John Dowdall; Richard Fitz Roland; Stephen Gernon
17 July 1388	Robert Clinton; Thomas Fleming, baron of Slane ('Chief Keeper'); Michael Taam
25 May 1390	Matthew Tanner; Geoffrey White
24 November 1400	Reginald Hadsor; Thomas Talbot; Bartholomew Verdon; James White
4 November 1401	Janico Dartas [Meath and Louth]
22 November 1402	John Babe; John Clinton of Cappoge; Robert Gernon; Roger Gernon; Walter Plunket
24 January 1409	Nicholas Fleming, archbishop of Armagh; Nicholas, prior of Louth; Janico Dartas; Roger Gernon; Walter Plunket; Richard Verdon
26 June 1409	Christopher, prior of Louth; John Bellew; John Clinton of Cappoge; John Darcy; Janico Dartas; Walter Plunket
27 August 1412	John Darcy; Nicholas Taaf; Matthew Tanner; James Verdon; Richard Verdon
11 March 1415	John Clinton of Cappoge; Roger Gernon of Gernonstown; Nicholas Taaf; Bartholomew Verdon
26 April 1420	John Swayne, archbishop of Armagh; John Lyde, prior of Louth; John Bellew, sen.; John Bellew, jun.; John Clinton of Cappoge; Roger Gernon of Gemonstown; Walter Plunket
6 July 1420	John Bellew, jun.; Walter Plunket; Nicholas Taaf; Matthew Tanner, sheriff of Louth; Bartholomew Verdon
27 July 1420	John Bellew, sen.; John Bellew, jun.; John Clinton of Cappoge; Roger Gernon; John Kenefer; Walter Plunket
24 April 1421	Richard Bagot; Roger Gernon of Gernonstown; Roger Gernon of Kane (?); Nicholas Taaf; Bartholomew Verdon
21 June 1425	John Swayne, archbishop of Armagh; abbot of Mellifont; John Lyde, prior of Louth; Stephen Bray; Janico Dartas; John Hadsor; John Kenefer; Nicholas Taaf; Bartholomew Verdon
18 June 1431	William Hadsor, bishop of Meath [Louth and Meath]
*c.*1449	John Mey, archbishop of Armagh

[1] Gernon was murdered in Oct. 1310. See Smith, *Colonisation and Conquest*, 131–2.
[2] Hauberge was replaced temporarily in 1312 by Richard Taaf: NAI RC 8/6, 209.

members of the main, Dundalk, branch of the Dowdalls took wives from the families of Gernon, White, and Napton, while the Dowdalls of Termonfeckin forged ties of marriage with the families of Stokes, Bocombe, and also with the Gernons.[86] The four successive heads of the branch of the Gernon family based at Killincoole between the 1330s and 1400s took wives from the families of Chapman, Hadsor, Cruys, and Taaf.[87] In 1334 Richard Taaf of Braganstown, who would later serve as sheriff of Louth, married the recently widowed Anne Cogan. Two years earlier, Anne and her then husband Henry Mandeville, had paid the crown for Richard's marriage while he was still a minor.[88] A century later, Richard's great-granddaughter, Patricia, daughter of Sir Nicholas Taaf, married Thomas Babe, nephew and heir of John Babe, lord of Darver.[89]

Such marriages, which brought together families of roughly equal status, were more difficult to arrange for members of the premier family in late medieval Louth, the Verdons. Thomas son of Nicholas Verdon (d.1375), who had been raised in England in the household of Henry, duke of Lancaster, married Joan Hartort who appears to have been English by birth, and left as his heirs two daughters, Matilda and Anna.[90] The former married Peter Howth, lord of Beaulieu, and following his death John Cruys, while the latter married John Bellew. Bellew had purchased some of the Verdon lands in Louth that had been partitioned on the death of Thomas Verdon's uncle, Theobald Verdon, in 1316, and his marriage to Anne Verdon was perhaps designed to reunite parts of a greater family inheritance. Any such scheme was negated by the death of Anne at an early age without children.[91] Thomas's cousins, Richard and James, the sons of Milo Verdon, who both died in 1383, married respectively Alice Stanley and Isabella Gaydon.[92] Isabella subsequently married Thomas Talbot, but had a son, James, by her first marriage who, before his own death in 1412, arranged that his son and heir, Christopher, who was a minor, should be placed in the custody of Thomas Waley—whose activities appear to be unrecorded in surviving records—with the understanding that Christopher would in due course marry his guardian's daughter.[93]

An example of a successful marriage alliance of the type that eluded the Verdons was the union between Christophe Plunket and Joan Cusack which by 1402

---

[86] COA Rep. Records of the Exchequer, 1–10 Richard II, 504 (Richard Dowdall (d.1385) and Isabella Napton); *RCH* 130 no. 71 (John Dowdall and Isabella Gernon, 1386); *Reg. Mey*, 374–5 (Sir John Dowdall and Elizabeth Stokes, 1454).

[87] COA Rep. Records of the Exchequer, Henry IV, 274, 277; COA Rep. Records of the Exchequer, 1 Henry V–39 Henry VI, 4–5.

[88] TNA E 101/239/26; *RCH* 40 no. 124; *Rep. DKI* 45, 29, 30, 31. Richard was the son of Nicholas Taaf of Braganstown: NLI MS G[enealogical] O[ffice] 191, 60.

[89] *RCH* 259 no. 11. The Taaf ancestry is uncertain. A John son of Richard Taaf was active in Louth in the 1370s: *Reg. Sweteman*, 247. The Nicholas son of John Taaf of Braganstown who received a pardon in 1404 was possibly Patricia's father: *CPR 1401–5*, 374.

[90] For Thomas's career see below, 35, 63–5.

[91] COA Rep. Records of the Exchequer, 1–10 Richard II, 524–6.

[92] COA Rep. Records of the Exchequer, 1–10 Richard II, 405, 483–4, 499; *RCH* 140 no. 132.

[93] *RCH* 120 no. 37; COA Rep. Records of the Exchequer, 10–22 Richard II, 89–90; COA Rep. Records of the Exchequer, Henry IV, 473–4. James was dead by Feb. 1413, but had been acting as a keeper of the peace in Louth as recently as Aug. 1412: *RCH* 201 no. 123.

Table 2. The Verdon Family

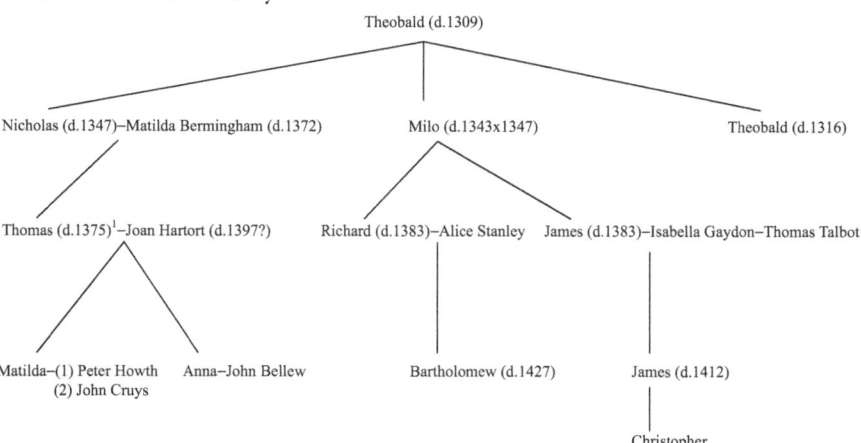

¹ Thomas also had illegitimate issue, William Verdon.

had brought together the estates of two of the oldest settler families in Louth and Meath, and which laid the foundations for the rise of the Plunkets to national importance later in the fifteenth century.[94] Joan was the daughter of Luke Cusack, who was in turn the son of Walter Cusack and Joan Tuyt. Luke's right to inherit his father's estates had been imperilled in the 1360s by the annulment of his parents' marriage on the grounds of consanguinity.[95] The tendency of the settlers of Louth and Meath to marry among themselves gave rise to many other instances of marriage within forbidden degrees.[96] In 1347, John Napton and Isabella Jordan petitioned the pope successfully for permission to remain married on the grounds that they had wed in ignorance of their close relationship, and in 1415 Archbishop Nicholas Fleming was commanded by the pope to grant dispensation to four men and four women of his diocese to marry within the fourth degree of kindred or affinity. That the individuals concerned were from Louth is suggested by the names of those who had petitioned the pope about the matter, Barnaby Gernon and Alice Verdon.[97] In 1441, the daughter of this union, Katharine Gernon, was herself at the centre of a similar case when her husband, Thomas Skreen of Dundalk, sought to divorce her on the grounds that they shared a common great-great-grandparent.[98] In 1422, Christopher Fleming, the son and heir of the baron of Slane, was granted permission to marry Elizabeth Wogan notwithstanding the fact that she was related to him, and in the following year, Sir John Dowdall of Termonfeckin and Anne Bocombe were permitted by the pope

---

[94] *RCH* 164 no. 151.
[95] For the uproar occasioned by the unhappy marriage of Walter and Joan see below, 47–8.
[96] Art Cosgrove, 'Consent, Consummation and Indissolubility: Some Evidence from Mediaeval Ecclesiastical Courts', *Downside Review* (Apr. 1991), 94–104.
[97] *Vetera Monumenta*, 287–8; *Reg. Fleming*, 246–8.
[98] *Reg. Mey*, 46–7.

to separate and remarry upon confessing to having married while aware that they were related within prohibited degrees.[99]

There is much in this brief account of some of the characteristics of politics and society in late medieval Louth that will appear familiar to students of localities in England in the same period.[100] Louth was part of a larger English world, and retained close ties with England, and in particular north-west England, throughout this period. It was a county in which great magnates did not hold substantial amounts of land, but its small size and position between the liberties of Ulster and Trim meant that its leading men looked to the Mortimers, earls of March, who held both liberties from the 1360s, for protection and patronage.[101] The Church was a major landowner in the county, and the residence within its borders of the archbishop of Armagh afforded that ecclesiastic a leading role in the affairs of Louth. Armagh was in constant communication with the papacy, and Louth's openness to contact with the outside world was also ensured by the presence within it of the major port of Drogheda, which was erected as a county in its own right in 1412. Finally, Louth was a border county, and its politics, society, and economy were decisively shaped by its interactions with the neighbouring Irish lordships of south Ulster with which it was in a state of potential—and often actual—warfare.

The settlers of late medieval Louth never tired of proclaiming their Englishness, and it is natural to seek to identify a county or region in England with which Louth might productively be compared. Its distinguishing characteristics, however, defy attempts to point to anything approaching a perfect match on the other side of the Irish Sea. The primary importance of the border in its fortunes draws the eye towards the far North of England, but Scotland was a very different type of enemy than the lordships of the Irish of south Ulster. Louth was not—apart from some very brief interludes after 1330—a liberty, and no local family equivalent to the Percys emerged in Louth to lead local resistance and rise to national prominence.[102] A more appropriate, though at first sight unlikely, comparison might be with a southern coastal county of England such as Kent or Hampshire, where the Church was a significant landowner and in which were located busy ports that attracted the unwelcome attention of the king's continental enemies.[103] As historians begin to focus on the medieval 'English world' as a subject of enquiry, it is possible that the sea will come to be viewed as the unifying feature of this entity, and that Bordeaux, Calais, Southampton, Exeter, Bristol, Waterford, Dublin, and Drogheda will be identified as key points on one of the main routes of communication that gave it meaning. Such an approach also has the advantage of reducing the tendency

---

[99] *CPL 1417–31*, 221; *Dowdall Deeds*, 169–71. Their children were declared to be legitimate.

[100] See the relevant essays in Raluca Radulescu and Alison Truelove (eds), *Gentry Culture in Late Medieval England* (Manchester, 2005).

[101] As we shall see, the Verdon and Gernon families also had strong links to the house of Lancaster. A full-scale study of the Mortimers and their estates throughout the British Isles, similar to those that have been undertaken for the dukes and duchy of Lancaster, would be of enormous benefit. For the possibilities see Davies, *Lords and Lordship*.

[102] Holford and Stringer, *Border Liberties and Loyalties*, 291–355.

[103] Peter Fleming, 'The Landed Elite, 1300–1500', in Sweetinburgh, *Later Medieval Kent*, 209–33.

to view Louth as 'peripheral' to some English 'core'. Not only was it within easy reach of the headquarters of English power in Ireland at Dublin, but the county also enjoyed a level of contact with the English crown and those who wielded power around it that stood comparison with that enjoyed by many of the shires of southern England.

The layout of the book requires a word of explanation. It is divided into two parts, with a narrative section followed by three thematic chapters. The purpose of the first section is not only to outline the main events of the period 1330–1450 as they impinged upon Louth, but also to suggest that the history of late medieval Ireland itself looks rather different when viewed not from the centre, or from above, but from a local or regional perspective. The cast of characters in most accounts of the Irish Middle Ages is noticeably small in number, though of impeccable breeding, and those 'below stairs'—including those only slightly below—have rarely attracted much attention. Magnate lordship was without question of fundamental importance in late medieval Ireland, but it was rooted in relationships between these great lords and their tenants and retainers about which we still know far too little. The troubled governorship of William Windsor in the 1370s, and the power-struggle between John Talbot and James Butler, earl of Ormond, for control of the Irish administration from the 1410s to the 1440s involved constitutional issues of great importance that merit further consideration. But they also involved the intense interaction of these powerful men with the people who mattered in counties such as Louth and towns such as Drogheda, as they sought to bolster their own position and undermine that of their foes. And of that interaction we know almost nothing.

As well as serving to introduce new actors to the historical stage, the local perspective also has the potential to challenge traditional interpretations of national developments. It is hardly surprising that 'decline' has been the theme of most historical comment on the Lordship in the late Middle Ages, since it is the sentiment that dominates contemporary settler comment on their situation. Yet the geographical extent of English lordship in Louth barely changed in the period under consideration in this book, and in 1450 the mood of the settlers appears to have been at least as bullish as it had been in 1330. In like manner, the tendency among some historians to see cultural assimilation with the Irish, or 'Gaelicization', as characteristic of this period draws upon contemporary settler hand-wringing about the dilution of English identity in the colony. It was, rather, their assured Englishness that allowed the Louth settlers to adopt and adapt some aspects of native culture. A detailed account of the history of the area between 1330 and 1450, and of the careers of some of those who wielded power there at that time, can help resolve apparent paradoxes such as these, and should at least serve to highlight the case for a more regional approach to late medieval Irish history.

The second section of the book owes its contents and omissions to a lifelong regard for the story of Perseus and Medusa. While I have no wish to decapitate those who comprised the political elite of late medieval Louth, I am sufficiently wary of them to avoid direct eye contact. I have sought to contemplate their reflection, instead, in the polished shields of the Church, the towns, and the marches.

Such an approach no doubt fails to capture these figures in all their complexity and energy, but it might at least provide a starting point for future enquirers of a less timid disposition. I have kept the frontiers between these three chapters as porous as possible, in recognition of the extent to which the themes they address overlapped and interacted with each other in the lives of contemporaries. For this reason the early section of the chapter on the towns retains the previous chapter's focus on the Church, while the chapter on the marches commences with discussion of the role of towns on the Irish frontier.

* * *

I have used 'Airgialla' when referring to the MacMahon lordship. Contemporary records use the terms 'Uriel' and 'Louth' interchangeably, and I employ the latter. Until 1412, Drogheda on either side of the Boyne had separate constitutional standing, being referred to as 'Drogheda in Louth [or Uriel]', and 'Drogheda in Meath'. Gaelic sources draw a distinction between 'Gall' (foreigner), a settler of English origin, and 'Saxon', a native of England. Gaelic surnames that exist in modern English form are given in that form with the Gaelic original in brackets on the first occurrence. Settler surnames that have assumed different forms since the Middle Ages, such as 'Repenteny–Pentony' are given in their medieval version. Where Christian names among the Irish represent borrowings from Anglo-French names they are given in English rather than Irish form. Thus 'John', not 'Seán', and 'Henry', not 'Énrí'. Christian names of Irish origin such as 'Toirdelbach' are left unchanged. Finally, 'm' stands for 'marks', a monetary sum equivalent to two-thirds of a pound.

PART I

CRISIS AND SURVIVAL

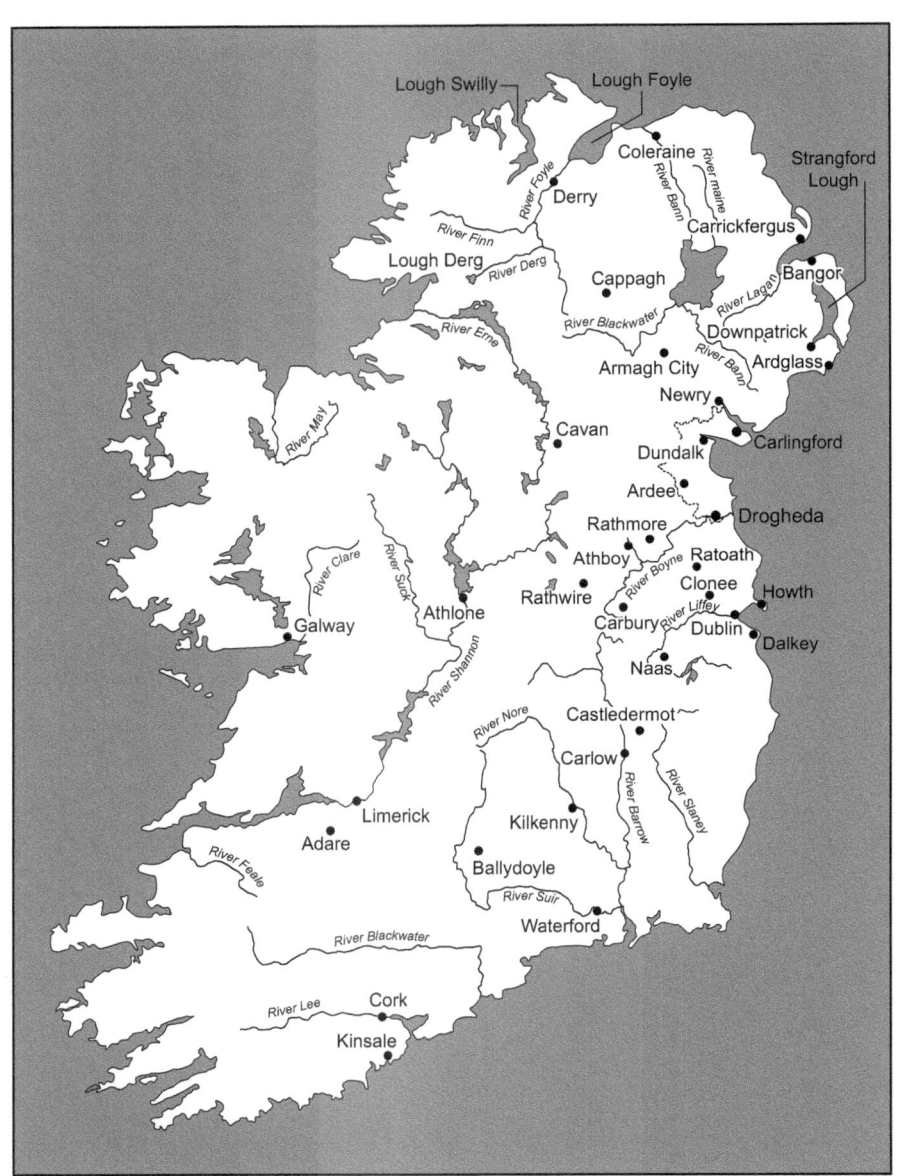

Map 2. Louth and Ireland

1
False Dawn: 1330–1369

For the English settlers of Louth, the execution of Roger Mortimer, earl of March, at Tyburn on 29 November 1330 appeared to provide a suitably gory finale to a troubled chapter in their history.[1] Mortimer had been intimately connected with the several traumas that they had endured in the early fourteenth century, starting with a settler rebellion against the crown in 1312 and concluding with the murder of the earl of Louth and many of his family and followers in 1329. Although not a landowner in the county, Roger had as recently as June 1330 engineered the grant to himself of royal jurisdiction in Louth and Meath, to add to the rights he already enjoyed as lord of the liberty of Trim. He held the latter by right of his marriage in 1301 to Joan Geneville, co-heiress of the Lacy lordship of Meath, and the marriage the next year of his sister, Matilda (d.1312), to Theobald Verdon (d.1316), lord of the other half of Meath and the greatest landowner in Louth, had further increased his interests in this part of Ireland.[2] When Theobald's younger brothers became involved in a large-scale rebellion in Louth in 1312 Mortimer was instrumental in bringing them back into the king's peace, and he worked effectively with them again during the Scottish invasion of 1315–18 to ensure the eventual defeat of the king's enemies. As Irish justiciar (1319–20), he also secured the promotion to the newly established earldom of Louth of John Bermingham, the leader of the force that had defeated Edward Bruce at Faughart in Louth in October 1318. Bermingham, however, sided with the king against Mortimer in the civil war that erupted in England and Wales in 1321–2, and as justiciar of Ireland from August 1321 to February 1324, confiscated the property of Mortimer in Ireland. When in June 1329 Bermingham and his entourage were slaughtered at Braganstown by a local force led by the sheriff of county Louth, Mortimer who with Queen Isabella now ruled England in the name of the young Edward III (1327–77) did nothing to punish those involved, and within a year had secured Louth as a liberty for himself.[3]

---

[1] For what follows see Smith, *Colonisation and Conquest*, chs 5–7.
[2] Mark S. Hagger, *The Fortunes of a Norman Family: The de Verduns in England, Ireland and Wales, 1066–1316* (Dublin, 2001), 16, 115–16.
[3] Ian Mortimer, *The Greatest Traitor: The Life of Sir Roger Mortimer, Ist Earl of March, Ruler of England 1327–1330* (London, 2003); Paul Dryburgh, 'The Last Refuge of a Scoundrel? Edward II and Ireland, 1321–7', in Gwilym Dodd and Anthony Musson (eds), *The Reign of Edward II: New Perspectives* (Woodbridge, 2006), 119–39; Paul Dryburgh, 'Roger Mortimer and the Governance of Ireland, 1317–20', in Smith, *Ireland and the English World in the Late Middle Ages*, 89–102.

Mortimer's downfall, therefore, held out the promise of more stable times for the inhabitants of Louth, who now resided once more under the direct lordship of their king. The young Edward III worked hard and with considerable success in the first years of his reign to re-establish the prestige of a monarchy badly tarnished by the behaviour of his father, Edward II (1307–27), but the wounds inflicted on the English body-politic in the early fourteenth century would take time to heal.[4] In Louth, the reverberations of earlier upheavals continued to be felt long after Mortimer's death. The financial penalty imposed by the crown upon the community of the county in the aftermath of the Verdon rebellion of 1312, for instance, continued to be collected well into the 1330s, and the involvement of specific individuals in the revolt was still being noted in exchequer records into the next decade.[5] The suspicion that collaboration with the Scots during the Bruce invasion had been more widespread than had been recognized at the time also persisted. An inquiry held by the justiciar, Ralph Ufford, at Drogheda in December 1344—twenty-seven years after the incident occurred—found that Sir Richard Mandeville had led Robert and Edward Bruce and their forces into county Louth in the spring of 1317, resulting in the burning of towns and the deaths of eighty men, women, and children of settler stock.[6]

Nor did Mortimer influence in Louth end with Roger's death. Edward III did not wish the earl's downfall to encompass his wife and children, and allowed Joan Mortimer (Geneville), to pursue claims to her own, and her late husband's, property in Ireland.[7] As early as October 1331, an inquisition was held at Drogheda at her behest by the Irish justiciar, Anthony Lucy, to determine her rights in a manor in Meath, and in the summer of 1333 she was awarded arrears of rent from the site of the town and castle of Drogheda, which had belonged to her ancestors and had not been paid since Roger's death in November 1330.[8] In 1347, Joan, in a petition to the crown, noted that she had not been in Ireland for thirty years, and in the same year she was allowed to enfeoff her grandson, Roger, with the castle of Trim and the family property in Drogheda.[9] This marked a key moment in the rehabilitation of the Mortimer dynasty; by the time Joan died in 1356, Roger had established his reputation as a great warrior and friend of Edward III and had had his claim to the earldom of March and its estates in Ireland and elsewhere recognized. Although his own death at the age of 31 in 1360 left Mortimer influence in Ireland in abeyance until the majority of his son and heir, Edmund, in 1372, the efforts of

---

[4] Seymour Phillips, *Edward II* (New Haven, 2010), 607–13.
[5] *Rep. DKI 43*, 52. TNA SC 8/18/866. (A summary of this petition is at Connolly, 'Ancient Petitions', 9.) *Rep. DKI 53*, 24, 26.
[6] TNA C 260/60/9. A summary of this document is at Connolly, 'List of Irish Material... (C. 260)', 12–13.
[7] Frame, *English Lordship in Ireland*, 119, 205–6. Gillian Kenny, 'The Power of Dower: the Importance of Dower in the Lives of Medieval Women in Ireland', in Christine Meek and Catherine Lawless (eds), *Studies on Medieval and Early Modern Women* (Dublin, 2003), 59–74.
[8] *Inquisitions and Extents*, 135; *IEP* 358; *CCR 1343–6*, 627; G. H. Orpen, 'The Site of Castle Blathach', *Journal of the Royal Society of Antiquaries of Ireland*, 6th ser. 4/2 (June 1914), 167–70.
[9] *CCR 1346–9*, 314; *CPR 1345–8*, 349.

Joan Mortimer had ensured that the execution of her husband did not signal the end of the family's power in Ireland.[10]

In defending the rights of her family, Joan came into conflict with the leading resident lords in county Louth, the brothers Nicholas and Milo Verdon. The parties were related, since Joan's grandmother, Maud, and the grandmother of the Verdons, Margery, were sisters.[11] The head of the Verdon family, Theobald, died in 1316, leaving as his heirs four underage daughters, and custody of the family's Irish estates in Louth, Meath, and Dublin was entrusted to his younger brothers, Nicholas and Milo Verdon.[12] The resistance offered by the brothers to the invading Scots earned them grants of land in Louth and Meath confiscated from those who had collaborated with the enemy, and they were content to exploit the downfall of their former patron, Roger Mortimer, to gain possession of a number of his manors in Meath after 1330.[13] Joan Mortimer's efforts to regain these lands were prolonged, but apparently unsuccessful. She first petitioned for the return of Rathfeigh (bar. Skreen, co. Meath) and Rathwire (bar. Farbill, co. Westmeath) in 1332, but these manors were in the possession of Nicholas Verdon until at least 1338 and possibly up to his death in 1347.[14]

That Nicholas and Milo were able to frustrate attempts by Joan, and also on occasion by ministers of the crown in Ireland, to reclaim grants of land made to them in the 1310s and 1320s bore witness to their local importance and also to their ability to influence or obstruct the policies of the king and his council in England.[15] Nicholas Verdon in particular had been deeply involved in the rebellion in Louth in 1312 and in the years that followed was notorious for extorting protection-money from his less powerful neighbours in Louth and Meath.[16] The rental for the manor of Kells in 1351, for instance, recorded that some tenants had been accustomed to pay their rent not to the rightful lord, but 'to Nicholas Verdon for life, wishing to enjoy his better avowry [that is, protection]'.[17] His success in avoiding punishment for his misdeeds and retaining possession of his acquisitions in Ireland is remarkable, especially when compared to the fate of lesser contemporaries in Louth who had incurred royal displeasure for more venial offences. Benedict

---

[10] Davies, *Lords and Lordship*, 118, 149; Brendan Smith, 'Lordship in the British Isles, c.1320–c.1360: The Ebb Tide of the English Empire?', in Huw Pryce and John Watts (eds), *Power and Identity in the Middle Ages: Essays in Honour of Rees Davies* (Oxford, 2007), 158; Rowena E. Archer, '"How ladies...who live on their manors ought to manage their households and estates": Women as Landholders and Administrators in the Later Middle Ages', in P. J. P. Goldberg (ed.), *Women in Medieval English Society* (Stroud, 1997), 168–9, 180.

[11] *NHI* ix. 173.

[12] For this, and what follows, see Smith, *Colonisation and Conquest*; Brendan Smith, 'A County Community in Early Fourteenth-Century Ireland: The Case of Louth', *EHR* 108 (1993), 561–88.

[13] *CCR 1330–3*, 377; *CCR 1341–3*, 188; *CPR 1330–4*, 31, 264; *CPR 1340–3*, 386, 436; NAI RC 8/15, 607; TNA C 47/10/18.

[14] Sayles, *Affairs*, 151–2; *CCR 1333–7*, 591–2; *Clyn*, 240. An inquisition post mortem was ordered to be held into Nicholas's estate in Oct. 1351, but no record of it survives: *IEP* 481. Edward III confirmed Matthew Bath in possession of Rathfeigh in 1340: NAI RC 8/21, 488–90.

[15] Frame, *English Lordship in Ireland*, 205–6, 257–8.

[16] Smith, 'A County Community', 572–8.

[17] *Handbook and Select Calendar...Ireland*, 306 (TNA SC 6/1238/10).

Hauberge, for instance, had served as sheriff of Louth between 1307 and 1309, and at intervals between 1311 and 1314, but by 1319 was incarcerated in Dublin castle with outstanding debts from his periods in office totalling £260. By the time of his death in 1329, this had been reassessed at a daunting £449 5s 8d, and remained a burden on his family for generations.[18] The grant by his son Adam in 1340 of land in Stameen in Meath, south of Drogheda, to Richard Preston, a burgess of the town and member of an ambitious and acquisitive local family, may have been prompted by the need to raise money owed to the exchequer, and Benedict's relatives were still being hounded by the government for his debts as late as 1389.[19] This determined pursuit of its rights by the crown against an inconsequential local officer and his descendants stands in contrast to its relaxed approach to the disruptive activities of one of the locality's greatest men.[20]

Nicholas Verdon's success in retaining the king's favour despite his questionable conduct on many occasions was helped by the closeness of his ties with England and with those who wielded power there. He continued to hold estates in the Verdon heartland of Staffordshire, and was resident in England in 1332, 1336, 1338, and 1342–3. The grant to him of the important royal manor of Mansfieldstown (bar. Louth) at the York parliament of November 1338 added significantly to his landed endowment in Louth and testified to the influence of his political connections in England.[21] These connections had blossomed as a result of marriages made by his relatives in the 1310s and 1320s. His older brother, Theobald, had taken as his second wife in February 1316 Elizabeth, sister of Gilbert Clare, earl of Gloucester (d.1314), and widow of John Burgh (d.1313), son of Richard Burgh, earl of Ulster (d.1326).[22] Upon Theobald's death five months later, Elizabeth became entitled to one-third of her husband's estate, and this, in addition to the Irish lands she had acquired through her marriage to John Burgh, remained with her until her death in November 1360. Following the demise of her third husband, Roger Damory, in 1322, she remained unmarried, but used her vast wealth and influence to further the fortunes of her children and grandchildren.[23] These individuals included her son, William Burgh, earl of Ulster, who was murdered in 1333, and his daughter, also Elizabeth (d.1363), who would inherit her

---

[18] Smith, *Colonisation and Conquest*, 96, 137–8.
[19] Otway-Ruthven, 'Partition of the de Verdon Lands', 425; *Gormanston Reg.*, 39, 40, 41; NAI RC 8/27, 243–4; TNA E 101/243/12; TNA E 101/244/4; COA Rep. Records of the Exchequer, 10–22 Richard II, 252.
[20] For general discussion of this topic in its English setting: Musson and Ormrod, *Evolution of English Justice*.
[21] NAI RC 8/16, 15; NAI RC 8/23, 351; BL Egerton MS 75, 9; *CPR 1330–4*, 283; *CPR 1334–8*, 279; *CPR 1338–40*, 153; *CPR 1340–3*, 510; *CCR 1341–3*, 531; J. R. S. Phillips, 'The Anglo-Norman Nobility', in James Lydon (ed.), *The English in Medieval Ireland* (Dublin, 1984), 98–9.
[22] Scott L. Waugh, *The Lordship of England: Royal Wardships and Marriages in English Society and Politics, 1217–1327* (Princeton, 1988), 219; Phillips, *Edward II*, 269–70; Hagger, *Fortunes of a Norman Family*, 240–1.
[23] For a useful family tree and discussion see Given-Wilson, *English Nobility in the Late Middle Ages*, 40–2; Davies, *Lords and Lordship*, 153, 163–5. Gillian Kenny, *Anglo-Irish and Gaelic Women in Ireland, c.1170–1540* (Dublin, 2007), 135–6; Peter Coss, *The Lady in Medieval England, 1100–1500* (Stroud, 1998), 59–63.

grandmother's estates and who in 1341 was betrothed to Lionel of Antwerp, son of Edward III.[24] The marriages of Theobald's daughters further extended the circle of important individuals in England to whom Nicholas was now connected. Elizabeth Verdon (d.1360) married in or before 1321 Bartholomew Burghersh (d.1355), the older brother of Henry Burghersh (d.1340), bishop of Lincoln and chancellor of England between 1328 and 1330. Bartholomew, a founder-member of the Order of the Garter, was an important royal councillor and diplomat, who among other posts served as constable of Dover castle and guardian of the Cinque Ports, keeper of the forests south of the Trent, and chamberlain to the king.[25] Isabel Verdon (d.1349)—the sole offspring of Theobald's brief marriage to Elizabeth Clare—married before February 1331 Henry Ferrers (d.1343) who, like Burghersh was a councillor to Edward III and was appointed keeper of the Channel Islands in 1333.[26]

Nicholas's immunity from the king's displeasure was also a consequence of his continued usefulness to the crown. In 1335, he and Milo Verdon were among those who received individual summonses to fight in Scotland under the command of the Irish justiciar, John Darcy.[27] The expedition met with mixed success, but for the Verdons and their companions from Louth who had battled with the Scots on home soil in 1315–18, the opportunity to take the fight to Scotland itself twenty years later must have been enticing.[28] The fleet of some fifty ships assembled for the campaign gathered at Drogheda, and despite the prolonged presence in the town of armed retinues under the justiciar, the earl of Kildare, and the earl of Desmond, there was no repeat of the riots or complaints of extortion that had accompanied such campaigns earlier in the century.[29] Drogheda merchants had been attacked by Scottish naval vessels—one merchant was abducted at sea and held for ransom at Dumbarton, near Glasgow—and men from Drogheda were instrumental in the recapture of the Isle of Man from the Scots in 1337.[30]

Another of those personally summoned to fight in Scotland in 1335 was Domnall O'Hanlon (Ó hAnluain), leader of a family that during the Bruce invasion had attacked Dundalk and neighbouring parts of Louth. The appearance of Domnall

---

[24] W. M. Ormrod, 'Edward III and his Family', *Journal of British Studies*, 26 (1987), 398–422; Jennifer C. Ward, *English Noblewomen in the Later Middle Ages* (Harlow, 1992), 93–107.

[25] W. M. Ormrod, *The Reign of Edward III: Crown and Political Society in England, 1327–1377* (New Haven, 1990), 19, 108–9, 122–34; Michael Prestwich, *Plantagenet England, 1225–1360* (Oxford, 2005), 315–16; Hugh Collins, *The Order of the Garter, 1348–1461: Chivalry and Politics in Late Medieval England* (Oxford, 2000); David Green, *Edward the Black Prince: Power in Medieval Europe* (Harlow, 2007), 10–11, 46.

[26] Eric Acheson, 'Ferrers Family (per. c.1240–1445)', *Oxford Dictionary of National Biography* (Oxford, 2004; online edn, Jan. 2008).

[27] NLI MS 2, f. 61.

[28] Frame, *English Lordship in Ireland*, 142–8; Ranald Nicholson, 'An Irish Expedition to Scotland in 1335', *IHS* 13 (1963), 197–211.

[29] *IEP* 380, 623; *Clyn*, 216; *CCR 1339–41*, 518; Smith, *Colonisation and Conquest*, 152–3. Lack of shipping caused the earl of Desmond and his men to reside in Drogheda for a month in 1335: *RCH* 41 no. 40.

[30] *RCH* 42 nos. 7, 17; Tim Thornton, 'Scotland and the Isle of Man, c.1400–1625: Noble Power and Royal Presumption in the Northern Irish Sea Province', *SHR* 78 (1998), 5–6.

in Dundalk in May 1335, where as *Rex Erthir* he attached his seal to a grant of land in the Cooley peninsula to two Dundalk men, suggests the extent to which relations between the settlers and this Irish leader had improved in recent years.[31] Already, Domnall had agreed to hold his lands in the earldom of Ulster as a free tenant of the earl in 1331, and travelled to Dublin for talks with the government following the murder of William Burgh, earl of Ulster, in 1333.[32] He appears also to have been paying rent for land on the borders of Louth to the successors of Theobald Verdon (d.1316) into the 1330s, and by 1337 at the latest had entered into a formal treaty of peace with the English of the county.[33] The ability of the English of Louth to engage so fully in the crown's efforts against the Scots in the early 1330s was facilitated by this increase in security on one of the county's most dangerous borders. The fragility of this new accord, however, was demonstrated in September 1337 when it was found necessary to appoint a commission of local settlers to hold inquisitions to identify those in Louth who had already infringed, or were likely in future to infringe, this peace agreement.[34] Relations with other neighbouring Irish families in the 1330s were even less stable. John MacMahon (Mac Mathgamna) had allied with the English of Louth in 1331 to gain the chieftainship of Airgialla, but in 1336 the sheriff of Louth, John Clinton, was compensated for fighting against him 'and other Irish felons' in the marches of Louth.[35] 1330 had witnessed the death, in the Franciscan house he had founded at Cavan, of the aged chief of East Breifne, Gilla Ísa O'Reilly (Ó Raigillig). He had fostered close relations with the English during his reign, but his successor proved less accommodating. The justiciar, John Darcy, conducted a campaign against Richard O'Reilly at Kells in 1334, leading to negotiations the following year, while further west in 1335 Milo Verdon was engaged in hostilities with Irish families including that of O'Farrell (Ó Feargall).[36]

The renewal under Edward III of successful warfare against the Scots may have encouraged belief among the English in Louth in the years after the death of Roger Mortimer that the traumas of the early fourteenth century were yielding to a more stable, prosperous, period. Continued warfare on the marches of the county, however, served as a reminder of the persistence of underlying problems, and by the time Nicholas Verdon died and was buried with great pomp in Drogheda in March 1347, it was clear that any hopes for better times raised in the early 1330s had been

---

[31] *Chartul. St Mary's, Dublin*, ii. 297, 350; *Dowdall Deeds*, 52–3.
[32] BL Add MS 6041, no. 101; *Inquisitions and Extents*, 155; *CCR 1333–7*, 249–50; *IEP* 365; *Dowdall Deeds*, 51–2.
[33] Otway-Ruthven, 'Partition of the de Verdon Lands', 421–36; *RCH* 42 no. 6; Katharine Simms, 'The O Hanlons, the O Neills and the Anglo-Normans in Thirteenth-Century Armagh', *Seanchas Ardmhacha*, 9 (1978), 70–94.
[34] *RCH* 42 no. 6.
[35] *AFM* iii. 549; *Rep. DKI 43*, 53; *Inquisitions and Extents*, 155; *CCR 1333–7*, 249–50; *AU* ii. 467, 471; *A. Clon.* 293; *AC* 289.
[36] BL Landsdowne MS 315, 83; TNA E 352/130; *RCH* 39 no. 65, 41 nos. 22 and 41; *IEP* 616; *AFM* iii. 545, 559; *AC*, 269; Katharine Simms, 'The O Reillys and the Kingdom of East Breifne', *Breifne*, 5 (1976–81), 305–19.

misplaced.³⁷ The murder of William Burgh, earl of Ulster, by his own tenants in June 1333 was a crushing blow to English interests in Ireland, though its full impact was delayed by the effectiveness of the response it provoked from the crown and its Irish administration.³⁸ The earl's killers were dealt with speedily, and the most powerful of the Ulster Irish lords, Henry O'Neill (Ó Néill), was granted wide acres in Antrim in 1338 to encourage continuation of his traditional allegiance to the English. In 1341, in a sign of the crown's continued interest in the Ulster settlement, the infant heiress of the earldom was betrothed to Lionel of Antwerp, the second surviving son of Edward III.³⁹ Despite such decisive action, however, William Burgh's death left an important English lordship in Ireland without leadership at a particularly sensitive moment. English success in Scotland in the early 1330s had involved encouraging western Scottish leaders to abandon their allegiance to the Bruce dynasty. John MacDonald (Mac Domnaill) of the Isles was persuaded to side with the English and Edward Balliol against King David II, and even resided for a time at Drogheda.⁴⁰ In 1343, however, he switched allegiance again and proceeded thereafter to play the Scots and English off against each other in order to increase the independence of his own position as Lord of the Isles.⁴¹ A consequence for Ulster of these developments was the settlement at this time of a branch of the MacDonalds, Clan Alexander, around Ballygawley in Tyrone. The initiative for this permanent migration of Scots to Ireland lay with the senior segment of the O'Neill dynasty whose leaders demanded service from the MacDonalds as their galloglass in return for the lands they granted to them. By the 1360s the English of Louth were experiencing the repercussions of this strengthening of military power among the leading Irish family of Ulster.⁴²

The increasing danger posed to Louth from Ulster following the murder of William Burgh in 1333 did not arise from crown neglect of its responsibilities in the earldom. Not only did the justiciar, John Darcy, lead military expeditions that included contingents from Louth into Ulster in 1333, 1334, and 1335, but with the support of the king received permission from the pope in 1334 for his 4-year-old

---

³⁷ *Clyn*, 240. Given the Franciscan provenance of Clyn's annals, it is likely that Nicholas was buried in the Franciscan house in Drogheda.
³⁸ 'And now the tragedy occurred which may be regarded as closing this epoch of Irish history'. G. H. Orpen, *Ireland under the Normans* (Dublin, 2005), 557–9, quotation at 557.
³⁹ Frame, *English Lordship in Ireland*, 146–7, 217–18, 222–4; Simms, 'The O Hanlons, the O Neills and the Anglo-Normans', 91–2; *CCR 1337–9*, 142, 329, 363; Robin Frame, 'English Policies and Anglo-Irish Attitudes in the Crisis of 1341–42', in his *Ireland and Britain*, 124–5.
⁴⁰ Frame, *English Lordship in Ireland*, 144–52; *Rep. DKI 44*, 60; *CPR 1338–40*, 81.
⁴¹ R. Andrew McDonald, *The Kingdom of the Isles: Scotland's Western Seaboard, c.1100–c.1336* (East Linton, 1997), 187–9; Alexander Grant, 'Scotland's "Celtic Fringe" in the Late Middle Ages: The MacDonald Lords of the Isles and the Kingdom of Scotland', in R. R. Davies (ed), *The British Isles, 1100–1500: Comparisons, Contrasts and Connections* (Edinburgh, 1988), 129–31; Michael Penman, 'David II (1329–1371)', in Michael Brown and Roland Tanner (eds), *Scottish Kingship, 1306–1542: Essays in Honour of Norman Macdougall* (Edinburgh, 2008), 50–2.
⁴² Kenneth Nicholls, 'Scottish Mercenary Kindreds in Ireland, 1250–1600', in Seán Duffy (ed.), *The World of the Galloglass: Kings, Warlords and Warriors in Ireland and Scotland, 1200–1600* (Dublin, 2007), 97–9.

son, William, to marry Matilda Burgh, cousin of the late earl of Ulster.[43] Edward III's betrothal of his son Lionel to the heiress of the earldom in 1341 has already been mentioned, and before 1343 the king also gave his consent to the marriage of his kinswoman, Maud of Lancaster, the widow of William Burgh, to Ralph Ufford, younger brother of Robert Ufford, earl of Suffolk. Ralph was appointed as justiciar of Ireland in February 1344 and served there between June of that year and his death at Dublin in April 1346.[44] The interests of his wife and of the crown combined to prompt the campaign he launched in Ulster the spring of 1345, and the English of Louth were heavily involved in the fierce fighting that marked its early stages.[45] Although his foray was deemed a success by contemporaries, Ufford's decision to depose Henry O'Neill of the Clandeboy (Clann Aeda Buide) branch and replace him with Aed O'Neill of the senior line of the family—under whose patronage the MacDonald galloglass were at that time settling in Tyrone—was to prove detrimental to the future security of the settlers both in Ulster and Louth.[46]

Despite the efforts of the crown to fill the vacuum left by the murder of the earl of Ulster, the dangers facing the English of Louth from these neighbours were greater by the middle of the 1340s than they had been even ten years before. Infighting among the O'Neills had particularly serious consequences for the Irish of south Armagh whose lands bordered those of Louth and who now looked to the English for support. In March 1346, the sheriff of Louth was ordered to inquire in the county whether it would be to the profit of the king and of 'the men of the march of the parts of Dundalk' to grant the petition of 'Auly and Petrus Orogan, Irishmen, with their adherents' that they be received into the king's peace, while in the following month the king granted protection to three leading members of the O'Hanlon family 'and their lands, rents and possessions, during good behaviour'.[47] The major focus of concern, however, was the family of MacMahon, which in a period of marked instability was led by four different men between 1342 and 1344.[48] In June 1346, Brian MacMahon, whose father was one of those who had ruled Airgialla in these years, launched the most destructive attack on Louth that had been seen since the Bruce invasion. Before dismissing the figure of 300 settler-dead given by the Irish annals in its report of the campaign as implausibly high, it should be borne in mind that it was repeated and on occasion pitched even higher by contemporary colonial chroniclers, and was also mentioned in a petition sent to

---

[43] TNA C 59/14, m. 9; NAI RC 8/18, 608; *RCH* 41 no. 21; Frame, *English Lordship in Ireland*, 222–4.

[44] For this and what follows, Robin Frame, 'The Justiciarship of Ralph Ufford: Warfare and Politics in Fourteenth-Century Ireland', *Studia Hibernica*, 13 (1973), 7–47.

[45] Katharine Simms, 'The Dating of Two Poems on Ulster Chieftains', in Alfred P. Smyth (ed.), *Seanchas: Studies in Early and Medieval Irish Archaeology, History and Literature in Honour of Francis J. Byrne* (Dublin, 2000), 385.

[46] *Account Roll of Holy Trinity, Dublin*, 95; *Clyn*, 230; *Chartul. St Mary's, Dublin*, ii. 385; *AC* 301; Robin Frame, 'The Defence of the English Lordship, 1250–1450', in Thomas Bartlett and Keith Jeffery (eds), *A Military History of Ireland* (Cambridge, 1996), 92–4; Kenneth Nicholls, *Gaelic and Gaelicised Ireland in the Middle Ages* (Dublin, 1972), 129.

[47] *RCH* 49 no. 48, 50 no. 70.

[48] *NHI* ix. 146; *AC* 289, 297.

England later in the year by the local community.⁴⁹ The strategies that had deterred Irish attacks on Louth for some thirty years had run their course; the death within nine months of MacMahon's incursion of Nicholas Verdon, who for the same three decades and more had dominated local political life, served to reinforce the sense that English Louth was entering a new phase of its history.⁵⁰

On 26 August 1346, two months after the MacMahon raid on Louth, the English won a remarkable victory over the French at Crécy in Picardy. It was the beginning of a period in which England's armies proved irresistible in France, culminating in their great success at the battle of Poitiers in September 1356, in which the French king was made captive.⁵¹ The contribution of the king's lieges in Ireland to these enterprises was small, but some individuals from the Louth/Meath area did participate in the fighting. In August 1347, John Teeling, a chaplain who was later to become involved in a prolonged dispute about a benefice at Stabannan in Louth, was pardoned at Calais on account of his good service in France for homicides committed in Ireland, and in the following month, for the same reason, John Bacon was restored to the serjeanty of Meath which he had lost almost ten years before as a result of making a false return to the steward of Trim.⁵² More spectacular was the success in battle of Robert Clinton, whose part in the capture of the bishop of Le Mans/Sens at Poitiers in 1356 was adjudged to be worth £1,000, and who was rewarded by the king with grants of land in Kildare and Dublin to add to his possessions at Navan in Meath and Collon in Louth.⁵³ Clinton's career serves as a reminder of the variety and intensity of the links that continued to bind the part of Ireland from which he came to England and the English crown in the middle of the fourteenth century. He had spent lengthy periods in England since at least 1351, and was already in receipt of royal grants in Ireland before his exploits at Poitiers.⁵⁴ His prowess encouraged the king to retain him in his presence for life at an annual fee of £20 in 1359, and in 1361 he took his place in the retinue of knights that accompanied Lionel of Antwerp, earl of Ulster, to Ireland.⁵⁵ In 1355, he had served as attorney in Ireland for Edward, Lord Montagu, brother of William Montagu, earl of Salisbury (d.1344), and in 1365 acted in the same capacity

---

⁴⁹ *AC* 299; *Clyn*, 238; *Chartul. St Mary's, Dublin*, ii. 389; Connolly, 'Ancient Petitions', 66 (TNA SC 8/208/10390); Sayles, *Affairs*, 186–7.

⁵⁰ Milo Verdon was still active in 1343, but appears to have died before his brother. *RCH* 45 no. 78.

⁵¹ Clifford J. Rogers, *War Cruel and Sharp: English Strategy under Edward III, 1327–1360* (Woodbridge, 2000); Andrew Ayton and Sir Philip Preston, *The Battle of Crécy, 1346* (Woodbridge, 2005); David Green, *The Battle of Poitiers, 1356* (Stroud, 2002).

⁵² *CPR 1345–8*, 525, 535, 411; *CPR 1338–40*, 248; *CCR 1343–6*, 286; G. O. Sayles, 'Ecclesiastical Process and the Parsonage of Stabannon in 1351: A Study of the Medieval Irish Church in Action', *PRIA* 55 (1952), C, 1–23; Potterton, *Medieval Trim*, 124, 375.

⁵³ TNA E 101/244/9; TNA SC 8/227/11345, calendared in Connolly, 'Ancient Petitions', 73, and printed in Sayles, *Affairs*, 223–4; *CPR 1358–61*, 63, 440; *RCH* 85 no. 10; Chris Given-Wilson and Françoise Bériac, 'Edward III's Prisoners of War: The Battle of Poitiers and its Context', *EHR* 116 (2001), 832–3; James B. Leslie, 'The Clinton Family in County Louth', *CLAJ* 2 (1911), 399–400.

⁵⁴ *CPR 1350–4*, 122; *Admin. Ire.*, 251–5 (TNA E 368/125, m. 24).

⁵⁵ *CPR 1358–61*, 213, 441; *Handbook and Select Calendar…Ireland*, 312–13 (TNA E 101/28/18).

for Joan, widow of Thomas Furnival, who had inherited part of the Verdon estates in Ireland.[56] He was dead by March 1369, leaving an estate of sufficient value to attract the interest of the justiciar, William Windsor, who acquired its wardship during the minority of Robert's son and heir, also Robert.[57]

Robert Clinton's links with the wider English world were unusually extensive, but reflected the degree to which the part of Ireland from which he came continued to form part of this larger entity. Louth and Meath still attracted new English settlers in the first half of the fourteenth century, as the case of the Darcy family demonstrates. John Darcy of Knaith in Lincolnshire (d.1347)—who fought alongside King Edward III at Crécy—had first been appointed justiciar of Ireland in 1323, and subsequently acquired interests in Meath and Louth for himself and his family that would endure.[58] In 1329, he was granted wardship of the lands of John Bermingham, earl of Louth, in Ardee and Donaghmoyne (bar. Farney, co. Monaghan), and in 1340 the Irish estates of Ralph, count of Eu, including the manor of Louth, which had been confiscated on account of Ralph's adherence to the king of France, were awarded to him and his heirs.[59] These remained in the possession of the main line of the family until 1465, but did not comprise the entirety of Darcy holdings in Ireland. William Darcy, the child of John's second marriage to Joan Burgh, widow of the earl of Kildare, acquired Platin (bar. Lower Duleek, co. Meath), in the vicinity of Drogheda, and established a branch of the family that settled permanently in Ireland.[60]

While no other noble family in England matched the level of commitment to newly acquired Irish lands displayed by the Darcys in the mid-fourteenth century, absentee lords with property in Louth ensured that their interests in the county were safeguarded and, on occasion, extended. The Verdon heiresses and their husbands and children, for instance, continued to cultivate their Irish connections. Elizabeth (d.1360), wife of Bartholomew Burghersh, saw such links significantly strengthen in 1347 with the marriage of her daughter, Elizabeth, to Maurice fitz Thomas, earl of Kildare (d.1390). Her sisters, Margaret (d.1377), wife, successively, of William le Blount (d.1337), Mark Husee (d.1346), and John Crophull (d.1383), and Joan (d.1335), wife of Thomas Furnival (d.1339), also continued

---

[56] *CPR 1354–8*, 262, 265; *CPR 1364–7*, 171; *Dowdall Deeds*, 92, 94, 95; Otway-Ruthven, 'Partition of the de Verdon Lands', 440–1; Ormrod, *Reign of Edward III*, 107.

[57] *CPR 1367–70*, 125, 245; *CFR 1369–77*, 4; BL Add MS 4790, f. 40b. Robert Clinton's three sons, Robert, John, and Thomas, all died without heirs. His lands passed to John son of Simon Clinton, his cousin. Windsor was ordered to pass the estate to John Clinton in July 1373: COA Rep. Records of the Exchequer, 42–51 Edward III, 87–8, 91.

[58] Frame, *English Lordship in Ireland*, 96–8 and *passim*; W. M. Ormrod, 'Darcy, Sir John (b. before 1284, d.1347)', *Oxford Dictionary of National Biography* (Oxford, 2004; online edn, Jan. 2008).

[59] *CFR 1327–37*, 143; *CPR 1338–40*, 441–2, 458; *Rep. DKI 47*, 22.

[60] Harold O'Sullivan, 'The March of South-East Ulster in the Fifteenth and Sixteenth Centuries: A Period of Change', in Raymond Gillespie and Harold O'Sullivan (eds), *The Borderlands: Essays on the History of the Ulster–Leinster Border* (Belfast, 1989), 59; John P. Clarke, 'Notes on the Devolution of Title to the Manors of Louth, Castlering and Ash, County Louth', *CLAJ* 21 (1987), 267–73. William Darcy's widow, Margery or Matilda Burgh, married William London—her third husband—sometime before Sept. 1356: *RCH* 64 no. 9.

to take an interest in their Irish lands.⁶¹ Absentee lords could send servants from England to administer their Irish lands, but the employment of local men of substance in Louth and Meath as estate officials and attorneys was also common.⁶² Such men might find it necessary on occasion to cross the Irish Sea in connection with their duties, as did John Rauf, or Ralph, of Dundalk who acted as attorney for Joan Verdon and her husband Thomas Furnival, and who was in England in 1333.⁶³ Elizabeth Clare (d.1360), widow of John Burgh and Theobald Verdon continued to employ officials to protect her rights at Duleek and Kells up to the time of her death, while her daughter-in-law, Maud of Lancaster, countess of Ulster (d.1377), widow of William Burgh (d.1333) and Ralph Ufford (d.1346), was exploiting the interests she had acquired in Drogheda, Ratoath in Meath, and Carlingford through her first marriage long before her second husband led an army through Louth into Ulster in 1345.⁶⁴

Maud further strengthened her involvement in Louth by acquiring in 1347 the wardship of Thomas, son and heir of Nicholas Verdon, an award she was permitted to pass on to her brother Henry, earl and later duke of Lancaster (d.1361), in 1348 when she entered a convent.⁶⁵ Nicholas Verdon's widow, Matilda Bermingham, remained in Ireland, but Thomas spent some years in the Lancastrian household in England, where it is likely that he had contact with his female cousins, the daughters and heiresses of Theobald Verdon.⁶⁶ Maud was also responsible for engineering an English career for Nicholas Gernon, a Louth man who in return for good service had received a life-grant from the king in 1341 of £20 from forfeited land in Drogheda.⁶⁷ He served in the retinue of Maud's husband, Ralph Ufford, in Ireland in 1344–6, receiving an additional grant from the revenues of Drogheda as reward for his endeavours, and soon after was one of those chosen by Maud to act as her

---

⁶¹ For Elizabeth Verdon, *Chartul. St Mary's, Dublin*, ii. 390; *Inquisitions and Extents*, 195; Frame, *English Lordship in Ireland*, 282–3, 342. For Margaret, *CPR 1358–61*, 302. For Joan, TNA E 101/240/15; *Rep. DKI 44*, 58.

⁶² Frame, *English Lordship in Ireland*, 60–72; W. M. Ormrod, *Political Life in Medieval England, 1300–1450* (Basingstoke, 1995), 41.

⁶³ *CPR 1330–4*, 150, 432; Otway-Ruthven, 'Partition of the de Verdon Lands', 423, 428, 433, 436.

⁶⁴ For Elizabeth Clare, Otway-Rutheven, 'Partition of the de Verdon Lands', 437–9, 440–1; *IEP* 350; *Handbook and Select Calendar…Ireland*, 304–6; TNA E 101/244/9; *RCH* 79 no. 120. For Maud, *RCH* 49 no. 47, 50 no. 85; *CCR 1333–7*, 249–50; *CCR 1337–9*, 172; *Dowdall Deeds*, 51–2. At first sight this undated document, with its mention of a 'velvet bed-spread with the arms of England, Gloucester and Damory' which among other goods found at Carlingford was to be returned to the unnamed recipient of the letter, seems to refer to Elizabeth Clare (d.1360). Robin Frame, however, has argued that the addressee was Maud of Lancaster and dates from 1345, rather than c.1334 as suggested by the editors of the document. Frame, 'Justiciarship of Ralph Ufford', 23 n. 97.

⁶⁵ *CPR 1348–50*, 86.

⁶⁶ *CPR 1345–8*, 333; *CPR 1364–7*, 322–3; *CPR 1367–70*, 152, 461. Thomas Verdon had been granted his father's lands by 1352: TNA E 101/242/13. His first recorded visit to Ireland came in 1355: *CPR 1354–8*, 278. How Matilda Bermingham was related to John Bermingham, earl of Louth (d.1329) is unclear. She was, of course, not his daughter, Matilda, who married Eustace le Poer in 1331: *Clyn*, 202; COA Rep. Records of the Exchequer, 42–51 Edward III, 180, 183.

⁶⁷ Otway-Ruthven, 'Partition of the de Verdon Lands', 432; *CPR 1340–3*, 386; *Rep. DKI 54*, 31.

attorney when she retired to the convent.⁶⁸ In 1382, as an old man dwelling in the Franciscan house of Bruisyard in Suffolk, which Maud had founded in 1367, Nicholas was still receiving his money from Drogheda, having striven for many years to prevent this grant being revoked.⁶⁹ It is possible that he did not visit Ireland again after his patroness returned to England in 1346, although it was as 'Nicholas Gernon, knight, of the diocese of Armagh' that he was identified in a papal letter of 1357 permitting him to choose his own confessors.⁷⁰ He was careful to appoint attorneys in Ireland on a regular basis from the late 1340s onwards, and the surnames of many of those chosen by him to act in this capacity between 1348 and 1383—Stokes, Teeling, Babe, de la Feld—attest to their Louth provenance. The appearance in their number of no fewer than four Gernons, John, Hugh, Simon, and Roger, suggests the importance of family ties in uniting different regions of the English world at this level of society at this time.⁷¹

It was perhaps the success of great ladies such as Elizabeth Clare and Maud of Lancaster in maintaining their Irish estates that encouraged Queen Philippa to seek custody in 1346 of the Burgh lands in Ireland—her son had been betrothed to Elizabeth, heiress of Ulster, in 1341—and she added to her interests in Louth and Meath by acquiring the wardship of the heir of John Darcy of Knaith on his death in 1347.⁷² Despite the low level of involvement of the English of Louth in the king's French wars in the 1340s and 1350s, and despite the non-residence of the major landowners in the county, what all this suggests is that some of the greatest lords in England, including members of the royal family, maintained or increased their involvement in this part of Ireland at this time. The restoration to Roger Mortimer (d.1360) in 1354 of his grandfather's title and estate, including the liberty of Trim, accorded with an established policy towards Ireland and anticipated the arrival of Lionel of Antwerp, earl of Ulster, at Dublin as lieutenant in September 1361.⁷³ This appointment marked a fusing of Edward III's personal

---

⁶⁸ Robin Frame does not appear to think that Gernon had Irish connections before Ufford's justiciarship. Frame, *English Lordship in Ireland*, 265; Frame, 'Justiciarship of Ralph Ufford', 13–15; *CPR 1345–8*, 41.

⁶⁹ *CCR 1354–60*, 493; *CPR 1367–70*, 219; *CPR 1370–4*, 116, 327; *CCR 1377–81*, 8; *CPR 1377–81*, 237, 603; *CPR 1381–5*, 161. In his old age Nicholas had also received a grant of land in the Ards peninsula from Edmund Mortimer, earl of March (d.1381), *CPR 1381–5*, 269; Walker, *Lancastrian Affinity*, 107 and n. 158, 270.

⁷⁰ *CPL 1342–62*, 588. The diocese of Armagh included Louth.

⁷¹ *CPR 1348–50*, 7, 369, 559; *CPR 1350–4*, 537; *CPR 1354–8*, 377, 574; *CPR 1358–61*, 472; *CPR 1361–4*, 187; *CPR 1364–7*, 24, 168; *CPR 1367–70*, 361, 375; *CPR 1370–4*, 325; *CPR 1374–7*, 122; *CPR 1377–81*, 265, 528; *CPR 1381–5*, 159, 275.

⁷² Frame, *English Lordship in Ireland*, 323; *CPR 1358–61*, 441; *CPR 1361–4*, 269; *CFR 1356–8*, 8; TNA E 101/243/12; *CCR 1354–60*, 406. For discussion of Queen Philippa's acquisitions in England, Christian Liddy, *War Politics and Finance in Late Medieval English Towns: Bristol, York and the Crown, 1350–1400* (Woodbridge, 2005), 62–80. For her reputation as a spendthrift see W. Mark Ormrod, *Edward III* (New Haven, 2011), 126–31.

⁷³ George A. Holmes, *The Estates of the Higher Nobility in XIV Century England* (Cambridge, 1957), 14–16; Frame, *English Lordship in Ireland*, 295–326; Peter Crooks, '"Hobbes", "Dogs" and Politics in the Ireland of Lionel of Antwerp', *Haskins Society Journal*, 16 (2005), 117–48; Potterton, *Medieval Trim*, 103–4.

interests, as father-in-law of the heiress to the greatest of the Irish earldoms, with his role as *dominus Hiberniae*, lord of Ireland.

Ties not only of lordship, but also of government, bound Louth to a larger English world. With the exception of the ten years (1319–29) in which John Bermingham had held Louth as a liberty, and the five months in 1330 in which Roger Mortimer had held it in like manner, Louth had operated since the early thirteenth century as a royal shire answerable directly to the crown and its officers in Dublin and Westminster, and administered at a local level through a royally appointed sheriff and his staff.[74] John Darcy was not the only English senior official of the Irish lordship to acquire property and other interests in Louth and Meath in this period, despite royal ordinances prohibiting its ministers in Ireland from indulging in this practice.[75] An associate of Darcy's, the Bedfordshire man John Morice, held the post of Irish escheator between 1329 and 1336, and in the 1340s served for periods as deputy justiciar, justiciar, and chancellor. While in office, he procured custody of two-thirds of the manor of Ardee, as well as custody of the lands of an important Meath sub-tenant, Walter de la Hyde, and the marriage of his heir, James.[76] Men from Louth and Meath, meanwhile, also helped staff the administration of the lordship in Dublin, and in particular its judicial branch. To take three examples, John Gernon served as chief justice of the common bench in the 1340s and 1350s, while John Keppok and Richard Plunket both began acting as king's serjeants at law in Dublin in the late 1350s.[77] All three spent time in England either before taking up office or during their time in post.[78]

Aristocratic lordship and royal government were only two of the ties that bound Louth to England and the English world in the middle of the fourteenth century. Another strand of the relationship centred on trade, and in this regard the town of Drogheda was of supreme importance. The revival of English authority in the Irish Sea after 1327 benefited the town, and its central role in the campaigns against Scotland in the 1330s has been noted.[79] The extent of Drogheda's trading network at this time is suggested by the recorded presence of its ships at Antwerp, Bristol, Bordeaux, and London between 1339 and 1342.[80] Closer to home, Drogheda and its hinterland had particularly strong links with north-west England. One dimension of this

---

[74] The origins of the county are discussed in Brendan Smith, 'Tenure and Locality in North Leinster in the Early Thirteenth Century', in Terry Barry, Robin Frame, and Katharine Simms (eds), *Colony and Frontier in Medieval Ireland: Essays Presented to J. F. Lydon* (London, 1995), 29–40.

[75] Frame, *English Lordship in Ireland*, 75–123.

[76] *CFR 1327–37*, 237; *Rep. DKI 44*, 38–9; *CCR 1333–7*, 565; *CFR 1337–47*, 296, 329; TNA E 101/241/9; Robin Frame, 'Morice, Sir John (d.1362)', *Oxford Dictionary of National Biography* (Oxford, 2004; online edn, Jan. 2008).

[77] *IEP* 415; *CPR 1348–50*, 38; *CPR 1350–4*, 84. Keppok was one of the executor's of Gernon's will: *IEP* 467. *NHI* ix. 522; *Admin. Ire.* 160–81; Paul Brand, 'The Birth and Early Development of a Colonial Judiciary: The Judges of the Lordship of Ireland, 1210–1377', in W. N. Osborough (ed.), *Explorations in Law and History: Irish Legal History Discourses, 1988–1994* (Dublin, 1995), 32–6.

[78] Frame, *English Lordship in Ireland*, 247; Sayles, 'Ecclesiastical Process and the Parsonage of Stabannon', 11–12; *CPR 1340–3*, 570, 572; *CPR 1348–50*, 254; *CPR 1350–4*, 244; *IEP*, 470, 478, 500.

[79] See above, 29.

[80] *CCR 1339–41*, 334, 592, 624; *CCR 1341–3*, 697.

relationship was ecclesiastical, centring on the possessions in eastern Ireland of the abbey of Furness in Cumbria, one of the richest Cistercian monasteries in England. Walter Lacy had granted the community Mornington (Marinerstown) on the Meath side of the Boyne estuary, east of Drogheda, in 1234, and in 1332 the house of Beaubec in Normandy was permitted to alienate its Irish property, worth almost £400, to Furness.[81] This consisted of land in Kells, the manor of Beybeg (originally Beaubec), south of Drogheda, as well as properties within the town itself.[82] These original holdings were supplemented in the 1330s by gifts from Drogheda merchants of shops and messuages (house plots), the revenues from which were to be used to sustain the monks in their life of prayer.[83] Its new Irish acquisitions were considered sufficiently important for the abbot of Furness to appoint attorneys in England in 1341 to allow him to spend time in Ireland, dealing with the affairs of his house.[84]

While in Drogheda, it is possible that the abbot had dealings with members of the Preston family who, as their name suggests, came originally from the Lancashire town some 60 kilometres south-east of Furness, and who had settled in Ireland in the 1300s.[85] William Preston (d. c.1351), burgess of Drogheda, had been a member of the inquisition jury assembled in the town by the escheator, John Morice, in November 1332 to decide whether Beaubec should be allowed grant its Irish property to Furness, while his brother Richard, who in the early 1330s served as seneschal of Drogheda in Meath and constable of its castle, in 1336 quitclaimed property in the town to a fellow burgess who subsequently granted it to Furness.[86] William Preston was a merchant—one of his ships was attacked by Spanish forces in 1332—who acquired land in the hinterland of Drogheda, at Slane, Duleek, and Gaulstown (Fingalstown, bar. Lower Duleek) in the 1340s, while in the same decade Richard was the recipient of land at Stameen, just south of Drogheda.[87] A third brother, Roger (d. c.1350), whose wife was from Lancashire, maintained estates on both sides of the Irish Sea and pursued a legal career first in England and then in Ireland, where in the 1330s he served as one of the justices of the justiciar's bench and as an assize justice in Louth and Meath.[88] He accumulated property in

---

[81] *Gormanston Reg.*, 8, 180.

[82] *RCH* 45 no. 67; *CPR 1330–4*, 382; *CCR 1333–7*, 474–5; Aubrey Gwynn and R. Neville Hancock, *Medieval Religious Houses: Ireland* (Dublin, 1988), 128. Among those who witnessed the charter by which the abbot of Beaubec made the grant in 1333 was Milo Verdon: *CPR 1340–3*, 52–3.

[83] *CPR 1334–8*, 44, 224; *CPR 1338–40*, 16; 'Ancient Deeds', 25, 30 (TNA DL 25/538, TNA DL 27/135); TNA C 143/226, 243; *Inquisitions and Extents*, 135; *The Coucher Book of Furness Abbey*, ed. J. C. Atkinson and J. Brownhill, Chetham Society (Manchester, 1886–1916), ii/3. 726–7; Paul Brand, 'King, Church and Property: Mortmain in the Lordship of Ireland', *Peritia*, 3 (1984), 495–6.

[84] *CPR 1340–3*, 128.

[85] Smith, *Colonisation and Conquest*, 154. Robert Preston was accounting for revenues from the abbey's holdings in Meath at the Irish exchequer in the 1360s: TNA E 101/244/9.

[86] *Inquisitions and Extents*, 135; *Gormanston Reg.*, 55–9; *CFR 1347–56*, 314; TNA E 101/239/26; *IEP* 363; 'Ancient Deeds', 24–5; James Moynes, 'The Prestons of Gormanston, c.1300–1532: An Anglo-Irish Gentry Family', *Ríocht na Midhe*, 14 (2003), 26–55.

[87] 'Lord Chancellor Gerrard's Notes on his Report on Ireland', 216–17, 250–1; *Gormanston Reg.* 39–40, 52, 55–9; TNA E 101/242/13.

[88] *Gormanston Reg.*, v–vi; Frame, *English Lordship in Ireland*, 95; *Admin. Ire.*, 169–70; *CCR 1333–7*, 188; *IEP* 373–4.

Drogheda and in 1343 received a royal grant of the holdings at Brittstown (Brettonstown, bar. Upper Slane) in Meath, which had been confiscated from the Scottish Cistercian house of Dundrennan.[89] Roger's son, Robert (d.1396) received his legal training in England but was active in Ireland by the mid-1340s, when with his father he was granted a lease for life by Eustace le Poer of the third of the manor of Ardee which had come to him through his wife.[90]

By the time Lionel of Antwerp arrived in Ireland in 1361, Robert Preston was a wealthy and influential man. Not only had he inherited his father's possessions in Drogheda and its environs, but he had also been the recipient of grants from his uncles, Richard and William, and had been awarded the custody of lands previously granted to them by the crown.[91] His links with England remained close: he received special permission to export grain from Drogheda to England in May 1355, at a time when such exports were forbidden, and continued to involve himself in the land market in Preston in the 1350s. In the same period he also received numerous grants of property in Drogheda and adjacent parts of Meath.[92] His legal career in Ireland flourished in the same years. He served as a serjeant at law between 1348 and 1358; was one of those given a commission of oyer et terminer in 1351 to deal with disturbances in the earldom of Desmond; and in 1358 was appointed as chief justice of the common bench.[93] In 1353 he married Margaret Bermingham, daughter of a former justiciar, Walter Bermingham (d.1350), and on her death in 1361 succeeded to the Bermingham estates on the troubled Meath–Kildare–Offaly border centred on Carbury.[94] He was also a popular choice as attorney for absentee lords with Irish interests in the 1350s, acting in this capacity for, among others, the former Irish escheator, Roger Darcy, Elizabeth Meynell, widow of Roger's older brother John Darcy 'le fitz' (d.1356), and Roger Clifford (d.1389), lord of a portion of the Clare lands.[95] In another indication of his high standing and influence he was also chosen to act as his attorney in Ireland by the justiciar, Thomas Rokeby, on his departure for England in August 1355.[96]

Drogheda, it is clear, continued to provide opportunities to ambitious English families to advance their status in an Irish setting in the middle of the fourteenth century, and was an important point of contact between the settlers in Louth and

---

[89] *Reg. Kilmainham*, 86; *Gormanston Reg.*, 38, 75; *CFR 1337–47*, 332; TNA E 101/241/9, 14, 18, 20.

[90] Frame, *English Lordship in Ireland*, 275; Eustace had married Matilda, eldest daughter of John Bermingham, earl of Louth, in 1331: *Clyn*, 202. Their son, Arnold, was a minor in 1358 and was dead before 1366: *RCH* 70 no. 76, 73 no. 40; TNA E 101/244/9.

[91] *Gormanston Reg.*, 40, 41, 53, 55–9, 79–80; *CFR 1347–56*, 314; TNA E 101/242/13; TNA E 101/243/1, 4, 11, 12; TNA E 101/244/4, 9.

[92] *Gormanston Reg.*, 45, 70–1, 72, 76, 77–8; 79–80, 88, 89, 90–3; *RCH* 62 no. 106.

[93] *NHI* ix. 522; *Admin. Ire.*, 162; *CPR 1350–4*, 84.

[94] Moynes, 'Prestons of Gormanston', 33–4; A. J. Otway-Ruthven, *A History of Medieval Ireland* (London, 1968), 263–7. Margaret was buried in the Dominican church in Drogheda: *Chartul. St Mary's, Dublin*, ii. 395.

[95] *CPR 1350–4*, 383, 398; *CPR 1354–8*, 203, 375, 412, 577; *CPR 1358–61*, 93, 236, 458, 461; Frame, *English Lordship in Ireland*, 60, 97; Henry Summerson, 'Clifford, Roger, Fifth Baron Clifford (1333–1389)', *Oxford Dictionary of National Biography* (Oxford, 2004; online edn, Jan. 2008).

[96] *RCH* 58 no. 155.

the wider world. It was its very openness to such contact, however, that brought disaster in late July or early August 1348 with the appearance of plague in the town.[97] Contemporary Franciscan chroniclers in Kilkenny and Nenagh (co. Tipperary), who can be expected to have kept in regular contact with their confrères in Drogheda, made plain the devastation that quickly ensued. Writing independently, they asserted that Dublin and Drogheda had been almost destroyed and left uninhabited by the first onslaught of the disease, with twenty-five Franciscans alone succumbing in Drogheda between summer and Christmas 1348.[98] There is no reason to doubt that the loss of life in the town was substantial, and when combined with the death-toll resulting from the MacMahon raid of 1346, it seems likely that county Louth in the two-and-a-half years before the end of 1348 saw its population reduced by a significant amount.[99] It was almost certainly in response to a high mortality rate among his clergy that sometime before January 1351 Archbishop Richard Fitz Ralph of Armagh (1346–60) successfully petitioned the pope for permission to dispense from disqualifications including illegitimacy sixty men so that they might be ordained and take up benefices in his province. In the wake of trauma on such an unprecedented scale the appearance in the area by November 1349 of 'flagellantes' should come as little surprise.[100] Some sense of the impact of the epidemic within the first few years of its appearance on a local economy already suffering as a result of Irish raids can be gleaned from a variety of contemporary financial records. The account of Elizabeth Clare's receiver of Kells, John Burri, for 1352–3 noted that a portion of the payments due from John Roche for the previous two years had been suspended 'as the town has been brought to nothing by the plague, and the mill has been burnt to the ground by the Irish', while an inquisition held at his manor of Nobber (bar. Morgallion, co. Meath) before Archbishop Fitz Ralph in November 1351 found that the manor had yielded no revenue whatsoever since December 1349.[101]

The arrival of plague in 1348 marked the beginning of an era in which the disease appeared on many occasions in Louth and Meath, with some later outbreaks being regarded by contemporaries as even more devastating in their impact than the first assault. The Register of Clogher, in recording the death of Bishop Brian Mac Cathmhaoil, probably in 1358, reports that 'he died in the city of Clogher of the common plague by which all Ireland was afflicted and the city of Clogher almost entirely depopulated'.[102] The Dublin annalist described the outbreak of

---

[97] Maria Kelly, *A History of the Black Death in Ireland* (Stroud, 2001), 22.

[98] *Clyn*, 246, 250; 'The Annals of Nenagh', ed. Dermot F. Gleeson, *Anal. Hib.* 12 (1943), 160.

[99] A recent estimate puts the death-rate from the disease in England before the end of 1349 at between 30 and 40%: Jim Bolton, '"The World Turned Upside Down": Plague as an Agent of Economic and Social Change', in Mark Ormrod and Phillip Lindley (eds), *The Black Death in England* (Donington, 2003), 22–6.

[100] *CPL 1342–62*, 311, 387. For the death-rate among the clergy in England see Christopher Harper-Bill, 'The English Church and English Religion After the Black Death', in Ormrod and Lindley, *Black Death in England*, 79–123.

[101] *Handbook and Select Calendar...Ireland*, 304–6; *Reg. Sweteman*, 244–6.

[102] 'The Register of Clogher', ed. Kenneth Nicholls, *Clogher Record*, 7 (1971–2), 393 and n. 66 where the editor suggests 1361—a year of great plague throughout Europe—as the year of death.

1370, 'in which many nobles, townsmen, and innumerable children died', as the worst that Ireland had seen and listed among those who died that year Simon Fleming, baron of Slane, and John Cusack, baron of Culmullin (bar. Upper Deece, co. Meath).[103] In 1367 Milo Sweteman, archbishop of Armagh (1361–80), wrote to the pope that since he became archbishop in 1361 his province had been destroyed, 'primo per pestilentiam continuam et postea per continuam guerram'. In 1375, in a grant of the manor of Iniskeen (bar. Farney, co. Monaghan), Milo included the provision that the grantee be compensated 'if the manor yields him no profit through the ravages of pestilence or the king's enemies'.[104]

Repeated and severe occurrences of plague from the middle of the fourteenth century affected many aspects of life in Louth, but did not lead to any weakening of the ties between the area and England. Instead, the economic dislocation caused by the rapid and sizeable decrease in population in England after 1348 led to a new reliance on Irish resources, and to efforts to integrate more closely the economies of both sides of the Irish Sea. Drogheda was elevated to the status of a staple port in 1353 at the same time as Exeter, Bristol, Carmarthen, Dublin, Waterford, Cork, and other ports in England.[105] In Dublin in March 1362, the lieutenant, Lionel of Antwerp, authorized a series of measures to help Drogheda on account of its having been 'damaged recently by a great and horrible pestilence', to the detriment of its sea merchants and burgesses. The town was permitted to retain a portion of the money raised from the sale of goods within its confines in order to pay for the repair of its streets, walls, a fallen tower, and its bridge.[106] Such initiatives made good economic sense from an English perspective since it was from Drogheda that much of the grain from Meath and Louth—'the granary of the empire' as one nineteenth-century local historian put it—was exported to help feed the king's subjects closer to home as the century progressed.[107] As early as November 1351, royal licences were being granted to Drogheda merchants to allow shipment of corn to England, and in July 1352 Archbishop Fitz Ralph of Armagh was permitted to ship corn from Ireland to succour his old friend and patron, John Grandison, bishop of Exeter (1327–69).[108] Some realization of the strain placed on Irish resources by the scale of this trade was displayed in the mid-1350s when ports between Carlingford and Dublin were prohibited from exporting corn or fish 'because of their high price and scarcity, and the oppression and complaint of the

---

[103] *Chartul. St Mary's, Dublin*, ii. 397–8.
[104] *Reg. Sweteman*, 136–7, 154.
[105] *Statutes of the Realm*, i. 333; *PROME* v. 71.
[106] *CPI* 78, 82, 89. The grant, initially for six years, was repeated in 1385 and 1392.
[107] Dalton, *History of Drogheda*, i. 137; Richard Britnell, 'English Agricultural Output and Prices, 1350–1450: National Trends and Regional Divergences', in Ben Dodds and Richard Britnell (eds), *Agriculture and Rural Society After the Black Death: Common Themes and Regional Variations* (Hatfield, 2008), 21–31; John S. Lee, 'Grain Shortages in Late Medieval Towns', in Ben Dodds and Christian D. Liddy (eds), *Commercial Activity, Markets and Entrepreneurs in the Middle Ages: Essays in Honour of Richard Britnell* (Woodbridge, 2011), 63–80.
[108] *CPR 1350–4*, 192, 305, 356; Katherine Walsh, *A Fourteenth-Century Scholar and Primate: Richard FitzRalph in Oxford, Avignon and Armagh* (Oxford, 1981), 64–70; Gearóid Mac Niocaill, *Na Buirgéisí, XII–XV Aois*, 2 vols (Dublin, 1964), i. 351–2.

common people', but by the late 1370s, as food shortages continued in parts of England, the crown was once more urging the authorities in Drogheda to facilitate the transport of 'wheat or other kinds of corn' to England, and continued to grant licences to individual Drogheda merchants to encourage the same trade.[109] The monks of Furness were allowed import grain from Ireland—no doubt via Drogheda—for their own use in 1383 because the Furness peninsula was said to be destitute of corn.[110]

Drogheda's sufferings in 1348, and its ability in the decades that followed to benefit from the economic upheavals wrought by the disaster of that year, reflected its openness to the outside world. County Louth as a whole shared in this openness, as the career of its most famous medieval son, Richard Fitz Ralph, archbishop of Armagh between 1346 and 1360, demonstrated.[111] Fitz Ralph was born in Dundalk some time shortly before 1300 and studied at Oxford from about 1315 to 1328. After a short spell at Paris he was elected chancellor of Oxford in 1332, a post he held until 1334 when he made the first of several lengthy sojourns at the papal court at Avignon. He was chosen to be their new archbishop by the canons of Armagh in May 1346, a choice confirmed by Pope Clement VI two months later. He arrived in Ireland in early 1348, delivering his first recorded sermon in the country at Dundalk in April of that year, some three months before the plague arrived at Drogheda. A break in his otherwise full sermon-diary for the period between May 1348 and March 1349 suggests a suspension of his normal routine as a result of the pestilence, but by August 1349 he was at Avignon, where he preached before the pope. He had been sent by King Edward III to explain the difficulties faced by his subjects on account of warfare and plague in taking advantage of the Jubilee Indulgence granted by the pope to coincide with the Holy Year of 1350. Fitz Ralph's reflections in this sermon on the impact of the plague of 1348, which place the Irish experience in the context of the king of England's wider realms, speak to the cosmopolitan nature of his own career to this point.[112]

Fitz Ralph was among many young men from Ireland who studied in England in the fourteenth century. In 1346, the commons of Louth, seeking vengeance for the raid of MacMahon of that year, had petitioned that all native Irish scholars then at Oxford should be arrested for the wrongdoings of their relatives back in Ireland. The curt reply of the king's council—'La peticion nest pas resonable'—reflected in part the degree to which the presence of such scholars at Oxford was seen as routine and desirable.[113] As archbishop of Armagh, Fitz Ralph ensured that the connections of his province with the outside world were not only maintained

---

[109] *RCH* 57 nos. 130 and 144, 60 no. 44; *IEP* 473; *CCR 1374–7*, 318; *CPR 1374–7*, 301, 304, 305.

[110] *CPR 1381–5*, 329.

[111] For what follows, Katherine Walsh, 'Fitzralph, Richard (b. before 1300, d. 1360)', *Oxford Dictionary of National Biography* (Oxford, 2004; online edn, May 2010); Aubrey Gwynn, 'Richard Fitz-Ralph, Archbishop of Armagh', *Studies: An Irish Quarterly Review*, 22 (1933), 389–405.

[112] Aubrey Gwynn, 'The Black Death in Ireland', *Studies: An Irish Quarterly Review*, 24 (1935), 25–42; Aubrey Gywnn, 'The Sermon-Diary of Richard Fitzralph, Archbishop of Armagh', *PRIA* 44 (1937–8), C, 42–3.

[113] Sayles, *Affairs*, 186–7.

but strengthened, both by continuing to visit Avignon and by using his international renown to attract pilgrims from Europe to St Patrick's Purgatory on Lough Derg in Donegal. En route to the famous cave, pilgrims from Hungary, France, and Italy passed through Louth in the 1350s.[114] Richard Fitz Ralph died at Avignon in late November 1360. His bones were returned to Ireland, where they were interred in the church of St Nicholas, Dundalk, 'where he had preached'.[115] Not since St Malachy (Máel Máedoc Ó Morgair, d.1148) had befriended St Bernard of Clairvaux and overseen the introduction of the Augustinian and Cistercian Orders into Ireland in the 1140s had the holder of the see of Patrick enjoyed such a high profile on the European stage.[116] While none of his successors were to emulate Richard's stature as an international figure, his death did not mark any weakening of links between Armagh and the western Church, any more than the appearance of plague in 1348, and its recurrence thereafter, reduced the strength of the bonds between Louth and England.

Within a year of Fitz Ralph's death, in September 1361, Lionel of Antwerp, earl of Ulster and son of King Edward III, accompanied by his wife, Elizabeth Burgh, arrived in Dublin as his father's lieutenant of Ireland.[117] His advent reflected a willingness on the part of the English crown to engage with the fortunes of its Irish lordship more thoroughly than had been the case for many decades, if not generations.[118] It was prompted by a cessation in the war with France in 1360, and by the death in the same year of the grandmother of Lionel's wife, Elizabeth Clare, which brought to him yet more Irish estates in Ulster and elsewhere. It also resulted from a successful campaign on the part of the settler community in Ireland to convince the king that the security situation in the country had declined to such an extent that only the dispatch 'd'un bone chiefteyn suffisant' would save the lordship from utter ruin.[119] Undoubtedly Irish pressure on the English settlement had increased since the first appearance of plague in 1348, but Louth and Meath were not considered by the authorities to face as serious a threat from the king's enemies as other parts of the country.[120] In the 1350s, it was Munster and Leinster that absorbed the attention of the chief governor, and his armies were seen infrequently further north as a result.[121] The MacMahon attack of 1346, however, was not an isolated incident,

---

[114] Walsh, *Fourteenth-Century Scholar and Primate*, 304–18; Shane Leslie, *St Patrick's Purgatory* (London, 1932), 19–20; Michael Haren, 'Two Hungarian Pilgrims', in Michael Haren and Yolande de Pontfarcy (eds), *The Medieval Pilgrimage to St Patrick's Purgatory: Lough Derg and the European Tradition*. Clogher Historical Society (Enniskillen, 1988), 120–68.
[115] *AC* 319; *Chartul. St Mary's, Dublin*, ii. 393.
[116] Smith, *Colonisation and Conquest*, 17–25; Marie Therese Flanagan, 'St Mary's Abbey, Louth, and the Introduction of the Arrouaisian Observance into Ireland', *Clogher Record*, 10 (1980), 223–34.
[117] *Chartul. St Mary's, Dublin*, ii. 395.
[118] Robin Frame, *Colonial Ireland, 1169–1369* (Dublin, 2012), 128–53.
[119] Frame, *English Lordship in Ireland*, 323–5; *Parls. & Councils*, 19–22, quotation at 21.
[120] James Lydon, *The Lordship of Ireland in the Middle Ages* (Dublin, 1972; new edn, 2003), 147–52; James Lydon, *Ireland in the Later Middle Ages* (Dublin, 1973), 77–85.
[121] A. J. Otway-Ruthven, 'Ireland in the 1350s: Sir Thomas Rokeby and his Successors', *Journal of the Royal Society of Antiquaries of Ireland*, 97 (1967), 47–59; Frame, *English Lordship in Ireland*, 295–326; Robin Frame, 'English Officials and Irish Chiefs in the Fourteenth Century', in his *Ireland and*

and the Irish on their borders presented serious dangers to the inhabitants of Louth and east Meath at a time when government resources were being expended elsewhere. Hugh Golding was held hostage by O'Reilly in 1346 and parleys with this Irish leader and with the Irish of Ulster, conducted in part by Archbishop Fitz Ralph, were still ongoing in 1349.[122] A fragment of an Irish chronicle preserved in a fifteenth-century episcopal register from Armagh records the burning of St Mary's abbey, in the town of Louth, in 1350 by Magnus MacMahon, king of Airgialla—'a lamentable, detestable, horrible and pernicious deed (*exemplum*), the like of which had not been perpetrated in Ireland in memory'.[123]

In response to this attack, which the English authorities believed had been carried out by MacMahon in alliance with Aed O'Neill and his military commander, Mac-Quillin (Mac Uigilín), the justiciar, Thomas Rokeby, in the following year assembled an armed force 'in Uriel against Eth Inell and other Irish enemies'.[124] In the years that followed, Rokeby spent most of his time in Munster and south Leinster, but did conduct negotiations with O'Reilly before Easter 1353 that led to the latter returning to the king's peace. The justiciar declared that he had acted 'in the most subtle way he could' on this occasion, a subtlety that extended to paying £5 9s to O'Reilly to encourage his cooperation.[125] In 1354 it fell to the Irish treasurer, William Bromley, to undertake business of this sort; in that year he was awarded £20 for expenses incurred 'in going and staying in parts of Kilkenny, Meath and Uriel to conduct various parleys in the marches with the Irish enemies of the king for the restoration of the peace and the defence of the marches against hostile attacks'.[126] Particular attention appears to have been paid to placating Brian MacMahon—the leader of the assault on Louth in 1346—who was granted the king's peace twice in 1355.[127] On 28 April 1355, while conducting a visitation of the diocese of Meath at Trim, Richard Fitz Ralph, archbishop of Armagh, received a letter from Rokeby ordering him to proceed at once to Dundalk, which was under threat of attack from Aed O'Neill, and to negotiate a settlement with him. He seems to have succeeded in this task, and had resumed his visitation, at Kells, by 14 May.[128]

Britain, 249–77; Frame, 'Military Service in the Lordship of Ireland', 279–99. For Munster see Robin Frame, 'Lordship Beyond the Pale: Munster in the Late Middle Ages', in Roger Stalley (ed), *Limerick and South-West Ireland: Medieval Art and Architecture*. British Archaeological Association Conference Transactions, 34 (Leeds, 2011), 5–18. For Leinster see O'Byrne, *War, Politics and the Irish of Leinster*, 96–102; Robin Frame, 'Two Kings in Leinster: The Crown and the MicMhurchadha in the Fourteenth Century', in Barry et al., *Colony and Frontier in Medieval Ireland*, 165–8.

[122] *RCH* 50 no. 105; NAI RC 8/24, 446–7.

[123] *Reg. Octaviani*, ii. 487–8. In describing the de Verdon rebellion of 1312 the same fragment contains in Gaelic script the Gaelic words *Luguad do luscud uli*: '[the town of] Louth was entirely burnt'. The editor has transcribed the entry slightly differently, as *luguad de lorcud uli*.

[124] NAI RC 8/25, 562–4; *IEP* 435, 442, 454; Katharine Simms, *From Kings to Warlords: The Changing Political Structure of Gaelic Ireland in the Later Middle Ages* (Woodbridge, 1987, repr. 2000), 138–9.

[125] *IEP* 448, 449; Robin Frame, 'Thomas Rokeby, Sheriff of Yorkshire, Justiciar of Ireland', *Peritia*, 10 (1996), 274–96.

[126] *IEP* 454.

[127] *RCH* 56 no. 34, 57 no. 135. He may have received a similar grant in Nov. 1356: *RCH* 64 no. 17.

[128] *RCH* 62 no. 100; Walsh, *Fourteenth-Century Scholar and Primate*, 339–40, 343–4; Katharine Simms, 'The Archbishops of Armagh and the O'Neills 1347–1471', *IHS* 19 (1974), 45.

The circumstances of the threat to Dundalk in 1355 are revealing: Aed O'Neill was responding to a significant defeat inflicted upon him the previous year by the Clandeboy branch of the O'Neills, in alliance with the English of Dundalk.[129] It was at this time that the Clandeboy O'Neills completed their separation from the main line of the dynasty, concluding a physical relocation eastwards from southeast Derry across the river Bann into Antrim that had begun a generation earlier. The English of Dundalk had spotted an opportunity in these internal dissensions among the O'Neills in 1354 to strike back at Aed O'Neill, who had attacked Louth four years earlier, by supporting his enemies in Clandeboy. They had their archbishop and fellow-Dundalkman, Richard Fitz Ralph, to thank for being spared a reckoning for their endeavours in 1355.[130] During his reign of twenty years (1345–64), Aed O'Neill rarely targeted Louth, concentrating instead on having his authority as king of Ulster recognized by the other Irish families of the province. A notable success in this campaign was the victory he achieved over the Maguires (Méig Uidir) of Fír Manach (Fermanagh) and MacMahons of Airgialla in 1358.[131] In the previous year O'Neill's ally in the 1350 attack on Louth, Magnus MacMahon, had died, to be succeeded by his uncle, Philip. On Philip's death in 1362 he was succeeded by Brian MacMahon, who had led the assault on Louth in 1346.[132]

Two years after Brian MacMahon (d.1371) became chief, Aed O'Neill died and MacMahon took advantage of the subsequent succession dispute among the O'Neills to increase his own power in south Ulster.[133] It was his potential usefulness as an obstacle to O'Neill expansionism in Ulster that brought MacMahon to the attention of Lionel of Antwerp (after November 1362 duke of Clarence), and he was rewarded in 1364 for having accompanied the lieutenant on an expedition in the midlands in the spring of that year.[134] Lionel had earlier entered into an indentured peace agreement with Aed O'Neill which the latter had abrogated by seizing the horses of Lionel's constable, Geoffrey White, at Greencastle (bar. Mourne, co. Down). The lieutenant's response was limited to requesting that the archbishop of Armagh, Milo Sweteman, excommunicate O'Neill and his son, Domnall, and he seems to have exerted little or no influence on the course of the O'Neill succession dispute that began on Aed's death in 1364.[135] The winner of

---

[129] *A. Clon.*, 298–9.
[130] James Hogan, 'The Irish Law of Kingship, with Special Reference to Ailech and Cenél Eoghain', *PRIA* 40 (1931–2), C, 226–7.
[131] *AFM* iii. 613. For discussion of Aed's seal, with its heraldic motif of a hand on a shield, which proclaims him to be 'king of the Irish of Ulster', see Freya Verstraten, 'Images of Gaelic Lordship in Ireland, *c.*1200–*c.*1400', in Linda Doran and James Lyttleton (eds), *Lordship in Medieval Ireland: Image and Reality* (Dublin, 2007), 62–7, with a sketch of the seal at 74.
[132] *A. Clon.* 300; *AU* ii. 505, 515; *AC* 299.
[133] *AC* 325.
[134] *Handbook and Select Calendar…Ireland*, 316 (TNA E 101/28/21. Particulars of account of Walter Dalby, 1361–4); Otway-Ruthven, *History of Medieval Ireland*, 289.
[135] *Reg. Sweteman*, 229–30. The entry is incomplete and undated. The description of Domnall as son of O'Neill implies that Aed O'Neill is intended. This dates the indenture to in or before 1364. Jay Gundacker, 'Absolutions and Acts of Disobedience: Excommunication and Society in Fourteenth-Century Armagh', *Traditio*, 64 (2009), 183–212.

this contest, Niall son of Aed, who defeated his brother, Domnall, in 1370, would pose a far greater threat to the English of Louth than his father had done.

In 1358, before his appointment as Irish lieutenant, Lionel had shown some concern for the fortunes of that part of his earldom which overlapped with county Louth by successfully petitioning his father for the grant of a weekly market and annual fair at Carlingford, but he did not sustain this level of interest in Ulster while in Ireland.[136] He visited Drogheda twice, in February 1362 and December 1365, but for most of the four-and-a-half years he spent in the country between September 1361 and November 1366, his energies were focused on safeguarding Leinster.[137] The death of his wife, Elizabeth Burgh, in 1363 removed a direct connection with Ulster and his remarriage, shortly before his death in 1368, to a Milanese aristocratic lady pointed to a further reduction in his Irish interests.[138] Lionel's first marriage, however, had produced a daughter, Philippa (1355–78), and the plans he made for his granddaughter's future suggest that Edward III continued to devote careful consideration to the question of how to maintain the English position in Ulster. In 1358 the king secured the betrothal of Philippa, then aged 3, to the 6-year-old Edmund Mortimer (1352–81), heir to the earldom of March and extensive properties in Ireland, including the lordship of Trim.[139] Lionel heard pleas at Trim in January and February 1362 and in July and November 1366, suggesting an interest on his part in the fortunes of the estates of his future son-in-law.[140] In 1368 the marriage of Edmund and Philippa took place, at which point Mortimer was allowed to accede to his title and lands even though he had not yet reached his majority. It seems clear that Edward III saw the best hope for Ulster as lying in its union with Trim under the authority of one of the greatest magnate families in the British Isles.[141]

While he did not spend a great amount of time in Meath or Louth when acting as lieutenant of Ireland, Lionel did have sustained contact with some important individuals from these counties. The baron of Slane, Simon Fleming (d.1370), held land in Cornwall and Devon and had spent considerable periods of time in England since the late 1340s. He succeeded in 1355 in regaining Slane, which had been confiscated in 1352, and remained by Lionel's side in Ireland, having

---

[136] *CPI* 60; *RCH* 75 no. 95.

[137] Otway-Ruthven, *History of Medieval Ireland*, 286–95; NAI RC 8/28, 64 and 8/29, 33–6; Otway-Ruthven, 'Partition of the de Verdon Lands', 440–1. A puzzle is presented by the document in *Reg. Sweteman*, 31–2, a charter issued by Lionel at Downpatrick on 13 May 1366. The lieutenant was in Clonmel in Apr. and at Kilmallock on 20 May.

[138] W. M. Ormrod, 'Lionel, Duke of Clarence (1338–1368)', *Oxford Dictionary of National Biography* (Oxford, 2004; online edn, Jan. 2008); Ward, *English Noblewomen*, 100, 161.

[139] George Holmes, 'Mortimer, Edmund (III), Third Earl of March and Earl of Ulster (1352–1381)', *Oxford Dictionary of National Biography* (Oxford, 2004; online edn, Jan. 2008).

[140] Philomena Connolly, 'Pleas Held Before the Chief Governor of Ireland, 1308–76', *The Irish Jurist*, 18 (1983), 127–8.

[141] Davies, *Lords and Lordship*, 143, 151. There is a confusion in Davies's account of the date of this union which as editor of this posthumously published work I should have spotted and corrected. Given-Wilson, *English Nobility*, 42; K. B. McFarlane, *The Nobility of Later Medieval England* (Oxford, 1973), 86 and n. 3; G. L. Harriss, *King, Parliament and Public Finance in Medieval England to 1369* (Oxford, 1975), 485.

accompanied him to the lordship.¹⁴² In 1363–4, when complaints from Ireland reached the king about the conduct of Lionel and his ministers in the country, Fleming was one of those appointed to investigate and report on a matter which Edward III declared he had 'very much at heart'.¹⁴³ Soon after his arrival in Ireland, Lionel knighted a number of settler leaders with whom Fleming would have been familiar, including Robert Preston, Robert Holywood, Walter Cusack, and James de la Hyde, all of whom had or would soon have significant landed interests in Louth/Meath.¹⁴⁴

In the 1350s, the jusiticiar, Thomas Rokeby, had addressed the issue of absenteeism—which had featured in the rhetoric of Anglo-Irish relations since the time of the Bruce invasion—with a new determination, and the continuation of this approach under Lionel began to have an impact on landholding in Louth and Meath during his lieutenancy.¹⁴⁵ In August 1363, Amaury St Amand, who had been Irish justiciar in 1357–9 and who had accompanied Lionel to Ireland in 1361, granted his manor of Gormanston (bar. Upper Duleek, co. Meath) to Robert Preston, who worked closely with Lionel during his lieutenancy.¹⁴⁶ A year later, William Ferrers, son and heir of Isabel, daughter of Theobald Verdon and Elizabeth Clare, alienated his lands in Louth and Meath to Robert Holywood, a senior administrator in the colonial government with a long history of land acquisition in Ireland, while by August 1366 William Furnival of Sheffield, heir to another portion of the Verdon estates, had granted his Louth and Meath lands to one of his former attorneys in Ireland, John Bellew.¹⁴⁷ Such alienations broke landholding links between this part of Ireland and England that in some cases were of long standing, but were clearly popular with those settlers who stood to gain from them new estates and increased status.

Far less appealing to local tastes were Lionel's attempts to exploit the resources of the liberty of Trim, which had been in the hands of the crown since 1360 and which was destined to be united with his own earldom of Ulster, to the advantage of his entourage in Ireland. This was a policy that led to armed conflict involving another of those whom Lionel had knighted in 1361–2, Walter Cusack.¹⁴⁸ Lionel

---

¹⁴² NAI RC 8/25, 633–5; *RCH* 63 no. 136; *CPR 1348–50*, 380; *CPR 1350–4*, 353, 356, 488; *CPR 1361–4*, 155; *CCR 1364–9*, 58; *CPR 1364–7*, 154, 182; *CFR 1377–83*, 159; Robin Frame, 'King Henry III and Ireland: The Shaping of a Peripheral Lordship', in his *Ireland and Britain*, 45 n. 92.

¹⁴³ *CPR 1361–4*, 369, 537; *CCR 1364–9*, 58.

¹⁴⁴ *Chartul. St Mary's, Dublin*, ii. 395–6.

¹⁴⁵ Frame, 'Thomas Rokeby', 286–90; Frame, *English Lordship in Ireland*, 52–60; Beth Hartland, 'Absenteeism: The Chronology of a Concept', in Björn Weiler, Janet Burton, Phillipp Schofield and Karen Stöber (eds), *Thirteenth Century England XI* (Woodbridge, 2007), 215–29.

¹⁴⁶ *NHI* ix. 474; *Handbook and Select Calendar…Ireland*, 312–13; *Gormanston Reg.* 18–22; *CPR 1364–7*, 68; Robin Frame, 'St Amand, Almaric, Third Baron St Amand (1314–1381)', *Oxford Dictionary of National Biography* (Oxford, 2004; online edn, Jan. 2008).

¹⁴⁷ Otway-Ruthven, 'Partition of the de Verdon lands', 417, 441–3; *CPR 1364–7*, 218; *Dowdall Deeds*, 96–7. For Holywood, Frame, *English Lordship in Ireland*, 101–2.

¹⁴⁸ For tensions between the king's subjects from England and those living in Ireland in the 1360s, see Crooks, '"Hobbes", "Dogs" and Politics'. More generally, James Lydon, 'The Middle Nation', in Lydon, *The English in Medieval Ireland*, 1–26. Repr. in Peter Crooks (ed.), *Government, War and Society in Medieval Ireland: Essays by Edmund Curtis, A. J. Otway-Ruthven and James Lydon* (Dublin, 2008), 332–2. For Trim in the 1360s, Potterton, *Medieval Trim*, 104–6.

had appointed Roger Berde, who had accompanied him to Ireland, as constable of Trim castle soon after his arrival in the country, but by May 1363 Berde had been dismissed and a commission given to a number of important individuals from Meath, including John Bellew and Walter Cusack, to enquire into aspects of his behaviour, including his possible complicity in the death in captivity at Trim of Art MacMurrough (Mac Murchada), king of Leinster, and his *tánaiste* (likely successor), Domnall Riabach MacMurrough.[149] Walter's marriage to a member of another respectable Meath family, Joan Tuyt, had proved unhappy and the union was annulled some years before 1363.[150] Joan had subsequently married Henry Ferrers, who was possibly a member of the family into which one of the Verdon heiresses had married earlier in the century, and who served as a knight in the retinue of Lionel of Clarence in 1364 before being appointed marshal of Ireland.[151] Walter appears to have feared that the son of his marriage to Joan, Luke, might be disinherited as a result of Joan's remarriage, and in 1363 appealed to Milo Sweteman, archbishop of Armagh, who was conducting a visitation of the diocese of Meath, to reverse the annulment. Milo agreed and ordered Joan to return to Walter. On her refusal to do so, Milo ordered the bishop of Meath to excommunicate her in February 1364, leading Joan and Henry to appeal to the pope, who in October 1364 ordered the bishop, dean, and archdeacon of Clonmacnoise to adjudicate in the case.[152] The tensions between Walter and Henry led to them being arrested and ordered to pursue their dispute by legal means, but in the autumn of 1366 the affair spilled over into violence when a force of Meath notables led by Walter Cusack and James de la Hyde—the son of a former sheriff of Meath and another of those knighted by Lionel in 1361–2—'assuming to themselves the royal power', expelled Henry and Joan from their lands. Henry was wounded in this affray and was then besieged in his manor of Clonee on the Meath/Dublin border until relieved by a force led by Lionel in one of his final acts before leaving Ireland for the last time on 7 November 1366.[153]

By the time of his departure, Lionel had learnt the dangers of antagonizing the local settler elites of Louth and Meath. Despite his attempts to show them goodwill

---

[149] Potterton, *Medieval Trim*, 216–7; *CPR 1361–4*, 368; Emmett O'Byrne, '"A Divided Loyalty": The MacMurroughs, the Irish of Leinster and the Crown of England 1340–1420', in Thomas McGrath and William Nolan (eds), *Carlow: History and Society* (Dublin, 2008), 282. For the position of the *tánaiste*, Simms, *From Kings to Warlords*, 41–59.

[150] For what follows see Brendan Smith, 'Lionel of Clarence and the English of Meath', *Peritia*, 10 (1996), 297–302.

[151] Philomena Connolly, 'Lionel of Clarence and Ireland, 1361–1366', Ph.D. thesis, University of Dublin, Trinity College (1977), 307; TNA E 101/28/18; *CPR 1364–7*, 12. It is not certain that Joan's husband was the Henry son of Ralph Ferrers mentioned in 1380 (*CPR 1377–81*, 496). Ralph was attorney in Ireland for some of the Verdon heirs, and served as a justice of the justiciar's bench in the early 1360s: *Dowdall Deeds*, 90–1, 92, 94 (*bis*), 95; *Admin. Ire.*, 172–3.

[152] *Gormanston Reg.*, 29; *Reg. Sweteman*, 226–7; *Vetera Monumenta*, 327–8.

[153] *CPR 1364–7*, 326; TNA E 101/243/4. Henry and Joan remained married and retained their Irish lands, and on Joan's death Henry married another settler lady, Maud. He spent an increasing amount of time away from Ireland after 1366 and cut his Irish ties in 1386 when he granted his lands in Meath to the ubiquitous Robert Preston: *CPR 1367–70*, 185. 186; *CPR 1374–7*, 342–3, 436–7; *CFR 1377–83*, 6; *CPR 1377–81*, 13, 270, 392, 496, 528; *Gormanston Reg.*, 29–30.

by knighting several of their number in 1361 and by acquiescing in the transfer to them of property from English absentees thereafter, he seems never to have gained their trust or full cooperation. In May 1363, in response to complaints from the settlers, Edward III established a commission to investigate the actions of Lionel and his ministers in Ireland. As well as the three settler earls, Ormond, Kildare, and Desmond, its membership comprised four men from Meath/Louth: Simon Fleming, baron of Slane, John Hussey, baron of Galtrim, John Cusack, and William London. The ties between these men could hardly have been closer since the wives of three of them, Fleming, Hussey, and London were sisters—the daughters of Simon Geneville and Joan Fitz Leones—while Cusack's wife appears to have been their niece.[154] Simon Fleming's career has already been mentioned, and while his fellows lacked comparable landed interests in England, they remained important figures both within their locality and beyond. Hussey, Cusack, and London, for instance, all served as seneschals of Trim between 1348 and 1354, and it was probably in connection with discharging their duties in this capacity that Cusack and London spent time in England in these years.[155]

Fleming was also a member of the next commission established because of concerns about how Ireland was being governed, which operated from April 1364. Among its other members was Richard Plunket, a man with extensive interests in Louth and Meath who served as one of the king's serjeants at law in Ireland from the late 1350s and who had been visiting England regularly since the early 1340s.[156] Before word of this new commission arrived in Ireland, however, Fleming and Plunket had left for England in the company of the earl of Kildare, John Hussey, and Richard White, the recently appointed chief justice of the justiciar's bench, who also hailed from Meath. The purpose of Fleming's journey was to administer his English estates, but the business of the other voyagers, who had been 'chosen by certain of the commons of Ireland', was to bring to the king's attention the corruption of his Dublin-based representatives.[157] In September 1364 Edward III instituted yet another commission to investigate malpractice in the Irish administration, and the English-born chancellor and treasurer of Ireland, Thomas Burley and Walter Dalby, were dismissed. The commissioners on this occasion included not only Lionel and the earl of Kildare, but also John Hussey, baron of Galtrim, Robert Preston, and Richard White.[158]

---

[154] *Jacobi Grace, Kilkenniensis, Annales Hiberniae*, ed. Richard Butler (Dublin, 1842), 159, 161. For the Fitz Leones family, Otway-Ruthven, *History of Medieval Ireland*, 106.
[155] *CCR 1349–54*, 626; TNA E 101/241/18; Potterton, *Medieval Trim*, 371; *CPR 1348–50*, 107; *CPR 1350–4*, 244.
[156] *CPR 1361–4*, 537; *Admin. Ire.*, 178–81; *CPR 1340–3*, 570, 572; *CPR 1348–50*, 254; *CPR 1350–4*, 244; *CPR 1354–8*, 29; *IEP*, 470, 478, 494, 499, 500.
[157] *CCR 1364–9*, 58; *Admin. Ire.* 179 n. 9. Richardson and Sayles call him 'of Clonegall' (co. Carlow). He is referred to as 'Richard White of Clongell' in a separate commission—of which James de la Hyde was also a member—of Apr. 1364 (*CPR 1361–4*, 533). Rather than Clonegall in Carlow, this is more likely to have been Clongall (bar. Upper Moyfenrath), in co. Meath. Crooks, '"Hobbes", "Dogs" and Politics', 129–32.
[158] *CPR 1364–7*, 68.

From the perspective of the English of Louth and Meath, the presence in Ireland of the longed-for 'bone chiefteyn suffisant' had proved more problematic than might have been expected. Lionel was well-funded from English resources, but assumed that the settlers would contribute financially to his campaigns. He also believed himself entitled to reward his associates from England with government positions and landed estates in Ireland.[159] Neither of these expectations sat easily with the settlers, who in the course of the previous three decades had seen their local power increase and whose success in meeting grave challenges to their position had increased their self-confidence. By the late 1360s, powerful families in Louth had gained possession of most of the Verdon inheritance that had been in the hands of absentee English lords for half a century, while members of the local elite also staffed important branches of the crown's Irish administration. By this time, also, the shire community had long experience of making its wishes known at Westminster through its participation in the Irish parliament and by joining in the dispatch of petitions to England.[160] Since 1330 the settlers of Louth had fought for the king in Scotland, and to a lesser extent in France, and they had helped feed his subjects in north-west England in the years of grain shortage that followed the first onslaught of plague. They believed that they had fully earned the support of the crown, and were acutely aware that with the murder of William Burgh, earl of Ulster, in 1333 they were vulnerable as never before to Irish attacks. The MacMahon and O'Neill campaigns of 1346 and 1350 testified to the increasing military capacity of the native lords of south Ulster and suggested that only internal divisions and the existence among them of other priorities prevented a more sustained native assault on the colony in this part of Ireland. Anxiety generated by a growing sense of military insecurity, combined with a developing sense of their own importance, may in part account for the tensions that arose between the settlers and Lionel of Clarence, and also help explain why relations with the next lieutenant sent from England, William Windsor, broke down so quickly and so completely.

---

[159] To take one example; in Feb. 1362 Lionel appointed John Virley, one of his valets, as serjeant of Meath, a post usually held by members of local families such as the Bacons: NAI RC 8/28, 64.
[160] Robin Frame, 'English Policies and Anglo-Irish Attitudes', 123–9.

2

Friends Like These: William Windsor and Edmund Mortimer, 1369–1381

William Windsor's tenure of the chief governorship, which lasted for most of the period between 1369 and 1376, was marked by bitter conflict between him and sections of the English community in Ireland. Serious as this dispute was, it should be remembered that there was no disagreement among the contending parties about what constituted the main priority of government: the duty to combat the increasing power of the Irish. There was much less agreement about how this was to be paid for, but before examining how this issue coloured Windsor's relations with the settlers in Louth, it is necessary to gauge the level of threat posed to the county by the Irish of Ulster in these years.

During Lionel's lieutenancy Louth had not been attacked by its Irish neighbours to the north and west, not least because of tension between the MacMahons and O'Neills, and after 1364 within the O'Neill family itself. By the time Windsor's involvement in Ireland ended, however, its security situation was much more serious. To some extent, our perception of this development is shaped by the unusual wealth of the evidence for this period, and in particular the survival of the first episcopal register from Armagh, that of Archbishop Milo Sweteman (1361–80). It is likely, however, that the end of internal strife among the O'Neills in 1370 and the lack of a resident lord of either Ulster or Trim in these years did encourage the Irish of south Ulster to adopt a more aggressive attitude towards the settlement. Not all of the Irish families on the borders of Louth with which Milo Sweteman was most concerned were involved during his episcopate in attacks on the county. His extensive dealings with the O'Reillys of East Breifne, for instance, for the most part concerned the misbehaviour of the bishop of Kilmore, Richard O'Reilly, whose diocese was coterminous with the O'Reilly territory, and who was a kinsman of its ruler, Philip O'Reilly. Milo and Philip, who ruled his lordship for almost twenty years until his death in 1384, appear to have cooperated successfully to bring Richard to confess and seek absolution from the excommunication imposed upon him for adultery and incest before his death in 1369.[1] Philip O'Reilly's attitude to the settlers on his borders was not consistently pacific. In June 1375 Sir Walter Cusack, seneschal of Trim, was unable to attend parliament at Kilkenny because he was defending the marches of Westmeath against a confederacy of Irish

---

[1] *Reg. Sweteman*, 67–71, 73–4, 119–20; *AC* 337, 339.

families, for the most part from Connacht and the midlands, but also including the O'Reillys.[2]

The O'Hanlons, by contrast to the O'Reillys in the 1360s, engaged in frequent violent attacks upon the archbishop of Armagh's men and property. These attacks centred on the city of Armagh rather than on Louth but Milo, as well as imposing excommunication upon them—whereupon, he remarked, they behaved worse than before—was prepared to threaten his enemies with English power should they fail to desist. In December 1366, he wrote to his official at Armagh ordering him to arrange for a number of O'Hanlons to appear at Raskeagh, on the northern fringes of co. Louth. They were to be given the opportunity to persuade him why he should not proceed against them with extreme measures involving 'the support of the secular arm' (*invocacionem brachii secularis*).[3] In a letter to the dean of Armagh dated 9 September 1367, Milo wrote of the 'tyranny' (*tyrannidem*) of O'Hanlon and his ally Domnall O'Neill and on 18 September wrote directly to Malachy O'Hanlon, chief of the family, threatening to take council with the magnates of Ireland with a view 'to procuring his destruction' (*deliberare intendimus ad vestrum exterminium*).[4]

More menacing to Louth than the O'Reillys and O'Hanlons in the 1360s and 1370s were the MacMahons and O'Neills. Brian MacMahon, who had become chief of his family in 1362, campaigned with Lionel in 1364 but failed to take advantage of the competition for leadership of the O'Neills which began that year upon the death of Aed O'Neill. In 1365, Brian even managed to unite against him the rival O'Neills, Niall and Domnall, by treacherously slaying Somairle MacDonald, the leader of O'Neill's galloglass forces. Joined by a rival MacMahon, Domnall drove Brian from his territory in that year, while Niall O'Neill inflicted another defeat upon him on his return to Airgialla in 1368.[5] It may have been his weak position that persuaded Brian MacMahon in 1369 to seek absolution from the sentence of excommunication passed upon him by Archbishop Sweteman for an earlier attack on his tenants, but the resolution of the succession dispute among the O'Neills in 1370 increased his vulnerability: Niall O'Neill marked his victory in that contest with a particularly savage raid on Airgialla that involved 'many being drowned and destroyed'.[6] In the following year, 1371, MacMahon, described by one annalist as 'the man who killed the most Galls and Gaels in his time in Ireland', was slain by one of his own galloglass while on his way 'to give battle to the English'.[7] He was buried in the monastery of Louth, which suggests some otherwise undocumented connections between him and the house of Augustinian canons there which one of his predecessors had burnt in 1350.[8] Brian's son and successor, Philip Ruad, who ruled until 1403, in general avoided conflict with the

---

[2] *Parls. & Councils*, 71–3; *AC* 351. [3] *Reg. Sweteman*, 131.
[4] *Reg. Sweteman*, 95–6, 205–6.
[5] *AFM* iii. 631; *AC* 327, 335.
[6] *Reg. Sweteman*, 109–10; *AC* 339.
[7] *AC* 341; *AFM* iii. 365. These annals date events ahead by one year at this point.
[8] *AU* ii. 557. The house had been founded by Donnchad Ó'Carroll [Ó Cerbaill], king of Airgialla, in 1142. Brian's choice of burial-place was an assertion of MacMahon claims to rightful succession to the O'Carroll lordship. Smith, *Colonisation and Conquest*, 20–1.

settlers in Louth, but exerted only limited control over his more bellicose Mac-Mahon relatives.[9]

Niall Mór (the elder) O'Neill and his son Niall Óc (the younger) had attacked and occupied lands in Armagh and east Tyrone belonging to the archbishopric during the power struggle with Domnall O'Neill in the late 1360s, but did not threaten Louth until the early 1370s.[10] The scale of that threat is revealed in an open letter written by Milo Sweteman on 15 July 1373 setting out the terms of a peace agreement concluded that day under his auspices and in his presence between the Irish of south Ulster and the English of Louth and Meath.[11] The English party was led by the justiciar, Robert Ashton of Long Ashton near Bristol, who in early June had been holding hearings at Drogheda into the conduct of his predecessor, William Windsor.[12] It included the sheriff of Louth, John Dowdall, Geoffrey White, who had served as Lionel's constable in Ulster in the 1360s, and the most important members of the Verdon family, Thomas son of Nicholas and James son of Milo. The Irish contingent led by Niall Mór O'Neill consisted of his brother Toirdelbach, the MacDonald leader of O'Neill's galloglass, Magennis (Mac Aengusa), and MacMahon.[13] By the terms of the agreement, both sides swore to keep the peace and to refer any future disputes for adjudication rather than resort immediately to war. Matters touching the rights of the king were to be notified to the justiciar, while those concerning the rights of the Church were to be brought to the attention of the archbishop.

The agreement appears to have bolstered O'Neill's self-confidence both within his own territories and in his attitude towards the settlers. In August 1374, Milo Sweteman wrote to his dean and chancellor at Armagh that he had been informed of actions on O'Neill's part which, if true, implied that he had lapsed into heresy: since Milo's most recent visit to Armagh, in August 1373, O'Neill, 'like some pope or emperor' (*si esset papa vel imperator*), had threatened to leave the archbishop with nothing in Armagh save the cathedral itself, and to build a manor near the city on Church property. Milo professed himself reluctant to believe such reports, and extended an olive branch to 'his lay friend' (*amicum nostrum laicum*), by ordering his chancellor to take actions against a cleric who had given false information against O'Neill.[14] Three months later O'Neill wrote to Sweteman to inform him that Geoffrey White and other men from Dundalk had broken the peace agreement of the preceding year, a message that the archbishop passed on to the chief

---

[9] *NHI* ix. 146.
[10] *Reg. Sweteman*, 122–3, 205–6.
[11] For the details of the agreement outlined below, see *Reg. Sweteman*, 14–15.
[12] Clarke, 'William of Windsor in Ireland', 115–16. Ashton was in Drogheda for much of period 20 May–15 July 1373: NAI RC 8/31, 305–7; COA Rep. Records of the Exchequer, 42–51 Edward III, 67, 84.
[13] For the identification of Toirdelbach, see Simms, 'The Archbishops of Armagh and the O'Neills', 46 and n. 30. For the possible identity of the MacDonald participant see Nicholls, 'Scottish Mercenary Kindreds in Ireland', 98.
[14] *Reg. Sweteman*, 11–12, 241–2.

governor, John Keppok, in the hope that he might be able to provide a peaceful solution.[15] Before any mediation could take place, however, O'Neill and Magennis attacked Downpatrick in the heart of the English settlement in Ulster, killing Sir James de la Hyde in the course of a great victory over the settlers.[16] James, with Walter Cusack, had besieged Lionel of Clarence's client, Henry Ferrers, at Clonee in 1366, but had gone on to serve as Irish escheator and was at Downpatrick in 1374 in his capacity as representative there of the interests of the earl of March and Ulster, Edmund Mortimer.[17] The sheriff of Louth, John Dowdall, reported that after the battle of Downpatrick the Irish 'destroyed and plundered the county of Uriel and the king's lieges of that county', but were repulsed from the marches after he had 'assembled the whole power of the county' to confront them.[18] As they had done in 1355, the inhabitants of Dundalk had attacked their Irish neighbours without reference to the authority of the king's representative in Ireland. On the former occasion, the intervention of the archbishop of Armagh had forestalled retaliation—in 1374 the settlers were not so lucky.

It was in this context of increased tension with the Irish on their borders that the English of Louth responded to the policies pursued by William Windsor, who was appointed lieutenant of Ireland on 3 March 1369 and served until April 1372, and was subsequently appointed chief governor and keeper in September 1373, a post he filled until June 1376.[19] Windsor had served in Ireland under Lionel of Clarence in 1362–3 and 1364–5, and had been associated with Lionel's protégé in Meath, Henry Ferrers, even before his appointment as lieutenant. He held that office for less than a week when he acquired wardship on 10 March 1369 of the lands of Sir Robert Clinton in Meath until the majority of his heir, which suggests a keen interest on his part in the opportunities this part of Ireland might provide for his personal enrichment.[20] In his capacity as the king's representative, Windsor was present in the country from June 1369 to March 1372, and again between April 1374 and June 1376.[21] In all this time William appears never to have visited Louth, concentrating his military endeavours instead on Munster and Leinster. The fact

---

[15] *Reg. Sweteman*, 7–9. Milo appears to have passed O'Neill's message on in some haste: Keppok's title was chief governor and keeper, not justiciar as Milo had it. Edward III was also incorrectly referred to by him as 'king of Ireland'.

[16] James died of his wounds at Downpatrick priory: COA Rep. Records of the Exchequer, 1–10 Richard II, 204.

[17] Katharine Simms, 'The Ulster Revolt of 1404: An Anti-Lancastrian Dimension?', in Smith, *Ireland and the English World*, 143–4; *CFR 1369–77*, 245–6; *AC* 345, where James de la Hyde is misrepresented as 'James of Malahide, the king of England's lieutenant'.

[18] *Dowdall Deeds*, 103, where '43rd year of the king [1369]' should read 48th year: 1374.

[19] *NHI* ix. 474; Herbert Wood, 'The Office of Chief Governor of Ireland, 1172–1509', *PRIA* 36 (1921–4), C, 207, 212, 228–9.

[20] *CPR 1367–70*, 185, 245; *CFR 1369–77*, 4.

[21] Philomena Connolly, 'Windsor, William, Baron Windsor (1322x8–1384)', *Oxford Dictionary of National Biography* (Oxford, 2004); *Admin. Ire.*, 90–1; Peter Crooks, 'Negotiating Authority in a Colonial Capital: Dublin and the Windsor Crisis, 1369–78', in Seán Duffy (ed.), *Medieval Dublin IX* (Dublin, 2009), 136 n. 29; S. Harbison, 'William of Windsor, the Court Party and the Administration of Ireland', in James Lydon (ed.), *England and Ireland in the Later Middle Ages: Essays in Honour of Jocelyn Otway-Ruthven* (Dublin, 1981), 153.

that in November 1374 Archbishop Sweteman passed on the letter he had received from O'Neill not to Windsor but to his deputy, John Keppok, may suggest that a decision had been taken to allow William to concentrate his energies in the south of the country. If Windsor would not go to Louth, however, then Louth must go to Windsor: from the outset of his time as king's representative in Ireland, William displayed an interest in the affairs of Louth and Meath that, as we shall see, required representatives from these counties to undertake an unprecedented number of lengthy journeys around Ireland at the governor's command.

The various inquisitions into Windsor's behaviour in Ireland conducted between 1372 and 1376 produced allegations of serious wrongdoing on his part in relation to the king's lieges in Louth and Meath that were said to have commenced soon after his arrival in the country in July 1369. An inquisition taken at Drogheda on 20 May 1373, for instance, heard that on 29 October 1369 Windsor had ordered the arrest of a ship in the town that had been freighted by two local merchants with hides for the king's staple. This cargo was then replaced with hides belonging to Windsor upon which no custom duty was paid, to the loss of the king and the merchants concerned. Seven months later on 6 May 1370, the inquisition was told, Windsor ordered one of his close associates, James Pickering, the chief justice, to arrest at Dalkey two ships and their cargo of salt that had been purchased by another group of Drogheda merchants. The lieutenant then proceeded to sell the confiscated salt and keep the proceeds.[22] Even more serious were the allegations heard at this inquisition relating to Windsor's dealings with George Teeling, a member of a family that held the manor of Siddan (bar. Lower Slane, co. Meath), a particularly sensitive location on the marches between the English and the Irish.[23] Further details concerning this matter were heard at a second inquisition held at Drogheda on 9 June 1373, and it also featured in the case outlined against Windsor before the king's council in England in July 1376.[24]

Before setting out for Ireland in June 1369, it was said, the lieutenant had been instructed by the king's council in England to refuse a charter of pardon to George Teeling who had been indicted of the murder of his nephew, Walter Teeling, 'captain of his nation', in the previous year. Already in the mid-1360s George had appeared before the chief justice, John Keppok, at Drogheda, on a charge of leading an attack on his neighbours in Meath that involved the abduction of Nesta, the heavily pregnant wife of the prominent government official and local landowner, Robert Holywood. George escaped further punishment for his trespass on this occasion by agreeing to pay £20 to the injured parties.[25] Upon being indicted for

---

[22] Clarke, 'William of Windsor in Ireland', 116–19.
[23] This small corner of Ireland is fortunate to have found its historian: Linda Clare, *On the Edge of the Pale: The Rise and Decline of an Anglo-Irish Community in County Meath, 1170–1530* (Dublin, 2006).
[24] For what follows see Clarke, 'William of Windsor in Ireland', 84, 98–9, 107, 113–14, 116.
[25] *Admin. Ire.*, 173. A note in Sweteman's register from 6 Jan. 1368 that is largely illegible refers to a murder in the orchard of George Teeling. The dead man appears to have been a priest who was killed *martiro Christi* while blessing the fruit. The note can be read in such a way as to assign responsibility for the murder to Teeling: *Reg. Sweteman*, 207. Nesta, widow of Robert Holywood, was alive in 1380: *RCH* 109 no. 73.

having slain Walter, the son of his older brother, in order to gain his inheritance, valued at 100m per year, George pleaded clergy, and at the time of Windsor's arrival in Ireland was in the prison of the bishop of Meath. Before being imprisoned, however, he had given his manor of Crowmartin (bar. Ardee, co. Louth), some 10 kilometres north of Siddan, to another brother, Thomas, to enable him to procure for him a charter of the king's peace.[26] It was alleged that Thomas offered before Windsor and his council to pay 100m for such a charter. The offer was accepted, and in March and May 1370 Thomas made separate, secret, and substantial payments to Windsor, James Pickering, the chief justice, and Edmund Laurence, another of Windsor's confidants.[27]

Whatever the veracity of these and other charges levelled against Windsor—and he was able to brush some of them aside with ease—they show that his relationship with a substantial portion of the English political community of Louth and Meath had broken down soon after his arrival in Ireland in June 1369.[28] It should be acknowledged that Windsor was always likely to feel the impact of resentment towards the king's ministers that was running particularly high in this part of Ireland even before his appointment. It was at Trim in June 1368, for instance, that the justiciar, Gerald fitz Maurice, earl of Desmond, felt obliged to grant a request from the commons of Meath that he reissue a letter patent, first witnessed by Edward III in February 1367. In it, the king asserted that he had learnt from the 'prelates, magnates and people of Ireland' that they had been treated 'arbitrarily and unjustly' by his ministers. He, 'desiring the tranquillity and quiet of Ireland', now ordered that his lieges in Ireland not be treated 'otherwise than persons in England'.[29] Such fine words did nothing to address the problems that Windsor faced on his arrival. Paramount among these was his need for money to fulfil his responsibilities as the king's lieutenant. Unlike Lionel of Antwerp, Windsor was not a wealthy man, and could not supplement grants made to him at Westminster and Dublin from his personal resources.[30] His urgent need to close the gap between expenditure and income ensured that 'tranquillity and peace' would remain distant prospects.

Conflict with the citizens of Drogheda began as early as August 1369 when at his first parliament, convened at Dublin, Windsor allegedly extracted money from their representatives for his personal use and that of his associate, James Pickering.[31]

---

[26] In 1334, Philip Teeling proffered 53s 4d on behalf of Crowmartin as part of the communal fine imposed on the county for the Verdon rebellion of 1312: TNA E 101/240/4. George Teeling's possessions in Crowmartin were in the king's hands by Dec. 1368: COA Rep. Records of the Exchequer, 42–51 Edward III, 23, 337.

[27] In 1365, Thomas Teeling had acted as one of Nicholas Gernon's attorneys in Ireland: *CPR 1364–7*, 168. Gernon's other attorney on this occasion, John Troy, who was treasurer of Ireland between 1364 and 1367, also stood as pledge for Thomas in 1368–9 to receive custody of the estate of Hugh Hauberge in Louth: COA Rep. Records of the Exchequer, 42–51 Edward III, 9; *Admin. Ire.*, 104.

[28] For Windsor's response in June 1373 to various charges see Sayles, *Affairs*, 229–31.

[29] *Dowdall Deeds*, 97–8.

[30] Philomena Connolly, 'The Financing of English Expeditions to Ireland, 1361–1376', in Lydon, *England and Ireland in the Later Middle Ages*, 114; Robin Frame, 'English Political Culture in Later Medieval Ireland', *History Review*, 13 (2002), 7–8.

[31] Clarke, 'William of Windsor in Ireland', 119. For parliamentary taxation in Ireland under Windsor see Richardson and Sayles, *Irish Parliament*, 80–7, 113–18. For the dispute with Drogheda

Six months later, in February 1370, Windsor sent a writ to Drogheda ordering a number of its prominent burgesses to remove themselves to Limerick by Easter (14 April). At least two of these men paid substantial sums to be spared this imposition—which was probably the point of the exercise—and the incident no doubt contributed to the mistrust of the lieutenant that became apparent at the Dublin parliament of late April 1370.[32] On that occasion, the elected representatives of Drogheda in Louth refused to grant a subsidy on account of the heavy burden of the new customs regime imposed on Irish towns in the previous year.[33] Windsor responded to such opposition by having the seneschal of Drogheda in Meath, John Ashwell, and a fellow burgess arrested and kept in prison until they agreed 'under coercion' to contribute 20m from the town towards the subsidy. Arrest was also the fate of the knights elected for county Louth, Roger Gernon and Richard Vernon, upon their refusal to agree to the subsidy, and this harsh treatment was enough to persuade their equivalents for Meath, James de la Hyde and John Fitz John, to agree to pay, despite the promises they had made at the time of their election at Trim to withhold such consent.[34]

In response to their resistance, Windsor also commanded the mayor, seneschal, and bailiffs of Drogheda in Louth and Meath to come to him in person at Dublin, together with twelve of the better burgesses on 20 May 1370. When they arrived, he refused to allow them to leave the city until they had paid him £40, and they secured their release only by making extra payments to Windsor's associates, including James Pickering, to gain their goodwill.[35] Windsor continued his attack on the seneschal of Drogheda in Meath, John Ashwell, who was ordered to appear before him at Naas on 29 July 1370. Once there he was compelled to agree to contribute from the town five archers to accompany the lieutenant's retinue to Limerick. Despite the archers serving as required before being discharged, Windsor on 3 March 1371 ordered the arrest of certain burgesses of Drogheda who were in Kilkenny to meet him on the grounds that the archers had not been provided. Predictably, the burgesses were not freed until they paid a fine on behalf of themselves and the community of the town.[36]

From Naas Windsor moved to Munster, and by 8 August 1370 was campaigning at Adare in Limerick. From there he wrote to the authorities in Drogheda demanding that they either lend him £200 or else, under penalty of forfeiture, come to him in person, together with thirty men-at-arms, to serve for three months with his retinue in the district.[37] The failure of the Drogheda men to respond to this command—they later claimed that the relevant writ had never arrived in the

---

see Chiara Buldorini, 'Drogheda as a Case Study of Anglo-Norman Town Foundation in Ireland, 1194–1412', 2 vols. Ph.D. thesis, University of Dublin, Trinity College (2009), i. 285–92. I am grateful to Dr Buldorini for making her thesis available to me.

[32] Clarke, 'William of Windsor in Ireland', 118.
[33] Clarke, 'William of Windsor in Ireland', 117; RIA MS 12 D 10, 171.
[34] Clarke, 'William of Windsor in Ireland', 113–15.
[35] Clarke, 'William of Windsor in Ireland', 117.
[36] Clarke, 'William of Windsor in Ireland', 120
[37] Clarke, 'William of Windsor in Ireland', 117; Otway-Ruthven, *History of Medieval Ireland*, 298.

town—was not forgotten by the lieutenant, and in the following spring he ordered the mayor of Drogheda in Louth, John Frombold, and several other burgesses to be at Kilkenny on 3 May 1371 to explain their failure to comply with his order. Once there he forbade them to leave the town until they agreed, against their will, to pay him £100 on behalf of the community of Drogheda. Frombold subsequently made his way to the exchequer at Carlow and paid £50 of this sum, 'which was taken by extortion'. This was the third time since the start of the year that senior burgesses from Drogheda had been required to make the long journey to Kilkenny: in January 1371 they had attended a parliament convened there by Windsor at which, 'against their will', they contributed over £42 towards a subsidy granted to him by the commons of Ireland worth £3,000.[38] In early 1371, Windsor also resorted to a ploy that had worked well the previous year by again ordering individuals from Drogheda to be in residence at Limerick by Easter (6 April). The men concerned travelled to Kilkenny to plead with the lieutenant to be spared this cruel fate, only to be informed that he intended to arrest them if they came before him. Their response was to flee to England, where they remained for some time at their great expense.[39]

Representatives of both towns of Drogheda, as well as of Louth and Meath, were required to travel south for a fourth time in a little over six months in 1371 when Windsor convened a parliament in June of that year at Ballydoyle, south-east of Cashel in Tipperary.[40] This was a place without accommodation, 'a wasteland' (*locum vastatum*), and after three days of resistance the representatives of the towns and counties were worn down and agreed to the lieutenant's demand for a subsidy of £2,000. The commons of Meath, on being informed that they must contribute £500 of this sum decided to send an emissary, Stephen Bray, to the king in England to inform him of Windsor's behaviour.[41] The response of the king and the English council was sympathetic: on 10 September 1371 Edward III wrote to Windsor, ordering him to cease levying 'unlawful fines and tolls'. He had been informed by the mayor and community of Drogheda that the lieutenant had forced certain men of the town to reside at Kilkenny and Limerick until they paid great fines to be allowed to return home, and that at the Ballydoyle parliament he had imposed 'tallages, fines, extortions and imposts not to be borne it is said, to the impoverishment of the king and his people of the said city'.[42] This was followed by a more strongly worded royal letter of 12 November 1371 in which Windsor was commanded under pain of forfeiture to cease proceedings in the Irish courts against the towns of Dublin and Drogheda and the communities of the counties of Dublin, Louth, Meath, and Kildare, on the grounds of their opposition to the collection of

---

[38] Clarke, 'William of Windsor in Ireland', 117; Connolly, 'Financing of English Expeditions to Ireland', 114.

[39] Clarke, 'William of Windsor in Ireland', 119.

[40] Peter Crooks, 'Representation and Dissent: "Parliamentarianism" and the Structure of Politics in Colonial Ireland *c.*1370–1420', *EHR* 125 (2010), 9 and n. 57.

[41] Clarke, 'William of Windsor in Ireland', 115, 117–18; James Lydon, 'William of Windsor and the Irish Parliament', *EHR* 80 (1965), 258.

[42] *CCR 1369–74*, 246.

those 'tallages, fines, ransoms and imposts' which the king had recently suspended.[43] A third letter, of 8 December 1371, was addressed to the Irish treasurer and barons of the exchequer at Carlow. The king was 'moved to anger' to learn that the lieutenant 'in contempt of the king and his commands' had ordered the arrest of the mayor of Drogheda, John Frombold, for non-payment of sums which had been unlawfully imposed upon the town. Again, under pain of forfeiture, the Irish ministers were ordered to immediately release Frombold if he was then under arrest.[44]

It appeared that a clear victory had been won over Windsor. He was recalled to England early in the following year, leaving Ireland in March 1372, and was replaced as the king's representative in the country. Inquisitions were ordered into the conduct of his administration and in May and June 1373 the justiciar, Robert Ashton, and the chief justice of the common bench, Robert Preston, took sworn statements from eight juries at Dublin, Drogheda, Waterford, and Cork that detailed a vast range of alleged abuses on the part of the lieutenant and his ministers.[45] This, however, proved to be the high-water mark in the campaign of those settlers who resisted Windsor in Ireland. Ashton may have been conscientious in his enquiries into William's behaviour but showed little interest in contributing to the case against him that was being considered by the council at Westminster.[46] Edward III concluded that the charges against Windsor were for the most part baseless and on 20 September 1373 reappointed him as head of the Irish administration with the title of 'governor and keeper'. The king's letters to his ministers and lieges immediately thereafter were very different in tone from those dispatched to the same recipients two years before. On 20 December 1373, Edward ordered that the residue of the £5,000 granted at the Kilkenny and Ballydoyle parliaments was to be collected immediately since 'the king has particular information by nobles and other credible persons of Ireland that those sums were at the said parliaments freely granted as aforesaid in aid of the expenses of the war in Ireland'.[47] This was followed by letters sent on 20 March 1374 to the mayor and other officers in Drogheda and to various sheriffs including those of Louth and Meath, ordering them to proceed with the collection of the £5,000 and to aid Windsor in so doing.[48]

Even before his return to Ireland on 18 April 1374, Windsor had taken advantage of the renewal of the king's favour to strike a blow against those who had opposed him in Louth and Drogheda during his first term in office. In November 1373, writs were sent to the sheriff of Louth ordering him to extract from twenty-three individuals, or their pledges, payments for charters of peace.[49] In eighteen

[43] *CCR 1369–74*, 259.
[44] *CCR 1369–74*, 265.
[45] The findings of only six inquisitions survive. The proceedings of hearings almost certainly held at Cork and Waterford are missing. Clarke, 'William of Windsor in Ireland', 58 and n. 17.
[46] Harbison, 'William of Windsor's Administration', 159–61; Michael Jones, 'Ashton, Sir Robert (d.1384)', *Oxford Dictionary of National Biography* (Oxford, 2004; online edn, Jan. 2008).
[47] *CCR 1369–74*, 530.
[48] *CCR 1374–77*, 10.
[49] COA Rep. Records of the Exchequer, 42–51 Edward III, 114–17.

cases the payment demanded was 40s; four individuals were required to pay 20s; while one man, Richard Mole, was expected to produce 100s for being pardoned his 'trespass and contempt'. Mole had been one of the burgesses of Drogheda who in February 1370 had been ordered to attend the lieutenant at Limerick and who in 1371 had been detained by him at Kilkenny before being required to be present at the parliament at Ballydoyle. William Roth of Drogheda, who was obliged to pay 40s to regain the king's peace, was another of those who had refused to obey Windsor's command to lend him £200 or serve in person at Adare for three months in the autumn of 1370.[50] Several more of those required to pay for charters of peace in November 1373 are also recorded as having opposed Windsor in the past. John Walsh, for instance, had complained in May 1373 that the customs officials appointed by William in Drogheda had in 1371 extorted money from him to permit him to export fish to England, while Robert Sexton alleged at the same hearing that he and other Drogheda merchants had been defrauded in May 1370 when Windsor's lieutenant, James Pickering, commandeered ships at Dalkey containing salt for which they had already paid.[51]

In addition to the twenty-three individuals deemed to require charters of peace in November 1373, a further thirty-three were named as their pledges, and in that capacity might be called upon to pay the sums adjudged to be owed by those for whom they stood as guarantors.[52] Among this group of thirty-three were yet more men from Drogheda and Louth with a history of opposition to William Windsor. Robert Babe, who stood as pledge for two men, was among those who refused the summons to Adare in August 1370, while Robert Dover, who acted in the same capacity for three men, testified in May 1373 that in October 1369 a ship that he and another Drogheda merchant had freighted was arrested on Windsor's orders to their considerable loss. He was among the six Drogheda burgesses detained at Kilkenny by the lieutenant in May 1371, as were two others of those who stood pledge for those requiring charters of peace in November 1373, Nicholas Fitz Hugh and Thomas Skinner.[53] In total, Windsor's campaign against those who had opposed him in Drogheda and Louth encompassed fifty-six individuals. Had all the payments demanded been received they would have amounted to £45. For such a paltry sum, Windsor was prepared to reopen old wounds even before he returned to Ireland in April 1374.

Windsor's efforts upon his arrival to collect the £5,000 voted almost three years earlier met with little success and in June 1375 the king and council decided to send a special royal agent, Nicholas Dagworth, to ensure that the settlers contributed a realistic amount to their own defence.[54] Anticipating that his mission might

---

[50] *CCR 1369–74*, 246; Clarke, 'William of Windsor in Ireland', 116–19.
[51] Clarke, 'William of Windsor in Ireland', 116–19.
[52] COA Rep. Records of the Exchequer, 42–51 Edward III, 114–17.
[53] Clarke, 'William of Windsor in Ireland', 116–19.
[54] Otway-Ruthven, *History of Medieval Ireland*, 302–6; Connolly, 'Financing of English Expeditions', 116–17.

fail, the king had provided Dagworth with letters, which he produced at a parliament at Kilkenny in October 1375, ordering the towns, dioceses, and counties of Ireland to send elected representatives to England in the following February to consult about the government of the country.[55] Amidst blunt statements from, among others, Milo Sweteman, archbishop of Armagh, that men elected in Ireland were not bound to travel to England, elections were duly held but in almost all instances, as happened in Meath and Louth, the electors sought to frustrate the purpose of the exercise by withholding from their representatives 'the full power' (*plena potestas*) to agree to taxation on their behalf.[56] The representatives of the settlers used their time in England in the spring of 1376 to good effect, however, repeating their complaints about the government of Windsor, who as a result was summoned to England with Robert Holywood, chief baron of the exchequer, and William Carlisle, second baron. At the same time Nicholas Dagworth was sent to Ireland a second time, on this occasion to investigate Windsor's conduct.[57] Charges against him were heard in London in June 1376, but apart from the dismissal at this time of the officers appointed by him, he remained unscathed. Windsor left Ireland for the final time in September 1376, but soon thereafter the political winds at Westminster changed again and, despite attempts by some of the citizens of Dublin to injure his career as late as 1378, moves to hold William to account for his behaviour in Ireland were allowed to fade away.[58]

Rough wooing with regard to grants of parliamentary taxation was but one of the ways in which the English of Louth felt the impact of Windsor's rule in Ireland. In the same manner as his predecessors, Lionel of Antwerp and Thomas Rokeby, William put pressure on absentee lords to either defend their Irish lands or sell them, and this had the consequence in Louth of accelerating the trend by which property was transferred into the hands of local men.[59] This process was not always a smooth one: in February 1374, for instance, Windsor was ordered to restore to Sir John Crophull, third husband of Margaret, daughter of Theobald Verdon, lands near Dundalk and elsewhere in Louth and other parts of Ireland that he had confiscated under legislation targeting absenteeism.[60] John Bellew, who had already acquired the Furnival portion of the Verdon inheritance, and who was regularly summoned to parliament in the early 1370s, had farmed the lands forfeited by Crophull, and appears to have relinquished them with ill grace.[61] Before 1380, however, Crophull liquidated his Irish interests, thus concluding the process by which the inheritance of Theobald Verdon (d.1316) came into the hands of

---

[55] *CPI* 69.
[56] Clarke, 'William of Windsor in Ireland', 123–7; Crooks, 'Negotiating Authority in a Colonial Capital', 136–8.
[57] Harbison, 'William of Windsor's Administration', 164–6.
[58] *CCR 1374–7*, 469; W. Mark Ormrod, 'The Trials of Alice Perrers', *Speculum*, 83 (2008), 377–80; Crooks, 'Negotiating Authority in a Colonial Capital', 139–42.
[59] Harbison, 'William of Windsor's Administration', 156–8.
[60] *CPR 1370–4*, 417; *Parls. & Councils*, 74–8; 'Lord Chancellor Gerrard's Notes on his Report on Ireland', 232–4.
[61] *IEP* 538–9; *CPR 1364–7*, 218; *Dowdall Deeds*, 96; Betham, *Origin and History*, 311–13, 315–16; Lynch, *View of the Legal Institutions*, 324.

resident lords in Ireland.[62] Another of those who had acquired former Verdon land was Robert Holywood, who as a senior member of the Dublin administration was closely associated with William Windsor and who was still answering accusations about his conduct during Windsor's term of office as late as 1378.[63] Robert had considerable interests in Louth, and these appear to have been protected by Windsor during his time as lieutenant and governor.[64] In 1375, for instance, Holywood petitioned for the review of an earlier judgement that had deprived him of land in the barony of Ferrard in Louth. Windsor allowed this and summoned a new jury which awarded the land to Robert.[65]

Even those members of the English community in Louth with whom Windsor clashed most directly might find themselves benefiting from his control of royal resources in the county and his commitment to improving security in the area. Roger Gernon, for instance, had been one of those representatives of Louth at the Dublin parliament of April 1370 imprisoned on Windsor's orders for refusing to assent to a subsidy.[66] Archbishop Milo Sweteman signalled his support for Gernon's intransigence by choosing him as one of his proctors at the Kilkenny parliament of January 1371, and soon thereafter Windsor demonstrated his willingness to put earlier disagreements to one side.[67] In February 1371 the lieutenant, on behalf of the king, granted to Gernon and his heirs in perpetuity the royal manor of Donaghmoyne and the lands of Farney attached to it.[68] Donaghmoyne had come to the crown in the early fourteenth century when the Pipard family swapped its Irish lands for estates in England, but by then was already under the effective control of the MacMahons.[69] It had been included in the liberty of Louth established for John Bermingham in 1319, and after his murder in 1329 was granted first to John Darcy and then, for life, to a leading local figure, John Clinton, who held it until at least 1360.[70] At the time of the 1371 grant these lands were said to be 'in the hands of the king's Irish rebels', and Roger received them 'provided that he by no means make any feoffment thereof to any Irishmen and that he build within the twenty years next coming a competent fortalice against the king's enemies and rebels'.[71] It was of a piece with his receipt of this important grant on the marches of Louth that Roger should act as one of the representatives of the county in the truce agreed with the Irish of Ulster in July 1373, and two years later

---

[62] *CCR 1374–7*, 546, 552; *CCR 1377–81*, 320; Otway-Ruthven, 'Partition of the de Verdon Lands in Ireland', 417.
[63] Sayles, *Affairs*, 249–50.
[64] *CPR 1370–4*, 325; *CPR 1374–7*, 122; *Dowdall Deeds*, 99, 118; *RCH* 109 no. 73.
[65] *Dowdall Deeds*, 104–5.
[66] Clarke, 'William of Windsor in Ireland', 117–18.
[67] *Reg. Sweteman*, 107–8; *Parls. & Councils*, 37.
[68] Shirley, *History of the County of Monaghan*, 16. Shirley's account should be treated with caution.
[69] Brendan Smith, 'The Medieval Border: Anglo-Irish and Gaelic Irish in Late Thirteenth and Early Fourteenth Century Uriel', in Gillespie and O'Sullivan, *Borderlands*, 41–53.
[70] *CFR 1327–37*, 143, 329; *CFR 1337–47*, 66, 228; NAI RC 8/28, 256–8; TNA SC 8/168/8354; Connolly, 'Ancient Petitions', 54; TNA E 101/241/1; NAI M 999/184/18.
[71] *CPR 1374–7*, 340.

Archbishop Sweteman gave him a further stake in the fortunes of the march by granting him a five-year lease on the archiepiscopal manor of Iniskeen (bar. Farney, co. Monaghan), adjoining Donaghmoyne.[72]

Two months before William Windsor had him imprisoned in April 1370, Roger Gernon was appointed to act as one of his attorneys in Ireland by his relative Nicholas Gernon, whose close links with the house of Lancaster had seen him build a career in England since the 1340s.[73] Roger was in England in the summer of 1376, and in September of that year received confirmation from the king of the Irish letters patent by which he had been granted Donaghmoyne five years before.[74] His close ties with England were shared by another important local figure with whom William Windsor came into contact during his time in Ireland, but whose fate was far less happy—Sir Thomas Verdon.[75] Verdon, like Nicholas Gernon, moved within Lancastrian circles in England, having been placed in the care as a minor of Maud of Lancaster and then Henry, earl and later duke of Lancaster, in the years following the death of his father, Nicholas Verdon, in 1347.[76] He attained his majority sometime before April 1352 and appears to have divided his time between England and Ireland in the decade that followed.[77] In September 1358 he succeeded in regaining possession of the manor of Mansfieldstown, which his father had held in chief of the king but which had been alienated to Thomas by his mother, Matilda Bermingham, without royal licence.[78] By 1359, however, Thomas had been outlawed in Ireland for failing to appear before the justices of the bench in Dublin to answer a charge by a former baron of the exchequer, William Epworth, who claimed that he was owed money by the late Nicholas Verdon. In response to a petition from Thomas that he could not answer William in Ireland as he was about to depart from England on the king's service elsewhere, Edward III ordered the suspension of the outlawry on condition that Thomas compensate William.[79]

Thomas's Irish interests and revenues were limited on account of the longevity of his mother, who continued to reside in Louth after the death of her husband in 1347 and lived at Rathdrumin, which was part of the Verdon manor of Clonmore, until her death in 1372.[80] He was temporarily outlawed again in 1366, but had returned to the king's peace by 1370.[81] Thomas was present at the archbishop of

---

[72] *Reg. Sweteman*, 13–15, 154.
[73] *CPR 1367–70*, 361.
[74] *CPR 1374–7*, 338, 340.
[75] Verdon was a member of a jury empanelled by the sheriff of Meath that convened before Windsor at Kilkenny in Jan. 1371: *COD 1413–1509*, 363.
[76] *CPR 1348–50*, 86.
[77] TNA E 101/242/13; E 101/243/1, 4, 11, 12; E 101/244/4; *CPR 1354–8*, 201, 278, 458; *CPR 1358–61*, 211.
[78] *RCH* 73 no. 41.
[79] *CCR 1354–60*, 649; *Admin. Ire.*, 62–3; 253–7; Frame, *English Lordship in Ireland*, 256–8; Philomena Connolly, 'The Proceedings Against John de Burnham, Treasurer of Ireland, 1343–49', in Barry et al., *Colony and Frontier in Medieval Ireland*, 59–62.
[80] COA Rep. Records of the Exchequer, 42–51 Edward III, 395–6; *CPR 1345–8*, 333; *CPR 1364–7*, 322–3; *CPR 1367–70*, 152, 461; *Dowdall Deeds*, 81.
[81] COA Rep. Records of the Exchequer, 42–51 Edward III, 180, 183.

Armagh's manor of Dromiskin (bar. Louth) on 2 January 1370 when 'about the ninth hour' a royal writ arrived ordering Milo Sweteman to attend the parliament at Dublin summoned by William Windsor, and he was also with Milo in July 1373 when a peace agreement was reached between the English of Louth and Meath and the Irish of south Ulster.[82] Very soon thereafter, however, a serious dispute arose between Thomas and Milo concerning provision to the vicarage of the church of Feld. Thomas and some associates went so far as to occupy the church, and on failing to appear before the archbishop to answer for their conduct were declared heretical by him in their absence. This so infuriated Verdon that on the following day he confronted Milo in the chapel of his manor at Termonfeckin (bar. Ferrard) and, upon the sentence of heresy being repeated in his presence, replied to Archbishop Sweteman: 'And I, Thomas Verdon, pronounce and denounce you as a heretic' (*Et ego Thomas de Verdon te… pronuncio et denuncio hereticum*).[83] It was possibly this incident which led to Thomas's earlier outlawry being revived, and in April 1374 a commission was given to James Bellew and the sheriff of Louth, John Dowdall, to inquire by jury into the extent of Thomas Verdon's manor of Clonmore, 'in the king's hand for his outlawry'.[84] In July 1374 the custody of all Thomas's lands in Louth was granted to his cousins James and Richard Verdon, sons of Milo Verdon, but by September 1374 the former justiciar, Robert Ashton, who fourteen months before had led the English side that included Verdon in the treaty talks with the Irish, had secured from the crown a grant of Thomas's land for as long as they were in the king's hand.[85] On 6 May 1375 Thomas's outlawry was pardoned, but two weeks later William Windsor presided over proceedings whereby land believed to have been part of Thomas's manor of Clonmore (bar. Ferrard), and therefore in the king's hand, was adjudged instead to belong to his old ally, Robert Holywood.[86] In July 1375, Thomas undertook to pay sums owed by Richard and James Verdon incurred during their custody of all his lands in Louth, but he was still in debt to the king when he died shortly before 14 February 1376.[87]

As a deceased debtor, Thomas Verdon's lands were seized by the crown, and their custody was awarded to Richard Verdon on 16 October 1376.[88] Thomas left a widow, Joan Hartort, who received her dower of Rathmore in co. Meath by June 1379, and an illegitimate son, William Verdon, who had received some lands from his father near Clonmore and who acted as attorney for Richard and James

---

[82] *Parls. & Councils*, 29–30; *Reg. Sweteman*, 13–15, 42–3.

[83] *Reg. Sweteman*, 246–9, quotation at 248. The date of the incident is uncertain, though it is difficult to see how it could have happened before the treaty with the Irish was agreed. The 'Master Bartholomew, official of the bishop of Meath' who witnessed Verdon's outburst was probably Bartholomew Dullard, canon of Limerick, who took up the post in Meath in 1366 or shortly thereafter: *Reg. Sweteman*, 177. Another of those present, John Aubrey OP, was elected bishop of Ardagh in Sept. 1373, though not provided until the following Apr.: *NHI* ix. 272.

[84] COA Rep. Records of the Exchequer, 42–51 Edward III, 49; Leslie, *History of Kilsaran*, 150.

[85] COA Rep. Records of the Exchequer, 42–51 Edward III, 53; *CFR 1369–77*, 258. For James Verdon see Otway-Ruthven, 'Partition of the de Verdon Lands in Ireland', 445. For Richard son of Milo, *CPR 1367–70*, 33; *Reg. Sweteman*, 152–3.

[86] *Dowdall Deeds*, 104–5.

[87] COA Rep. Records of the Exchequer, 42–51 Edward III, 234, 276.

[88] *CFR 1369–77*, 366.

Verdon.⁸⁹ Thomas also had two legitimate daughters, Matilda and Anna, who were both minors at the time of his death, and he had made a determined effort in 1374 to ensure that his estate should not pass in the female line but instead go to his cousins, Richard and James, the sons of Milo Verdon, and their male descendants.⁹⁰ Anna Verdon married John son of John Bellew, but died without issue. Matilda Verdon married, first, Peter Howth, and following his death John Cruys of Merrion, and in 1386 she and her second husband succeeded in regaining the inheritance of Thomas Verdon from Bartholomew son of Richard Verdon and James son of James Verdon.⁹¹ Thomas's debts to the crown were finally pardoned in 1416, by which time Bartholomew Verdon had regained possession of what remained of the family estates in Louth. He, like Thomas and his father Nicholas before him, was to have a sometimes difficult relationship with royal authority and with his neighbours in Louth.⁹²

It was Robert Preston rather than Thomas Verdon who proved to be the most influential individual with whom William Windsor had dealings in this part of Ireland during his period in office. Already a senior figure in the Irish administration, the early 1360s had seen Robert knighted by Lionel of Antwerp and acquire the manor of Gormanston from Amaury St Amand.⁹³ He continued to augment his holdings in Drogheda throughout the 1360s and also continued to act as attorney for English-based lords with lands in Ireland.⁹⁴ A fellow-attorney for one such lord, John Gurney, in 1365 was Walter Cusack, with whom Robert had been knighted in 1361–2, and who had come into conflict with Lionel of Antwerp in the autumn of 1366. Cusack had granted Preston a life interest in land in Meath including Cusackstown (bar. Skreen) sometime before August 1366 and in that month added Rogerstown (bar. Upper Duleek) to the original grant in lieu of rent owed to Preston. Five years later, in August 1371, Walter and his son and heir, Luke, alienated these properties permanently to Robert and his heirs.⁹⁵ Cusack was summoned personally to parliament regularly in the 1370s, and on these occasions had dealings with members of the Irish council, one of whose senior members was Robert Preston.⁹⁶

---

⁸⁹ COA Rep. Records of the Exchequer, 42–51 Edward III, 22, 25, 52, 74, 343. Joan's surname is found at COA Rep. Records of the Exchequer, 10–22 Richard II, 89–90. She died sometime before 21 May 1397: COA Rep. Records of the Exchequer, Henry IV, 10.

⁹⁰ Details of the entails are to be found at COA Rep. Records of the Exchequer, 1–10 Richard II, 524–6. The date of the entail is provided at COA Rep. Records of the Exchequer, 10–22 Richard II, 301.

⁹¹ The estate had again come into the hands of the crown on the death of Richard Verdon in 1383, at which time his son and heir, Bartholomew, was still a minor. Its custody was initially assigned to John Cruys of Merrion: COA Rep. Records of the Exchequer, 1–10 Richard II, 483–4, 499.

⁹² *PKCI* 196–9; *Rotuli Selecti*, 47.

⁹³ See above, 38–9; John A. Watt, 'The Anglo-Irish Colony under Strain, 1327–99', in *NHI* ii. 361–2.

⁹⁴ Robert had residences in Drogheda on both sides of the river Boyne: *Gormanston Reg.*, 72–3, 78–9; *CPR 1364–67*, 118.

⁹⁵ *Gormanston Reg.*, 28–9.

⁹⁶ Betham, *Origin and History*, 311–13, 315–16, 322–3; Lynch, *View of the Legal Institutions*, 324.

The death of his wife, Margaret Bermingham, in 1361, resulted in Robert Preston acquiring property on the borders of Meath, Kildare, and Offaly, but his rights there were contested by a cadet branch of the Bermingham family in the years that followed.[97] Matters came to a head in 1367 when 'there began great warfare between the Berminghams of Carbury [co. Kildare] and the men of Meath' (*incepit magna guerra inter les Bermynghames de Carbry et homines de Midia*).[98] Preston garrisoned the castle of Carbury and captured James Bermingham, who was incarcerated at Trim. In the following year, however, the Berminghams took several important officials hostage, including the sheriff of Meath and the Irish chancellor, Thomas Burley, and James Bermingham had to be freed and traded for their release. It was perhaps a perceived lack of support for his efforts to gain control of his late wife's lands on the part of William Windsor that led to the difficult relations that appear to have existed between the latter and Preston. In 1376, it was alleged that Windsor had led his forces to Carbury very soon after his arrival in Ireland in June 1369, and had chastized the English marchers of the area for having taken cattle from the Irish during a truce. There was no mention of any attempt to support Preston's claims in Carbury.[99] On 21 March 1372, shortly before his first departure from Ireland, Windsor, in the king's name, awarded custody of the lands of Simon Fleming, baron of Slane, who had died of plague in 1370, to Stephen Fleming during the minority of Simon's son and heir, Thomas.[100] In October of the same year, Windsor's successor, the justiciar Robert Ashton, overturned this decision, and the wardship, including Thomas's marriage, was sold to Robert Preston for 300m.[101] Preston paid a further 100s to have this award confirmed by the king in May 1373, the same month in which he and Ashton began the process of taking inquisitions into Windsor's conduct during his time as lieutenant.[102]

The inquisitions held before Preston at Drogheda heard evidence of wrongdoing on Windsor's part involving inhabitants of the town with whom the chief justice was closely connected. One of those in Drogheda, to whom the lieutenant had written in the late summer of 1370 demanding that they lend him £300 or else serve with men-at-arms for three months at Adare in Limerick, was Robert Babe.[103] Babe had strong English connections, being granted a licence to export wheat to England or Wales from Drogheda in 1351, and acting as the Irish attorney of Nicholas Gernon on several occasions in the 1370s, in conjunction with Roger Gernon and Robert Holywood.[104] His mercantile interests explain his choice of a quayside residence on the Louth side of the Boyne in Drogheda, and he served as

---

[97] Moynes, 'Prestons of Gormanston', 33–4.
[98] *Chartul. St Mary's, Dublin*, ii. 396.
[99] Clarke, 'William of Windsor in Ireland', 83; Otway-Ruthven, *History of Medieval Ireland*, 297.
[100] *Chartul. St Mary's, Dublin*, ii. 397. Stephen stood as pledge on 20 Mar. for John Porter, to whom Windsor awarded custody of the manor of Dysart in Meath, which was in the king's hand: *CPR 1374–7*, 295. He also acted as attorney in Ireland for the widow of Bartholomew Burghersh: *CPR 1374–7*, 460.
[101] *CCR 1369–74*, 395–6; *CPR 1370–4*, 247.
[102] Ashton and Preston had acted as attorneys for John Gurney in 1365: *CPR 1364–7*, 118.
[103] Clarke, 'William of Windsor in Ireland', 117.
[104] *CPR 1350–4*, 192; *CPR 1367–70*, 361, 375; *CPR 1370–74*, 325.

mayor of the town in 1358.[105] He was acting as an attorney for members of the Preston family in Drogheda as early as 1348, and witnessed Hugh Hauberge's grant of land in Stameen (bar. Lower Duleek, co. Meath) to Robert Preston at Drogheda in 1360.[106] He had acquired the manor of Darver in the barony of Louth sometime before February 1372 when he was among those summoned by name by the sheriff of Louth to attend a parliament that convened in Dublin shortly before Windsor's departure from Ireland.[107]

Preston's ability to combine his government position with his local influence in Drogheda to oppose William Windsor, should he so choose, is demonstrated even more clearly in his dealings with Nicholas Starkey. On the same day that the first of the inquisitions before Preston and Ashton was held at Drogheda, 20 May 1373, Robert entered into an indenture with Nicholas Starkey whereby he made the latter a life grant of land in Stameen in return for the rent of a rose annually 'provided that Nicholas in war as well as peace shall remain with Robert and his heirs against all persons except the king'.[108] Starkey was a Lancashire man from Preston and a long-time associate of Robert's with a chequered past. Sometime before 20 September 1356, he was outlawed for the murder of a certain Richard Breton but succeeded in persuading the Black Prince to secure a pardon for him by pretending to be Richard Starkey, who had served with the Prince in Gascony. His deception was uncovered, and on 11 August 1357 the king revoked the pardon.[109] His difficulties over this matter may have encouraged Starkey to consider a future in Ireland and by 1363 he and his wife Matilda appear to have moved to Drogheda, while still retaining property interests at Preston.[110] In November 1375, no doubt with the support of his indentured lord, Robert Preston, from whom he had acquired grants of land in Meath, Starkey was one of the two men elected—without power to consent to a subsidy—by the community of Drogheda to travel to England the following spring at the king's command.[111] The hostility towards Windsor demonstrated in the Good Parliament of 1376 had beneficial consequences for Starkey who, in July of that year, was given licence to ship large amounts of wheat from Dublin and Drogheda to England, 'to make his profit thereof'.[112]

Preston was in a position to undermine Windsor's attempts to use the Irish parliament as a way of raising revenue both because of his ability to influence the election of representatives and because as chief justice of the common bench he also attended parliament in person as a member of the governor's council.[113] On

---

[105] *Gormanston Reg.*, 69–70; *Dowdall Deeds*, 87–8.
[106] *Gormanston Reg.*, 41, 53.
[107] BL Add MS 4790, f. 212b; Lynch, *View of the Legal Institutions*, 321. Darver had been held in chief by Richard son of Richard d'Exeter, but had come into the possession of Sir William Comyn at the end of the 1350s: *RCH* 79 no. 94.
[108] *Gormanston Reg.*, 41.
[109] *CCR 1354–60*, 371–2.
[110] *Gormanston Reg.*, 92.
[111] *RCH* 91 no. 80; Clarke, 'William of Windsor in Ireland', 126.
[112] *CPR 1374–7*, 301; Crooks, 'Negotiating Authority in a Colonial Capital', 138–9; George A. Holmes, *The Good Parliament* (Oxford, 1975).
[113] Richardson and Sayles, *Irish Parliament*, 135–6.

this council were several other men with connections in Louth and Meath whose cooperation Windsor needed if his plans were to succeed. As discussed above, Robert Holywood, chief baron of the Irish exchequer, associated himself closely with William, as did the Irish treasurer, John Colton, dean of St Patrick's cathedral, Dublin, and future archbishop of Armagh.[114] Less compliant appears to have been John Keppok, chief justice of the justiciar's bench, whose surname, derived from Cappoge in the barony of Ardee, reveals his family connections with county Louth.[115] John may have been following a family tradition in pursuing a legal career, and his advocacy on behalf of John Teeling, who claimed the rectory of Stabannan (bar. Ardee), involved him in journeys to England as early as 1351.[116] Another of Keppok's clients in the early 1350s was Walter Cusack, who was knighted with Robert Holywood and Robert Preston by Lionel of Antwerp in 1361–2, while John's association with Preston was already strong by the early 1360s, at which time he was employed as a king's serjeant.[117]

In August 1363, Preston and Keppok were among those to whom Amaury St Amand granted his manor of Gormanston, and in July 1370, Keppok and the other grantees, John Plunket the elder and Richard Plunket, made over all their interests in the manor to Preston.[118] In February 1364 Keppok was appointed chief baron of the exchequer, but this appointment did not become effective and, in 1365–6, he served as second justice of the justiciar's bench. While holding this position he continued to receive fees for his labours as an advocate from Milo Sweteman, archbishop of Armagh.[119] The extent to which his official role and his local status in Louth overlapped was further demonstrated in 1373 when the king, in granting to the men of Ardee financial concessions to enable them to wall their town, allowed them to account annually not at the Irish exchequer but directly to Keppok and the sheriff of Louth.[120] In the same year, Keppok also stood as pledge for two of those required to purchase royal pardons on account of their opposition to William Windsor during his first term of office, an act that suggests sympathy for his neighbours in their dealings with the lieutenant.[121] Between 1367 and 1377, John served at various times as chief justice and second justice,

---

[114] Crooks, 'Negotiating Authority in a Colonial Capital', 141–2; Dorothy B. Johnston, 'Colton, John (d.1404)', *Oxford Dictionary of National Biography* (Oxford, 2004; online edn, Jan. 2008); John A. Watt, 'John Colton, Justiciar of Ireland (1382) and Archbishop of Armagh (1383–1404)', in Lydon, *England and Ireland in the Later Middle Ages*, 196–8.

[115] *Admin. Ire.* 164, 173. For Cappoge as Keppok see *Dowdall Deeds*, 47; *CPR 1381–5*, 544.

[116] John Keppok the advocate, possibly the father of the chief justice, had played an important role in the events leading up to the murder of John Bermingham, earl of Louth, and scores of his companions at Braganstown, 5 kilometres north of Cappoge, in June 1329: *CPR 1327–30*, 532; James Lydon, 'The Braganstown Massacre, 1329', *CLAJ* 19 (1977), 11, 13; Sayles, 'Ecclesiastical Process and the Parsonage of Stabannon in 1351', 11–12; Sayles, *Affairs*, 302. For Keppok's legal training in England: Paul Brand, 'Irish Law Students and Lawyers in Late Medieval England', *IHS* 32 (2000), 164.

[117] *CCR 1349–54*, 475. Brand, 'Birth and Early Development of a Colonial Justiciary', 32–3. John and his wife Matilda were among those chosen to act as executors of his will by the Louth man John Gernon, justice of the common bench, who died before Aug. 1350: *IEP* 467.

[118] *Gormanston Reg.*, 20, 22.

[119] *CPR 1361–4*, 468; *Admin. Ire.*, 113 n. 5, 173. *Reg. Sweteman*, 301. The document is undated, but Peter Repenteny is named as sheriff, a post he held in 1365–6: TNA E 101/244/9.

[120] *CPI* 73, 77.

[121] COA Rep. Records of the Exchequer, 42–51 Edward III, 114–17.

and attended parliament as a member of the council alongside Robert Preston, Robert Holywood, and Richard Plunket.[122] Between November 1373 and April 1374 he was chief governor of Ireland, a post he appears to have shared with William Tany, prior of Kilmainham.[123] In November 1376 he was appointed with James Butler, earl of Ormond, Maurice fitz Thomas, earl of Kildare, Nicholas Dagworth, and Richard White to investigate Windsor's administration, but the inquiry provoked so much unrest in Dublin that it was allowed to lapse before the end of 1378.[124]

William Windsor was not without his supporters in Ireland, but his insistence that the settlers should contribute to their own defence put him at a disadvantage, since he could only secure grants of taxation on the scale required in parliament.[125] An analysis of the careers of Roger Gernon, Robert Babe, Nicholas Starkey, Robert Preston, and John Keppok suggests that the connections between the ministerial element in the Irish parliament and the localities from which they came, and which sent representatives to that institution, could not have been closer.[126] Windsor's crude approach to gaining assent to his demands ensured that both these components of parliament would oppose him, and when he also alienated its third component, the nobility, in the person of James Butler, earl of Ormond (d.1382), it was clear that his governorship had no future.[127]

For the settlers in Louth Windsor's period of office had seen no sustained effort to combat the growing threat from the Irish, but had at least provided opportunities to strengthen contacts with similar communities elsewhere in Ireland and with parliament in England. Located as they were between the lordship of Trim and the earldom of Ulster, united since 1368 by the marriage of Edmund Mortimer and Philippa Plantagenet, it appeared obvious to them who would best protect their interests. That Mortimer was content to encourage this sentiment is suggested by his appointment in May 1375 of Sir Walter Cusack—whose clashes with Windsor's supporter, Henry Ferrers, continued into the 1370s—as seneschal of his liberty of Trim.[128] Long before Windsor's final departure from Ireland in June 1376 the English of Ireland had petitioned for his replacement by one of the king's sons or a great noble such as Lord Latimer, and for the dispatch to Ireland to defend his lands of Edmund Mortimer, 'earl of March and Ulster, lord of Clare, Trim and Connacht'.[129]

---

[122] *Admin. Ire.*, 173; *CPR 1377–81*, 31; *Parls & Councils*, 51–2; Richardson and Sayles, *Irish Parliament*, 302–5; Betham, *Origin and History*, 322–3.

[123] *NHI* ix. 474; *Admin. Ire.*, 90–1.

[124] *CPR 1374–7*, 394, 416; *CCR 1374–7*, 469. The chancery rolls in error name Gerald fitz Maurice as earl of Kildare. He was earl of Desmond. My thanks to Peter Crooks for advice on this point.

[125] Richardson and Sayles, *Irish Parliament*, 111–18; Connolly, 'Financing Expeditions to Ireland'.

[126] The landholding ties between Roger Gernon and John Keppok in Louth in the 1350s, centred around Mullanstown in the barony of Ardee, were particularly close: *RCH* 75 no. 109.

[127] Crooks, 'Representation and Dissent', 22–4.

[128] COA Rep. Records of the Exchequer, 42–51 Edward III, 141, 209.

[129] For the use by Edmund Mortimer of his full title in an Irish document, Hogan, *Priory of Llanthony*, 347; *The Irish Cartularies of Llanthony Prima and Secunda*, ed. Eric St John Brooks. Irish Manuscripts Commission (Dublin, 1953), 175–6. For the importance of titles to the English aristocracy, Davies, *Lords and Lordship*, 21–9, 58–61. Harbison, 'William of Windsor's Administration', 160–2.

Mortimer agreed to serve as lieutenant of Ireland in June 1379, receiving letters patent of appointment in October of that year and arriving in Ireland, at Howth, in May 1380.[130] He was the first head of the family to set foot in the country since the departure of Roger Mortimer in September 1320. He had shown an interest in the administration of his Irish lands before his arrival in the country, as is suggested by the indenture drawn up at Carlingford on 21 May 1375 between his treasurer of Ulster, Walter Brugge, and his receiver of revenues in Cooley and Carlingford, John Maryman, whereby John entrusted to Walter £35 5s 6½d of the issues of these lands collected since 1 November 1374.[131] In the same year, Edmund secured a licence to have grain transported from any port in Dublin, Meath, or Louth to Ulster for the provisioning of his castles there, and installed Walter Cusack as his seneschal of Trim.[132] His intervention with the young Richard II in April 1378 to secure a pardon for John Adyne, a follower found guilty of murder in co. Louth, suggests a degree of attention on his part to affairs in Ireland, revealed more explicitly in the following year when in anticipation of his sojourn there he ordered the compilation of an inventory of all his Irish possessions.[133] On his arrival in Ireland he set out almost at once for Trim, which he had reached by 17 May, and between then and his death on St Stephen's Day 1381 he devoted much of his energy to strengthening his liberty of Trim and his earldom of Ulster.[134] The English of Louth and their neighbours in Meath and Ulster at last had a king's representative who would prioritize their needs.

From Trim, Mortimer moved to Drogheda, where he conducted government business in late June and early July 1380, before advancing into Ulster.[135] Mortimer stationed himself at Downpatrick for two months, during which time he made the most determined effort to re-establish English authority in Ulster that had been seen since the death of William Burgh in 1333.[136] Earlier that year, the settlers of north Louth, in alliance with O'Hanlon, had been heavily defeated in battle by Art Magennis, king of Uí Echach (Iveagh = south Down), but Mortimer's presence, and that of his large army, was enough to persuade Irish chiefs from the borders of Meath and from south Ulster to come to him at Downpatrick to submit.[137] Among those who acknowledged his lordship were O'Hanlon, O'Reilly, Niall Mór O'Neill, and Art Magennis. The latter was 'treacherously taken prisoner' by Mortimer—he died of plague in the castle of Trim three years later—after which 'the Irish and many of the English stood very much in awe of [Mortimer]; and

---

[130] Dorothy Johnston, 'Chief Governors and Treasurers of Ireland in the Reign of Richard II', in Barry *et al., Colony and Frontier in Medieval Ireland*, 99. The indenture is transcribed at 113–15.
[131] BL Egerton Charter 7228.
[132] *RCH* 97 no. 230; COA Rep. Records of the Exchequer, 42–51 Edward III, 209.
[133] *CPR 1377–81*, 186. A John Adyn, burgess of Termonfeckin, mentioned in a deed of 1443, may have been a descendant of this man: *Dowdall Deeds*, 182. For the inventory see Herbert Wood, 'The Muniments of Edmund de Mortimer, Third Earl of March, Concerning his Liberty of Trim', *PRIA* 40 (1932), C, 312–55; Simms, 'Ulster Revolt of 1404', 144.
[134] Hogan, *Priory of Llanthony*, 347.
[135] *RCH* 107 no. 1; NAI RC 8/33, 118–19. Mortimer was at Kells on 29 June: *RCH* 107 no. 6.
[136] He spent some days at Carrickfergus in mid-July: *RCH* 109 no. 73.
[137] *AFM* iv. 677.

seeing themselves at his mercy, they resolved not to cultivate any familiarity with him'.[138] This was an incident that lived long in the memory of the Magennises: in March 1395, as he contemplated the possibility of submitting to Richard II at Drogheda, Muirchertach Magennis, head of the family, wrote to the king asserting that Edmund Mortimer had been responsible for the death of his brother and son.[139]

In August or September 1380, Edmund sought to capitalize on the fear he had inspired among the Irish, and assert his provincial dominance, by leading his forces on a destructive raid as far into north-west Ulster as Donegal. It was probably at this juncture that a bridge was built across the river Bann at Coleraine, using timber imported from the Mortimer lordship of Usk in Wales, and that Irish cattle were exported by Roger for the use of the monks at Wigmore, the Augustinian abbey in Herefordshire that had been patronized by his family for generations.[140] Before he could translate temporary supremacy into something more permanent in his own inheritance, however, Edmund was required to deal with the threat to English rule elsewhere in Ireland. He was not to visit Ulster again. He travelled south to Athlone and from there to Kells, where he resided in late September and early October. By the end of the month he was at Trim, and from there made his way to Dublin where he convened a parliament in November 1380.[141] He was at the town of Louth on 8 February 1381 and at Dundalk at the end of the month, but spent most of the year in Leinster and Munster, before dying at Cork at the age of 29 on 26 December.[142] In his will he left money to 'the convent of Ulster'—probably the Benedictine house at Downpatrick—and in the same document expressed his pride in the arms of Mortimer and Ulster.[143]

Edmund Mortimer's short, dynamic, sojourn in Ireland demonstrated the continued strength of the network of support that an earl of Ulster and lord of Trim might call upon should he choose to pursue his ambitions in the country. Edmund's most important officers, such as Ralph Poley and Walter Brugge, were Englishmen whose attachment to the house of Mortimer or to the royal family brought them occasional service in Ireland. Poley, who acted as Edmund's seneschal of Trim during his time in Ireland, had previously served as his seneschal of Ulster in the late 1360s.[144] Brugge was a royal clerk whose Irish connections were established during Lionel of Antwerp's lieutenancy, when the king secured for him a pension from the archbishopric of Armagh.[145] He was Edmund's treasurer of

---

[138] *AFM* iv. 677; *A. Clon.* 308.
[139] Curtis, *Richard II in Ireland*, 85–90, 173–9.
[140] Davies, *Lords and Lordship*, 35; Robin Frame, 'War and Peace in the Medieval Lordship of Ireland', in his *Ireland and Britain*, 239.
[141] 'Ancient Deeds', 29; *RCH* 107 nos. 8, 9; Otway-Ruthven, *History of Medieval Ireland*, 314.
[142] *RCH* 108 nos. 31, 52; *Dowdall Deeds*, 109.
[143] *A Collection of all the Wills, Now Known to Be Extant, of the Kings and Queens of England, Princes and Princesses of Wales, and every Branch of the Blood Royal, from the Reign of William the Conqueror, to that of Henry the Seventh Exclusive: With Explanatory Notes and a Glossary*, ed. J. Nichols (London, 1780), 104–17, at 111, 112.
[144] *Reg. Sweteman*, 39–40; Hogan, *Priory of Llanthony*, 347; *Dowdall Deeds*, 122–4.
[145] *Reg. Sweteman*, 24, 29.

Ulster in 1375 and in the same year was ordered to arrest the sheriff of Ulster, John White, and to oversee the election of a successor.[146] He served as receiver-general of the Mortimer estates in the 1380s and 1390s, and before his death in 1401 had acquired not only a canonry at York, but also prebends at Trim and Howth, as well as the archdeaconry of Meath. Following Edmund Mortimer's death in 1381, Brugge continued in the service of his son and heir, Roger.[147]

Edmund also had at his disposal in Ireland local men with family traditions of service to the Mortimers or to the crown. James de la Hyde, son of a sheriff of Meath, had been knighted by Lionel of Antwerp in 1361 and as seneschal of Trim died at the hands of Magennis while defending Edmund Mortimer's interests at Downpatrick in 1374.[148] The John Maryman who was acting as Edmund's receiver in Cooley and Carlingford in 1375 was a member of a long-established Louth family that held its land of the earls of Ulster. Inquisitions held at Dromiskin in 1334 and Carlingford in 1342 into the extent of the lands of the late William Burgh, and the dower of Maud, countess of Ulster, respectively, found that Adam Maryman held land and a watermill in Cooley and owed suit at the earl's court at Carlingford every two weeks.[149] In 1356, John Maryman served on a jury at Dundalk that supported the wish of the people of Carlingford to endow a Dominican friary in their town, and in 1382 he was granted custody of the watermill at Carlingford, which was in the king's hands on account of the minority of the heir of Edmund Mortimer.[150]

In like manner, when in 1377 Edmund and Philippa employed as their attorneys in Ireland Richard Plunket and Stephen Bray, they were calling on the services of experienced individuals with whom they were already familiar.[151] The two had been among those appointed by the king in 1364 to inspect all indictments in Ireland on the grounds that they had been instigated maliciously by royal officials, and Bray had been chosen by the commons of Meath to protest on their behalf before the king following their treatment by Windsor at the Ballydoyle parliament of June 1371.[152] His long career as a lawyer extended into the 1410s, by which time he had been appointed chief justice of the king's bench.[153] Two cousins, both called Richard Plunket, were prominent in Ireland at this time, and it is not always clear which one is being referred to in the records. Aspects of the career of the Richard Plunket who saw service as a serjeant at law in the 1350s, made frequent visits to England, and had close connections with Robert Preston

---

[146] BL Egerton Charter 7228; COA Rep. Records of the Exchequer, 42–51 Edward III, 159, 267.

[147] Davies, *Lords and Lordship*, 186, 188; R. R. Davies, *The Revolt of Owain Glyn Dŵr* (Oxford, 1995), 42–3; *CPR 1377–81*, 555, 589; *CPR 1388–92*, 370, 380; *CPR 1396–9*, 8; *CPL 1396–1404*, 404.

[148] Simms, 'Ulster Revolt of 1404', 144; Potterton, *Medieval Trim*, 371.

[149] *Inquisitions and Extents*, 137, 138; TNA C 47/10/20 no. 14.

[150] *Inquisitions and Extents*, 185–6; COA Rep. Records of the Exchequer, 1–10 Richard II, 306; *Reg. Sweteman*, 97–8.

[151] *CPR 1374–7*, 432.

[152] Crooks, '"Hobbes", "Dogs" and Politics', 131–2.

[153] *CPR 1361–4*, 537; Clarke, 'William of Windsor in Ireland', 114–15; Richardson and Sayles, *Irish Parliament*, 312–17.

have already been mentioned.¹⁵⁴ In 1358 Lionel of Antwerp had appointed the other Richard Plunket as one of his attorneys in Ireland, and it was he who was summoned to parliament in 1374 where, of course, he would have met his cousin and namesake who sat on the council.¹⁵⁵ Which Richard was in Ulster on the king's business in 1375, in the aftermath of O'Neill's victory at Downpatrick, is not clear, nor can one be certain that the Richard Plunket chosen alongside Walter Brugge, Mortimer's treasurer of Ulster, by Bartholomew Pigot, executor of the will of Lionel of Antwerp, to act as his attorney in Ireland in March 1377 was the same individual selected to act in this capacity by Edmund and Philippa a month earlier.¹⁵⁶

The power of the earl of Ulster and lord of Trim in his own lordships was expressed most obviously and regularly in the sittings of his court, and it appears that the liberty court of Trim was busy during the period of Edmund Mortimer's lieutenancy in Ireland.¹⁵⁷ Richard Plunket was among the judges appointed by Mortimer to hear cases at Trim in 1380 and 1381, while Sir Walter Cusack had the distinction of appearing as a judge at one session, and a defendant at another.¹⁵⁸ An earlier Walter Cusack—probably the grandfather of Edmund's judge—as well as acting as a senior legal officer for the king in Ireland had been the seneschal of Trim under Roger Mortimer (d.1330), and was suspected of offering his lord support during his disgrace in 1323, while his son, John, was seneschal between 1348 and 1350.¹⁵⁹ Walter Cusack's dispute with Lionel of Antwerp's supporter, Henry Ferrers, in 1366, did not adversely affect his career, and he in turn served as seneschal of Trim in 1375–6 and 1378.¹⁶⁰ Finally, John Bermingham, who as one of Mortimer's judges at Trim heard the case of Peter Ryse (Rice) against Walter for recovery of land in Meath in 1381, had acted previously as Edmund's escheator of the liberty of Trim and went on to serve as a justice of the king's bench at Dublin in the early fifteenth century.¹⁶¹

To have their lord among them strengthened the attachment of the settlers in the liberty of Trim and earldom of Ulster—many of whom also held land in Louth—to Edmund Mortimer.¹⁶² He showed awareness of the power of personal lordship by bringing with him to Ireland his young son and heir, Roger. The appointment of this 7-year-old child as lieutenant of Ireland in January 1382, four weeks after his father's death, has attracted the ire of some historians on account of its impracticality.¹⁶³ The simultaneous appointment of his uncle, Thomas Mortimer,

---

¹⁵⁴ See above, 49.
¹⁵⁵ Lynch, *View of the Legal Institutions*, 267–9, 324.
¹⁵⁶ *IEP* 535; *CPR 1374–7*, 430.
¹⁵⁷ Potterton, *Medieval Trim*, 117–42.
¹⁵⁸ Hogan, *Priory of Llanthony*, 347; *Dowdall Deeds*, 122–4.
¹⁵⁹ Smith, *Colonisation and Conquest*, 112, 117, 133; TNA E 101/241/18.
¹⁶⁰ *Parls. & Councils*, 71–3; Potterton, *Medieval Trim*, 371.
¹⁶¹ *Reg. Fleming*, 181–2; *COD 1413–1509*, 352.
¹⁶² The decline of 'the liberty's traditional importance for local society', with reference to 14th-cent. Tyndale, is explored in Holford and Stringer, *Border Liberties and Loyalties*, 309–17.
¹⁶³ Otway-Ruthven, *History of Medieval Ireland*, 316, describes the appointment as an 'absurdity' and suggests that it was greeted by the leaders of the settlers 'with stupefied incredulity'. Lydon sees it

as his deputy prevented any collapse of authority, and although his direct participation was no doubt slight, the young Roger did preside over many sessions of assizes, including one at Drogheda in May 1383, before his return to England later that summer.[164] Roger's appointment served to convey the message that in Richard II's view, Edmund's lieutenancy had been a success, and that on reaching his majority, Roger Mortimer could be expected to play a major role in Irish affairs. The settlers in Louth would have taken reassurance from such a message. Their bruising disputes with William Windsor made them more anxious than ever to have as their governor an English lord with sufficient financial resources to spare them from the necessity of funding their own defence. Furthermore, unlike Windsor, the Mortimer earls were great fonts of patronage, and might further advance the fortunes of those settler families in Louth whose members held local and national office and who had completed the acquisition of absentee property in the county. But above all, the Mortimer earls of March and Ulster could be expected to provide military leadership of the highest order. The power of Niall O'Neill, father and son, had grown apace in south Ulster in the 1370s, and by the time of Edmund Mortimer's death in 1381 represented a potentially lethal challenge to the settlement in Louth. The twenty years that followed would see warfare in the area become endemic, with important consequences for its inhabitants and their political fortunes.

---

as 'the final blow' to attempts within Ireland to find a suitable successor to Edmund: *Lordship of Ireland*, 165. Hartland says Richard II 'was rather maverick to say the least' to make the appointment: Beth Hatland, 'Policies, Priorities and Principles: The King, the Anglo-Irish and English Justiciars in the Fourteenth Century', in Smith, *Ireland and the English World*, 135. Wood, 'Office of Chief Governor', 230.

[164] *Dowdall Deeds*, 113–14. Roger had acted in his capacity as lieutenant at a meeting of the king's Irish council at Trim in Mar. 1382: *RCH* 117 no. 48.

Map 3. Louth connections beyond Ireland

3
Richard II and his Legacy, 1382–1405

The 1380s demonstrated the vulnerability of Louth to attacks by land and sea launched by enemies of the king resident in Ireland or elsewhere. The Dublin administration acted swiftly to arrest a Spanish ship driven on to the Ulster coast by a storm in February 1383, but its main focus of concern in the northern reaches of the Irish Sea was the Scots.[1] Schemes by the English government in 1375 to regulate what was clearly a significant illicit trade between Ulster and Scotland proved as fruitless as its efforts seven years later to deter attacks on Scottish shipping during a period of truce between Scotland and England.[2] Attempts to separate the MacDonald Lord of the Isles from his allegiance to the Scottish crown, ongoing since the 1330s, continued, with Drogheda merchants being permitted to trade with 'John del Ontyles' in April 1375 and William Symcock of Drogheda receiving a licence in December 1386 to transport wine to the Hebrides (*ad insulas Scocie*).[3] Earlier in 1386, the authorities in Drogheda were commanded to take to the seas to capture those Scots who had caused damage along the Irish coast, and the extent to which Louth lay open to Scottish attack was demonstrated in the summer of 1388 when the lord of Nithsdale, Sir William Douglas, with a large force, plundered Carlingford before rejoining the main Scottish army in its assault on the north of England.[4]

Edmund Mortimer's belligerence in the north of Ireland in 1380, followed by his sudden and unexpected death the next year, left the English in Louth and Meath in an especially vulnerable position. It is conceivable that Niall O'Neill's raid into the MacMahon territory of Airgialla in 1381 was undertaken at Mortimer's behest, since MacMahon was conspicuous among those who had not submitted to Edmund the previous year, but it is more likely that it represented an attempt by O'Neill to reassert his own dominance over other Irish lordships in south Ulster following Mortimer's departure for Leinster and Munster. Niall's pres-

---

[1] TNA E 101/246/3.
[2] COA Rep. Records of the Exchequer, 42–51 Edward III, 159; *CCR 1381–5*, 35.
[3] *RCH* 96 no. 218, 136 no. 199.
[4] *RCH* 127 no. 243; Otway-Ruthven, *History of Medieval Ireland*, 321; Alastair J. Macdonald, 'Douglas, Sir William, Lord of Nithsdale (c.1360–1391)', *Oxford Dictionary of National Biography* (Oxford, 2004). The royal service proclaimed at Carlingford on 12 July 1388 was probably a response to this attack: COA Rep. Records of the Exchequer, 10–22 Richard II, 98; Otway-Ruthven, 'Royal Service in Ireland', 175. The mill at Carlingford, which needed repair at some point between May 1388 and Aug. 1391, may have been damaged during this raid: TNA E 101/247/1.

tige among these families had perhaps been damaged by his submission to Mortimer, and his raid into Airgialla met with stiff resistance.[5] In October 1382, Geoffrey White was compensated for 'the damages, labours and expenses incurred by him in resisting O Neill and other Irish enemies in Ulster after the death of the lieutenant, from day to day', and by 1384 Niall was sufficiently confident of his power to launch a major assault on Carrickfergus as a result of which, an Irish annalist claimed, he 'acquired great power over the English'.[6] In November 1384, the sheriff of Meath, Thomas Chambers, was rewarded for his 'great labours and expenses in treating with Oneel in Ulster, and in arraying and sustaining knights to resist him', and these labours resulted in O'Neill agreeing to a truce with the settlers.[7] Within a year, however, the prior of Louth and the abbot of Knock made 'clamorous report' to the council that MacMahon and others, at the instigation of O'Neill, intended to raze their houses, and they were permitted to negotiate with MacMahon to help avert this catastrophe.[8]

By the mid 1380s, the Irish backlash against Edmund Mortimer's endeavours in Ulster had reached proportions that the Dublin administration could not hope to contain. Archbishop Milo Sweteman, whose close contact with the leading native dynasties of his province had helped protect the settlement in the 1360s and 1370s, had died in August 1380 and his successor, John Colton, who did not gain the temporalities of Armagh until 1383 and who was not permanently resident in Ireland, could not hope to emulate his predecessor's role as a local peacemaker.[9] In July 1385 the lieutenant Philip Courtenay, and other members of the council, were ordered to journey to Carlingford and Dundalk with a company of men to overawe the king's enemies. The clerks assigned to purvey victuals for their campaign, however, reported by the end of the year—a year marked by the return of plague—that various granaries in Louth, Meath, Kildare, and Dublin had refused to conduct business with them, and in the absence of necessary supplies the campaign was abandoned.[10] Lacking any prospect of a military solution to the problems of the marches, the Dublin government encouraged the conclusion of local, temporary, truces between the settlers of Louth and Meath and their Irish neighbours. Thomas Fleming, baron of Slane, was licensed to treat with the king's enemies in Louth and Meath in February 1386 and February 1388; in January and May 1387

---

[5] *AFM* iv. 683. Edmund Mortimer's presence in Louth and Dundalk in Feb. 1381 may have been in part in response to an attack on Haggardstown, south of Dundalk, on 25 Jan. in which corn, houses, and movables were destroyed: *RCH* 108 no. 33.

[6] TNA E 101/246/7. Immediately after Mortimer's death a force of thirty-three archers, funded for six weeks, was sent by the Irish council to Ulster 'for the restoration of the peace between the English and Irish, and for the safety and security of those parts': *RCH* 117 no. 48. *AFM* iv. 695; *RCH* 120 no. 30.

[7] COA Rep. Records of the Exchequer, 1–10 Richard II, 495; *RCH* 120 no. 30.

[8] *RCH* 127 no. 210.

[9] *NHI* ix. 270; *RCH* 127 no. 230. The Avignon pope, Clement VII, provided Thomas Ó Calmáin to Armagh in Jan. 1381 but this did not take effect. Charles Burns, 'Papal Letters of Clement VII of Avignon (1378–94) Relating to Ireland and England', *Collectanea Hibernica*, 24 (1982), 24.

[10] *RCH* 126 no. 195, 127 no. 218. The payment to the men of Dublin in Sept. 1386 of £40 in recognition of the large force from the town that had travelled to Louth to resist the Irish was probably made in connection with this campaign: *RCH* 128 no. 12. For plague, see *Dowling*, 25.

John Darcy, sheriff of Meath, and John Cruys were similarly empowered; and in August 1388 Edmund London, the newly appointed constable of Greencastle and Carlingford castle, had the same commission in Ulster and the Cooley peninsula.[11] In a public manifestation of his self-confidence and regional superiority Niall O'Neill in 1387 constructed a house in the vicinity of the city of Armagh 'for the entertainment of the learned men of Ireland'.[12] Some Irish lords in Ulster chafed under such dominance and sought to distance themselves from the hegemony of O'Neill. In August 1388 Magnus O'Hanlon and his following (*sequela*) were taken into the king's protection and in the following month two O'Reilly leaders were given permission to reside among the English.[13]

That such initiatives did not succeed in eliminating all armed conflict on the marches in the late 1380s is demonstrated by the confrontation that occurred in 1387 between the Dundalk settlers and the Clandeboy O'Neills, but the outcome of this encounter—Concobar son of Brian Carrach O'Neill was slain and his brother, John, was to remain in the custody of Geoffrey White, one of the keepers of the peace for Louth, until at least June 1391—also suggested that local communities remained willing and able to defend themselves by force when required.[14] An even greater success for the settlers appeared to have been achieved in the autumn of 1389 with the capture by Edmund London of Niall Óc O'Neill while the latter was raiding in Louth.[15] Niall Óc, who was by this time joint ruler with his father of the lands under O'Neill control, and who had been active in extending the power of his family since the 1360s, was taken initially to the small town of Louth, and then to Drogheda.[16] The justiciar, John Stanley, was at Drogheda on 21 January 1390 and at Dundalk on 24 January, probably to begin negotiations with Niall Mór about the future of his son.[17] Perhaps it was some threat of immediate and terrible war on the part of Niall Mór that persuaded Stanley to seal an indenture with him at Trim on 20 February whereby Niall Óc was released in exchange for a ransom and seven other hostages, including Niall Óc's eldest son, Brian.[18] These hostages were taken first to Trim and then to Dublin castle, but any hope the justiciar might have had that peace had been secured by this policy failed to take account of the anger felt by O'Neill at his treatment by the settlers.[19] Irish exchequer records for the period reveal some of the desperate measures taken by the English in Louth as they awaited O'Neill's next move. The archdeacon of

---

[11] *RCH* 127 no. 224, 142 no. 225, 136 no. 211, 141 no. 211; COA Rep. to Records of the Exchequer, 10–22 Richard II, 38–9.
[12] *AFM* iv. 709.
[13] *RCH* 141 nos. 212, 214.
[14] *AC* 357; *AFM* iv. 709; TNA E 101/247/1; Frame, 'Commissions of the Peace', 21.
[15] Simms, 'Ulster Revolt of 1404', 147; Simms, 'The Archbishops of Armagh and the O'Neills', 49, where '1398' should be '1389'; *RCH* 138 no. 43.
[16] Simms, *From Kings to Warlords*, 52; *Reg. Sweteman*, 122–3; TNA E 101/247/1.
[17] *CPR 1388–92*, 275, 300.
[18] *RCH* 147 no. 240. Stanley's presence at Trim on 20 Feb. is suggested by the issuing of other chancery letters there on that date: *RCH* 146 no. 214. The agreement (*concordia*) reached by Stanley was approved by the Irish parliament that met at Castledermot on 12 Mar.: *RCH* 147 no. 222.
[19] 'Lord Chancellor Gerrard's Notes on his Report on Ireland', 214; *IEP* 547.

Armagh, Maurice Sweteman, nephew of the late Archbishop Milo, held many parleys with O'Neill, MacMahon, and O'Hanlon at great personal risk. Sir Thomas Fleming, baron of Slane, was ordered to organize the defence of the marches of Louth to resist an O'Neill attack, while the keepers of the peace in Meath were authorized to treat with the Irish within the baronies of Kells and Morgallion.[20]

When the attack came it was devastating. As Roger Mortimer explained to the king in a letter of 1391 complaining about the decision to release him, Niall Óc's first act on securing his freedom had been to destroy the English settlements in Ulster and a 'graunde partie de vos terres el counte de Uriell'.[21] The size of the Irish force involved in the campaign of 1390 is suggested by the compensation awarded in the following year to Robert Clinton for his labours 'in resisting O'Neill, Magennis and O'Hanlon who came burning and destroying the county of Louth'.[22] In February 1391, the king did order an investigation into Stanley's conduct as justiciar, and in particular the circumstances of Niall Óc's release.[23] The fact that one of those commissioned to hear evidence from 'good and lawful men' in different parts of the country, including Ulster, Louth, and Meath, was Walter Brugge suggests that Roger Mortimer also had some influence in the selection of commissioners.[24] Brugge and his colleagues held an inquisition at Drogheda in June 1391 that heard evidence from, among others, O'Neill's captor, Edmund London, the sheriff of Meath, John Darcy, and Thomas Fleming, baron of Slane, about the catastrophic nature of Niall Óc's raid.[25]

The inquisition was premature, given that Irish attacks on the settlement persisted. Before the end of the year war had broken out between the O'Reillys and the English of Meath. The Irish gained the upper hand and the Dublin administration was forced to sanction the payment by the settlers in Meath of 84m to O'Reilly to persuade him to cease his attacks on the settlement.[26] In the following year, 1392, O'Neill launched another military campaign. A royal service was proclaimed in February to assemble at Carlingford on 17 March 1392, but little resistance was offered to the Irish.[27] O'Neill was accompanied by 'the chiefs of the whole province of Ulster', and his assault was directed specifically against the Cooley peninsula and the inhabitants of Dundalk.[28] 'He acquired power over them on this occasion',

---

[20] TNA E 101/247/1; *RCH* 146 no. 210.
[21] Sayles, *Affairs*, 261–2. The attack took place sometime after 20 Mar. 1390, the date on which Stanley and the O'Neills entered into an indenture concerning the rights of Roger Mortimer in Ulster: *RCH* 147 no. 240. Stanley was at Drogheda on 30 June 1390: *Dowdall Deeds*, 126.
[22] TNA E 101/247/1.
[23] Stanley presided over a session of the council at Drogheda on 26 Jan. 1391: *Dowdall Deeds*, 128.
[24] *CPR 1388–92*, 404–5.
[25] TNA E 101/247/1.
[26] *PKCI* 192–6; Frame, 'Commissions of the Peace', 25, 26; *RCH* 148 no. 42.
[27] COA Rep. Records of the Exchequer, 10–22 Richard II, 147. This does not appear in the list provided in Otway-Ruthven, 'Royal Service in Ireland', 175.
[28] In 1394–5, Stephen Gernon, to whom the property of the abbey of Newry in Cooley had been awarded in Feb. 1392, reported that 'the lands are destroyed by Oneel, an Irish enemy': COA Rep. Records of the Exchequer, 10–22 Richard II, 229.

the Irish annalist tells us, 'and Seffin [Geoffrey] White, who had engaged with him [in single combat], was slain by him'.[29] Geoffrey White of Dundalk has the distinction of being the first English settler in Louth below the rank of magnate to be mentioned by name in an Irish annal. By the time of his death he had been involved in recorded clashes with the O'Neills for almost thirty years.[30] Niall Óc's grandfather, Aed, had seized horses belonging to him in 1364 when he was acting as Lionel of Antwerp's constable at Greencastle, and ten years later Niall Mór O'Neill identified him and the men of Dundalk as responsible for breaking the truce negotiated between the English and Irish by the archbishop of Armagh in 1373.[31] Geoffrey served as a keeper of the peace for Louth on at least three occasions between 1380 and his death, and his acquisition of a substantial part of the manor of Roche, and the manor of Dungooley, both on the Louth–Armagh border, in the mid-1380s suggests that he was willing to accept the perils associated with holding land in the marches.[32] His death in single combat at the hands of Niall Óc O'Neill in 1392 demonstrated how real those dangers were.

In confronting the threats they faced in the early 1390s, the settlers in Louth received support from an unexpected source. Philip Darcy, third Baron Darcy of Knaith, as well as holding significant property in Meath and Dublin, was lord of Louth, Ash, and Castlering, and thus a major landowner on the frontiers of co. Louth.[33] These properties had come into the hands of John Darcy (d.1347) in 1340, but were placed in the custody of Queen Philippa during the series of minorities that followed his death. In 1362, John's 10-year-old grandson Philip succeeded to the property, and on Queen Philippa's death in 1369 the Darcy custody was awarded to Edmund Laurence, later Irish escheator. Finally, in 1374 the king allowed Philip to enter into his inheritance.[34] He had already proved himself to be an accomplished warrior, fighting alongside John of Gaunt in Picardy in 1369 at the age of 17, and became a member of Edward III's household thereafter.[35] His military worth—he saw service in Brittany in 1380–1 and Scotland in 1384 and 1385—secured exemption for him from the requirement to defend his Irish lands in person, but he was careful to maintain his interests there. To this end he called upon the services of his cousin, John Darcy of Platin, who was a frequent visitor to England and who not only served as sheriff of Meath and as a justice of

---

[29] *AFM* iv. 723, 725.

[30] He held land at Castletown, on the north-west fringes of Dundalk. *Dowdall Deeds*, 116.

[31] *Reg. Sweteman*, 7–9, 229–30.

[32] Frame, 'Commissions of the Peace', 21; *RCH* 121 no. 57; COA Rep. Records of the Exchequer, 1–10 Richard II, 470. His interest in acquiring lands on the marches of Louth places him in the company of other local men who had embraced this challenge in the 14th cent., such as John Clinton, John Bellew, Edmund London, and Roger Gernon. See below, 209–10.

[33] For what follows see Clarke, 'Notes on the Devolution of Title to the Manors of Louth, Castlering and Ash, County Louth'.

[34] *Admin. Ire.* 129 and n. 7; 'Ancient Deeds', 56.

[35] Anthony Verduyn, 'Darcy Family (per. c.1284–1488)', *Oxford Dictionary of National Biography* (Oxford, 2004); Chris Given-Wilson, *The Royal Household and the King's Affinity: Service, Politics and Finance in England 1360–1413* (New Haven, 1986), 209, 310.

the peace, but also acted as Philip Darcy's attorney in Ireland.[36] Philip Darcy set out for Ireland in October 1392, 'to recover his inheritance and the king's lordships, as well as to defend the same against the Irish rebels'.[37] The four months he spent in the country on this occasion did not allow him to achieve all of these goals, but he did work closely with the justiciar, James Butler, earl of Ormond, who was his cousin, to shore up the defences of his lands. He also secured practical assistance for his tenants in Louth by gaining for them a rent-reduction on account of their 'poverty and innocence'.[38] He returned to Ireland in the summer of 1398, but was back in England at the time of his death in April 1399.[39] His son, John (d.1411), appears not to have visited Ireland, and was succeeded by a minor who died before he had reached his majority.[40] The brief flicker of interest shown by the Darcys in their estates in Louth had been extinguished, but Philip's Irish interlude had served to demonstrate the continued capacity of personal lordship to make a significant contribution to the fortunes of the settlers in Louth.

In July 1392, in the midst of the ongoing conflict between the O'Neills and the settlers in Louth and Meath, James Butler was appointed justiciar of Ireland for three years.[41] He convened sessions of the Irish council at Trim in December 1392 and early March 1393, and was at Drogheda for most of March and part of April.[42] During this period he led a major assault on the territory of the O'Hanlons, and at the same time opened negotiations with Niall Óc O'Neill about the future of the hostages who had been handed over to secure his release in 1390.[43] On 18 March 1393, Ormond issued letters patent to the effect that he had granted safe conduct to Úna, Niall's wife, to meet with him and the king's council at Drogheda within the week. She was to be accompanied by twelve men and women and Butler commanded that they, their servants, horses, equipment, goods, and chattels were to be protected and no damage or insult done to them upon pain of forfeiture.[44] In 1391 Mortimer had warned the king that his officers in Ireland were considering releasing Brian son of Niall Óc O'Neill in return for 1,000 cattle and ten hostages

---

[36] *CPR 1377–81*, 9, 79, 82, 269, 274, 393; *CPR 1385–9*, 47, 276, 450; *CPR 1389–92*, 14; *CPR 1391–6*, 183; Frame, 'Commissions of the Peace', 25, 27. In 1378 Philip granted John Darcy and his heirs an annual rent of over £20 from his lands in Dublin, Meath, and Louth in return for their service: *RCH* 213 no. 137.
[37] *CPR 1391–6*, 189; Otway-Ruthven, *History of Medieval Ireland*, 323–4.
[38] *PKCI* 159–61, 163–8. Ormond's mother, Elizabeth (d.1390) was the daughter of the John Darcy who died in 1347: C. A. Empey, 'Butler, James, Third Earl of Ormond (c.1360–1405)', *Oxford Dictionary of National Biography* (Oxford, 2004).
[39] *CCR 1396–9*, 273; *CPR 1396–9*, 356, 378, 382, 587.
[40] *CPR 1401–5*, 155; *CPR 1405–8*, 176; *Rotuli Selecti*, 63; Verduyn, 'Darcy Family (per. c.1284–1488)'.
[41] Johnston, 'Chief Governors and Treasurers of Ireland', 106–7.
[42] *Dowdall Deeds*, 131; *PKCI* 63–6, 159–61; 175–220, 234–6; *CPR 1391–6*, 286.
[43] *Misc. Ir. Annals*, 147. The O'Hanlons were divided in their loyalties at this time. Magnus O'Hanlon had been allowed into the king's peace in 1388 but in June 1391 his son was said to be in the custody of O'Neill. The fact that Magnus was 'restored to the king's peace' in Oct. 1391 may suggest that he had felt obliged to support O'Neill for a time. The death at the hands of his own kinsmen in the same year of the unnamed leader of the O'Hanlons (possibly Magnus) seems to have restored O'Neill overlordship of the family: *AC* 365; TNA E 101/247/1; *RCH* 141 no. 214, 148 no. 55.
[44] *PKCI* 191–2.

'de petite ou nulle value', and in the spring of 1393, probably as part of an agreement reached with Úna, the exchange was completed.[45] Richard II declared that this had happened contrary to his wishes, and in response allowed Mortimer, who at the age of 19 was still a minor and who would have to wait until the following year to obtain his English and Welsh estates, to receive full custody in June of all his Irish properties and rights, including the remaining hostages of O'Neill in Ireland.[46] Plans for Mortimer to go to Ireland for the second time in his young life in July 1392 came to nothing, and he made his way to the Lordship for the first time since 1382 in 1394 as one of the most important supporters of his cousin, the king.[47]

Richard II landed at Waterford on 2 October 1394, and by the middle of January 1395 was at Drogheda. Roger Mortimer was already active in the area by then, using Trim as a base from which to overawe the Irish of Westmeath and Longford, as well as those of south Ulster. The entry in the Annals of Clonmacnoise for 1394 makes no mention of Richard's advent, noting instead that '[t]he earle of March arived in Ireland of a purpose to get his rents of the inhabitants of the kingdome'.[48] The entry also includes the information that Brian MacCabe (Mac Cába), constable of MacMahon's galloglass, died that year, and it is possible that his death resulted from a settler raid on the territories of MacMahon and O'Reilly.[49] The aggression displayed by the young earl of Ulster, combined with the urgings of John Colton, archbishop of Armagh, encouraged the Irish of Ulster to begin negotiations with Richard II. On 6 January 1395, Niall Óc O'Neill wrote to the king from Maddan, near the city of Armagh, notifying him that he had appointed his father as his proctor and given him permission to return lands and rights taken from the earl of Ulster. These included the bonnacht (*buannacht*) of Ulster—the prerogative by which the earls had once billeted their mercenary troops on each of the Irish chiefs of the province.[50] On 8 January, Richard II could write of the 'pleasant news' that O'Neill and others were preparing to surrender to him, and at the Dominican house at Drogheda on 20 January the process of submission began.[51] On that day, Niall Mór O'Neill became the king's liegeman on behalf of himself, his family, and subjects, by words spoken in Irish and repeated in Latin and English, and sworn on the Gospels and on the cross of St Patrick carried before the

---

[45] Perhaps the twenty cows 'of the fine of Onell' delivered to John Colton, archbishop of Armagh, at this time were from this herd of cattle: *IEP* 547.

[46] Sayles, *Affairs*, 261–2; *CCR 1392–6*, 157–8; R. R. Davies, 'Mortimer, Roger (VII), Fourth Earl of March and Sixth Earl of Ulster (1374–1398)', *Oxford Dictionary of National Biography* (Oxford, 2004; online edn, Jan. 2008).

[47] Otway-Ruthven, *History of Medieval Ireland*, 323; James Lydon, 'Richard II's Expeditions to Ireland', in Crooks, *Government, War and Society in Medieval Ireland*, 225.

[48] *A. Clon.* 316.

[49] *Misc. Ir. Annals*, 153. John O'Reilly entered into an indenture with Mortimer at Kells on 12 Dec. 1394: *RCH* 165 no. 233.

[50] Curtis, *Richard II in Ireland*, 85–90, 173–9. For the bonnacht see Katharine Simms, 'Gaelic Warfare in the Middle Ages', in Bartlett and Jeffery, *Military History of Ireland*, 108–9.

[51] *Anglo-Norman Letters and Petitions from All Souls Ms 182*, ed. M. Dominica Legge (Oxford, 1941), 210–11; Otway-Ruthven, *History of Medieval Ireland*, 328–9.

archbishops of Armagh. He also surrendered the bonnacht of Ulster to Roger Mortimer, but a dispute arose in the king's presence between him and Mortimer concerning the overlordship of the other Irish families of Ulster. Richard promised to arbitrate on this matter by 24 June, and insisted that Niall Óc O'Neill must come in person to submit to him in either Dublin or Drogheda.[52]

The king had returned to Dublin by 1 February, but his appearance in Louth continued to have repercussions in Ulster, and in particular threatened the authority wielded by O'Neill over the other Irish of the province. On 25 February, Eoin Mael MacDonald, leader of O'Neill's galloglass, using the title 'constable of the Irish of Ulster', wrote from Armagh to Richard promising to serve him even if O'Neill refused to do so.[53] On the following day, Niall Óc O'Neill wrote, also from Armagh, to Archbishop John Colton, explaining how, on Colton's advice, he had assembled the Irish of Ulster and envoys from native families from elsewhere in Ireland, and how this gathering had advised him not to submit to the king.[54] By 5 March 1395, Richard II was back in Drogheda—this time residing among the Franciscans rather than the Dominicans—where 'in a room set apart for him' he asked a notary to make copies of letters received from Irish chiefs, including one from Muirchertach Magennis, lord of Uí Echach. On 9 March, Magennis wrote again, promising to come to perform homage and requesting permission to bring his men and goods to the marches of Dundalk. This was necessary, he wrote, because of the attacks upon him launched by O'Neill and O'Hanlon from the west, and by the seneschal of Ulster, Edmund Savage, from the east. Finally, he expressed the hope that the earl of Ulster would be present at his submission.[55]

The first of the Irish of Ulster to submit in March 1395 was not Magennis but John MacMahon, who appeared before the king on 10 March. He promised to attend parliament when summoned, and agreed to be bound by a penalty of £1,000 should he break his allegiance.[56] Niall Óc O'Neill wrote to Richard at this time acknowledging receipt of a letter from the king containing the assertion that he 'had come to Ireland in part to do justice to every man'. Niall Óc complained that he had sustained many injuries at the hands of 'the marchers of Uriel' (*marchiales Uriel*) since his father had submitted to Richard. He wished to come to the king 'with my poor retainers and goods', but asked that he first receive satisfaction from the marchers for their actions against him.[57] On 14 March, Richard II received the submissions of no fewer than seven Irish chiefs, mostly from the western and southern borders of the liberty of Trim, but including two O'Reillys: Gilla Ísa and Mael Morda.[58] A large number of Irish also submitted on 16 March, among them

---

[52] Curtis, *Richard II in Ireland*, 105–7, 144–6, 190–2, 223–4; Edmund Curtis, 'Unpublished Letters from Richard II in Ireland, 1394–5', *PRIA* 37 (1927), C, 287; Dorothy Johnston, 'Richard II and the Submission of Gaelic Ireland', *IHS* 22 (1980), 1–20.
[53] Curtis, *Richard II in Ireland*, 87–8; Kenneth Nicholls, 'Anglo-French Ireland and After', *Peritia*, 1 (1982), 386–7.
[54] Curtis, *Richard II in Ireland*, 143–4, 221–3; Simms, *From Kings to Warlords*, 70–1.
[55] Curtis, *Richard II in Ireland*, 85–90, 173–9, 219–20; Simms, 'Ulster Revolt of 1404', 150.
[56] Curtis, *Richard II in Ireland*, 102–3, 188–9.
[57] Curtis, *Richard II in Ireland*, 126–7, 129–31, 208, 210–11.
[58] Curtis, *Richard II in Ireland*, 101–2, 116–18, 187–8, 199–201.

Muirchertach Magennis, Eoin Mael MacDonald, and two O'Hanlons, Cú Ulad and Niall, the last of whom agreed to pay 2,000m to the papal camera should he default on the terms of his submission.[59] This was also the date on which Niall Óc O'Neill finally took the oath of allegiance to Richard II.[60]

From Drogheda Richard travelled briefly to Dundalk where, in the Franciscan church on 19 March, he received the submissions of six more Irish chiefs, including Brian O'Brien of Thomond, Philip and Aed MacMahon, and MacCabe, the constable of the galloglass of Airgialla.[61] By 21 March, the king was back in Drogheda, and was probably in Dublin on 24 March when Niall Óc O'Neill wrote to him from 'nostre mansionis' at Lisslanly (bar. Tiranny, co. Armagh). In his letter Niall repeated his readiness to serve the king anywhere, and professed himself willing to send his eldest son and heir as guarantee of his goodwill. He asked that another son, Feidlimid, be released from Trim castle and brought to the king, and that the other boy prisoners there be entrusted to the care of other great men, as earlier agreed.[62] Otherwise, he assured the king, these hostages would die, since those guarding them at Trim cared nothing for them, 'even as they cared nothing for the lives of the dying who are and have been tortured with divers dire and dread torments'. He also informed Richard that his own people were turning against him, believing that he was abandoning them in favour of the king.[63] Soon thereafter O'Neill became aware of the rumour that Richard was about to leave Ireland, and sent two further letters to the king, one dated 14 April and written near the marches of Dundalk, expressing his fears about what might occur following his departure. Referring to himself as 'knight by your creation'—the knighting of O'Neill is also referred to in Irish annals—Niall Óc repeated his request for the transfer of Feidlimid and his other captive sons from the custody of Mortimer, and stated that he had heard that the latter intended to attack him once the king left Ireland.[64]

O'Neill had good reason to be worried. No doubt with his lord's assent the constable of the Mortimer liberty of Ulster, Edmund Savage—whose own loyalty was sufficiently in doubt to necessitate the keeping of his son as a hostage by Mortimer—had employed Janico MacQuillin, head of a mercenary band based in north Antrim, to attack O'Neill's ally, Magnus O'Kane (Ó Catháin), in neighbouring Derry. This had occurred since Niall Mór O'Neill submitted to Richard II in January 1395 and therefore, according to O'Kane, was against the king's peace.[65] This got to the heart of the matter, since Mortimer rejected the notion of O'Neill overlordship of the other Irish of Ulster: if O'Kane had not himself submitted to

---

[59] Niall O'Hanlon had been accepted into the king's protection in Oct. 1391: *RCH* 148 no. 55.
[60] Curtis, *Richard II in Ireland*, 58–9, 60, 68–9, 70–1, 149–51, 152, 159–60, 161.
[61] Curtis, *Richard II in Ireland*, 97–8, 184–5; M. V. Ronan, 'Some Medieval Documents', *Journal of the Royal Society of Antiquaries of Ireland*, 67 (1937), 229–30, 233.
[62] The young age of some of the hostages for O'Neill in English custody is confirmed by the need to transport nurses for four of them from Dundalk to Dublin in 1394: *RCH* 151 no. 19.
[63] Curtis, *Richard II in Ireland*, 133–4, 213–14.
[64] Curtis, *Richard II in Ireland*, 124–5, 134–6, 205–6, 214–16; *Misc. Ir. Annals*, 153.
[65] Curtis, *Richard II in Ireland*, 142–3, 220–1; *CCR 1392–6*, 157–8; NLI MS 4, f. 65–65v.

the king, then he could not be covered by O'Neill's submission. O'Neill, on the other hand, admitted only with the greatest reluctance that the earl of Ulster was his overlord, arguing instead that he should and did hold his lands directly from the crown.[66] Richard II left none of the parties concerned in any doubt about where he stood on these issues by appointing Roger Mortimer as lieutenant of Ireland before his departure from Waterford on 15 May 1395. Presumably at Roger's request he also assigned to him special responsibility for the Mortimer lands of Ulster, Connacht, and Meath, leaving Louth, Munster, and Leinster in the care of a justiciar, William Scrope.[67]

For the rest of 1395 peace prevailed, in part because of a soothing letter sent by Richard to O'Neill in November in which he thanked him for his continued good service, urged him to come to Westminster, and guaranteed that Mortimer would treat him 'graciously and well'.[68] The worth of such assurances became obvious in the following year when Roger launched a full-scale military campaign in the parts of Ireland under his direct command. The precise details of the assault were no doubt finalized shortly before action commenced, but the recovery of the family patrimony in Ireland was a Mortimer imperative, and one that Richard did nothing to impede. Already on his arrival, the Irish annalist knew that Roger had come 'of a purpose to get his rents of the inhabitants', but he was probably unaware of the poem commissioned by Mortimer from his Welsh bard, Iolo Goch, in 1393 in which the earl was urged to 'claim completely the land of Ulster' and to capture O'Neill, that 'Ulster dog'.[69]

The first Irish families to be attacked in 1396 were the O'Farrells of Longford and the O'Reillys of East Breifne, who had already experienced Mortimer aggression in 1394–5. Then came a raid on O'Neill, followed by a sustained assault on the city of Armagh. Leading a force of native Irish and settlers that included the earls of Ormond and Kildare, Mortimer plundered Armagh for a fortnight before burning it together with its cathedral church.[70] According to the annalist, the English 'took sway over Ulaid [Ulster] after that', and by the time he died in 1397 Niall Mór O'Neill must have wondered whether his quarter-century of success against the settlers of Ulster and Louth was in the process of being permanently reversed.[71]

---

[66] Simms, 'Ulster Revolt of 1404', 146–7, 149–50.
[67] Wood, 'Office of Chief Governor', 231.
[68] Dorothy Johnston, 'The Interim Years: Richard II and Ireland, 1395–1399', in Lydon, *England and Ireland in the Later Middle Ages*, 179–81. I am less inclined to view Richard's behaviour as even-handed than is Dr Johnston. See also Peter Crooks, 'State of the Union: Perspectives on English Imperialism in the Late Middle Ages', *Past and Present*, 212 (2011), 33–4.
[69] Simms, 'Ulster Revolt of 1404', 148; R. R. Davies, *The Age of Conquest: Wales 1063–1415* (Oxford, 1991), 408 (first publ. as *Conquest, Coexistence and Change: Wales 1063–1415* (Oxford, 1987)); Davies, *Revolt of Owain Glyn Dŵr*, 38, 41; Rachel Bromwich, 'The Earlier *Cywyddwyr*: Poets Contemporary with Dafydd ap Gwilym', in A. O. H. Jarman and Gwilym Rees Hughes (eds), rev. Daffyd Johnston, *A Guide to Welsh Literature, 1282–c.1550* (Cardiff, 1997), 138–9.
[70] *Misc. Ir. Annals*, 155, 157. Archbishop Nicholas Fleming was still appealing for funds to repair his cathedral church, 'burnt long before we came to it', in 1405: *Reg. Fleming*, 3, 4–5. Mortimer's success in Armagh may have been facilitated by infighting among the O'Hanlons. In 1396 the O'Hanlon chief 'was treacherously slain by a party of his own people [*fine*]': *AFM* iv. 745. Douglas Biggs, *Three Armies in Britain: The Irish Campaign of Richard II and the Usurpation of Henry IV, 1397–1399* (Leiden, 2006), 36–9.
[71] *A. Clon.* 319; *AU* iii. 39.

Had he lived for a further three years he would have witnessed a dramatic decline in the fortunes of his enemies: in July 1398 Roger Mortimer was slain in Carlow by the O'Byrnes, while in February 1400 Richard II was murdered on the orders of his cousin, Henry Bolingbroke, having been deposed five months earlier on his return from a second expedition to Ireland.[72] Meanwhile, Niall Óc O'Neill, who succeeded Niall Mór without opposition, had quickly regained the initiative against those who had threatened the power of his family in Ulster. In 1398, the annals record that '[t]he English and Irish of the province of Ulster (O'Donnell only excepted) went into the house of O'Neill and gave him hostages and other pledges of submission', and in the following year he pressed home his advantage by leading a force 'against the English, so that the greater number of them was plundered and expelled by him'.[73]

Not all O'Neill attacks on the settlers in 1399 proved successful, as the belligerent attitude towards the Irish displayed by Roger Mortimer continued to influence settler responses to the threat posed by their enemies. The sons of Niall Óc's brother, Henry, were routed by the settlers of Dundalk that year after having attacked the town, and Domnall son of Henry was sent as a prisoner to England.[74] This victory must have heartened the settlers of Louth, Meath, and Ulster as they came to terms with the death of Mortimer at the age of 24. Not only had he defeated their Irish enemies in 1395 and 1396, but in 1397, after routing the Irish of Leinster, he had demonstrated yet again the power of Mortimer lordship by knighting seven of their leading men, including Christopher Preston, John Bellew, Edmund London, and Walter de la Hyde.[75] In so doing, Roger almost certainly sought to imitate the actions of his grandfather, Lionel of Antwerp, earl of Ulster, who, following a similar victory over the Irish in 1361–2, had knighted a cohort of important settlers that included Christopher Preston's father, Robert, and James de la Hyde, who seems to have been the father of Walter.[76] Roger Mortimer had been brought to Ireland as a child by his father in 1380, and his own son and heir, Edmund, who was 6 years old at the time of his father's death in July 1398, was with Roger in Ireland during his lieutenancy.[77] This cyclical reaffirmation of their

---

[72] O'Byrne, *War, Politics and the Irish of Leinster*, 112; Alistair Dunn, 'Richard II and the Mortimer Inheritance', in Chris Given-Wilson (ed.), *Fourteenth Century England II* (Woodbridge, 2002), 159–70. The author's remark that Mortimer 'returned to the British mainland' in Jan. 1398 suggests the degree of caution with which this article should be read. Nigel Saul, *Richard II* (New Haven, 1997), 405–34.

[73] *AFM* iv. 757, 765.

[74] *AFM* iv. 765.

[75] 'Henry Marleburrough's Chronicle of Ireland', 218.

[76] *Chartul. St Mary's, Dublin*, ii. 395–6.

[77] Wood, 'The Office of Chief Governor of Ireland', 231; Otway-Ruthven, *History of Medieval Ireland*, 335–6. While Roger was in England in late 1397 and early 1398 his wife, Eleanor Holland, and presumably the young Edmund, remained in Ireland. The Catalan pilgrim, Ramon de Perellós, when returning from the Purgatory at Lough Derg celebrated Christmas with O'Neill and saw in the New Year with the countess of March 'in one of her castles'—presumably Trim: D. M. Carpenter, 'The Pilgrim from Catalonia/Aragon: Ramon de Perellós, 1397', in Haren and de Pontfarcy, *Medieval Pilgrimage to St Patrick's Purgatory*, 118. Mortimer had entered into an indenture with James Butler, earl of Ormond, at Trim on 23 Nov. 1397: 'Private Indentures for Life Service in Peace and War, 1278–1476', ed. Michael Jones and Simon Walker, *Camden Miscellany*, 32 (1994), 121–2.

commitment to their Irish interests by the Mortimers, and their employment from generation to generation of the same settler families as their officials in the country, helped mitigate to some extent the instability associated with the long minorities that followed the deaths of Edmund in 1381 and Roger in 1398.

Roger's decision to confer knighthood on his most important tenants in 1397 was also a response to the unsuccessful attempts of Richard II to make many of the same men knights some eight years earlier. Between October and December 1389, the king ordered eighteen prominent individuals from Meath and Louth to take up knighthood before the justiciar in the following spring on the basis that each of them had lands worth over £40 per annum. None of those thus identified was willing to accept this valuation of their estates, and the inquisitions taken as a result of their stance found that only two of the eighteen, Christopher Plunket and John Rochfort, in fact met the property qualification. Of the others, four—Christopher Preston, John Bellew, Edmund London, and Robert Cadell—were, however, content to accept knighthood from Roger Mortimer in 1397.[78] While it is possible that the estates of these men had risen in value since 1387, thus making it unproblematic for them to be knighted, the fact that, as late as May 1397, Christopher Preston had sought and received an exemption for life from being made a knight against his will, only to accept knighthood from Mortimer later in the same year, suggests that the deciding factor for these men was not financial but personal, and constituted an acknowledgement on their part of the prestige and power of Mortimer lordship.[79]

If the Mortimer earls of Ulster and lords of Trim and Connacht therefore provided a crucial element of continuity in terms of lordship and patronage for important sections of the settler community in Ireland in the late fourteenth century, the visits to his Irish lordship of Richard II in 1394–5 and 1399 offered them the most convincing proof possible that they remained an integral part of a larger English world. The settlers of Louth enjoyed unprecedented access to their ultimate earthly lord in the early months of 1395 as Richard resided among them at Drogheda in January and at Drogheda and Dundalk in March. The king had come to Ireland with a force of at least 5,000 soldiers, and while most of these were stationed in Leinster at the time of his sojourns in Louth, he would have been accompanied there by his own armed retinue, as well as by a sizeable household and administrative staff.[80] Added to this would have been the military and household personnel accompanying the large number of great lords, both temporal and spiritual, who travelled to Louth with the king.[81] No doubt the forces of the earl of March and Ulster, raised both in England and Ireland, dwarfed those of the other English magnates present at Drogheda and Dundalk, but Thomas Mowbray, marshal of England and earl of Nottingham, who was also a landowner in Ireland, probably

---

[78] COA Rep. Records of the Exchequer, 10–22 Richard II, 166–7, 169, 173–4, 223, 227, 257–8.
[79] *CPR 1396–9*, 147. For the ceremony of knighting as 'a visual act of aristocratic bonding', see Davies, *Lords and Lordship in the British Isles*, 68–9.
[80] Lydon, 'Richard II's Expeditions to Ireland', 223–9.
[81] For what follows see Curtis, *Richard II in Ireland*.

travelled with a substantial party, while the future earls of Worcester and Wiltshire, Thomas Percy and William Scrope, respectively steward and under-chamberlain of the royal household, would also have had supporters with them.[82] Also to be taken into account were the domestic and administrative servants of the archbishop of York and the bishops of London, Chichester, and Llandaff, who witnessed the submissions in Louth. To this list of English-based figures who brought retainers to the county can be added, from Ireland, the earl of Ormond and the bishop of Waterford and Lismore, as well as the archbishop of Armagh, who normally resided in Louth.

On 14 and 16 March in Drogheda, and 19 March in Dundalk, the presence of numerous Irish chiefs who had come to submit to Richard II—at least twenty did so—each accompanied by a small body of supporters, swelled the numbers of great men in these towns still further. The Dominican house at Drogheda and the Franciscan house at Dundalk provided the venues for the submissions received by the king in these towns, while 'a room set apart for him' in the Franciscan house at Drogheda was used by Richard as a space in which he could order the copying of key documents and engage in correspondence. It is likely that the castle at Drogheda, the residence in the town of the archbishop of Armagh, and the various religious houses both there and in Dundalk afforded shelter to some of the visiting dignitaries during their time in these towns. The mayor of Drogheda and sheriff of Louth had been ordered in June 1394 to prevent the export of goods from the area in anticipation of the royal visit, but providing suitable food and lodging for such a large contingent of elite guests—and for their horses—must have stretched local resources to their limits, even as it offered opportunities for profit to urban entrepreneurs.[83]

The English of Louth and Meath in the fourteenth century had frequently petitioned the king of England at Westminster, and they did not miss the opportunity offered by his presence amongst them to raise issues of local concern. On 7 January 1395, shortly before leaving Dublin for Drogheda, Richard II confirmed a grant by Edward III to the burgesses of Drogheda in Meath of escheated land in the town and further granted that it be held free of rent for ten years.[84] While he was in the town on 16 and 17 March, the king granted privileges to the bishop of Meath and confirmed a charter granting fishing rights to the Cistercian house of Mellifont dating from 1348.[85] It was also while Richard was at Drogheda that

---

[82] In 1394 Roger Mortimer came to Ireland with 100 men-at-arms, including two bannerets and eight knights, 200 mounted archers and 400 archers on foot. Otway-Ruthven, *History of Medieval Ireland*, 336.

[83] *CCR 1392–6*, 220; *CPR 1391–6*, 421 For a fascinating account of the impact of itinerant courts on local economic activity see James Masschaele, 'Town, Country, and Law: Royal Courts and Regional Mobility in Medieval England, *c.*1200–*c.*1400', in Richard Goddard, John Langdon, and Miriam Müller (eds), *Survival and Discord in Medieval Society: Essays in Honour of Christopher Dyer* (Turnhout, 2010), 127–44.

[84] *CPR 1422–9*, 419–20.

[85] *CPI* 92; *CPR 1399–1401*, 509–10. On 22 Feb. 1395 Richard II granted 35m per annum to the Dominicans living in Dublin, Waterford, Cork, Limerick, and Drogheda: *CPR 1399–1401*, 334.

Walter Tanner of Dundalk recovered in the king's court possession of substantial property in Dundalk against John Tanner and Thomas Golding.[86] Already, in February 1395, while at Dublin, the king had pardoned John Dowdall, a former sheriff of Louth, the outlawry he had incurred for failing to appear before his judges to answer William Stone in a case of debt.[87]

Even before coming to Ireland Richard had been accustomed to grant to his favourites the office of the serjeanty of Louth, and in 1394 he also made to one of his esquires, John Humbleton, a grant for life of the lands and tenements in the county forfeited by Richard Netterville and John Napton, as well as custody of John's cousin and heir, Elizabeth Netterville.[88] These lands and Elizabeth's custody had been petitioned for by John Darcy of Meath and Thomas Butler, the brother of the earl of Ormond, in 1393 and despite Darcy's argument that Elizabeth was 'young and of little value', they were obviously much sought after.[89] In like manner, at Dublin on 31 January 1395, Richard granted for life to one of his esquires, Richard Burgh, the annual fee-farm of £40 which the town of Drogheda in Louth was accustomed to pay to the Irish exchequer, and on 22 March, at the behest of his uncle Thomas, duke of Gloucester, confirmed the rights of the Augustinian house of Llanthony in Gloucester to the advowsons of the church of St Mary's and chapel of St Nicholas's in Drogheda in Meath.[90]

Richard may have had a particular interest in visiting Drogheda while in Ireland since in 1388 the Merciless Parliament in England, in seeking to curb his power, had sent two of his supporters among the judiciary, Robert Bealknap and John Holt, in exile to the Irish town for the rest of their lives. These sentences were revoked in January 1399 as part of the campaign of revenge the king pursued against those who had humiliated him a decade before.[91] Richard also made decisions during the last five years of his reign that affected the constitutional position of Drogheda and Louth and their inhabitants. Shortly before leaving Ireland in May 1395 he appointed Roger Mortimer as lieutenant with special responsibility for Meath, Ulster, and Connacht, and William Scrope, who had been given the post of chamberlain of Ireland, as justiciar with care of Munster, Leinster, and Louth; an arrangement he confirmed in April 1396 and January 1397.[92] Already, on 20 February 1395, Scrope had been granted Louth to hold as a liberty for life, and on 20 March, Drogheda on both sides of the Boyne was added to this grant.[93]

---

[86] *Dowdall Deeds*, 135. [87] *Dowdall Deeds*, 126–7, 133–4.
[88] *CPR 1389–92*, 101, 223; *CPR 1391–6*, 406, 416, 661; *Handbook and Select Calendar…Ireland*, 141.
[89] *PKCI* 176, 210–11. John Napton had, along with the earl of Ormond, Nicholas Dagworth, Stephen Bray, and John Cusack, been commissioned in 1377 to investigate complaints against William Windsor in Ireland: *CPR 1377–81*, 52, 87.
[90] *CPR 1399–1401*, 159–60, 173–4; Buldorini, 'Drogheda as a Case Study of Anglo-Norman Town Foundation', 316–22.
[91] *PROME* viii. *Richard II, 1385–1397*, 117–18; John L. Leland, 'Bealknap, Sir Robert (d.1401)', and Anthony Goodman, 'Holt, Sir John (d.1418/19)', both in *Oxford Dictionary of National Biography* (Oxford, 2004; online edn, May 2011); Christopher Fletcher, *Richard II: Manhood, Youth, and Politics, 1377–99* (Oxford, 2008), 257.
[92] *CPR 1391–6*, 715; *CPR 1396–9*, 58. In Mar. 1397 Mortimer was appointed lieutenant on his own. Johnston, 'The Interim Years', 176, 188.
[93] *CPR 1396–9*, 174.

No record of any actions William may have taken in his new liberty survives, and the king's wish to keep him by his side led in September 1396 to his brother, Stephen, being appointed to act in his place in Munster, Leinster, and Louth until the following Easter.[94] By that time a petition had been sent from Ireland which included charges of peculation against William Scrope and criticisms of his associate, James Cottenham.[95] In response, Scrope was relieved of his duties as justiciar of Ireland, and on 25 April 1397 surrendered the royal grants made to him of Louth and Drogheda. He was not, however, required to account for the revenues of these places during his time as their lord, and was instead permitted to collect money owed to him from them.[96] Nor was he required to surrender the Irish hostages—including several O'Neills—whom he had acquired and who were still in his possession in May 1399.[97] That Richard was not intent on punishing Scrope and his subordinates is suggested by his appointment of James Cottenham in April 1397 as keeper of various castles in Leinster, and grant to him for three years of the profits of Louth and Drogheda on both sides of the Boyne.[98] Between 1397 and Richard's downfall, Scrope also received the title of earl of Wiltshire as well as properties in north Wales and the March of Wales escheated by the king's defeated enemies.[99]

Nor did Scrope's return of Louth and Drogheda to Richard in April 1397 end the king's plans for these places. It was 'on the information of William Lescrope, earl of Wiltshire' that on 1 March 1399 Richard granted to his nephew, Thomas Holland, duke of Surrey, 'the county of Uriel with the town and customs of Drogheda as fully as James Cotyngham had the same'.[100] Holland had been appointed lieutenant of Ireland in succession to his brother-in-law, Roger Mortimer, in July 1398 and was given wardship of the latter's lands in Ireland following his death at the hands of the O'Byrnes that summer.[101] On arriving in Ireland in October 1398, Holland appears to have based himself and his family at Trim, where his sister, the countess of March, may still have been in residence. That her dower consisted of the lordship of Cooley may have intensified Holland's interest in the affairs of county Louth.[102] He was in Ireland when Richard II arrived on his second expedition there in June 1399 and returned with him to England in late July to face Henry Bolingbroke. Following the victory of the latter, Holland was stripped

---

[94] *CPR 1396–9*, 23.
[95] Sayles, *Affairs*, 264–9; Johnston, 'The Interim Years', 186–8.
[96] Connolly, 'Ancient Petitions', 80 (TNA SC 8/252/12556); *CPR 1396–9*, 174.
[97] 'Ancient Deeds', 43 (TNA E 210/2431).
[98] *CPR 1396–9*, 187.
[99] Brigette Vale, 'Scrope, William, Earl of Wiltshire (1351?–1399)', *Oxford Dictionary of National Biography* (Oxford, 2004; online edn, Jan. 2011); Michael J. Bennett, 'Richard II and the Wider Realm', in Anthony Goodman and James L. Gillespie (eds), *Richard II and the Art of Kingship* (Oxford, 1999), 198; Michael Bennett, *Richard II and the Revolution of 1399* (Stroud, 1999), 106.
[100] *CPR 1396–9*, 483; *PKCI* 265.
[101] James L. Gillespie, 'Holland, Thomas, Sixth Earl of Kent and Duke of Surrey (c.1374–1400)', *Oxford Dictionary of National Biography* (Oxford, 2004; online edn, Oct. 2008).
[102] *RCH* 181 no. 40.

of all titles and grants he had acquired since 1397, including those in Ireland. Thomas's wife had remained at Trim in the summer of 1399 and at the end of August she delivered to representatives of Bolingbroke royal treasure stored in the castle by Richard II, as well as the persons of Bolingbroke's sons, Henry of Monmouth, the future Henry V, and his brother, Humphrey, who had been brought to Ireland by Richard as hostages for their father.[103]

The years of Richard II's close involvement with his Irish lordship also witnessed the deaths of a number of the most important settlers in Louth, and the emergence of a new generation of local leaders. The death at the hands of Niall Óc O'Neill in 1391 of Geoffrey White of Dundalk removed a man who had led resistance against the neighbouring Irish for three decades, but his son and successor, James White, was destined also to have a long career of service in defence of the settlement in Louth and Ulster.[104] Robert Preston's death in 1396 brought to an end a career of over half-a-century that had seen him acquire wealth and status in Drogheda and Meath, as well as national prominence as a senior judge and member of the king's council in Ireland.[105] At the outset of Richard's reign in 1377, Preston had been associated with the efforts of those in the Good Parliament who had sought to destroy William Windsor, and a decade later he again found himself in opposition to the king's wishes in Ireland.[106] In April 1388, he was one of three members of the Irish council appointed by the Merciless Parliament in England to put into force in the Lordship the sentence of treason passed upon Richard's favourite, Robert de Vere, lately marquis of Dublin and duke of Ireland, and at the same time was appointed as keeper of the great Irish seal with the fee usually allocated to the chancellor.[107] Confirmation of this appointment in 1391 suggests that Richard bore no ill-will towards Robert Preston, and on his death his son, Christopher, succeeded to his father's estate without trouble.[108]

Christopher Preston was knighted by Roger Mortimer in 1397, and it was perhaps some residual uncertainty on his part about his standing in the king's eyes that encouraged him to compile a register of his family's title-deeds in 1397–8.[109] He had been associated with his father's activities since the late 1360s, and his marriage to a co-heiress of William London had made him a wealthy man even before he succeeded to Robert Preston's estate in 1396.[110] Christopher spent time in England in the early 1390s and in 1392 acquired Roche in Pembrokeshire from David Fleming, a member of the family that also held substantial lands in Meath as barons of Slane.[111] He maintained traditional family links with north-west England

---

[103] Dorothy Johnston, 'Richard II's Departure from Ireland, July 1399', *EHR* 98 (1983), 785–805; Biggs, *Three Armies in Britain*, 40–2.
[104] Frame, 'Commissions of the Peace', 21–2; Simms, 'Ulster Revolt of 1404', 152.
[105] See above, 38–9.
[106] *CPR 1377–81*, 52, 87. See above, 65–8.
[107] *CPR 1385–9*, 436, 438, 441; Anthony Tuck, 'Anglo-Irish Relations, 1382–1393', *PRIA* 69 (1970), C, 23–7.
[108] *CPR 1389–92*, 474; *CPR 1396–9*, 147; *Gormanston Reg.*, 81.
[109] *Gormanston Reg.*, iii; 'Henry Marleburrough's Chronicle of Ireland', 214.
[110] *Gormanston Reg.*, xi, 72–3.
[111] *CPR 1391–6*, 193; *Gormanston Reg.*, 168.

by gaining land at Preston in 1399.[112] The reign of Richard II also saw the Verdon family recover to some extent from the outlawry that had befallen Thomas Verdon in the 1370s.[113] In 1384, Bartholomew, son of Richard Verdon, to whom the bulk of the remaining family lands in Louth had descended, was allowed to marry by the king despite being a minor in royal wardship, and by February 1386 had attained his majority.[114] In 1391 he made the first of at least two visits to England undertaken in the 1390s, but was in Ireland in the period 1395–7 when he acted as one of two deputies appointed by William Scrope during the time that he held Louth as a liberty.[115]

For the English of Louth and adjoining areas the 1390s had left a mixed legacy. On the one hand the vigorous efforts of Roger Mortimer to regain from the Irish what had been lost to his family in the lordships of Ulster and Trim, and the sustained interest displayed by Richard II in Louth and its resources, undoubtedly strengthened the ties that bound this part of Ireland to the wider English world. On the other hand, Richard II's policy of awarding Louth and Drogheda to a succession of favourites to be held as a liberty presented a potential challenge to traditional patterns of lordship and power in the area, while the limited nature of the successes achieved by such substantial forces against the O'Neills and their allies emboldened the latter to continue and intensify their pressure upon the colony. Ominously, Richard II had barely departed from Ireland for the final time when O'Neill assembled a great host 'pur guerrir et destruir tout la paiis'.[116]

With Richard's overthrow, Louth and Drogheda returned to their accustomed constitutional positions, but in other ways Henry IV's approach to ruling this part of his new realm was marked by a high degree of continuity with the policies of his predecessor. This was apparent in the personnel deployed by the king to govern Ireland in the earliest part of his reign, many of whom had already formed contacts with Louth as servants of Richard II. In December 1399, John Stanley, who had been recalled from his position as Irish justiciar in October 1391 following the complaints of Roger Mortimer about his release from captivity of Niall Óc O'Neill, was appointed as lieutenant of Ireland for three years.[117] His policies on his arrival in the lordship in the following spring were reminiscent of his previous term of office. In April 1400, he convened a local council at Skreen in Meath that granted a subsidy for the defence of their marches and in July, at Dundalk, presided over a similar gathering for Louth that granted a subsidy to resist 'Nelanus Onell, captain

---

[112] *Gormanston Reg.* 94.

[113] See above, 63–5.

[114] *RCH* 120 no. 53; 133 no. 119.

[115] *RCH* 148 no. 66; *CPR 1396–9*, 174, 203; Connolly, 'Ancient Petitions', 80 (TNA SC 8/252/12556). The John Verdon who was a justice of the peace and justice of oyer and terminer in Staffordshire in 1392, and who had served as sheriff of the county in 1382, was presumably a distant relative of Bartholomew: *CCR 1392–6*, 66, 95.

[116] *PKCI* 262–3.

[117] Stanley's career in Cheshire, and his sponsorship of other Cheshiremen who staffed the higher reaches of the Irish administration in the late 14th cent., such as Laurence Merbury, is discussed in Bennett, *Community, Class and Careerism*, 199–200, 215–19. For the history of the family: Coward, *The Stanleys*.

of the Irish of Ulster'.[118] Henry IV's decision in May 1401 to appoint his 12-year-old son, Thomas of Lancaster, as lieutenant in Stanley's place was also of a piece with Richard's acceptance of the case argued by his subjects in Ireland that the preservation of the lordship required the presence there of a royal prince. In appointing as Thomas's deputy Stephen Scrope—who arrived in Ireland in August 1401, three months earlier than the new lieutenant—Henry again drew on the pool of Irish administrative experience nurtured by his predecessor.[119] Stephen was the younger brother of William Scrope, earl of Wiltshire, who had been executed at Bristol in July 1399 for his role in the attempt to disinherit Henry Bolingbroke.[120] He had served as William's deputy in Louth, Meath, and Munster in 1396 and had accompanied Richard II back to England in the summer of 1399, remaining loyal to him even as the king fell into the clutches of Bolingbroke at Conway castle in the middle of August.[121]

A further demonstration of Henry's willingness to show clemency to adherents of the old regime with Irish experience came in his treatment of another of Richard's companions at Conway, Janico Dartas.[122] Dartas had distinguished himself against the Irish in Richard's expedition of 1394–5 and had been awarded lands in south Dublin which, he joked in a letter to his patron, the bishop of Salisbury, would have been worth a great deal were they nearer to London.[123] In 1399 Janico was again in Ireland, fighting under the command of Thomas Holland, duke of Surrey, and at this time also became betrothed to Joan Taaf, a member of an important family in Louth and Meath. Richard II granted him 110m from the fee-farm of Drogheda before the two men left Ireland, and this was confirmed by Janico's new master, Henry IV, before the end of the year.[124] This was followed at the end of May 1400 by a grant of the custody of Trim during the minority of Edmund Mortimer, and by a further grant in September of the keeping of the most important Ulster hostage still in English hands, Cú Ulad son of Cú Ulad O'Neill, who in May 1399 had been transferred by William Scrope to the custody of Thomas Percy.[125] In November 1400, he was one of nine men appointed as justices of the peace and commissioners of array for Meath, but left Ireland soon

---

[118] *RCH* 158 no. 119, 159 no. 7; Otway-Ruthven, *History of Medieval Ireland*, 339–41.
[119] *CPR 1399–1401*, 135, 507.
[120] Anthony Tuck, *Crown and Nobility, 1272–1461* (Oxford, 1986), 213–15; Alistair Dunn, *The Politics of Magnate Power: England and Wales, 1389–1413* (Oxford, 2003), 142–51.
[121] *CPR 1396–9*, 23; Jean Creton, 'Metrical History of the Deposition of King Richard the Second', ed. J. Webb, *Archaeologia*, 20 (1824), 322.
[122] Given-Wilson, *The Royal Household and the King's Affinity*, 224–5. For Henry's treatment of Richard's adherents among the nobility, Douglas Biggs, 'The Reign of Henry IV: The Revolution of 1399 and the Establishment of the Lancastrian Regime', in Nigel Saul (ed.), *Fourteenth Century England I* (Woodbridge, 2000), 195–210.
[123] Curtis, 'Unpublished Letters from Richard II in Ireland', 288; *RCH* 154 no. 52. For an excellent account of Janico's career: Simon Walker, 'Janico Dartasso: Chivalry, Nationality and the Man-at-Arms', *History*, 84 (1999), 31–51.
[124] Walker, 'Janico Dartasso', 40–1; *CPR 1399–1401*, 74, 247.
[125] 'Ancient Deeds', 43; *CFR 1399–1405*, 62; *CPR 1399–1401*, 327, 330. By the time he was granted custody of the liberty of Trim in May 1400, numerous hostages, both Irish and English, had escaped from Trim castle: *CPR 1399–1401*, 289.

afterwards.[126] Having served with distinction in Scotland in the mean time, in April 1401 Janico was chosen to accompany the new lieutenant, Thomas of Lancaster, to Ireland, where he rejoined his comrade from the dying days of Richard's reign, Stephen Scrope, who was acting as Lancaster's deputy.[127] Henry's magnanimity also encompassed settlers who had been patronized by the late king and his officers. In November 1400, Bartholomew Verdon, who had served as one of William Scrope's deputies in Ireland, was appointed as one of the keepers of the peace for Louth, and in June of the following year was commissioned along with several other prominent men from Louth and Meath to deal with the aftermath of an incident of unrest that had recently occurred in the latter county.[128]

The nature of this incident suggests that, despite Henry's attempts at pacification, the events of the previous years had increased the potential for serious disturbance in this part of Ireland. On 5 April 1401, the chief baron of the exchequer, Richard Rede, while travelling from Drogheda to Trim to meet the lieutenant, John Stanley, was ambushed at Rathfeigh, near Skreen, by Thomas Fleming, baron of Slane, and imprisoned in a nearby castle belonging to Thomas's son, Christopher. He was detained there until he paid a ransom of £1,000 to Christopher, and was robbed of goods worth £200 as well as 'divers records of the king' that were in his custody.[129] What lay behind this attack is obscure, though it is likely that it was connected with the fate of the lands in Meath that had come to Elizabeth Netterville while a minor in the early 1390s.[130] Richard II had granted these lands, and custody of Elizabeth, to his esquire, John Humbleton in 1394, only for Elizabeth to be abducted by a number of leading Meath settlers, including John Darcy and Thomas Cusack, who were clearly unhappy with this arrangement.[131] She was soon released, but as late as September 1400 Richard II was still being informed that some of his lieges in Meath were 'scheming to deprive the heir'. By then Humbleton had granted the lands and custody of Elizabeth to Richard Rede, who married his ward soon thereafter.[132] This did not end the tensions surrounding Elizabeth and her inheritance since in July 1401, shortly after the attack on Rede, Henry IV was receiving reports of further attempts to deprive Elizabeth of her lands.[133]

Evidence linking Thomas and Christopher Fleming to those opposed to Richard Rede's marriage to Elizabeth and with it acquisition of the Netterville/Napton lands in Meath is wanting, but the seriousness of the incident was beyond

---

[126] *RCH* 160 no. 17.

[127] *CPR 1399–1401*, 131, 466; Walker, 'Janico Dartasso', 42–3'; Edmund Curtis, 'Janico Dartas, Richard the Second's "Gascon Squire": His Career in Ireland, 1394–1426', *Journal of the Royal Society of Antiquaries of Ireland*, 7th ser. 3 (1933), 192–3.

[128] Frame, 'Commissions of the Peace', 21–2; *CPR 1399–1401*, 519.

[129] *RCH* 160 no. 15; *Handbook and Select Calendar…Ireland*, 167–8 (TNA E 28/11/21). Stanley left Ireland in May 1401: Otway-Ruthven, *History of Medieval Ireland*, 341.

[130] See above, 89.

[131] *CPR 1391–6*, 406, 416, 427, 520.

[132] *CPR 1391–6*, 661; *CCR 1399–1402*, 176–7, 215; *Handbook and Select Calendar…Ireland*, 141 (TNA C 1/69/50).

[133] *CCR 1399–1402*, 410. Richard and Elizabeth were acquiring land in Louth as late as 1416: *Dowdall Deeds*, 160.

doubt: a minister of the crown had been attacked by a leading settler who, as recently as November 1400, had been appointed a keeper of the peace for Meath.[134] Initially it appeared that the response of the government would be severe: on 14 June 1401, a commission of seven notables from Meath and Louth, including Bartholomew Verdon, James Verdon, John Bellew, Edmund London, and Walter Plunket, was established to arrest and imprison Thomas Fleming and his wife Elizabeth, Christopher Fleming, and ten other named individuals.[135] In like manner, on 18 October, a petition from Richard Rede urging that 'suitable punishment be applied for the wrong, riot, and rebellion' orchestrated by the Flemings 'so that an example be made to all who plan or attempt such a thing' was endorsed by the king's council at Westminster.[136] Almost immediately thereafter, however, this harsh approach was abandoned, and on 22 October 1401 the king, in return for a fine of £30, pardoned Christopher Fleming for his involvement in the plot to capture and imprison Richard Rede.[137]

This pardon was issued by Stephen Scrope, who arrived in Ireland in August 1401 as deputy for the new lieutenant, Thomas of Lancaster. He appears to have believed that confrontation with settlers in this part of Ireland was unwise at a time when he was attempting to negotiate peace agreements with neighbouring Irish families.[138] In pursuing such a policy he was to some extent continuing an initiative begun in the reign of his former master, Richard II, but one now made more urgent by the increasing dominance of Niall Óc O'Neill in Ulster. Less than two months after the grant of pardon to Fleming, on 13 December 1401, Scrope arranged for Lancaster to enter into an indenture with Echaid son of Philip MacMahon, king of Airgialla, whereby in return for promising to use his power against the king's enemies, the Irish chief was granted for life the land and lordship of Farney, on the borders of the baronies of Louth and Ardee, with the exception of its castle, for an annual rent of £10.[139] Twenty years later, this agreement was still the subject of indignant protests from the settlers in Louth, who insisted that it had allowed the MacMahons to spy upon them and plot their destruction, and its immediate impact was to negate the grant of Farney made to Roger Gernon and his descendants in 1371.[140] Any sentiments of discontent expressed at the time by the settlers went unheeded, and in February 1402, an indenture was concluded between the lieutenant and the chief of the O'Reillys of Breifne, whereby the latter

---

[134] *RCH* 160 no. 17; Frame, 'Commissions of the Peace', 27.
[135] *CPR 1399–1401*, 519.
[136] *Handbook and Select Calendar... Ireland*, 168.
[137] *RCH* 160 no. 15.
[138] Otway-Ruthven, *History of Medieval Ireland*, 341–2.
[139] *RCH* 165 no. 232. A fuller version is at NAI Lodge MS 17, 15.
[140] BL Cotton Titus B xi, 26 (formerly f. 13). Published in *Proceedings and Ordinances*, ii. 49–50, and *Cal. Carew Mss: Miscellaneous Papers: The Book of Howth*, 387–9; see above. For the dating of the petition from Louth to 1421 see Elizabeth Matthew, 'Henry V and the Proposal for an Irish Crusade', in Smith, *Ireland and the English World in the Late Middle Ages*, 166–7. Otway-Ruthven misdates the document to 1416: *History of Medieval Ireland*, 350–1.

swore to abide by the terms of the agreement reached between his predecessor and Roger Mortimer in 1394.[141]

In the light of yet another Mortimer minority which was set to continue for many years, and given the fragile nature of Henry IV's grip on power, the priority given by the English government in Ireland in the early 1400s to reaching some form of accommodation with powerful Irish families of south Ulster and elsewhere was understandable. However, the hostility displayed by the settlers in Louth towards the agreement with MacMahon, following swiftly as it did the attack on a senior member of the Dublin administration in Meath, suggested that some of the king's leading lieges in this part of Ireland were operating in a dangerous state of alienation from the crown and its ministers. The extent of this alienation became apparent in September 1402 when the sheriff of Louth, John Dowdall, was murdered by some of the most important settlers of the county.[142]

John Dowdall of Newtown, near Termonfeckin in the barony of Ferrard, was a member of a junior line of one of the most significant settler families in medieval Louth, the main branch of which was based in Dundalk. Nothing in the surviving records suggests a history of conflict on his part with those held responsible for taking his life in an ambush at Dunleer, but the evidence to indicate that it was the result of careful thought rather than unplanned violence is overwhelming.[143] The contemporary chronicle of Henry Marlborough, for instance, was clear that the plotters planned their attack to coincide with a meeting of parliament at Dublin, presumably to draw maximum attention to their actions.[144] In its response, the government also made plain its view that there was associated with the murder a political symbolism that it intended to confront and overcome. At Ardee, on 13 December 1402, the lieutenant, Thomas of Lancaster, who was visiting the town in connection with the murder, granted land in Louth worth £10 per annum to Thomas Scargill in recognition of his services to the crown. The grant stated that the land had been forfeited by Thomas White on account of his participation in the sedition called 'Verdonsgame'.[145] This reference to the Verdon uprising of 1312, in which many of the leading settlers in co. Louth had defied the king and his ministers for several months, was not made lightly: the lieutenant wished to convey the message that, while in the intervening ninety years the settlers of Louth might have bestowed on this act of rebellion an affectionate, heroic, nickname, the crown had neither forgotten nor forgiven the affront presented to its authority on that occasion, and viewed the murder of the sheriff as an offence of similar propor-

---

[141] *RCH* 165 no. 233. A fuller version is at NAI Lodge MS 17, 15.

[142] For what follows see Brendan Smith, 'The Murder of John Dowdall, Sheriff of Louth, 1402', in Seán Duffy (ed.), *Princes, Prelates and Poets: Essays in Honour of Katharine Simms* (Dublin, 2013). The murder of an official of the crown by fellow-settlers in Louth was not without precedent in the period 1330–1450. Sometime before Sept. 1349 this fate had befallen the coroner of the county, Philip Hauberge: *RCH* 55 no. 1; *CPR 1350–4*, 173.

[143] Dunleer is named as the location of the murder in a document from 1407–8: COA Rep. Records of the Exchequer, Henry IV, 274, 277.

[144] 'Henry Marleburrough's Chronicle of Ireland', 215; *RCH* 176 no. 154.

[145] *RCH* 173 no. 36.

tions.¹⁴⁶ By deliberately linking the events of 1402 and 1312 through reference to 'Verdonsgame', the authorities sought to attribute the latest disturbance in Louth primarily to the unpredictable actions of an influential but volatile family with a tradition of local influence and lawlessness stretching back many years. As recently as November 1400 Bartholomew Verdon—one of Dowdall's murderers—had been appointed as one of the keepers of the peace for Louth, and this office had also been held by Nicholas Verdon at the moment in 1312 when he put himself at the head of a rebellion begun by his brother, Robert.

This 'official' interpretation of what lay behind the murder of the sheriff of Louth in September 1402 is plausible to some extent, but fails to explain the widespread nature of the conspiracy that led to Dowdall's death, and—as was no doubt its intention—distracts attention from the possibility that an element of opposition to the rule of Henry IV was also present in the attack on the sheriff.¹⁴⁷ In the investigations that followed the murder, more than thirty individuals from Louth were identified as having played some role in the attack itself or in the sheltering of those who had committed the crime. Among these were several of the most important settlers in the county. Thomas Gernon of Killincoole, for instance, had acted in 1400 as one of the collectors in the barony of Louth of the subsidy agreed to by the community of the county in order to resist Niall O'Neill, while Stephen Gernon had served as a keeper of the peace for Louth in the 1380s and was constable of the castles of Greencastle and Carlingford between April 1400 and March 1401. In like manner, James White, the son of Geoffrey White, and Reginald Hadsor had been appointed as keepers of the peace at the same time as Bartholomew Verdon in November 1400.¹⁴⁸

By the time Dowdall was murdered in September 1402, some of these individuals had already placed themselves beyond the law. James White appears to have 'adhered to the king's Irish enemies and ridden against his lieges, and robbed and burned them in the... county of Louth' before the murder, while the inability of Stephen Gernon's pledges to produce him at chancery in late November 1401 suggests both that his conduct had already given cause for concern and that he was by then evading the authorities.¹⁴⁹ Gernon had been replaced as constable of Greencastle and Carlingford in March 1401, which might have led to resentment on his part towards the crown, while the White family had a tradition of service to the earls of Ulster even before the earldom came into the hands of the Mortimer family. It is possible that the gathering of opposition to Henry IV in England at this time around the figure of the young Edmund Mortimer, earl of March, son of the Roger Mortimer who had died in 1398, might have attracted the sympathy of James White.¹⁵⁰

---

¹⁴⁶ Smith, *Colonisation and Conquest*, 97–105.
¹⁴⁷ Simms, 'The Ulster Revolt of 1404', 152.
¹⁴⁸ Frame, 'Commissions of the Peace', 21–2; *RCH* 156, no. 62, 158 no. 119, 160 no. 12.
¹⁴⁹ *CPR 1401–5*, 242; *RCH* 161 no. 54. White had already required a pardon for unspecified misbehaviour in Mar. 1400: *RCH* 155 no. 11.
¹⁵⁰ Harriss, *Shaping the Nation*, 496–7.

Convincing evidence for anti-Lancastrian sentiment among Dowdall's killers, however, is lacking. The Verdons and Gernons had enjoyed the patronage of the house of Lancaster during the fourteenth century and they invoked this connection to their advantage in the aftermath of John Dowdall's death. Bartholomew Verdon, Christopher White, James White, and Stephen Gernon fled to England immediately after the murder and, with the exception of Verdon, were captured and imprisoned at the Lancastrian castle of Tutbury in Staffordshire, not far from the ancestral Verdon estates at Alton. They appear not to have been kept under strict guard, as by the summer of 1403 they had escaped from Tutbury and rejoined Bartholomew Verdon who in the meantime had found service against Owain Glyn Dŵr under the banner of Henry of Monmouth, prince of Wales. Only four years before, Prince Henry had resided at Trim during Richard II's expedition to Ireland, and it is not unlikely that he and Verdon first encountered each other at that time.[151] By proving their usefulness in the field against the Welsh to Henry of Monmouth, Verdon and his associates showed great political acuity, and managed to salvage a position in Ireland that appeared beyond redemption.

The response of the government in the Lordship to the murder of the sheriff of Louth had been swift and harsh. Prince Henry's younger brother, Thomas of Lancaster, had arrived in Ireland as lieutenant in November 1401 and by the following August was in such desperate financial straits that the Irish council informed King Henry IV that his 14-year-old son 'had not a penny in the world'.[152] The murder of the sheriff of Louth in the following month presented him with opportunities to replenish his coffers and exercise power and patronage that he was not slow to exploit. On 25 September 1402 John Clinton of Cappoge was appointed as Dowdall's successor as sheriff of Louth, only to be replaced on 21 October by the more influential John Bellew.[153] On 26 September, a panel of senior justices which included John Darcy, Edward Perrers, Laurence Merbury, Stephen Bray, Stephen Scrope, and Janico Dartas, was appointed to investigate the 'treasons' in Louth, and on 2 October John Dowdall's lands were taken into the hands of the king on account of his debts to the crown.[154] Thomas of Lancaster had witnessed the appointment of John Bellew as sheriff of Louth at Dublin on 21 October and had reached Trim by 28 October. By this time the process of distributing the confiscated lands and chattels of those indicted of the murder of John Dowdall had begun, and was supervised in the months that followed by Lancaster and his officials with a thoroughness that encompassed even the granting away of two of Bartholomew Verdon's millstones.[155] The lieutenant remained at Trim for four weeks before travelling to Ardee, which he had reached by 4 December 1402 and

---

[151] Smith, 'Murder of John Dowdall'.
[152] *Royal and Historical Letters during the Reign of Henry IV*, ed. F. C. Hingeston (London, 1860), i. 73–6; Art Cosgrove, *Late Medieval Ireland, 1370–1541* (Dublin, 1981), 31–2.
[153] *RCH* 165 no. 215, 166 no. 1.
[154] *RCH* 165 no. 215, 166 nos. 1 and 254, 171 no. 98, 172 no. 2; Peter Crooks, 'Factionalism and Noble Power in English Ireland, *c*.1361–1463', Ph.D. thesis, University of Dublin, Trinity College (2007), 266–7.
[155] *RCH* 173 no. 46.

where he resided until at least 20 December. In January and February 1403, he spent time at Drogheda, Dublin, and Trim and in April and May, visited Drogheda and Kells. The numerous pardons that Lancaster issued during these months explicitly excepted any involvement on the part of the recipients in Dowdall's killing, and distribution of the forfeited estates of the men convicted of his murder proceeded at the same time. Meanwhile, the chief justice, Stephen Bray, repeated at Drogheda in February 1403 the sentences of outlawry passed on the most notable of those who had killed the sheriff five months earlier. The outlawries were proclaimed again by the sheriff and coroner of the county at Carlingford on 12 March 1404, the town of Louth in May 1404 and at Ardee and Drogheda in June 1404. It appeared that the murderers of the sheriff of Louth had been dealt with comprehensively and finally.[156]

The four leading conspirators—Bartholomew Verdon, James White, Christopher White, and Stephen Gernon—who had fled to England in the aftermath of Dowdall's death, had sufficient influence there to begin to reclaim their position in Ireland within a year of murdering the sheriff of Louth. This was not a straightforward process, with contradictory decisions being made about the fate of these individuals by the Irish administration in the spring of 1403. On 21 April, for instance, Christopher White was pardoned 'for all manner of trespasses and outlawries' only to have his lands at Jenkinstown, to the east of Dundalk, granted in perpetuity by the lieutenant, Thomas of Lancaster, to John Darcy and his heirs two weeks later on account of 'the various high seditions' that he had committed in Louth.[157] In July 1403, at Dublin, Thomas of Lancaster, at the request of John Dowdall's widow, Joan, repeated the order to the sheriff of Louth to attach the goods of these men, but in the same month Henry IV, under the privy seal, issued letters patent pardoning them for this and other crimes.[158] While action against them continued in Ireland they successfully petitioned the English parliaments of January and October 1404 and March 1406 for pardon of their offences and the return of their estates in Ireland.[159] Joan, the widow of John Dowdall, was pursuing action against her husband's killers as late as May 1406, and Stephen Gernon was still fighting in Wales in January of that year, but the prohibition against the former outlaws returning to Ireland was lifted in February 1407, by which date they were already in receipt of new grants from the crown in Louth and Meath.[160]

---

[156] Smith, 'Murder of John Dowdall'.
[157] *RCH* 176 no. 147 and 169 no. 9.
[158] TNA C 260/118/31, calendared in Connolly, 'List of Irish Material … (C. 260)', 17.
[159] *PROME* viii. *Henry IV, 1399–1413*, 260–2 (Jan. 1404), 301–2 (Oct. 1404), 350–1 (Mar. 1406); *CPR 1401–5*, 240, 242, 388, 481; *CPR 1405–8*, 176, 284, 294, 295, 296, 443; TNA SC 8/29/1415 and 1416; SC 8/113/5618, calendared in Connolly, 'Ancient Petitions', 10, 39.
[160] TNA C 260/118/31; *CPR 1405–8*, 176. Thomas of Lancaster, for instance, granted to 'his dear esquire' James White custody of manors of Fore and Belgard in Meath in Feb. 1406: COA Rep. Records of the Exchequer, Henry IV, 215; *RCH* 185 no. 61. The pardon to Stephen Gernon was repeated in 1415 (*RCH* 212 no. 79) and the outlawry of Thomas Gernon of Killincoole was still in place in 1422 (COA Rep. Records of the Exchequer, 1 Henry V–39 Henry VI, 619).

If involvement in the murder of John Dowdall encompassed a large number of settlers in Louth, there was also no shortage of men with local interests willing to seek and accept grants of the forfeited lands of those convicted of his death. Janico Dartas, a member of the commission established in September 1402 to investigate the incident, received a grant in October 1402 of 120 oak and ash trees from Bartholomew Verdon's manor of Mansfieldstown, while another member of the commission, John Darcy of Platin, went further, receiving several substantial grants of White and Verdon lands in the period from October 1402 to May 1403, including lands at Philipstown, Balregan, and Bellurgan in the vicinity of Dundalk.[161] In February 1403, John More, who had succeeded Stephen Gernon as constable of Greencastle and Carlingford in March 1401, was made a perpetual grant of Reginald Hadsor's manor of Raskeagh, also north of Dundalk, while John Bellew, the sheriff of Louth, took the opportunity to extend his possessions at Roche—again, close to Dundalk—by acquiring land there in January 1403 forfeited by Christopher and James White.[162]

John More's grant noted that Raskeagh lay in the marches of Dundalk, near O'Neill, Magennis, and O'Hanlon, and had been utterly devastated by them, and the proximity of so many of the lands of the leading figures in the murder of John Dowdall to the frontier with the Irish, and the need to attend to their defence, may explain why Verdon, Gernon, and the Whites were so speedily rehabilitated and allowed to resume their careers in Ireland. In the eight months that followed the killing of the sheriff, an unusual number of important settlers with interests in Louth were permitted to visit England, including the priors of St Mary's, Louth, and St Leonard's, Dundalk, Thomas Fleming, baron of Slane, and John Darcy of Platin.[163] No doubt they carried with them reports of the instability that prevailed in Louth, and perhaps advocated to the English crown the rehabilitation of Dowdall's murderers as the only way to protect the settlement from Irish attack. It was surely more than coincidence that their return to favour in 1403 came at precisely the moment when English interests in the earldom of Ulster, from Coleraine in the north to Carrickfergus in the east, and Downpatrick in the south, came under sustained and heavy assault from a combination of Ulster Irish families led by Magennis and MacGilmore (Mac Gilla Muire).[164] The Irish council considered the plight of the burgesses of Carrickfergus, whose town had been 'totally burned by the king's enemies', on 2 July, the day before a royal pardon was issued in England to James White 'for all felonies, treasons, murders, conspiracies, confederacies and trespasses committed by him and especially for the death of John Dowdale, late sheriff of Louth in Ireland'.[165]

---

[161] *RCH* 169 no. 9, 174 no. 73, 175 no. 133; COA Rep. Records of the Exchequer, Henry IV, 466; BL Egerton MS 75, 38b.
[162] *RCH* 174 nos. 85 and 107.
[163] *RCH* 170 nos. 37, 79; 172 nos. 4, 5; 173 no. 41.
[164] *Misc. Ir. Annals*, 173; Simms, 'Ulster Revolt of 1404', 153.
[165] *RCH* 170 no. 74; *CPR 1401–5*, 242.

The Irish alliance that had overrun the settlement in Ulster, which included O'Hanlon in its number, contemplated an equally devastating attack on Louth and Meath in the summer of 1404, but was deterred by the vigorous actions of the settlers led by James Butler, earl of Ormond, who governed Ireland in the absence of both Thomas of Lancaster and Stephen Scrope.[166] Rehabilitating the murderers of John Dowdall may have formed part of a larger strategy to defend English interests in Louth against the Irish undertaken in this time of crisis, though there is some evidence that the appetite for this course of action was greater in England than among sections of the settler community in Louth. This may explain why the sentence of outlawry passed on Dowdall's killers was repeated by John Babe, sheriff of Louth, at Carlingford, Louth, Ardee, and Drogheda between March and June 1404.[167] As late as June 1407, Stephen Gernon still considered it necessary to seek a charter of pardon from England for John Dowdall's murder, while the grant of the late sheriff's estate to his son, John, in September of that year pointedly restated that the elder John had been killed by Sir Bartholomew Verdon, James White, Stephen Gernon, and others.[168] But by then, five years after the slaying of the sheriff of Louth, the need to preserve the settlement from destruction by its external enemies left little time or energy for the continued prosecution of internal disputes among the settlers.

The murder of the sheriff of Louth in 1402 did not result from anti-Lancastrian sentiment on the part of a segment of the local elite in Louth but was not unrelated to broader issues, being one of many manifestations throughout the lands of the king of England in the early years of the fifteenth century of the crisis caused by the violent change of royal dynasty in 1399.[169] The participation of Dowdall's well-heeled killers under the banner of Henry of Monmouth, prince of Wales, in the fight against Owain Glyn Dŵr was but one example of involvement by the settlers of Louth in English politics in these years. The invasion of Scotland launched by Henry IV in August 1400 ushered in a period of over ten years of intermittent Anglo-Scottish warfare in which Drogheda served as a base from which both raiding and trading across the Irish Sea might be conducted. It is possible that forces from the town were involved in the naval battle between the Scots and the constable of Dublin castle in Strangford Lough in 1400 in which 'many Englishmen were slaine and drowned', and Drogheda was shipping corn to the constable of Carrickfergus castle in 1402.[170] The defeat inflicted on the Scots at Homildon Hill in September 1402 was followed by a truce that Drogheda merchants sought to

---

[166] 'Lord Chancellor Gerrard's Notes on his Report on Ireland', 206–8; *PKCI* 270; Otway-Ruthven, *History of Medieval Ireland*, 343–4; Richardson and Sayles, *Irish Parliament*, 155–6.

[167] TNA C 260/118/31.

[168] *CPR 1405–8*, 443; COA Rep. Records of the Exchequer, Henry IV, 298.

[169] For this topic see the essays in Gwilym Dodd and Douglas Biggs (eds), *Henry IV: The Establishment of the Regime, 1399–1406* (Woodbridge, 2003). For violent competition among supporters of the new regime in the duchy of Lancaster: Castor, *King, Crown and Duchy of Lancaster*, 217–24. The extreme case of Cheshire is examined in Morgan, *War and Society*, 185–227.

[170] BL Add MS 4790, f. 26b; 'Henry Marleburrough's Chronicle of Ireland', 215; Simms, 'Ulster Revolt of 1404', 151–2.

exploit, with Robert White, for instance, being licensed to export wheat to Scotland in March 1404.[171] As Thomas Walton explained in a petition to the Coventry parliament of November 1404, however, entrepreneurship in such choppy waters could be dangerous.[172] In March of that year he had sailed 'in one of his ships laden with divers saleable merchandise' to the port of Loch Ryan—presumably Stranraer—in the lordship of the earl of Douglas, only to have his ship and goods confiscated by Alexander Campbell and the abbot of Glenluce.[173] In August 1404, fishermen from Minehead in Somerset were plying their trade near Carlingford when they were captured by a Spanish captain 'in a well-armed ship, arrayed for war' and taken to Scotland where they were imprisoned in Bothwell castle near Glasgow by an esquire of King Robert III of Scotland.[174] By the summer of 1405, any pretence of an Anglo-Scottish truce had been abandoned and following the capture of Scottish naval vessels at Greencastle and Dalkey in May, 'the merchants of Drogheda entered Scotland and took pledges and preys'.[175] The unusual decision of the lieutenant, Thomas of Lancaster, to land at Carlingford on his return to Ireland in August 1408 was probably taken in part to display English determination to maintain dominance of the Irish Sea, but the situation was still sufficiently dangerous in June 1409 for Janico Dartas's plan to build a warship at Drogheda to receive government support.[176]

The varied interests and activities of Dartas in Louth and Meath in the early fifteenth century serve as further evidence that links between this part of Ireland and the wider English world did not decline as a result of the overthrow of Richard II and accession of Henry IV. Having fought in Scotland the previous year, Janico accompanied Thomas of Lancaster to Ireland in April 1401 and immediately commenced a tussle with another of the king's esquires, Richard Burgh, about monies awarded to them from the fee-farm and various revenues of Drogheda by the king. In October 1402, he secured a fresh grant of 100m yearly from the fee-farm of the town, as well as £40 yearly from the fee-farm of Dublin.[177] In May 1400, Dartas had been awarded custody of the manor and lordship of Trim during the minority of Edmund Mortimer, and in May 1402, this was supplemented with a grant of the profits and revenues of the castle and lordship of Trim as a reward for the efforts he had made to repair the castle.[178] In November 1401, Dartas had been appointed as sole keeper of the peace for Louth and Meath with the title 'justice and supervisor'

---

[171] *RCH* 178 no. 89.
[172] This parliament also heard petitions from the murderers of John Dowdall for pardon of their offence.
[173] *Handbook and Select Calendar…Ireland*, 170 (E 28/14/67); *RCH* 201 no. 110.
[174] *Handbook and Select Calendar…Ireland*, 170–1 (E 28/15/86).
[175] 'Henry Marleburrough's Chronicle of Ireland', 216; Stephen Boardman, *The Early Stewart Kings: Robert II and Robert III, 1371–1406* (East Linton, 1996), 286.
[176] 'Henry Marleburrough's Chronicle of Ireland', 217; 'Late Medieval Irish Annals: Two Fragments', ed. Kenneth Nicholls, *Peritia*, 2 (1983), 98 (Annals of Duisk); *RCH* 193 no. 184.
[177] *CCR 1399–1402*, 355–6, 437; *CCR 1402–5*, 10; *CPR 1401–5*, 22, 162. The king confirmed his predecessors grant of £40 per annum for life from the farm of Drogheda to Richard Burgh in Mar. 1406: COA Rep. Records of the Exchequer, Henry IV, 177.
[178] *CFR 1399–1405*, 62; *Proceedings and Ordinances*, i. 182–3.

and that winter, with Stephen Scrope and Edward Perrers, conducted a campaign against the Irish that led to peace agreements being drawn up with MacMahon and O'Reilly.[179] His interest in the security of the marches of this region was personal, since in January 1402 he was identified, along with John Teeling, as holding the manor of Crowmartin (bar. Ardee), which bordered the lands of the Irish lords with whom these agreements had been reached.[180]

Dartas was still 'justice and supervisor' in Louth and Meath in September 1402 when John Dowdall, sheriff of Louth, was murdered, and he was appointed to the commission established in the aftermath of that event, on 26 September, to investigate unrest in Louth. One of the sheriff's murderers, Stephen Gernon, had been replaced as constable of Carlingford and Greencastle by John More in March 1401, and he and Thomas More were recorded as victualling both castles with grain from Louth in December 1401.[181] On 20 February 1403, John More took advantage of the seizures of land arising from John Dowdall's murder to secure for himself Reginald Hadsor's manor of Raskeagh, near Dundalk, and six days later received a new grant on better terms under the Irish seal of the castles of Carlingford and Greencastle.[182] It was with his acquisition in December 1405 of custody of the dower lands of Eleanor Holland, countess of March, late wife of Roger Mortimer (d.1398) in Cooley near Carlingford, that More's interests appear to have collided with those of Janico Dartas, who the previous month had received a similar grant of Eleanor's dower land in Meath.[183] One of Dartas's pledges on this occasion had been his old friend Stephen Scrope, who continued to act as Thomas of Lancaster's deputy in Ireland during the latter's absence in England. At some point in 1407 information reached Scrope—supplied no doubt by Dartas—that despite the requirement of the grant of February 1403 that More spend £10 per annum on the upkeep of each of the castles of Carlingford and Greencastle the buildings 'were ruinous, the halls in danger of falling, [with] no provision of bows, arrows, helmets or other arms existing within said castles'.[184]

The state of repair of castles in Ireland was a sensitive issue in these years: the award of Trim to Janico Dartas in May 1402 asserted that '[m]any of the castles in Ireland needed to resist the Irish enemies are badly governed and so ruinous as to be on the point of falling to the ground' and in May 1403, Janico and his wife Joan Taaf successfully petitioned to be allowed erect a fortalice at Liscartan, between Navan and Kells, to resist the attacks of Irish marchers.[185] On receipt of alarming rumours about the condition of the castles under John More's command, Scrope ordered Henry Stanihurst, second chamberlain of the exchequer, to enter the castles and investigate, and to enquire by oath about the behaviour of More as constable

---

[179] *RCH* 165 no. 233; Frame, 'Commissions of the Peace', 22; Walker, 'Janico Dartasso', 42–4.
[180] *RCH* 163 no. 135.
[181] *CPR 1399–1401*, 449; *RCH* 161 no. 53; see above.
[182] *RCH* 166 no. 11, 174 nos. 93 and 107.
[183] *RCH* 181 no. 40. More still held these lands in 1415–16: *Rotuli Selecti*, 45; *CFR 1405–13*, 21.
[184] Otway-Ruthven, *History of Medieval Ireland*, 343–5; TNA C 47/10/26 no. 1, ed. and tr. in Curtis, 'Janico Dartas', 203–4.
[185] *Proceedings and Ordinances*, i. 182–3; *RCH* 169 no. 21.

and how the castles might be improved. Stanihurst submitted his report to the Irish chancery on 13 December 1407, and its criticism of John More was harsh. John's deputy, Thomas More, had refused Stanihurst entry to the castle when he arrived in mid-November, upon which the latter had convened an inquest of the burgesses of the town. They reported that John More had been absent from Ireland for five years, that Carlingford was not garrisoned, and that the big hall in the great tower of Greencastle was destroyed for want of a roof. When More failed to appear at Drogheda in early January 1408 to answer these charges, custody of the castles was taken from him and given to Janico Dartas.[186] More was not without influence in Louth, having served as sheriff of the county in 1406, and had received a confirmation of his custody of the castles as recently as March 1407, but he could not resist the combined opposition of Scrope and Dartas and his petition to the crown seeking restoration of what he had lost to Dartas in 1408 was unsuccessful.[187]

A document from later that year reveals Janico's approach to executing his new responsibilities and how this complemented his larger ambitions at this time. On 31 December 1408 he entered into an indenture with Peter Dowdall whereby he farmed out to the latter custody of the castles of Greencastle and Carlingford for an annual payment of £18. In return, Peter undertook to give to Dartas a quarter of all profits made in warfare against the king's enemies, and half of the profits of any ransoms received. He also agreed to have quantities of lime ready for building repairs to the castles, to find eight men-at-arms 'of English nation' to guard the fortresses, and to ride in Janico's company in Louth, Meath, or Ulster at his own expense if given reasonable warning.[188] Dartas, who had been appointed admiral of Ireland in July 1404, understood the strategic significance of these coastal castles: from them attacks could be launched into the interior of Ulster and influence could also be wielded in western Scotland.[189] In September 1407, some eighteen months after the death of King Robert III of Scotland and the capture at sea by the English of his son and heir, James, Dartas, along with John Dongan, bishop of Down and former bishop of Sodor and Man, was commissioned to enter into negotiations with Domnall Mac Donald, Lord of the Isles, and his brother, Eoin Mór, who was married to Marjorie Bysset, heiress to English settler lands in the Glens of Antrim.[190] In May 1408 this commission was renewed, with Christopher Preston, taking John Dongan's place alongside Janico.[191] The establishment of good

---

[186] Curtis, 'Janico Dartas', 203–4.

[187] *RCH* 183 no. 106, 185 no. 71; Connolly, 'Ancient Petitions', 102 (TNA SC 8/331/15671). While still acting as constable of Carlingford and Greencastle in Sept. 1407 More was ordered to be placed in the custody of the marshal because of arrears in his account of the custody of the countess of March's dower lands in Cooley: COA Rep. Records of the Exchequer, Henry IV, 236.

[188] *Dowdall Deeds*, 152–3.

[189] *CPR 1401–5*, 406; *CPR 1405–8*, 309; Walker, 'Janico Dartasso', 44–5; John W. M. Bannerman, 'The Lordship of the Isles', in Jennifer M. Brown (ed.), *Scottish Society in the Fifteenth Century* (New York, 1977), 209–40.

[190] *CPR 1405–8*, 361; S. I. Boardman, 'Robert III (d.1406)', *Oxford Dictionary of National Biography* (Oxford, 2004); Simms, 'Ulster Revolt of 1404', 145–6, 153–4.

[191] *CPR 1405–8*, 487; Rymer, *Foedera*, viii. 527.

relations with the MacDonalds may have helped ensure the success of a raid launched in 1409 by Dartas in which eighty of the Irish of Ulster were slain, and in April 1410, Janico and his wife were given permission to marry their eldest son—who cannot have been older than 6 at the time—to the daughter of Eoin Mór, and their daughter to the latter's son, Eoin.[192]

Janico Dartas's exploits in the first decade of the fifteenth century demonstrated the continued capacity of Louth and Meath to provide opportunities for advancement to outsiders willing to engage in a determined fashion with the challenges posed by a frontier region, and illustrated the extent to which this part of Ireland remained linked to a wider English world. The instability of the region at this time, however, should not be underestimated. The attack by the baron of Slane on the chief baron of the exchequer in 1401, and the murder of John Dowdall in 1402 spoke to a general level of unrest among the settlers in Meath and Louth that that showed little sign of abating and that seems to have exasperated those sent from England to defend them against the Irish. On 6 September 1403, while conducting business at Ardee, Thomas of Lancaster established a commission of senior officials that included Stephen Bray and Janico Dartas, to hold inquisitions in Louth and Meath

> concerning all treasons, felonies, trespasses, mayhems, oppressions, extortions, falsities, deceptions, damages, grievances, conspiracies, confederacies, maintenance of false complaints, champerties, false allegations, encroachments, purprestures, usurpations, disinheritances of the king or his progenitors or ancestors former kings of England, escapes of thieves, concealments, contempts, forestallments, highway robberies, burnings, robberies, adherence to Irish enemies of the king and rebels, robberies, murders, homicides, alterages, receipts of felons and of outlaws, victuallers of the king's enemies, misprisions and excesses whatsoever, perpetrated by anyone within the said counties, both inside and outside liberties, before this time or in the future.[193]

The lieutenant's evident frustration with the behaviour of the king's lieges, and conviction that their actions constituted a grave threat to law and order, was fully shared by his father, Henry IV, who thundered in January 1405 that he had received

> information that divers treasons etc. have ofttimes been committed and are daily committed in Meath, and that although [those concerned], the king's subjects there dwelling are indicted, hitherto they were not taken or punished according to their deserts, but are suffered to go at large, in contempt of the king, and for a mischievous example to other evildoers; and the king's will is that the same shall not be left unpunished.[194]

---

[192] 'Henry Marleburrough's Chronicle of Ireland', 218; *CPR 1408–13*, 183; Curtis, 'Janico Dartas', 194.

[193] *RCH* 172 no. 114.

[194] *CCR 1402–5*, 419–20. Sometime in the period 1403–5 members of the Hussey family, which provided the barons of Galtrim in Meath, were accused of occupying lands in Meath 'in a warlike manner'. The sheriff of Meath and his officials had proved unwilling to take action against them: *Handbook and Select Calendar... Ireland*, 169 (TNA E 28/14/26); *RCH* 160 no. 20.

Enforcing the king's will in this part of Ireland, was becoming an increasingly difficult task, as the growing frequency and severity of Irish attacks combined with political instability in England to encourage the settlers to resort to violence to settle disputes among themselves more readily than had been the case since the reign of Edward II. The situation was not destined to become any easier as the finances of the Lancastrian monarchy contracted and the ambitions of Henry IV's son and heir and those of the political elite of England came once again to focus on France.

4
'The Poor Commons', 1405–1450

Henry IV's willingness to direct a portion of his limited resources towards the defence of his Irish lordship, and his policy of employing as his officers there capable men who had been associated with his predecessor, provided a degree of reassurance to the settlers that they would not be abandoned by the new dynasty, but could not distract from the increasingly unstable environment in which they lived. That the attack on the English of Ulster in 1403–4 failed to encompass their equivalents in Louth and Meath was the result not only of good generalship on the part of the earl of Ormond, but also of good fortune: at this moment, for the first time in over thirty years, there was a lack of united leadership among the greatest of the Irish families, the O'Neills. Late in 1403 Niall Óc O'Neill died, and he was followed to the grave early in the following year by his son and successor, Brian. The English were in a position to take advantage of this situation since in October 1402 the lieutenant, John Stanley, had released from captivity Domnall O'Neill, who had been captured by the English in the raid of 1399 on Dundalk. Following Brian's death in 1404, Domnall proceeded to contend for the leadership of the O'Neills with his cousin, Eógan son of Niall Óc, for the following thirty years.[1]

The absence of strong leadership among the O'Neills was not an unmitigated boon to the settlers, since it served to increase the likelihood of violent competition among and within the lesser Irish families on the borders of Louth and Meath for local supremacy, with unpredictable consequences for English interests. In general, however, the frequency and intensity of conflict between the Irish and the settlers in this part of Ireland waned in the years between 1404 and c.1413, as both sides adjusted to the state of disunity among the O'Neills, and the prolonged minority in the earldom of Ulster.[2] Already in February 1402 Eógan O'Reilly, 'chieftain of his lineage', had concluded a peace agreement with Thomas of Lancaster, but Irish annals note the election in the same year of Mael Morda O'Reilly as leader of the O'Reillys, and the banishment of his rival—possibly Eógan, who may have been installed by the English. Mael Morda exercised control over at least some of Breifne

---

[1] *Misc. Ir. Annals*, 167, 171; *AFM* iv. 765, 767; *CPR 1401–5*, 183. Eógan had also spent time in English captivity, appearing as 'John son of Niall' O'Neill in a list of hostages in the possession of William Scrope in May 1399: 'Ancient Deeds', 43; Simms 'Ulster Revolt of 1404', 160.

[2] Edmund Mortimer, earl of Ulster, was declared of age in June 1413: R. A. Griffiths, 'Mortimer, Edmund (V), Fifth Earl of March and Seventh Earl of Ulster (1391–1425)', *Oxford Dictionary of National Biography* (Oxford, 2004; online edn, Jan. 2008).

until his death in 1411 and appears to have avoided conflict with the settlers.³ The O'Reillys were not recorded among those who threatened to invade Louth and Meath in 1404, being instead the targets of a settler raid led by the sheriff of Meath in 1406 that resulted in the capture of many cows. It was not until 1413, after Mael Morda's death, that Thomas Óc O'Reilly raided Meath with his MacCabe galloglass, receiving for his troubles 'a javelin in the leg, in consequence of which he was lame ever afterwards'.⁴

More overtly hostile to the settlers in the first decade of the fifteenth century were the O'Hanlons. The escape from Trim castle in early 1400 of Magnus and Domnall O'Hanlon, who had been held hostage for several years, appears to have been the prelude to a period of aggressive action on the part of this family against Louth and Ulster.⁵ In February 1403 they were said to have 'utterly devastated' Raskeagh, north of Dundalk, in alliance with O'Neill and Magennis, and in the following year planned a major assault on Louth and Meath.⁶ In 1407 or 1408, Nicholas Fleming, archbishop of Armagh, excommunicated Ardgal O'Hanlon, 'captain of his nation', and others, 'for various injuries inflicted on him and his tenants', including the murder of his falconer, and while this in itself is unlikely to have discouraged further aggression on their part, there is no record of O'Hanlon attacks for several years thereafter. It is possible that they were the targets of Janico Dartas's successful campaign against the Irish of Ulster of 1409.⁷

The MacMahons presented a particular problem to the settlers in Louth, as they rarely acknowledged the authority of one leader. In December 1401, Thomas of Lancaster entered into an indenture with Echaid MacMahon, son of the ruling chief, Philip, whereby the Irishman promised to support the English in return for a grant of the lordship of Farney, which he was to hold for an annual rent of £10.⁸ A similar grant of Farney was issued in 1407 or 1408 to Cú Chonnacht MacMahon (d.1411), Echaid's brother, probably because of concerns about Echaid's behaviour, but seems not to have come into effect.⁹ Walter Plunket and John Clinton of Cappoge, who were appointed as keepers of the peace in Louth in November 1402, were commissioned to assist Echaid in his struggles against Irish enemies at that time and to assess the level and nature of support that could be offered to him by the settlers.¹⁰ MacMahon and his forces, however, refused 'such food and drink as

---

³ *RCH* 165 no. 233; *AC* 377, 413; *AU* iii. 45, 47; *Misc. Ir. Annals*, 165, 169. Fergal son of John O'Reilly was in English custody at Trim in Nov. 1402, presumably as a consequence of the February agreement: *RCH* 168 no. 3.

⁴ *Misc. Ir. Annals*, 179. The sheriff is named as Baron Hussey. This was probably Matthew Hussey, baron of Galtrim, who died in 1418 and was buried at the Dominican house at Trim: 'Henry Marleburrough's Chronicle of Ireland', 221; *AFM* iv. 815; COA Rep. Records of the Exchequer, Henry IV, 369.

⁵ *CPR 1399–1401*, 289.

⁶ *RCH* 174 no. 107; 'Lord Chancellor Gerrard's Notes on his Report on Ireland', 206–8.

⁷ *Reg. Fleming*, 17–18.

⁸ *RCH* 165 no. 232 (where the agreement is dated to Dec. 1402).

⁹ *RCH* 187 no. 12; *AC* 413.

¹⁰ Clinton had recently and briefly served as sheriff of Louth following the murder of John Dowdall: *RCH* 162 no. 215.

the poor commons use themselves', and proceeded to settle their families throughout the county where they were accused of acting as spies.[11] In 1403, Philip MacMahon died and was succeeded by his brother, Ardgal, who ruled until 1416.[12] Ardgal's son, Brian, involved himself in the succession dispute among the O'Neills, 'outrageously' taking Domnall O'Neill captive in 1410 and delivering him to his rival, Eógan.[13] In 1414, Brian 'and the English' captured Echaid MacMahon of Farney, which suggests that the settlers in Louth had at last found a way to rid themselves of that unwelcome guest introduced among them in 1401.[14]

Among the O'Neills, the struggle for supremacy between the cousins Eógan son of Niall Óc and Domnall son of Henry absorbed energies that might otherwise have been directed against the settlers, and provided the space that enabled another branch of the family, led by the sons of Cú Ulad Ruad son of Niall Mór O'Neill (d.1400), to carve out its own lordship around the city of Armagh, to the dismay of the archbishop of Armagh, Nicholas Fleming.[15] In 1380, Niall Mór O'Neill had given his 15-month-old grandson, Cú Ulad son of Cú Ulad Ruad, to Edmund Mortimer as a hostage for his good behaviour, and this young man was still in captivity in 1400 when he was delivered into the custody of Janico Dartas.[16] That this branch of the O'Neills was cultivating good relations with some of the settlers in Louth in this period is suggested by the permission granted in March 1410 to James son of Geoffrey White to foster his children with Muirchertach son of Cú Ulad Ruad O'Neill and to negotiate peace with him or members of his lineage 'Irish enemies in the marches of Ulster and co. Louth'.[17] This followed the granting of similar permissions to the Betagh family of the Meath/Louth borders to enter into relationships of fosterage and sponsorship at baptism with the MacCabes and O'Reillys.[18] The promise of more peaceful times held out by such alliances was not to be fulfilled: by 1413, when two leading members of the MacCabe family were killed by the settlers while raiding Meath with Thomas O'Reilly, accommodation had given way to renewed hostility on the frontiers of Louth and Meath, and a prolonged period of unrest ensued.[19]

Already the threat to the settlers from Ulster, which was in temporary abeyance, had been replaced by new dangers from the midlands. The O'Connor Faly

---

[11] *Proceedings and Ordinances*, ii. 49–50.   [12] *Misc. Ir. Annals*, 171; *AC* 431.
[13] *AC* 407; *AFM* iv. 801.   [14] *AC* 421; *AFM* iv. 819.
[15] Simms, 'The Archbishops of Armagh and the O'Neills', 50; *AC* 373; *Reg. Fleming*, 30–1, 36–7, 68–70, 150–1, 158–60, 189–90, where Cú Ulad appears as Catholicus.
[16] *RCH* 122 no. 29; 'Ancient Deeds', 43; *CPR 1399–1401*, 327, 330. The young Cú Ulad's sobriquet, *Gallda*, attests to his lengthy sojourn among the settlers, or *Gallaibh*. Simms, *From Kings to Warlords*, 108.
[17] *RCH* 196 no. 82; Simms, 'Ulster Revolt of 1404', 155–6. Geoffrey White had been killed by Muirchertach's uncle, Niall Óc O'Neill, in 1392: *AFM* iv. 723, 725.
[18] *RCH* 180 no. 5, 182 no. 72; BL Add MS 4797, f. 124b; BL Add MS 23693, 71; *AFM* iv. 861; Frame, 'Commissions of the Peace', 27; Simms, *From Kings to Warlords*, 94–5; Nicholls, 'Scottish Mercenary Kindreds in Ireland', 103–4.
[19] *AFM* iv. 815.

(Ó Conchobair Failge) family of Offaly had attacked the hinterland of Trim in 1410 and in the following year captured the sheriff of county Meath.[20] An assertive response on the part of the government to such challenges to its authority in the heartland of the colony was guaranteed, and was given added impetus by the declaration in June 1413 that Edmund Mortimer, earl of Ulster, had come of age.[21] On 8 June 1413, John Stanley, who had first been appointed as chief governor of Ireland in 1386, was given the position of Irish lieutenant for six years, landing in the country in September 1413.[22] He died at Ardee on 18 January 1414, but not before he had stirred up considerable trouble in Meath by plundering the lands of the foremost native poet of the region, Niall O'Higgins (Ó hUigin).[23] The aged archbishop of Dublin, Thomas Cranley, was elected by the Irish council as justiciar in Stanley's place, and Edward Perrers, Christopher Holywood, and Janico Dartas were appointed as 'governors of the king's wars'.[24]

Dartas had seen the grant of 1402 by which he was to receive 100m per annum from Drogheda suspended by Stanley during his brief tenure as lieutenant, and by 1415 had concluded that the opportunities for further advancement in Ireland were limited, especially in comparison with those likely to arise in France as a result of Henry V's projected campaign on the continent.[25] He joined the king's first French expedition in April 1415 and remained in France until 1423. He was present at the siege of Rouen between July 1418 and January 1419 where he was joined by a force from Ireland led by Thomas Butler, prior of Kilmainham.[26] The Annals of Connacht report that many men from Ireland (*Erennchaib*) died during the siege, noting in particular how 'a blue fly entered William Darcy's mouth, and afterwards his whole body swelled and he died thereof'.[27] This William, son and heir of John Darcy of Platin (d.1415), was a knight in the service of Thomas Butler's half-brother, James Butler, earl of Ormond, who was also present at Rouen. Janico Dartas also enjoyed the favour of Ormond, and both he and Darcy suffered as a result of the rivalry that had arisen in Ireland between James Butler and John Talbot, Lord Furnival and later earl of Shrewsbury.[28]

John Talbot was appointed lieutenant of Ireland on 24 February 1414, with the intention that he serve for six years.[29] His marriage in 1401 to Maud, only daughter

---

[20] *RCH* 197 no. 14; *AC* 411; 'Henry Marleburrough's Chronicle of Ireland', 218.
[21] Griffiths, 'Mortimer, Edmund (V)'.
[22] *CPR 1413–1416*, 38; *NHI* ix. 475–6.
[23] 'Two Old Drogheda Chronicles', ed. Diarmuid Mac Iomhair, *CLAJ* 15 (1961), 94; *AC* 423; Katharine Simms, 'Bards and Barons: The Anglo-Irish Aristocracy and the Native Culture', in Robert Bartlett and Angus Mackay (eds), *Medieval Frontier Societies* (Oxford, 1989), 183–5. Stanley had celebrated Christmas at Ardee: *RCH* 202 nos. 6, 7; 203 no. 15.
[24] Otway-Ruthven, *History of Medieval Ireland*, 348.
[25] *Select Cases in the Court of King's Bench*, vii. *Richard II, Henry IV and Henry V*, ed. G. O. Sayles. Selden Society (London, 1971), 240–2.
[26] Walker, 'Janico Dartasso', 45–6.
[27] *AC* 443.
[28] *AC* 425; *Rotuli Selecti*, 46; *RCH* 213 no. 137; TNA C 47/10/27, ff. i–iv, transcribed in Griffith, 'Talbot–Ormond Struggle', 394. For Talbot's treatment of Dartas: Walker, 'Janico Dartasso', 47–8.
[29] *RCH* 205 no. 86; Wood, 'Office of Chief Governor', 233.

of Thomas Neville, Baron Furnival (d.1407), gave him interests and family connections in Louth and Meath, since his wife brought with her part of the Verdon inheritance.³⁰ Prior to his appointment in Ireland, Talbot had spent time in the Tower of London as a consequence of a violent feud in which he had engaged with the earl of Arundel in Shropshire, and on his arrival in Ireland at Dalkey in November 1414 this 'harsh, self-seeking and aggressive soldier' quickly went on the offensive against the Irish. His earliest campaigns targeted the borders of Meath and Ulster, where his family interests and those of the earl of March were to be found.³¹ The scale of the task facing him was illustrated by the attack carried out by O'Connor Faly, and MacGeoghegan (Mac Eochucáin) on the English of Meath at Fore in Westmeath six months before his arrival, in which Thomas Mareward, baron of Skreen, was killed and Christopher Fleming, son of the baron of Slane, and John Dardiz (known to the Irish as 'the lawless') were taken captive.³²

In 1415, Talbot first defeated O'More (Ó Morda) in Laois and, having proclaimed royal service (that is, scutage payment) for a force to assemble at Carlingford, overcame O'Hanlon in south Armagh.³³ He then forced both these chiefs to fight alongside him with their forces against his main target, MacMahon, 'a greate Irishe enemie and a powerfull chieftaine of his nation in the partes of Ulvestre adjoyninge unto the county of Louth'.³⁴ Talbot spent much of September and October 1415 at Ardee arranging the purveyance of food and other necessities for his men and horses, before launching a prolonged campaign in Airgialla. His forces 'burnte and destroyed one of [Ardgal MacMahon's] chiefe places, with all his townes and corne aboute, and wounded and killed a greate multitude of his people, until he must of force yealde himself' to the king's peace 'and deliver divers English prisoners without ransome, which he and his people have taken'.³⁵ As part of an indenture into which MacMahon then entered with the lieutenant, he sent his brother, Magnus, with a large force to fight against O'Connor Faly. At this point O'Hanlon reneged on his agreement with Talbot, only for the lieutenant to cut a pass through his heavily wooded territory—an unprecedented feat that encouraged the submission not only of O'Hanlon but also O'Neill and several other of the most important Ulster chiefs.³⁶

---

³⁰ *Dowdall Deeds*, 117. Thomas Neville had married Joan, daughter and sole heir of Willliam, Lord Furnival: Anthony Tuck, 'Neville, John, Fifth Baron Neville (c.1330–1388)', *Oxford Dictionary of National Biography* (Oxford, 2004; online edn, Jan. 2008). Part of the Verdon inheritance that Talbot acquired through marriage was Alton in north Staffordshire, the original chief manor of the Verdon family: Castor, *King, Crown and Duchy of Lancaster*, 239 n. 68.

³¹ A. J. Pollard, 'Talbot, John, First Earl of Shrewsbury and First Earl of Waterford (c.1387–1453)', *Oxford Dictionary of National Biography* (Oxford, 2004; online edn, Oct. 2008); Harriss, *Shaping the Nation*, 514 (quotation).

³² 'Henry Marleburrough's Chronicle of Ireland', 219; *AFM* iv. 817.

³³ A. J. Otway-Ruthven, 'Royal Service in Ireland', in Crooks, *Government, War and Society in Medieval Ireland*, 175.

³⁴ *AC* 425; *Original Letters*, i. 57–8.

³⁵ *RCH* 211 nos. 56, 57, 67; 212 nos. 76, 79; 213 nos. 120, 121, 142; *Original Letters*, i. 57–8. Peter Crooks's remarks on the treatment of non-combatants during English-led campaigns in Ireland are highly relevant: Crooks, 'State of the Union', 32–4.

³⁶ *Original Letters*, i. 57–8.

Talbot's successes proved to be short-lived, as the victories in 1416 of O'Connor Faly over the English of Meath and MacMurrough over the English of Wexford demonstrated. The lieutenant was in England between February and June 1416, but failed to secure the funds he needed to underpin his earlier achievements, and by January 1417 the parliament that met at Dublin was drawing up complaints about the state of the country that included criticisms of the lieutenant and his officials.[37] Talbot sought to bolster his position by having a council that convened in June 1417 send a glowing report to the king about his achievements against the Irish two years before, but letters he dispatched later that year to Henry V's lieutenant in England, his brother the duke of Bedford, revealed that his most fundamental problem remained unchanged: he was desperately short of money.[38]

In June 1417, Talbot had sought to improve his finances by ordering the seizure of the estates of James Butler, earl of Ormond, for debts to the crown accrued by his ancestors.[39] Ormond, who had divided his time between managing his estates in England and fighting in Normandy since June 1416, had previously enjoyed Talbot's favour, but from 1417 the position of the earl and his supporters in Ireland came under increasing pressure from the lieutenant.[40] It was alleged in 1422 that, during Talbot's lieutenancy which ended in 1420, he had 'made areste with oute cause Petyr Dowdal squier of the saide Erlis [Butler] & held hym in prison in the castel of Trym tyl he moste gefe hym of sylver weschel & other goodis to the valu of xl li. & more'.[41] Some confirmation of Dowdall having incurred the lieutenant's displeasure at the same time as Ormond's estates were confiscated is found in a letter patent attested by Talbot at Naas in August 1417 granting Peter a general pardon with the reservation 'that he stand to right in the king's court if any one wish to implead him'.[42]

Peter Dowdall was the son of John Dowdall of Dundalk, who had served as a keeper of the peace for Louth in the mid-1380s and sheriff of the county in 1389–90.[43] His mother, Matilda Gernon, came from another of the most prosperous and long-established settler families in Louth, as did his wife, Joan White.[44] Peter displayed both his wealth and his ambition in 1408 when he entered into an indenture with Janico Dartas by which he received custody of the castles of Greencastle and Carlingford, and the lordship of the Mournes, in return for an annual payment of £18.[45] His local position was strengthened further in 1416 when Matthew Fleming of Dundalk granted to him the entirety of his substantial holdings in

---

[37] *AC* 431; Otway-Ruthven, *History of Medieval Ireland*, 351.
[38] Otway-Ruthven, *History of Medieval Ireland*, 351–3.
[39] C. A. Empey and Katharine Simms, 'The Ordinances of the White Earl and the Problem of Coign in the Later Middle Ages', *PRIA* 75 (1975), C, 164; Peter Crooks, 'Factions, Feuds and Noble Power in the Lordship of Ireland, *c*.1356–1496', *IHS* 35 (2007), 447.
[40] Crooks, 'Factionalism and Noble Power in English Ireland', 323–32.
[41] Griffith, 'Talbot–Ormond Struggle', 395.
[42] *Dowdall Deeds*, 162.
[43] *Dowdall Deeds*, xv, 127; Frame 'Commissions of the Peace in Ireland', 21.
[44] *Dowdall Deeds*, 154, 164–5, 183.
[45] *Dowdall Deeds*, 142–3, 152–3.

Louth.⁴⁶ The Dowdalls and the Flemings of Slane had been linked by marriage since the early fourteenth century, and in 1393 Thomas Fleming, son and heir of the baron of Slane, had granted to John Dowdall of Dundalk, Peter's father, an annual pension of 20s for life 'for his laudable service rendered and to be rendered in future to the said Thomas and his heirs'.⁴⁷ There is evidence that John Talbot also viewed Thomas Fleming—who was related to James Butler by marriage—unfavourably: in 1421, Talbot's appointee as under-treasurer of the Irish exchequer, William Tynbegh, ordered that a false entry be made in the White Book of the Exchequer altering the terms under which the barony of Slane was held. The consequence of this fraud was to render Fleming liable for substantial scutage payments when royal service was proclaimed.⁴⁸

His connections with Thomas Fleming and Janico Dartas brought Peter Dowdall—whose family connections, impressive as they were, were confined to Meath and Louth—to the attention of James Butler, fourth earl of Ormond. The role of king's butler in Ireland gave successive heads of the Butler family an interest in the trading fortunes—and in particular the wine imports—of Drogheda, Dundalk, and Carlingford. James Butler, third earl of Ormond (*c*.1360–1405), was a frequent visitor to Louth between 1392 and his death in 1405 in his capacity as chief governor of Ireland. In 1401, he requested an exemplification of deeds from the early thirteenth century by which his ancestors had acquired grants of land in south Armagh from the Verdons, to whom they were related.⁴⁹ Butler presided over at least one legal case involving Peter Dowdall's father, John, while acting as chief governor, and granted his brother, Thomas Butler, the wardship of Elizabeth Netterville, heiress to the Netterville and Napton lands in Louth and Meath, in 1393 only to see this trumped in the following year when Richard II awarded custody instead to his esquire, John Humbleton.⁵⁰

James Butler, fourth earl of Ormond (d.1452), who succeeded to his father's estates and title in 1405, imitated the third earl in seeking to exert influence in Louth. Nor was he the only member of his family to do so.⁵¹ His half-brother, Thomas Butler, prior of the Hospital of St John of Jerusalem at Kilmainham, outside Dublin, was appointed as his deputy by the lieutenant, Thomas of Lancaster, before his final departure for England in March 1409, and held this post until the

---

⁴⁶ *Dowdall Deeds*, 160–1, 163–4. At the time of his death in Oct. 1416 Fleming was an outlaw on account of 'various felonies and treasons': NAI RC 8/36, 29–30.

⁴⁷ *Dowdall Deeds*, 132; Clare, *On the Edge of the Pale*, 37.

⁴⁸ Malcolm Mercer, 'Exchequer Malpractice in Late Medieval Ireland: A Petition from Christopher Fleming, Lord Slane, 1438', *IHS* 36 (2009), 407–17. Dr Mercer's assertion that the arrests of Kildare and Preston in 1418 occurred at Slane (411) is incorrect. This took place at Clane, co. Kildare. Thomas Fleming's wife was Katherine Butler: *RCH* 257 no. 56.

⁴⁹ NLI D 971; *RCH* 63 no. 137; COA Rep. Records of the Exchequer, 42–51 Edward III, 46. The third earl's mother, Elizabeth, who died in 1390, was the daughter of John Darcy, who had been endowed in Louth earlier in the century: Empey, 'Butler, James, Third Earl of Ormond'.

⁵⁰ *Dowdall Deeds*, 131; *PKCI* 175–220, 234–6; *CPR 1391–6*, 286; Curtis, *Richard II in Ireland*, 129–31, 210–11; *Misc. Ir. Annals*, 157; 'Lord Chancellor Gerrard's Notes on his Report on Ireland', 207–8. *PKCI* 210–11, 214–16; *CPR 1391–1396*, 427.

⁵¹ Elizabeth Matthew, 'Butler, James, Fourth Earl of Ormond (1390–1452)', *Oxford Dictionary of National Biography* (Oxford, 2004; online edn, Jan. 2008).

arrival in Ireland of John Stanley as lieutenant in June 1413.[52] In May 1411, Thomas interceded with the king on behalf of John Clinton of Drumcashel (bar. Ardee), securing for him exemption for life from serving on juries or being appointed to local office in Louth, and in February 1412 he held a council at Drogheda that granted him a subsidy as a reward for his efforts as deputy.[53]

The displeasure evinced by John Talbot, Lord Furnival, towards Peter Dowdall may have arisen in part from a sense that he, rather than James Butler, was entitled to the loyalty of a member of a family that in previous generations had served the interests of the Furnivals in Louth. The Furnival arms had adorned the seal of the town of Dundalk since the middle of the fourteenth century, and William, Lord Furnival, the grandfather of Talbot's wife, had in the 1360s employed as one of his two attorneys in Ireland, John Dowdall of Dundalk, Peter Dowdall's grandfather.[54] William's other attorney on this occasion had been John Bellew, and in 1418 this man's son or grandson, John Bellew, also felt John Talbot's wrath. In June of that year, according to the chronicle of Henry Marlborough, Bellew was arrested by Talbot's brother and deputy, Thomas Talbot, along with the earl of Kildare and Sir Christopher Preston, and imprisoned at Trim.[55] The arrests were prompted by rumours of a plot involving Kildare, Preston, and Thomas Butler, prior of Kilmainham, to seize the deputy and kill his soldiers, and unearthed among Preston's possessions a copy of the constitutional tract *Modus Tenendi Parliamentum*, as well as a copy of the coronation oath.[56]

Although Bellew is not mentioned in the account of the incident provided to the crown by John Talbot in the following year, his involvement would appear to be confirmed by his inclusion, alongside Kildare and Preston, in a list sent to the lieutenant in November 1418 of those then imprisoned at Trim who were to be sent by him to appear at Westminster in the following January.[57] Bellew was lord of Bellewstown in Meath and, through acquisition by his family over time of parts of the Verdon inheritance, also lord of half of Dundalk (including Roche).[58] As we have seen, John Talbot also had Dundalk connections and, given his history of pursuing his family interests elsewhere in Ireland and in England with extreme vigour, it is possible to view his intimidation of Peter Dowdall and John Bellew in

---

[52] *NHI* ix. 476; Otway-Ruthven, *History of Medieval Ireland*, 346–7.

[53] BL Add MS 4790, f. 1; *pro suis immensis laboribus et expensis*: *Reg. Fleming*, 204. In his capacity as prior of Kilmainham, Thomas also made appointments to benefices in Louth, centred on Kilsaran (bar. Ardee) that had come to the Hospitallers following the suppression of the Templars in 1307–8: *Reg. Fleming*, 161–2, 256: Gwynn and Hadcock, *Medieval Religious Houses Ireland*, 327–43.

[54] Raghnall Ó Floinn, 'Two Medieval Seals from County Louth', *CLAJ* 22 (1992), 387–94; *Dowdall Deeds*, 92, 94, 95; *CPR 1364–7*, 218.

[55] 'Henry Marleburrough's Chronicle of Ireland', 220–1.

[56] For recent, significant, contributions to our understanding of the incident, containing references to other relevant scholarship, see Peter Crooks, 'The Background to the Arrest of the Fifth Earl of Kildare and Sir Christopher Preston in 1418: A Missing Membrane', *Anal. Hib.* 40 (2007), and Crooks, 'Representation and Dissent', 10–14, 27–32.

[57] *CCR 1413–9*, 472. Professor Otway-Ruthven did not believe that Bellew had been arrested: *History of Medieval Ireland*, 354 n. 30; A. J. Otway-Ruthven, 'The Background to the Arrest of Sir Christopher Preston in 1418', *Anal. Hib.* 29 (1980), 73 and n. 2.

[58] *Reg. Fleming*, 212; *Dowdall Deeds*, 96.

Louth in 1417–18 as a subplot in the larger story of his campaign against the earl of Ormond and his supporters for control of the Irish administration.[59] In this regard, it is worth remembering that Bellew and Christopher Preston were among those knighted in 1397 by Roger Mortimer, earl of March, at the end of a successful campaign against O'Byrne that the earl had led in conjunction with James Butler, earl of Ormond (d.1405).[60]

How can John Talbot's actions against some of the most important local settlers in Meath and Louth—William Darcy, Christopher Preston, Janico Dartas, Peter Dowdall, John Bellew, and Thomas Fleming—be reconciled with the enthusiastic support for his actions as lieutenant offered at the Irish parliament in June 1417 by, among others, members of the families of Clinton, Plunket, Taaf, and White?[61] Two crucial features of settler life are revealed by this apparent paradox: first, there were divisions in local societies such as that of Louth that could be exploited by both parties in the Talbot–Butler dispute and, second, attacks on the Irish—for which Talbot received such praise—could be used by each side to curry favour with the settlers. With regard to the first of these considerations, it was surely no coincidence that Talbot's lieutenancy witnessed the return to a position of prominence in Louth of his cousin, Bartholomew Verdon. For seven years after receiving a final pardon in May 1408

> for the death of John Doudall, sometime sheriff of the county of Louth in Ireland, killed in ambush aforethought, and for all treasons, felonies aforethought and others, murders, conspiracies, confederacies, trespasses, arsons, adherences to the king's Irish enemies, robberies, homicides, larcenies, insurrections, rebellions and champerties committed by him

Verdon disappears from the surviving records.[62] Then in March 1415, as Talbot prepared for his campaign against the Irish of Ulster, Verdon was appointed as one of four keepers of the peace in Louth—a post he had last held in 1400—with orders 'to assess and array all men of that county [and]...lead them to marcher areas of that county, where the greatest necessity demands it, against the enemies and rebels of the said marches, and to cause, distrain and compel them to stay there upon their defence until those enemies [etc.] restore themselves to the peace'.[63]

Further signs of favour for Verdon followed: in February 1416, following a visit to England, he received a letter patent absolving him from debts of over £700 accrued by the late Sir Thomas Verdon, and in July 1417 Talbot employed him as one of the messengers to transmit to Westminster the enthusiastic account of his lieutenancy elicited from the Irish parliament in June of that year.[64] Nor was Bartholomew the only member of the Verdon family to benefit from Talbot's first

---

[59] Smith, 'Late Medieval Ireland and the English Connection', 561–2; Anthony J. Pollard, *John Talbot and the War in France, 1427–1453* (London, 1983), 8–11.
[60] 'Henry Marleburrough's Chronicle of Ireland', 214.
[61] *Original Letters*, 62.
[62] *CPR 1405–8*, 435.
[63] *RCH* 209 no. 192; Frame, 'Commissions of the Peace', 21–2.
[64] *Rotuli Selecti*, 47; *RCH* 212 nos. 84 and 87; BL Cotton Titus B XI, no. 30.

period in office: in June 1417, his cousin Christopher, son of James Verdon, was pardoned over £600 of Thomas Verdon's debts.[65] The treatment of the Verdons at the hands of John Talbot clearly differed from that experienced by many of their contemporaries in Louth and ensured that James Butler could not take for granted the united support of local society in this part of Ireland in his conflict with the lieutenant.

Butler's successful response to this challenge was demonstrated by the manner in which he secured local support in Louth for the military operations he organized upon being appointed lieutenant of Ireland for the first time in the spring of 1420. His first campaigns were financed by subsidies agreed in parliaments that met in June and December, and another parliamentary subsidy was granted to him in October 1421.[66] Although these subsidies were granted by assemblies that included settler representatives from across Ireland, the actual returns they yielded revealed that only in the east and south of the country could the administration now expect to find communities 'fully responsive to its financial demands'.[67] Records of the process by which the subsidies were collected in Louth and Meath suggest that Ormond strove successfully to gain the cooperation of those in these counties to whom John Talbot had shown favour during his lieutenancy. The six assessors chosen to determine the level of subsidy to be paid by the community of Louth in June 1420, for instance, included Bartholomew Verdon and the three other keepers of the peace who had served to such good effect under John Talbot in 1415.[68] Further evidence of Ormond's determination as lieutenant to ease divisions within local society in Louth is found in the lists of names of those chosen to act as keepers of the peace in the county during his period in office, between April 1420 and April 1422. Keepers—with the title 'justices and keepers'—were appointed on four occasions in these two years, and included not only individuals known to be sympathetic to Butler, such as John Swayne, archbishop of Armagh, and John Bellew, but also Bartholomew Verdon and his three companions from 1415, John Clinton of Cappoge, Roger Gernon of Gernonstown, and Nicholas Taaf.[69] The appointment of Verdon, Gernon, and Taaf as justices and keepers of the peace in April 1421 was stated to be at the petition of the commons of county Louth,

---

[65] *Rotuli Selecti*, 50–1; COA Rep. Records of the Exchequer, Henry IV, 473–4.

[66] *Parls. & Councils*, 134–5, 143–4, 151–3, 171–2, 174–5, 177–8; Richardson and Sayles, *Irish Parliament*, 179–80.

[67] Matthew, 'Henry V and the Proposal for an Irish Crusade', 162. The geographical scope of representation at these parliaments is emphasized in Robin Frame, 'Exporting State and Nation: Being English in Medieval Ireland', in Len Scales and Oliver Zimmer (eds), *Power and the Nation in European History* (Cambridge, 2005), 147–8, and Frame, 'English Political Culture in Later Medieval Ireland', 6.

[68] *Parls. & Councils*, 134–5. A facsimile of the indenture for the 1421 subsidy in Meath is at *Facs. Nat. MSS Ire.*, iii, nos. xxxiv and xxxv.

[69] Frame, 'Commissions of the Peace', 22–3. Swayne and Preston were chosen by the Irish parliament in Apr. 1421 to carry letters of complaint about Talbot's conduct as lieutenant to England: Matthew, 'Henry V and the Proposal for an Irish Crusade', 167–9; Lynch, *View of the Legal Institutions*, 334–5.

which suggests that in showing them favour Ormond was working with the grain of local society.⁷⁰

Turning to the second feature of settler life exposed by the disputes between James Butler and John Talbot, the former realized that the surest way to gain the support in Louth of those favoured by the latter was to unite them with his own adherents in successful attacks upon the Irish. In 1418—the year of the imprisonment of Christopher Preston and John Bellew at Trim—Talbot had proclaimed a royal service for a force to assemble at Louth to prosecute a campaign against Magennis. A repeat of his successes against the Irish of 1415 initially looked likely, but Magennis and his allies, the Clandeboy O'Neills, rallied against Talbot's forces to such effect that at the end of the engagement it proved 'hard to estimate the number of Galls killed and captured there'.⁷¹ Talbot departed Ireland in 1420, 'carrying along with him the curses of many', and was succeeded as lieutenant by James Butler, earl of Ormond.⁷² Butler imitated his predecessor by immediately embarking upon a sustained campaign against the Irish. As had been the case with Talbot in 1415, he first turned his attention to the midlands before proceeding to Ulster, from whose settlers he had received a letter complaining bitterly about the depredations of Aed Magennis, whom Talbot had failed to subdue in 1418.⁷³ In the course of three months, the lieutenant overpowered O'Reilly, MacMahon, and Magennis, and gave the hostages of the latter to Domnall O'Neill, who had been residing among the Ulster settlers following defeat the previous year at the hands of Eógan O'Neill.⁷⁴

James Butler's attempts to exploit the ongoing divisions within the O'Neill dynasty at this time met with mixed success. Eógan quickly succeeded in banishing Domnall again, this time to Sligo, but in 1421 was himself taken hostage by the Clandeboy O'Neills while on his way to Dundalk to treat with the earl of Ormond.⁷⁵ This planned meeting with O'Neill explains in part why Ormond spent time in Drogheda in July, August, and September 1421, although the increasing danger posed by the MacMahons on Louth's western borders might also explain his presence there.⁷⁶ In May of that year, possibly upon learning of the death of John Bellew, lord of Roche, Brian MacMahon, who had submitted to Butler the previous year, 'did much hurt in Urgile by wasting and burning all before him'. In response to this attack, Ormond proclaimed a royal service at Louth on 14 July 1421.⁷⁷ This was the third time in six years that royal service had

---

⁷⁰ *RCH* 221 no. 112.
⁷¹ 'Lord Chancellor Gerrard's Notes on his Report on Ireland', 266; *AC* 439. The settler contingent from Meath in particular suffered losses: *AU* iii. 75.
⁷² A. J. Otway-Ruthven, 'The Chief Governors of Medieval Ireland', in Crooks, *Government, War and Society in Medieval Ireland*, 87.
⁷³ Otway-Ruthven, *History of Medieval Ireland*, 351 and 360, where the Ulster campaign is misdated to 1421; Simms, 'Ulster Revolt of 1404', 141, 155.
⁷⁴ Butler (ed.), *Annals of Ireland by Friar John Clyn and Thady Dowling*, 28; 'Henry Marleburrough's Chronicle of Ireland', 221; *AFM* iv. 845, 847; *AC* 441.
⁷⁵ *AFM* iv. 851.
⁷⁶ *RCH* 219 no. 49; 218 nos. 21, 23; 219 nos. 49, 70; 220 nos. 81, 96; *Parls. & Councils*, 183–6.
⁷⁷ 'Henry Marleburrough's Chronicle of Ireland', 222; TNA E 101/257/15; *RCH* 220 nos. 96 and 97.

been proclaimed in Louth: in the previous 100 years it had been proclaimed in the county only twice.[78]

A description of Butler's campaign on this occasion is provided in the *Gouvernance of Prynces* composed for the earl at this time by the Dublin notary, James Yonge.[79] From Dundalk the earl rode to the country of Magennis and then through the lands of the O'Hanrattys (Ó hInnrechtaig) of east Monaghan before attacking the heart of Brian MacMahon's lordship.[80] In language possibly modelled on the account of Talbot's attack on the same family some years previously, Yonge describes how Butler spent three nights in Airgialla, destroying MacMahon's 'stronge newe castell, his townes, his fayre toures, and his stronge plaases', and slaying many of his people. The lieutenant then moved south-east through Farney, the lordship of Brian's brother, Magnus MacMahon, as far as Ardee before turning back and burning Magnus's corn. From there Butler led his force into the lands of Clandeboy O'Neill before returning to Drogheda where he received the submission of MacMahon.[81]

Destructive of life, property, and foodstuffs Ormond's campaign may have been, but it appears to have impressed James Yonge more than it did the Irish against whom it had been directed. The Irish council found it necessary in March 1422 to sanction the collection of a subsidy to raise an army against O'Reilly, who had attacked Kells, and at the beginning of April it was reported that following the recent burning of the town of Louth by MacMahon 'the inhabitants fled for terror of them and…dare not return to re-inhabit the same town'.[82] Ormond left office the same month, having come no closer to either defeating or pacifying the Irish on the borders of Louth and Meath than had John Talbot. In October 1422 Talbot's brother, Richard, archbishop of Dublin, was appointed Irish justiciar, but the government had already lost the initiative in Louth and Meath, and was reduced to shoring up local defences against Irish attacks of increasing frequency and severity.[83] Trim was attacked by O'Connor Faly before the end of the year, and from January to July 1423 Eógan O'Reilly, who had assumed control of the family in 1418 and was to remain at its head for thirty years, campaigned throughout Meath.[84] A praise-poem commissioned by Eógan indicates the challenges awaiting

---

[78] The services of Carlingford, 1388–9 and 1392: Otway-Ruthven, 'Royal Service in Ireland', 173–6. Matthew, 'Financing of the Lordship of Ireland', 100.

[79] T. P. Dolan, 'Yonge, James (fl. 1405–1434)', *Oxford Dictionary of National Biography* (Oxford, 2004).

[80] The O'Hanratty lands, centred on Castleblaney, are identified at *AFM* iv. 862, note w.

[81] *Three Prose Versions of the Secreta Secretorum*, ed. Robert Steele. English Text Society (London, 1898), 203–4. Butler was in Drogheda, at the conclusion of the campaign, on 18 Dec. 1421: *RCH* 221 no. 118. The MacMahons were said to have been 'lately openly at war' in Oct. of that year: *RCH* 252 no. 31.

[82] TCD MS 3411, ff. 73v–74r, Irish Close Roll, 9 Henry V; *RCH* 180 no. 13; *AC* 465; Butler (ed.), *Annals of Ireland by Friar John Clyn and Thady Dowling*, 29.

[83] Elizabeth Matthew, 'Talbot, Richard (d.1449)', *Oxford Dictionary of National Biography* (Oxford, 2004).

[84] *RCH* 224 no. 9, 225 no. 29, 229 no. 96; *AC* 463.

any government attempting to negotiate with him during those periods when he could not be contained militarily:

> What matters it to the son of Seaán [i.e Eógan son of John] that there is a foreign charter to Inis Fail [Ireland]?... If, O Eoghan, a Gall [settler] produce a sealed charter from the Saxons [English of England] I think that thou shalt not surrender Leath Cuinn [the northern half of Ireland] at the command of the letter from London/ Thou shalt seek no other charter except thy own reliance on thy gallantry; to charge against the sharp spears that pierce thee is thy true charter to thy land.[85]

The government did succeed in detaching a branch of the O'Reilly family from its allegiance to Eógan, but in August 1423 resorted to granting permission to the abbot of the Augustinian house of St Mary's, Kells, to negotiate on its behalf with the Irish to bring them to peace. The abbot was himself an O'Reilly, and had first to be pardoned for treason and awarded the legal status of an Englishman before he would accept the role of peacemaker.[86]

An even greater threat to the settlers in 1423 was presented by the Irish of Ulster, among whom supremacy had been wrested from the faction-ridden O'Neills by Niall Garb O'Donnell of Tír Conaill (Donegal). In the previous year Niall had demonstrated his dominance in the north of Ireland by leading a force that included the rivals Eógan and Domnall O'Neill, as well as Maguire, MacMahon, and even the settlers of Ulster, on a major campaign in Connacht. Now he turned his attention to Louth.[87] At Ardee in July 1423 'the commons of Louth... gladly granted to the justiciar [Richard Talbot], for his expenses upon the defence of that county, £40', but to little avail.[88] Accompanied again by both O'Neills and by Brian Mac-Mahon, O'Donnell attacked Dundalk and the town of Louth and, after exacting tribute from their inhabitants and 'ruining a large part of Louth', entered Meath and defeated the justiciar.[89] In response to this crisis, the English council, ruling in the name of the infant Henry VI, turned once more for assistance to the Mortimer family, represented now by Edmund Mortimer, earl of March and Ulster, who had come of age in 1413. Edmund had appointed James White, one of the murderers of John Dowdall, sheriff of Louth, as seneschal of his Ulster earldom upon attaining his majority, but apart from seeking repayment of debts owed from Drogheda, had displayed little interest in his Irish lands, leaving the running of the liberty of Trim to his seneschal there, Thomas Talbot, who was both his kinsman and the

---

[85] *Aithdioghluim Dána*, ii. 71, 72, 73. I am grateful to Katharine Simms for pointing out to me that the editor of this poem omitted the words 'son of' before 'Seaán' in the first line quoted above.

[86] *RCH* 227 no. 49.

[87] Simms, 'The Archbishops of Armagh and the O'Neills', 50–1; *AU* 93; *AFM* iv. 855, 857. Eógan O'Neill had been freed from Clandeboy captivity earlier in the year by his wife and family: *AU* 91. Already, in Mar. 1423 the Dominican church at Carlingford was described as being 'disfigured by age and the incursions of enemies and robbers': *CPL 1417–31*, 261.

[88] *RCH* 230 no. 120.

[89] *AFM* iv. 859; *AU* iii. 95; *AC* 465 (quote). The Annals of Connacht misdate the attack to 1422. According to government sources the Irish had fled the battlefield 'for fear' when confronted in Louth by a force led by the mayor, bailiffs, and commons of Dublin: *RCH* 233 no. 20.

brother of John and Richard Talbot.[90] Following deliberations in the spring of 1423, on 9 May the English council appointed Edmund lieutenant of Ireland for nine years from the day of his landing in Ireland.[91] Mortimer, however, delayed his arrival until September 1424, appointing as his deputy in the mean time Edward Dantsey, bishop of Meath.[92]

Dantsey presented his letters of appointment at a meeting of the Irish council held in the Franciscan house at Drogheda on 24 September 1423, but the chancellor, Archbishop Richard Talbot, who had continued to act as Irish justiciar even after Mortimer's appointment as lieutenant in May, challenged his warrant of appointment and ordered the king's messenger, Sir Thomas Stynt, who questioned his actions, to depart for 'the marches to resist the malice of the Irish, enemies of the king'.[93] Dantsey did succeed in having his position as chief governor recognized, but the incident contributed to the belief in England that Mortimer was not treating the situation in Ireland with the urgency it deserved. Before the end of 1423, two members of the Irish council appeared before its English equivalent with letters explaining that the Irish, in alliance with the Scots and other enemies of the king, intended 'to lay waste and entirely destroy the land and people of Ireland'. In particular, it was said, 'the county of Uriel will be ransomed (*appaticiez*) to the rebels forever at eight hundred marks if it has not been recovered by 1 May next'. The council responded in January 1424 by reminding Mortimer of his responsibilities, but despite beginning preparations for his departure to Ireland the next month, it was to be September 1424 before the earl of March and Ulster arrived in the country.[94]

In May 1424, Dantsey was replaced as Mortimer's deputy by James Butler, earl of Ormond, who returned from England—where his bitter dispute with John Talbot before the king's council had been temporarily settled in November—with 'many Saxons...in consequence whereof the English (*Gallaibh*) of Ireland acquired great strength'.[95] Two years after his departure from office in the midst of Irish incursions into Meath and Louth which he failed to halt, Ormond now returned determined to take the offensive against the Ulster chiefs. In June 1424 he awarded the mayor and citizens of Dublin £40 in anticipation of their support in a campaign designed 'to curb the malice of McMaghone, McGenous, Neell Garrowe Odonyll and other enemies of the parts of Ulster' and by 8 July was at Navan, where he was joined by a force raised by the settlers in Meath.[96] Together they first attacked east Monaghan and Armagh before moving east to defeat and banish Magennis and destroy his castle. The efforts of Niall O'Donnell and Eógan and Domnall O'Neill to oppose them were undermined by the desertion to Butler's

---

[90] COA Rep. Records of the Exchequer, 1 Henry V–39 Henry VI, 484; *Reg. Fleming*, 266; Simms, 'Ulster Revolt of 1404', 152; NAI RC 8/37, 148–53.
[91] Otway-Ruthven, *History of Medieval Ireland*, 363–4.
[92] Wood, 'Office of Chief Governor', 234.
[93] The relevant documents are published in Richardson and Sayles, *Irish Parliament*, 311–17.
[94] *Handbook and Select Calendar...Ireland*, 190 (TNA E 28/43/52); *RCH* 234 no. 42.
[95] *AFM* iv. 861.
[96] *RCH* 233 nos. 12, 15, and 17.

side of the chief of the Clandeboy O'Neills, O'Hanlon, and Magnus MacMahon, brother of Brian.[97]

Ormond had prepared the ground well for the arrival of Mortimer who reached Ireland with John Talbot at the end of September 1424. Butler's victory over the Irish of Ulster made the latter amenable to the idea of entering into peace agreements with Mortimer, and with the probable encouragement of John Swayne, archbishop of Armagh, Domnall and Eógan O'Neill, Nechtain, the brother of Niall Garb O'Donnell, Brian, the head of the Clandeboy O'Neills, MacQuillin, and the head of the MacDonald galloglass, travelled to Trim to meet the newly arrived lieutenant.[98] The submissions of the Irish had been taken, but no formal indentures drawn up by the time Mortimer died of plague at Trim on 18 or 19 January 1425. His grandfather and father had both died in Ireland, and with Edmund's demise the male line of the Mortimer family ceased, its titles and estates passing to Edmund's nephew Richard, duke of York, who was 13 years old at the time.[99]

On Edmund Mortimer's death, John Talbot was chosen as justiciar by the Irish council. The Irish leaders present at Trim were seized, with some being released almost immediately and others taken as prisoners to Dublin by Talbot.[100] On 25 March 1425, at Trim, Talbot entered into an indenture with O'Connor Faly, whom he had first attacked ten years before. By the terms of the agreement O'Connor Faly promised to release English hostages captured in war, surrender 'all English lands and the tribute called "black rent"', and cease collection of the annuity of £40 he had imposed upon the English of Meath.[101] By this time, the English council had appointed James Butler, earl of Ormond, as lieutenant for one year, and upon taking up office on 28 April 1425 the new governor—as he had done in the past—showed himself willing to follow the policies of his predecessor and rival with regard to the Irish.[102] Within two weeks of assuming office, on 12 May, Ormond had entered into a detailed indenture with Brian MacMahon and his brothers Rudraige and Magnus.[103] The willingness of the MacMahons to come to terms may have been increased by a grant made at Trim on 7 February 1425 by which John Talbot had awarded the lordships of Donaghmoyne and Farney, held of the crown by the MacMahons since the early 1400s, to John St Leger, a member of an important Ardee family.[104]

---

[97] *AFM* iv. 861 863.
[98] Simms, 'The Archbishops of Armagh and the O'Neills', 51; *AFM* iv. 865; *AU* iii. 97, 99.
[99] Otway-Ruthven, *History of Medieval Ireland*, 363–4.
[100] *RCH* 239 no. 2; Wood, 'Chief Governors of Ireland', 234.
[101] *RCH* 238 no. 112.
[102] *NHI* ix. 476.
[103] A translation of the indenture and facsimile of the original (TNA E 30/1558) are published in *Handbook and Select Calendar... Ireland*, 216–22.
[104] TNA E 101/248/11. No place of issue is included, but other documents show that the justiciar was at Trim on 7 Feb.: *RCH* 165 no. 232, 235 no. 20. For John and William St Leger: *CPR 1413–6*, 253; *Inquisitions and Extents*, 207–8; *Reg. Octaviani*, ii. 59–61. John St Leger of Ardee was keeper of the rolls in 1430–1: *IEP* 567.

By the terms of the agreement, which was drawn up in the hospital of St John the Baptist, Ardee, the MacMahons were to vacate English lands (*terras Anglicanas*) occupied by them, and to render anew all services, including the bonnacht, which their ancestors had owed to the crown or the earls of Ulster. They were to release more than eighty hostages captured in a recent attack on the town of Nobber without payment of ransom, and to reveal to the lieutenant any plans of which they became aware for attacks on the settlers by 'the king's Irish enemies or any rebel Englishmen'. Three arbitrators from each side were appointed to settle future disputes within a fortnight of their occurrence, and the MacMahons undertook to pay a year's rent for Farney immediately, and continue to pay rent on a regular basis thereafter. The brothers and their men, properly equipped for war and at their own expense, were to serve with the lieutenant against Irish enemies and English rebels in Ulster and Breifne, while Brian MacMahon was to have his overlordship of Thomas Maguire and O'Hanlon recognized. When seeking out food and victuals, the men of the MacMahons were to be allowed to enter and exit the towns of Louth, Dundalk, and Ardee by the public highway only, though Irishmen engaged in trade might freely come and go. The MacMahons swore on the Gospels to observe these terms and seals were then affixed to the indenture by Brian MacMahon and the lieutenant. The document was witnessed by the priors of St Mary, Louth, and St John the Baptist, Ardee, and by many local settlers, of whom the most prominent fifteen were named. These included the sheriff, Sir James White, Sir John Bellew, Sir John Dowdall, Sir Bartholomew Verdon, and Sir Nicholas Taaf.[105]

Ormond spent June in Dublin, but was at Kells in the middle of the following month. On 23 July, at Dundalk, he entered into an indenture with Eógan O'Neill, whom he continued to favour over his rival, Domnall, for the leadership of the O'Neills.[106] In similar fashion to the terms agreed to by the MacMahons, Eógan undertook to cease enforcing 'black rent' and to render the bonnacht to the earl of Ulster or his representative. He also agreed not to prosecute any claims for damages against John Swayne, archbishop of Armagh, and to allow ecclesiastical visitations of his territories. Having handed over one of his sons as pledge for his observation of this treaty, O'Neill swore to uphold it in the presence of the archbishop and the bishop of Down, the prior of Louth, and the prior of St Leonard, Dundalk.[107] The agreement was witnessed by many unnamed laymen and by James White, who had ceased to be sheriff of Louth and had resumed his previous position as seneschal of Ulster; by his successor as sheriff, Sir John Bellew junior; and by Sir Bartholomew Verdon and Sir Nicholas Taaf.[108]

---

[105] *Handbook and Select Calendar...Ireland*, 216–22.

[106] *RCH* 237 no. 92, 238 no. 102. Katharine Simms, '"The King's Friend": O'Neill, the Crown and the Earldom of Ulster', in Lydon, *England and Ireland in the Later Middle Ages*, 219–20.

[107] The hostages Butler had in his custody at Trim in July 1426 included members of the O'Neill, O'Donnell, and MacMahon families: *RCH* 254 no. 14.

[108] *Handbook and Select Calendar...Ireland*, 222–3 (TNA E 30/1573); *Rec. Comm. Ire. Rep., 1811–15*, 54–6. For Bellew's appointment as sheriff in June 1425: *RCH* 236 no. 55.

For all the solemnity of the proceedings at Dundalk, it is possible that Eógan O'Neill regarded the treaty with the English of 1425 as less significant than the agreement he reached in the following year with his cousin, Domnall, which temporarily ended the conflict between the two men. Immediately thereafter, the annals inform us 'they proceeded to recover by force all the lands which had been alienated during their contentions'.[109] Certainly the indentures crafted by Talbot and Ormond failed to provide long-term security for the settlers in Meath and Louth: before the end of 1425 yet another inhabitant of Nobber had been kidnapped by the Irish and was being held to ransom, and in the following year Ormond found it necessary to enter the territory of the O'Reillys with an army and demolish the castle of Cavan.[110]

As the witness lists to the indentures of 1425 with the MacMahons and O'Neill suggest, in dealing with the deteriorating security situation that they faced in the 1420s, the settlers of Louth and Meath could look for leadership to local men who had accumulated decades of experience in frontier affairs. Nicholas Taaf, for instance, had first been appointed as serjeant of Meath in 1400 and served as sheriff of Louth and keeper of the peace there on several occasions in the 1410s, 1420s, and 1430s.[111] Bartholomew Verdon's appointment as keeper of the peace for Louth in April 1427 is the last reference in our sources to a career that spanned almost forty years, and that combined frequent visits to England with regular service on the marches of Louth.[112] James White had first been appointed a keeper of the peace in Louth in 1400, and in the 1430s was acting as seneschal of Ulster on behalf of Richard, duke of York.[113] Verdon and White, of course, had been convicted of the murder of the sheriff of Louth, John Dowdall, in 1402, and it is significant that another of the witnesses to the MacMahon indenture of May 1425 was the son of their victim, also called John Dowdall, who was later to serve as sheriff of Louth and seneschal of Ulster.[114] Twenty years after the slaying of the sheriff, and in the midst of a period of competition between Ormond and Talbot that according to John Swayne, archbishop of Armagh, had caused such divisions among 'jentyllmen and communes' that 'all this lond is severed', the political elite in Louth had put aside internal differences to defend its position against the Irish.[115]

In their travails, the settlers could expect little direct assistance from England, though the return to Ireland from service in France in 1423 of Janico Dartas, who

---

[109] *AFM* iv. 869.

[110] *Reg. Swayne*, 42; *AFM* iv. 873.

[111] *CPR 1399–1401*, 219–20; *Rotuli Selecti*, 59; TNA E 101/247/15; *IEP* 574, 578; *RCH* 201 no. 123, 209 no. 192, 221 no. 112. It is not impossible that this was the same Nicholas Taaf who witnessed an indenture between John Talbot and Henry O'Neill in 1446: *Handbook and Select Calendar...Ireland*, 226.

[112] *RCH* 120 no. 53, 239 no. 116, 242 no. 35.

[113] *RCH* 155 no. 11; *Reg. Octaviani*, ii. 101–2. It is probable that the Sir James White excommunicated in 1449 by Archbishop John Mey of Armagh for illegally occupying the palace of the bishop of Down is a different individual: *Reg. Mey*, 169, 170–4.

[114] *Dowdall Deeds*, xvi.

[115] *Reg. Swayne*, 111.

before his death three years later acted as keeper of the peace in Louth, seneschal of Ulster, and guardian of Carlingford and Greencastle, was a reminder that this part of Ireland remained of interest to men of ambition from beyond its shores.[116] In looking to their own resources, the settlers had recourse to strategies that had in the past helped improve relations with the Irish. In June 1426, Archbishop Swayne urged the pope to issue a dispensation to allow the marriage of Rudraige Mac-Mahon and Alice White to proceed, 'because therefrom probably peace will be strengthened between the English and the Irish'. The reason for invoking the pope's authority in the first place is instructive: 'the noble and puissant' Rudraige and Alice were closely related in several degrees, and together had already 'begotten many sons' who would be legitimized should their parents be allowed to wed.[117] Two contemporary poems extolling the merits of Rudraige's residence note that it had been built by 'craftsmen from every land', which suggests that Alice's fellow-settlers were involved in the construction of this family home, and speaks to a degree of routine cooperation across the frontier which has left little trace in our surviving written sources.[118]

At the same time the settlers also sought practical ways to strengthen their defences in the face of Irish raids of increasing frequency and ferocity. The Dublin parliament of November 1428 passed statutes concerned with the migration of servants and labourers from Ireland and also granted a subsidy of £10 to anyone in Louth who within five years would build a castle twenty feet in length, sixteen feet in breadth, and forty feet in height.[119] This is reminiscent of the 1371 grant of Farney to Roger Gernon, which was made on condition that he 'build within the twenty years next coming a competent fortalice against the king's enemies and rebels', but the shortened time-scale envisaged for construction of such an edifice fifty-seven years later speaks to the increase in danger to the settlement that had developed in the intervening period.[120] The castle-building subsidy—now extended to include Dublin, Meath, and Kildare—was repeated in the Dublin parliament of May 1430, and the parliament that convened at Dublin in November 1431 heard a petition from the commons of Louth stating that the county could not be defended 'unless certain castles and fortresses be made in the marches'. In response, the sheriff and keepers of the peace in Louth were permitted for three years to require all able-bodied men in the county for eight days each year 'to labour with their spades and shovels in the said marches... to carry stones and sand... and... to make the said castles or fortresses'.[121] The Dublin parliament of March 1435 in like

---

[116] Walker, 'Janico Dartasso', 46, 48; *CPR 1422–9*, 287–8, 488–9.

[117] *Reg. Swayne*, 45–6 where Rudraige appears as 'Roger'. Kenny, *Anglo-Irish and Gaelic Women in Ireland*, 80.

[118] Katharine Simms, 'Native Sources for Gaelic Settlement: The House Poems', in Patrick J. Duffy, David Edwards, and Elizabeth FitzPatrick (eds), *Gaelic Ireland c.1250–c.1650: Land, Lordship and Settlement* (Dublin, 2001), 252–4.

[119] *Stat. Ire., Hen. VI*, 17; J. T. Gilbert, *History of the Viceroys of Ireland* (Dublin, 1865), 326–7.

[120] *CPR 1374–7*, 340.

[121] *Stat. Ire., Hen. VI*, 33, 35, 45, 47; Terry Barry, 'The Last Frontier: Defence and Settlement in Late Medieval Ireland', in Barry et al., *Colony and Frontier in Medieval Ireland*, 217–28.

manner empowered Sir Christopher Fleming to employ forced labour in the baronies of Morgallion and Slane to fortify the towns of Nobber and Drumconrath.[122] Efforts were also made to strengthen defences that were already in place. In June 1437 a long-standing grant of murage and pavage to the community of Ardee to enable them to fortify their town was extended

> in consideration of the fact that the town is situated in the frontier of the marches of co. Louth and is the key to the county and surrounding countryside, and for the most part destroyed, and on account of the burdens that the provost [etc.] sustain daily in the war in that land and in defending against and resisting the Irish enemies in those parts, which burdens they cannot support without help and relief from the king.[123]

The need for urgent action of the type suggested by these initiatives had been signalled in letters to the king dispatched in late 1427 by Archbishop John Swayne of Armagh, who lived in the midst of the Louth settlers at Termonfeckin. Swayne asserted that the amount of land then obedient to the king's law in Ireland measured less than one shire in England and that with the exception of castles and walled towns the settlement would be entirely lost within months. More settlers had left Ireland for England and elsewhere within the previous few years than remained in it, he continued, while those who stayed had been subjected to crippling and illegal exactions from a succession of lieutenants.[124]

The situation described by the archbishop in 1427 was set to deteriorate further, with James White, in his capacity as constable of Carrickfergus, reporting rumours in March 1428 that O'Donnell had 'sent for a great multitude of Scots' with whom he intended to cause damage throughout Ireland.[125] In 1429 O'Connor Faly launched an attack from the midlands into Meath that reached as far as Duleek, 7 kilometres south-east of Drogheda, and resulted in the deaths of 'many husbandmen with their sons and servants'.[126] In the same year, the English of Meath joined forces with one branch of the O'Reillys in an attack on the leader of the main branch, Eógan. He in turn called on the support of O'Neill and together they defeated their opponents on the borders of Meath, killing or capturing the baron of Delvin in the process.[127] Spurred on by this success, Eógan O'Neill in 1430 led a large army into Louth 'and he plundered, laid waste, and burned the English settlements of the entire plain. He also burned the fortress of Traigh-Bhaile [Dundalk] and made the inhabitants of the town tributary and submissive to him; after which he returned home with victory and triumph.'[128] A sense of the lasting damage caused by this incursion to the economy of the area around Dundalk comes from testimony provided in 1439 in a case brought by Peter Dowdall

---

[122] *RCH* 258 no. 92; Lynch, *View of the Legal Institutions*, 197. A 'fortress of stone' was to be built at Drumconrath. Both towns are described as 'the key to the county'.
[123] NAI Ferguson Coll. iii. 152.
[124] *Reg. Swayne*, 107–11.
[125] *RCH* 246 no. 21.
[126] Mac Iomhair (ed.), 'Two Old Drogheda Chronicles', 91.
[127] *AFM* iv. 875, 877.
[128] *AFM* iv. 879.

concerning the ownership of a mill in the Cooley peninsula. One witness, Michael Rede, an 80-year-old burgess of Carlingford, asserted that four millers had been employed there 'until the army of Onell burnt the said mill and the vills of Coli for the greater part'.[129]

The early 1430s saw no lessening of military action on the marches. In 1431, Magnus MacMahon ambushed 'a large body of English cavalry' engaged in a raid into O'Reilly territory, and made a number of 'their chiefs prisoner, slew others, and returned home victoriously'.[130] A successful campaign in Louth in the following year garnered more hostages as well as noteworthy decorations for the garden of Magnus's residence at Carrickmacross. On his instructions, the heads of the settlers he had slain 'were placed upon the palisade of the town, so that it was very horrible…to behold the palisade of the town of Magnus, for the amount of heads of his foes and his enemies that was thereon'.[131] The events of 1432 demonstrated how closely interwoven the politics on either side of the Ulster frontier had by now become. The death that year of Domnall O'Neill at the hands of the O'Kanes at last left Eógan O'Neill as sole claimant to the leadership of his family, and he immediately set out to reassert the traditional supremacy of the O'Neills in Ulster by challenging O'Donnell. He was supported by Magnus and Rudraige MacMahon, but opposed by their brother, Brian, king of Airgialla, who allied with the settlers and by agreement moved his creaght (*caeraigecht* = herds of cattle and their attendants) into Louth. Together, Brian and the settlers then marched deep into Airgialla as far as Dartree before turning north-east and attacking Armagh. Only in return for 'great gifts from the clergy and students of the town', did they refrain from burning its churches before returning to Louth.[132] In the following year, O'Donnell and his ally MacQuillin, made 'a treaty of alliance and friendship' with the Meath settlers and the lieutenant, Sir Thomas Stanley, and together they embarked upon another raid on the city of Armagh. As part of this rapprochement, the Louth settlers agreed to allow MacQuillin, who had been banished from his territory in north Antrim by O'Neill, to billet his men in their midst.[133]

No doubt aware of the need to base the security of the settlement on firmer foundations than alliances with the competing Irish dynasties of Ulster, Archbishop Swayne and the treasurer, Thomas Strange, in February 1434 obtained royal permission 'to muster from time to time the men at arms and archers abiding in Ireland in the company of Thomas Stanley, king's knight, lieutenant of that land'.[134] At Drogheda in the following October all tenants holding by royal service were ordered to appear before the lieutenant at the town of Louth on 13 December in advance of a campaign in MacMahon's territory, and in preparation for this venture, Archbishop Swayne and Thomas Strange invoked the prerogative granted

---

[129] *Dowdall Deeds*, 177–80, quote at 178.   [130] *AFM* iv. 883, 885.
[131] *AFM* iv. 889; *AU* iii. 119. One version of the Annals of Ulster records the 'terror and loathing' induced by MacMahon's actions among the Irish poets and pilgrims present in the town.
[132] *AFM* iv. 887, 889, 891; *AU* iii. 119, 121, 123, 125; Katharine Simms, 'Nomadry in Medieval Ireland: The Origins of the Creaght or *Caoraigheacht*', *Peritia*, 5 (1986), 379–91.
[133] *AFM* iv. 895; *AU* iii. 127, 129.
[134] *CPR 1429–36*, 355.

to them in February.¹³⁵ At Mellifont in November they assembled a force of 400 men who were required to demonstrate their proficiency as archers. Although most of this force came from England, the inclusion in their number of men with such surnames as Plunket, Petit, O'Connell, O'Kelly, Cruys, O'Rogan, Teeling, 'Tege of Trim', Tuyt, Corre, Netterville, Clinton, and Nugent indicates that Stanley had also recruited to his retinue men from Meath and Louth of both native and settler stock.¹³⁶ That only twenty-four of the company of 400 men were considered to have performed unsatisfactorily at the muster probably bore witness to their employment in arms earlier in the same year. A dispute had erupted among the O'Donnells which led their chief, Niall, who only a year before had been allied with the settlers, to reach agreement with his old enemy Eógan O'Neill. Together they marched into Louth, taking rent and 'many articles of value' from the inhabitants of Dundalk before burning the settlement as far south as the hills around Slane, just north of the river Boyne. From there they moved deeper into Meath and attacked Nobber, but were forced to retreat by Thomas Stanley who captured Niall O'Donnell and imprisoned him on his estates in the Isle of Man.¹³⁷

Stanley's success in 1434 offered the settlers in Louth and Meath some years of respite after a decade and more of intense conflict with the Irish of Ulster—the royal service proclaimed at Louth in December of that year was the last of its kind in the fifteenth century.¹³⁸ One sign of more peaceful times was Archbishop Swayne's decision in 1435 for the first time to identify Eógan O'Neill and his son, Aed, as 'the church's secular arm' in the parts of Armagh among the Irish, and to describe them as 'watchful defenders of their Holy Church and its liberty and rights'.¹³⁹ This Aed was the founder of a branch of the O'Neills that in these years settled permanently in the Fews, the area of south Armagh adjacent to the Bellew lordship of Roche.¹⁴⁰ Aed's successful colonization of new land, accomplished to some extent at the expense of the O'Hanlons, mirrored the earlier achievement of the sons of Cú Ulad O'Neill, who at the beginning of the century had carved out a separate lordship for themselves around the city of Armagh.¹⁴¹

Another instance of attempts to defuse tension in the marches in the years after 1434 was the decision of the deputy lieutenant, Archbishop Richard Talbot of Dublin, to impose a harsh financial penalty on Nicholas Taaf and his companions for a cattle raid they conducted against the O'Reillys in 1436.¹⁴² Talbot, however, remained ready to resort to war in the marches of Louth and Meath when necessary or advantageous, as he demonstrated the following year when dispute flared again between Magnus and Brian MacMahon. While the former sought the support of Eógan O'Neill, the latter renewed his alliance with the settlers and Richard

---

¹³⁵ BL Add MS 4798, f. 30r–30v.   ¹³⁶ *Reg. Swayne*, 145–9.
¹³⁷ *AFM* iv. 897, 899, 901; *AU* iii. 131, 133; *AC* 477.
¹³⁸ Otway-Ruthven, 'Royal Service in Ireland', 175–6.
¹³⁹ *Reg. Swayne*, 159; Simms, 'The Archbishops of Armagh and the O'Neills', 51.
¹⁴⁰ Tomás Ó Fiaich, 'The O'Neills of the Fews', *Seanchas Ardmhacha*, 7 (1973), 1–64.
¹⁴¹ Simms, 'The Ulster Revolt of 1404', 155–6.
¹⁴² *RCH* 260 no. 34.

Talbot, now with the title justiciar, led a force late in 1437 against Magnus.[143] Magnus's position became yet weaker in 1441 when Eógan O'Neill and Eógan O'Reilly submitted to the new deputy lieutenant, James Butler, earl of Ormond, and it was with settler support that in 1442 O'Neill launched a campaign deep into O'Donnell's territory of Donegal.[144]

It was also in 1442 that Brian MacMahon, who had for the most part remained on good terms with the English since becoming king of Airgialla in 1416, died. His equability had most recently been encouraged by a subsidy of £20 granted to him by the commons and clergy of Louth in 1441, and there are reasons to believe that his usual policy of accommodation with the settlers was inspired neither by fear nor admiration, but because he considered them to be appropriately subservient to his authority.[145] It appears to have been during his period of rule that a tract on the rights of MacMahon was drawn up, of which only a copy dating from c.1600 now survives. In gloating terms it describes the tributes levied on the settlers of Louth and part of Meath by Brian MacMahon, which he demanded in return for his condescension in allowing them to occupy a portion of his territory of Airgialla. As well as exactions taken from the towns of Siddan, Drumconrath, Crowmartin, Ardee, Louth, and Dundalk, renders were also due from settler families such as the Taafs, Babes, Whites, Clintons, and Mores.[146] No doubt the strong element of fantasy in this account grew in the telling between c.1425 and c.1600, but the tract is reminiscent of the O'Reilly poem of the same period mentioned above in its tone of self-confidence and contempt for the settlers and for English power, and is a reminder of the intensity of ill-feeling that centred on the marches of late medieval Louth and Meath.[147]

The death in 1443 of Brian MacMahon's brother and rival Magnus, who had been a scourge to the settlers for many years, must also have encouraged the inhabitants of Louth and Meath to breathe more easily.[148] Magnus's demise did, however, evoke sympathy in some quarters: those same Irish annals that had described his use of the heads of his defeated foes to adorn his dwelling at Carrickmacross with such disgust in 1432 now lauded his record of hospitality and artistic patronage, and he received honourable burial at the Augustinian abbey of Sts Peter and Paul, Clones.[149] Brian was succeeded by his other brother, Rudraige, the husband of Alice White, and in 1445 the government demonstrated its support for his rule by granting his petition that he might have custody for fifty years of the lordships

---

[143] *RCH* 263 no. 10; *AFM* iv. 911.   [144] *RCH* 263–8; *AFM* iv. 927.
[145] NLI MS 2689, ff. 143–4.
[146] The family of Betagh of Kells, which was of Irish origin but was fully aligned with the settlers, was also under tribute.
[147] Séamus Pender, 'A Tract on MacMahon's Prerogatives', *Études Celtiques*, 1 (1936), 248–60; 'Cíos MacMathghamhna', ed. Seósamh Ó Dufaigh, *Clogher Record*, 4 (1962), 125–34; Linda Clare, 'Continuity and Change in North-East Meath, 1400–1540', *Ríocht na Midhe*, 18 (2007), 108–31. For discussion of the 'striking air of antiquity' that characterizes aspects of the tract: Simms, *From Kings to Warlords*, 67.
[148] *AU* iii. 151. The lieutenant, James Butler, earl of Ormond, was at Drogheda in Feb. 1443: TCD MS 1747, 111.
[149] *AFM* iv. 929; *AU* iii. 151, 153; Mac Firbis, *Annals*, 207.

of Farney and Donaghmoyne, which had been taken back into the king's hands by John Talbot in 1425.[150] This period of relative tranquillity for the settlers was disturbed in 1444 when '[a] great army was led by O'Neill...into the English settlements of Oriel, and he plundered and burned many of them'. Only in return for a payment of 60m and two tons of wine did Eógan refrain from burning Dundalk after he had ransacked it.[151]

It was probably in the aftermath of this attack that Peter Dowdall and his wife, Joan White, inserted an unusual clause into an indenture with another Dundalk merchant, William Brook, and his wife, dated 1 July 1444, concerning the farming out of a house in the town. Brook was required to return the property to Dowdall after twenty years and in the mean time 'to maintain the messuage "styff and staunche" and so surrender it unless burned by the rebels, the king's enemies, or by accidental fire'.[152] O'Neill's return to large-scale raiding of the settlement was a result of a breakdown in his relationship with James Butler, earl of Ormond, who since 1442 had been supporting Eógan's rivals for control of east Ulster, the Clandeboy O'Neills. O'Neill and Butler had become sufficiently close in the period preceding this dispute to allow for the marriage of Eógan's son and heir-designate, Henry, to Butler's niece, but in 1443 O'Neill showed his displeasure with Butler by urging the king to appoint to the vacant archbishop of Armagh the earl's enemy Richard Talbot, archbishop of Dublin.[153] This ploy proved unsuccessful, but O'Neill displayed his continued dominance over the Irish of south Ulster in 1446 when, on the death of Rudraige MacMahon, who had ruled Airgialla since 1442, he installed Rudraige's son, Aed Ruad, as his successor.[154]

Eógan O'Neill's unchallenged local supremacy provided the context in which his son, Aed, whose base was in the parts of Armagh adjacent to county Louth, sealed an indenture at Dundalk on 20 December 1446 with John Talbot, who had commenced his last period as lieutenant of Ireland in the previous month.[155] The indenture contained little that was new, but restated the commitment on the part of the O'Neills to render the bonnacht to the earl of Ulster who was now, of course, Richard, duke of York. It was followed in late January and early February 1447 by two separate indentures entered into at Trim by Talbot with Eógan O'Reilly, 'captain of his nation', and his brother Feidlimid. The latter agreed to support the lieutenant should he be at war with O'Reilly—a clause that suggests anticipation on the part of the English of future trouble with the head of this family, who was the first O'Reilly leader to recognize an O'Neill as his superior lord.[156]

---

[150] *CPR 1441–1446*, 343; see above.
[151] *AFM* iv. 935; Mac Firbis, *Annals*, 205.
[152] *Dowdall Deeds*, 183
[153] Simms, 'The King's Friend', 220–1; *Reg. Mey*, 297; John A. Watt, 'The Church and the Two Nations in Late Medieval Armagh', in W. J. Shiels and Diana Wood (eds), *Studies in Church History 25: The Churches, Ireland and the Irish* (Oxford, 1989), 43–4.
[154] In 1443 or 1444 Eógan had slain Eimír son of Brian MacMahon, a rival of Rudraige's. *AFM* iv. 929, 945; Mac Firbis, *Annals*, 206, 207.
[155] *NHI* ix. 477.
[156] *Handbook and Select Calendar...Ireland*, 226, 227; Simms, 'The King's Friend', 221–2.

Feidlimid, however, was identified by the government as dangerous in his own right and, in a repeat of the circumstances surrounding the submissions made by Irish leaders to Edmund Mortimer in January 1425, was taken prisoner by John Talbot while at Trim, dying of plague there shortly afterwards.[157] On 17 March 1449, Eógan O'Reilly died, and O'Neill's choice as his successor, his son John, was immediately challenged by a rival favoured by Ormond and the settlers, Fergal. The resultant battle saw a clear victory for John O'Reilly and his O'Neill sponsors, followed before the end of April by another raid by Eógan O'Neill and the O'Hanlons on Dundalk.[158]

On 6 July 1449, Richard, duke of York, who had been appointed lieutenant of Ireland at the end of 1447, landed at Howth.[159] Since the O'Neill successes of the spring Ormond and the archbishop of Armagh, John Mey, had been in negotiations with Eógan and his son, Henry O'Neill, who now ruled in conjunction with his father, about the possibility of concluding a formal peace agreement. Mey was at Armagh for much of July, and after his return to Termonfeckin wrote to Eógan to inform him that Richard's seneschal of Ulster would travel to Dundalk to parley with him. Mey assured O'Neill that he would also be present and would act as mediator.[160] In August, Richard moved to Drogheda, where he 'was greeted for the last time in Irish history by the mass voluntary submission of Irish chieftains to their legal overlord'.[161] In the course of that month, submissions were received from chiefs from various parts of Ireland, among whose number were Magennis, O'Reilly, MacMahon, and O'Hanlon. On 27 August, Henry O'Neill, acting on behalf of his father, entered into an indenture with the duke whereby he promised to restore to him all of his lands that he had usurped and to provide his share of the bonnacht of Ulster. His additional promise to surrender all lands conquered from the settlers and especially to return the Fews to John Bellew, lord of Roche, was so unrealistic as to cast doubt on the extent to which either party to the indenture actually expected its provisions to be fulfilled.[162] What the indenture did do, however, was signal acceptance on the part of the crown's government in Ireland of the argument that O'Neill stood in an intermediate position between the other Ulster chiefs and the earl of Ulster, and signal its willingness to support O'Neill against his enemies among the Irish. The stage was set for the long reign in Ulster of Henry O'Neill, who was to succeed his father in 1455 and rule until 1483, during which time attacks from Ulster on the settlers in Louth and Meath ceased almost entirely.[163]

---

[157] *AFM* iv. 953.   [158] *Reg. Mey*, 135–6; *AFM* iv. 963; *AU* iii. 163.
[159] Otway-Ruthven, *History of Medieval Ireland*, 377–9.
[160] *Reg. Mey*, 168–9, 176, 178–80.
[161] Simms, 'The King's Friend', 222.
[162] Edmund Curtis, 'Richard, Duke of York, as Viceroy of Ireland, 1447–1460: With Unpublished Materials for his Relations with the Native Chiefs', in Crooks, *Government, War and Society in Medieval Ireland*, 245, where Curtis remarks: 'Of this solemn treaty, we may remark that few of its positive clauses were carried out'. For Bellew's title, *Reg. Swayne*, 60; *Reg. Octaviani*, ii. 71–2. He had been granted the court of Dundalk and the hundred of the town in 1443: BL Add MS 43769, f. 64.
[163] Simms, 'The King's Friend', 223–4.

On 26 August 1449—the day before Richard, duke of York and Henry O'Neill entered into their indenture—another document was drawn up at Drogheda that offers an insight into settler priorities in mid-fifteenth-century Louth. This was a notarial instrument recording that Robert Fitz Rery had inquired as to the evidence given in a case held before another official of the Armagh diocese in March 1438. The evidence concerned, relating to ownership of the mill at Castletowncooley, had been assembled by Peter Dowdall as part of a long-running attempt to prove his right to the property. Dowdall had died sometime after July 1444 and his wife, Joan White, subsequently married Robert Fitz Rery who now took up the case.[164] In August 1449, John Mey, archbishop of Armagh, and his notaries were at Drogheda with the duke of York to conduct sensitive negotiations with the Irish leader who posed the greatest possible threat to English interests in this part of the country. For settlers such as Fitz Rery and Joan White, however, the presence in their midst of these great men provided the opportunity to gain advantage in a dispute over milling rights deep in the Cooley peninsula. This determination to advance their personal interests—preferably through legal means—combined with the political skills needed to bring those interests to the attention of those who wielded power, explains in large part why the English of Louth survived the most dangerous century in their history.

This survey of the history of late medieval Louth began with a reference to the execution of Roger Mortimer in 1330 and ends with an account of the presence of his descendant and the inheritor of his Irish estates, Richard, duke of York, at Drogheda in 1449. Roger had deposed the king of England, Edward II, in 1327, and Richard's son was to seize the throne as King Edward IV in 1460. Throughout this period of profound political and social change in both England and Ireland, the Mortimer connection had served to bind the fortunes of Louth, Meath, and Ulster closely to those of a wider English world. The unification of the Mortimer and royal titles under Edward IV ensured that this would continue to be the case, and offered the prospect of more intense English interest in the fortunes of this part of Ireland in the years ahead.

[164] *Dowdall Deeds*, xv, 177–80, 181, 185–6.

II
SETTLER SOCIETY

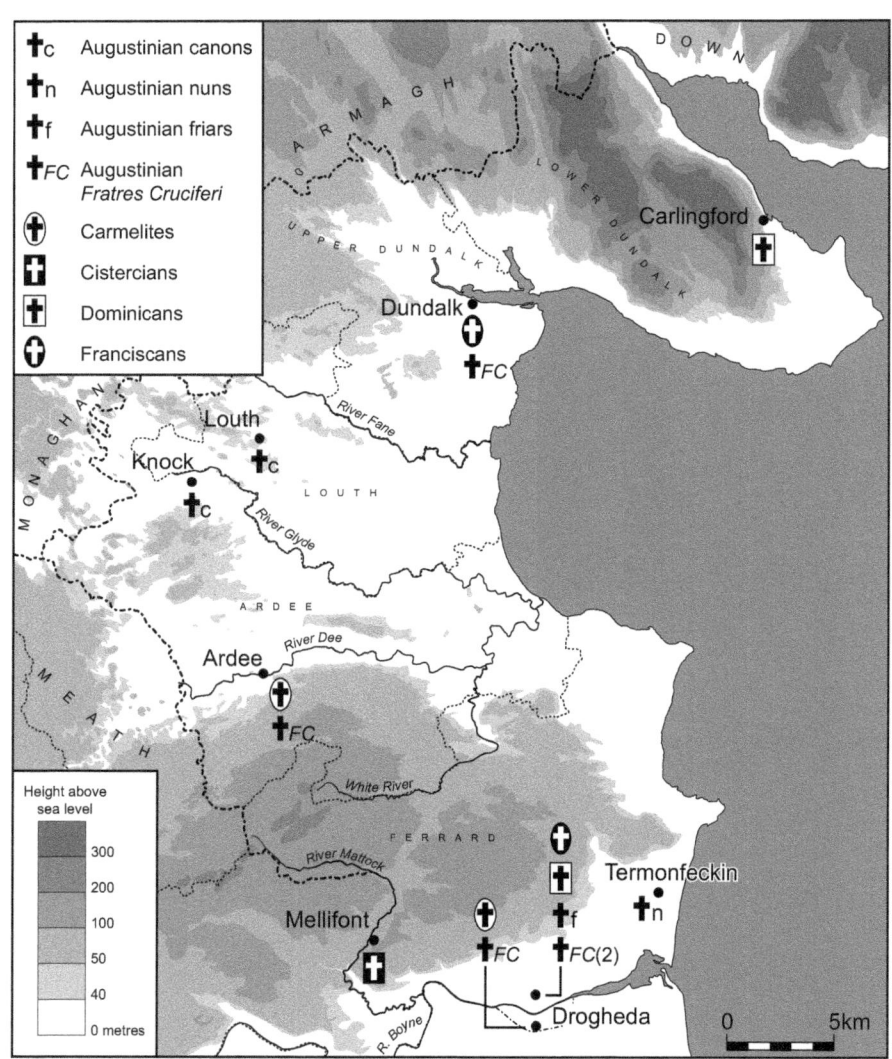

Map 4. Religious houses in Louth

5
The Church

If in political and cultural terms the settlers in Louth belonged to a larger English world, their religious identity ensured their membership of a still more extensive entity: western Christendom. This entity, of course, also embraced the Gaelic Irish, and the fact of a shared religion gave a particular character to relations between native and settler in this part of Ireland. The political map of Louth and its surrounding region rested uneasily on top of pre-existing Church structures that had not been established with later divisions between native and settler in mind. This disjuncture between political and religious boundaries meant that the Church and senior Churchmen would play a particularly significant role in the history of late medieval Louth.

Louth formed part of the diocese of Armagh—roughly coterminous with the modern counties of Louth and Armagh and the southern part of county Tyrone—which was itself pre-eminent within the ecclesiastical province of Armagh.[1] The province—one of four in Ireland—consisted of ten dioceses stretching from the Irish Sea in the east to the river Shannon in the west, and from the midlands in the south to the Atlantic ocean in the north. The province was undoubtedly remote from the centre of Christendom—the bishop of one of its dioceses, Clogher, described his see in the 1350s as being 'at the ends of the world'—yet it was far from isolated. Clogher, which bordered with Louth, contained at its western extreme the pilgrimage site of St Patrick's Purgatory, which in the fourteenth and fifteenth centuries drew pilgrims from Hungary, France, Italy, Aragon, and Wallonia, as well as England and other parts of Ireland.[2] Since these pilgrims were required to obtain the permission of the archbishop of Armagh to visit the Purgatory, they were obliged to spend time in Louth, where he normally resided. The 'travellers' tales' left by some of these pilgrims contain insights into conditions in the region not available in other sources. It is from the Catalan knight Ramon de Perellós, for instance, that we learn that Drogheda at the end of the fourteenth century was the same size as Tarragona. The Fleming, Gilbert Lannoy, who arrived from Scotland at Drogheda en route to the Purgatory in 1430, described Kells (*Kennelich*) as 'an ill-walled town still belonging

---

[1] Concerned with a later period, but containing many important observations on the late medieval situation, is Henry A. Jefferies, *Priests and Prelates of Armagh in the Age of Reformations, 1518–1558* (Dublin, 1997).

[2] See the contributions to Haren and de Pontfarcy, *Medieval Pilgrimage to St Patrick's Purgatory*. A list of known pilgrims is included at 5–6; the quotation is at 122–3; Katharine Walsh, '. . . *in Finibus Mundi*: The Late Medieval Pilgrims to St Patrick's Purgatory, Lough Derg, and the European Dimension of the Diocese of Clogher', in Henry A. Jefferies (ed.), *History of the Diocese of Clogher* (Dublin, 2005), 41–69.

to the king of England, seated on the frontier of the wild Irish. There is a poor abbey [there]'. From Kells he moved on to the town of Cavan (*Canaen*), which he characterized as 'a poor unwalled town belonging to King Auraly [Eógan O'Reilly] who lives in a wretched place and poor tower over the town'.³

Pilgrimage was an activity that not only attracted outsiders to Louth and Meath, but also encouraged men and women from these counties to leave Ireland and visit holy places elsewhere in Christendom and beyond. Archbishop Nicholas Fleming wrote to his clergy in the diocese of Armagh in 1410 encouraging them to induce their parishioners to grant alms to James Hall of the diocese of Meath who intended to make his way to the Holy Land and the Sepulchre of Christ.⁴ The Holy Land was also the proposed destination in 1413 of another of Fleming's flock, Christian Oferagaid, who by that date had already visited Rome and its pilgrimage sites on five occasions.⁵ The presence of a hospital dedicated to St James in the part of Drogheda south of the Boyne indicates a tradition of pilgrimage to Santiago de Compostela, but written sources relating to medieval Louth suggest that Rome was the most popular destination for pilgrims from this part of Ireland.⁶ Among the possessions left by John Brent, burgess and merchant of Drogheda, on his death sometime in the 1440s was 'a book in English about the stations of Rome' (*et alium librum de Anglico super stacionibus civitatis Romane*)—a volume that might have been of interest to those 'pilgrims of Armagh diocese' on whose behalf Archbishop Swayne wrote letters of recommendation in 1426 as they set off for Rome.⁷ On their arrival there it is probable that the travellers rested at the house of St Thomas the Martyr, 'founded long ago for the entertainment of poor pilgrims from England and Ireland', the proctors of which were permitted by Archbishop Fleming to seek alms in his diocese in 1406.⁸

If Rome attracted pilgrims in some numbers from among the laity of the diocese of Armagh, the papal court—whether situated at Rome or, as was the case

---

³ Carpenter, 'The Pilgrim from Catalonia/Aragon', 108; Leslie, *St Patrick's Purgatory*, 39. The town of Cavan had been burnt and its castle demolished by the justiciar James Butler, earl of Ormond, in 1427, and the town was burnt again in 1429, this time by the English of Meath and a rival branch of the O'Reillys: *AFM* iv. 873, 875. Cherry, 'Indigenous and Colonial Urbanization of Cavan Town', 87–8.

⁴ *Reg. Fleming*, 146.

⁵ *Reg. Fleming*, 236–7.

⁶ John Bradley, 'The Topography and Layout of Medieval Drogheda', *CLAJ* 19 (1978), 108–9; Roger Stalley, 'Sailing to Santiago: The Medieval Pilgrimage to Santiago de Compostela and its Artistic Influence in Ireland', in Bradley, *Settlement and Society in Medieval Ireland*, 397–420.

⁷ *Reg. Mey*, 241–2. Brent had been given permission to travel to England in 1415 (*RCH* 211 nos. 56, 57), and was one of the assessors for Drogheda of the subsidy granted to the lieutenant, James Butler, earl of Ormond, in Oct. 1421: *Parls. & Councils*, 174–5; *Reg. Swayne*, 43. Swayne's Roman career and connections are discussed in Katherine Walsh, 'The Roman Career of John Swayne, Archbishop of Armagh 1418–1439: Plans for an Irish Hospice in Rome', *Seanchas Ardmhacha*, 11 (1983–4), 1–21.

⁸ *Reg. Fleming*, 8–9. The chief officer of the court of Armagh, Thomas White, died in Rome in 1445 and was buried in the hospital of St Thomas the Martyr: *Reg. Mey*, 132. For the hospital of St Thomas, and the Irish in Rome, see Margaret Harvey, *The English in Rome 1362–1420: Portrait of an Expatriate Community* (Cambridge, 1999), 55–76, 89–90.

between 1309 and 1376, at Avignon—drew to it many members of the region's clergy. Proximity to the pope could have unexpected benefits for those clerics who had made the long journey to be near him: the presence at Avignon of David Mág Oireachtaigh (1334–46) in 1334 and Milo Sweteman (1361–80) in 1361, and at Rome of Nicholas Fleming (1404–16) in 1404 encouraged the pope to provide these men to the vacant see of Armagh, while John Swayne (1418–39), who had served as Fleming's proctor at the curia, was with Pope Martin V at Constance when the latter provided him to Armagh in 1418.[9] Fleming had been at Rome in his capacity as proctor for Archbishop John Colton (1381–1404), and John Prene (1439–43), who succeeded John Swayne as archbishop in 1439 had served as the latter's proctor at the curia in the late 1420s.[10] With the exceptions of Archbishop Richard Fitz Ralph (1346–60), who preached at Avignon in 1349 and remained there from late 1357 until his death in November 1360, and Archbishop John Colton, who represented Richard II at Rome between August 1398 and September 1399, serving archbishops of Armagh did not visit the curia.[11] Their previous curial experience and connections, however, ensured that Armagh's contact with the papacy and the wider Christian world remained close, and perhaps enhanced their ability to deal successfully with the secular rulers with whom they had to engage on behalf of their flock in Ireland.[12]

The most important of these secular rulers was the king of England, without whose assent the archbishop of Armagh could not take up his post. Of the nine consecrated archbishops who ruled Armagh in the period 1330–1450 only two, Stephen Segrave (1324–33) and John Colton, were from England, but of the remaining seven all but one—David Mág Oireachtaigh—spent time there either before becoming archbishop or during their prelacies.[13] Richard Fitz Ralph studied at the University of Oxford in the early 1320s and served as its chancellor between 1332 and 1334, while John Prene was permitted in 1415 to absent himself from Ireland for four years to study at Cambridge or Oxford.[14] Nicholas Fleming

---

[9] Walsh, *Fourteenth-Century Scholar and Primate*, 239–40; *Reg. Sweteman*, xiv. Fleming had been at the court of Rome in 1381: *Reg. Fleming*, xi; *RCH* 109 no. 115. Brendan Smith, 'Swayne, John (d.1439x42)', *Oxford Dictionary of National Biography* (Oxford, 2004); Harvey, *English in Rome*, 149–53. Matthew Mac Cathasaigh, chancellor of Armagh, was provided to the see of Clogher while at Rome in 1287, as was Brian MacCawell in 1356: Brendan Smith, 'The Late Medieval Diocese of Clogher, *c.*1200–1480', in Jefferies, *History of the Diocese of Clogher*, 73. The frequency with which the clergy of 15th-cent. Clogher travelled to Rome in pursuit of benefices in their diocese is discussed in this article and also in John A. Watt, 'The Medieval Chapter of Armagh Cathedral', in David Abulafia, Michael Franklin, and Miri Rubin (eds), *Church and City 1000–1500: Essays in Honour of Christopher Brooke* (Cambridge, 1992), 237–8.

[10] *Reg. Swayne*, 93–4, 95.

[11] Walsh, 'Fitzralph, Richard'; *Chartul. St Mary's, Dublin*, ii. 393; Johnston, 'Colton, John (d.1404)'.

[12] Archbishop Swayne had been rector of the University of Siena: Aubrey Gwynn, 'Anglo-Irish Church Life: Fourteenth and Fifteenth Centuries', in Patrick J. Corish (ed.), *A History of Irish Catholicism* (Dublin, 1968), ii/4. 36; R. Dudley Edwards, 'Conflict of Papal and Royal Jurisdictions in Fifteenth-Century Ireland', *PICHC* (1960), 3–9.

[13] It is not clear if Archbishop John Mey (1443–56) originated in England or Ireland. Katherine Walsh is dismissive of the suggestion that Mág Oireachtaigh had studied at Oxford: Walsh, *Fourteenth-Century Scholar and Primate*, 241.

[14] Walsh, *Fourteenth-Century Scholar and Primate*, 15–84; *RCH* 212 no. 76; NAI RC 8/36, 252–3. Prene may have spent longer than this away from Ireland. He next appears in our records in 1425: *Reg. Swayne*, 41. It is possible that Milo Swetman studied at Oxford: Gundacker, 'Absolution and Acts of Disobedience', 185.

received licence to spend two years in England in July 1403—presumably in pursuit of his studies—during which period he journeyed to Rome where he was provided to the archbishopric of Armagh in April 1404.[15] John Colton, John Swayne, and John Mey each spent time in England while serving as archbishop, not as students, but in connection with the disturbed state of Ireland. In 1386, Colton was licensed to travel to England, having been elected by the settlers 'to cross to the king for the consideration of the state of Ireland', and spent more than two years there between early 1388 and May 1390.[16] In May 1394 he was preparing to go to England again, no doubt in connection with the proposed visit of Richard II to Ireland, and in 1401 appeared before Henry IV 'in order to lay before him and the council the estate and grievances of Ireland', having been chosen to do so along with the archbishop of Dublin by the settler community in parliament.[17] Archbishop John Swayne was selected by the justiciar and council to cross to England 'upon public business' in early 1423, and remained there until the late summer, while Archbishop John Mey left for England 'in the king's service' at the end of 1449, returning to Ireland before 24 April the following year.[18]

Service to the crown on the part of the archbishops of Armagh was not limited to attending the king in England, or to representing him at the Roman curia. Archbishop Nicholas Fleming was empowered on three occasions between 1408 and 1414 to act in place of the Irish exchequer as the receiver of final accounts from the men of Dundalk and Ardee of grants made to them for the strengthening of the defences of their towns.[19] John Colton was appointed as seneschal of Ulster in October 1383—the earldom being vacant following the death of Edmund Mortimer in December 1381—and remained in that post for over a year.[20] Nicholas Fleming became the first archbishop of Armagh to serve as a keeper of the peace when he was appointed in that capacity for county Louth in 1409, and subsequently John Swayne in 1420 and 1425 and John Mey in c.1449 received similar commissions.[21] The Irish council might also call upon the archbishop to act on its behalf in an emergency, as in April 1355 when Richard Fitz Ralph was ordered to suspend his visitation of the diocese of Meath and hasten to Dundalk in order to parley with Aed O'Neill, who was threatening to attack the town.[22] Almost eighty years later, in February 1434, again in response to heightened concerns about the security of the settlement in Louth and Meath, the council commissioned Archbishop John Swayne and Thomas

[15] RCH 170 no. 63; CPL 1396–1404, 614–15.
[16] RCH 127 no. 230; 141 no. 187 (quotation); 146 no. 193; CPR 1385–9, 444, 447; CPR 1389–92, 196. Colton issued letters at Drogheda in Sept. 1387 and May 1390: Hogan, *Priory of Llanthony*, 366–8; *Reg. Fleming*, 225.
[17] COA Rep. Records of the Exchequer, 10–22 Richard II, 188; CCR 1399–1402, 366 (quotation).
[18] RCH 226 no. 43. Swayne was still 'in remote parts' on 24 July 1423 (RCH 230 no. 121), but attended a meeting of the Irish council held at Drogheda on 24 and 25 Sept.: Richardson and Sayles, *Irish Parliament*, 312–17. *Reg. Swayne*, 195, 196.
[19] *Reg. Fleming*, 262; RCH 200 no. 87, 203 no. 15; COA Rep. Records of the Exchequer, Henry IV, 407.
[20] COA Rep. Records of the Exchequer, 1–10 Richard II, 383, 495, 500; RCH 128 no. 14.
[21] Frame, 'Commissions of the Peace in Ireland', 22–3.
[22] RCH 62 no. 100.

Strange 'to muster from time to time the men at arms and archers abiding in Ireland in the company of Thomas Stanley', the lieutenant.[23]

This was as close to personal involvement in military action against the Irish as any archbishop of Armagh came in this period. In a letter of September 1367, Archbishop Milo Sweteman warned Malachy O'Hanlon, king of Airthir, that he was considering consulting with the magnates of Ireland about O'Hanlon's destruction (*ad vestrum exterminium*), but there was no implication that he would himself participate in any consequent military campaign.[24] The stance of the archbishops on this issue was summed up well in a letter of April 1449 from John Mey to the archbishop of Dublin in which he apologized for having failed to send a promised contingent to a military hosting at Tallaght, and explained that he would shortly be attending a parley between the lord deputy and O'Neill. While being willing to work for the public good and the benefit of the king's lieges by negotiation, Mey continued, he was determined to concern himself with spiritual rather than secular matters.[25] Such remarks on the proper role of a senior prelate in a warlike environment perhaps contained an implicit rebuke for their recipient, Archbishop Richard Talbot, who in his capacity as chief governor had led armies against the Irish within the province of Armagh more than once.[26] That they reflected deeply held beliefs on Mey's part is suggested by his willingness to share them with powerful men who might find them uncongenial. In a response to a request from the lieutenant, Richard, duke of York, in the summer of 1449 that he send a force of archers and footmen to Bray, the archbishop asked his unidentified correspondent to explain to the duke that 'we oweth nought to be a werriour or a fighter, but with the armys of God, that ys to sey with devout prayer, to pray for his blessyd astate'.[27]

Despite their status as the senior ecclesiastics in Ireland, few archbishops of Armagh sat on the king's Irish council. John Mey served briefly and ineffectually as deputy lieutenant for James Butler, earl of Wiltshire and Ormond, between September 1453 and March 1454, but none of his predecessors held high rank in the Irish administration while at the same time filling the see of Patrick.[28] John Colton was present at a meeting of the Irish council convened at Trim in October 1391 at which the bishop of Meath, Alexander Balscot, was sworn in as justiciar, and Nicholas Fleming was party to the decision of the council late in 1411 to send the archbishops of Dublin and Cashel to England to explain the plight of Ireland to the king.[29] John Swayne attended a meeting of the council at Drogheda in September 1423 and in January

---

[23] *CPR 1429–36*, 355.
[24] *Reg. Sweteman*, 96, 131.
[25] 'Et licet pro re publica et melioribus utilitate et pace domini nostri regis et suorum fidelium hiis partibus prompti fuerimus iuxta posse benivole ad | tractandum tamen ex onere assumpto in spiritualibus nobis commissis, omissis occupacionibus et intentis secularibus…': *Reg. Mey*, 135–6.
[26] Archbishop Talbot was at the head of campaigns against O'Reilly in 1423 and MacMahon in 1437: *RCH* 224 no. 9; 263 no. 10.
[27] *Reg. Mey*, 177–8.
[28] Otway-Ruthven, *History of Medieval Ireland*, 385–6; *NHI* ix. 477.
[29] *RCH* 148 no. 42; *Reg. Fleming*, 182–4.

1425 was formally appointed to the body by the lieutenant, John Talbot.[30] He complained in 1427 that as a result of his appointment he had 'laboured in various ways in the king's service at his own great costs without reward' and in January 1430 was awarded £20 annually for the duration of his membership of the council.[31] He was still a member in April 1436 when he sought exemption from attendance at a meeting in Drogheda on the grounds of ill-health.[32] His successor, John Prene, attended a meeting of the council at Drogheda in October 1443.[33]

Why archbishops of Armagh attended the council on some occasions and not others can be explained with reference to where the body convened: if meetings were held within the province of Armagh—at Trim or Drogheda—the archbishop attended; if they assembled in the province of Dublin he did not. This was one practical and serious consequence of the dispute about primacy within the Irish church between these two prelacies.[34] By the early fourteenth century contention had come to focus on the issue of the right of the archbishop of Armagh to have his episcopal cross carried before him in the Dublin province, and throughout the period under discussion successive holders of the see of Patrick attempted to have this right acknowledged. At Drogheda in November 1337 the justiciar, John Charlton, at the request of Archbishop David Mág Oireachtaigh, exemplified clauses in a bull of Pope Urban IV (1261–4) confirming Armagh's primacy, and in the following year Mág Oireachtaigh's right to have his cross carried before him as he attended a parliament in Dublin, unmolested by its archbishop, was firmly stated by Edward III.[35] Richard Fitz Ralph persuaded Edward III to affirm this decision soon after he became archbishop in 1346, but his attempt to give it practical effect ended badly in 1349 when after a three-day sojourn in Dublin he was forcibly ejected by its citizens.[36] Fitz Ralph's persistence, and the unrest it encouraged, exasperated the king, who in the early 1350s reversed his earlier decision and forbade the exercise by Armagh of any primatial rights in Dublin.[37] The response of Fitz Ralph's successor, Milo Sweteman, to this curtailment of his perceived rights after 1360 was one imitated by all subsequent archbishops of Armagh: he sidestepped royal efforts to force a compromise and continued to assert his claims to primacy while at the same time refusing to enter the province of Dublin, thereby avoiding an escalation of the issue into physical violence.[38]

As a former dean of St Patrick's cathedral, Dublin, Sweteman's successor, John Colton might have been expected to seek an amicable solution to the primacy dispute, but he was careful to use his title of primate in his correspondence and

---

[30] Richardson and Sayles, *Irish Parliament*, 312–17; TNA E 101/247/20.
[31] *RCH* 244 no. 33; *Reg. Swayne*, 121. He was present at a meeting of the council at Drogheda in Apr. 1429: *RCH* 248 no. 13.
[32] *Reg. Swayne*, 165.
[33] *PKCI* 295–303.
[34] Tomás Ó Fiaich, 'The Primacy in the Irish Church', *Seanchas Ardmhacha*, 21 (2006), 1–23.
[35] *CPR 1399–1401*, 506; *CCR 1337–9*, 286.
[36] St Patrick showed his support for his successor in 1349 by miraculously taking the life of Alexander Bicknor, archbishop of Dublin, later that year: *Reg. Octaviani*, ii. 478–9.
[37] *Alen's Reg.* 207–8; Gwynn, 'Anglo-Irish Church Life', 14–16.
[38] *Reg. Sweteman*, 128.

took the opportunity of an embassy to England in the summer of 1401 to revive the controversy at the highest level.[39] No doubt to the chagrin of the archbishop of Dublin, Thomas Cranley, who accompanied him on this mission, Colton succeeded in having Urban IV's bull acknowledging Armagh's primacy in Ireland exemplified before King Henry IV and entered on the English patent rolls.[40] The next archbishop, Nicholas Fleming, heightened the rhetorical pitch of the dispute further in his response to a summons to a parliament to be held at Dublin in 1409. He would be unable to appear personally, he lamented, 'on account of the rebellion of the archbishop and clergy of Dublin against him' (*propter contradictionem et rebellionem per archiepiscopum et clerum Dublinienses*) with regard to the carrying of his cross and the right of primacy in the province of Dublin.[41] The 'rebellion of the archbishop of Dublin' was also cited as a reason for his inability to attend parliaments and councils in the province of Dublin by Archbishop John Swayne in 1427, and both he and his successor, John Prene, objected to receiving writs of summons that failed to include the phrase 'primate of Ireland' in their address.[42]

John Mey's professed desire to avoid secular ensnarement has been noted above, but he was as assiduous as his predecessors in asserting his claims to spiritual primacy in Ireland.[43] The attendance at the parliament that assembled at Drogheda on 26 March 1451 of both Mey and the archbishop of Dublin, Michael Tregury, brought the primacy controversy to the boil once more. The provocation offered by Tregury's cross-bearer in openly carrying the cross before him as the party from Dublin made its way through Drogheda to their lodgings at Fromboll's Inn on St Laurence Street, inspired predictable outrage on the part of the townsmen. So serious was the incident considered to be by the deputy lieutenant, James Butler, earl of Ormond, that he convened a special meeting of the Irish council at the Franciscan friary in the town to discuss it. There Tregury explained that it had all been a misunderstanding and that he only had the cross with him because he wished to have it repaired by a Drogheda goldsmith. His account was accepted and, once he had purged himself in the presence of Mey and the members of the council, parliament resumed its business.[44] Reluctant he may have been to shoulder the burdens of secular office, but Archbishop Mey did not scorn to use his brief tenure of the chief governorship (September 1453–March 1454) to further the claims to primacy of Armagh. In a declaration of September 1453 he repeated the relevant clauses in the bull of Pope Urban IV concerning Armagh's primacy, and went on to argue that while in office he should also be allowed carry his cross before him wherever in Ireland he went.[45] How this declaration was received is unknown, but

---

[39] Hogan, *Priory of Llanthony*, 366–8; *CPR 1385–9*, 444; *CPR 1389–92*, 196; *Reg. Fleming*, 225.
[40] *CCR 1399–1402*, 366; *CPR 1399–1401*, 506.
[41] *Reg. Fleming*, 118.
[42] *Reg. Swayne*, 52–3, 144, 161–2, 188.
[43] *Reg. Swayne*, 193. For Mey's primacy: John Watt, '*Ecclesia inter Anglicos et inter Hibernicos*: Confrontation and Coexistence in the Medieval Diocese of Armagh', in Lydon, *The English in Medieval Ireland*, 46–64.
[44] *Reg. Mey*, 432–3; Watt, 'Church and Two Nations', 44.
[45] *Reg. Mey*, 424–5.

Dublin's opposition to Armagh's claims appears to have weakened as the fifteenth century progressed.[46]

The dispute over primacy had the capacity to inspire civil unrest in the towns of Drogheda and Dublin, and prevented the crown from calling upon the archbishops of Armagh to assist in governing its Irish lordship to the extent that it might otherwise have done. Particularly in the reign of Edward III the controversy was perceived by the English authorities as a significant hindrance to the effective running of the country. In several communications dating from 1363 to 1368 the king upbraided the archbishops of Armagh and Dublin for refusing to follow the example of their counterparts at Canterbury and York in finding a solution to the problem of primacy. Declaring that 'his heart is set upon a speedy agreement', he threatened them with his 'wrath' should they fail to come to an accord and appointed the lieutenant, Lionel, duke of Clarence, to mediate in the dispute.[47] Lionel's efforts came to nothing and the archbishops negated the royal threat to summon them before the council in London to settle the matter by pleading the necessity of their remaining in Ireland to defend their marches against the king's Irish enemies.[48] William Windsor made repeated but unsuccessful attempts to force Archbishop Sweteman to attend parliaments held within the province of Dublin in person, and on 18 January 1371—in the midst of his struggles to extract subsidies from an unwilling settler community—wrote to the archbishops of Armagh and Dublin again urging them to come to an agreement about primacy similar to that which had been reached between the archbishops of Canterbury and York. His efforts proved fruitless, and the archbishops of Armagh continued to avoid attendance at parliament outside the province of Armagh for the rest of the period.[49]

Rancour over the issue of primacy, however, did not prevent the archbishops of Armagh and Dublin from acting together as representatives of the settler community before the king in England, or from cooperating to defend their lands against Irish attacks.[50] Nor did it characterize those aspects of the relationship between the sees arising from the possession by numerous religious institutions in Dublin of benefices and estates in county Louth. Among these institutions was the priory of Holy Trinity, which was attached to one of Dublin's two cathedrals, Christ Church. Archbishop Albrecht Suerbeer of Armagh (1240–6) had sought to modify the rights claimed by Holy Trinity in the manors and churches of Drumshallon and Philipstown Nugent (bar. Ferrard), but a century later its prior was continuing to exercise these rights fully and in 1372 they were confirmed without reservation by Archbishop Sweteman.[51] Links between Holy Trinity and county Louth extended beyond property rights to issues of personnel: in 1411 Archbishop Nicholas Fleming confirmed the election by

---

[46] Ó Fiaich, 'Primacy in the Irish Church', 8.
[47] *CCR 1364–9*, 181; *Reg. Sweteman*, 23–4, 25–6, 45, 128.
[48] Sayles, *Affairs*, 227–8.
[49] *Parls. & Councils*, 26–7, 29–30, 31–2, 36–7, 38–9, 52–3, 73–4; *Reg. Sweteman*, 46.
[50] See above, 141.
[51] BL Add Charter 7041; *Alen's Reg.* 204; *Christ Church Deeds*, 82; *Account Roll of Holy Trinity, Dublin*, 2.

the Augustinian community of Sts Peter and Paul, Knock, as their new abbot of Simon, a canon of Holy Trinity, while in the following year Nicholas Staunton resigned as prior of the Augustinian house of St Mary's, Louth, in order to become prior of Holy Trinity.[52]

Dublin's other cathedral, St Patrick's, held no lands in Louth, but before 1431 was granted the right of presentation to the vicarage of Stabannan (bar. Ardee) by the king during the minority of the lord of Ardee, Thomas Faunt, to whom presentation belonged.[53] John Colton had been dean of St Patrick's before his elevation to Armagh, and his successor as archbishop, Nicholas Fleming, cooperated with his counterpart in Dublin, Thomas Cranley, in facilitating an exchange of benefices between Richard Ragg, archdeacon of Armagh, and Master William Pyrroun, precentor of St Patrick's, Dublin, in 1409.[54] Archbishop John Prene's willingness in 1440 to grant forty days' indulgence to those in his archdiocese willing to contribute alms towards the manufacture of a great bell for St Patrick's cathedral, Dublin, testifies to an underlying element of goodwill in the relationship between the churches of Armagh and Dublin in the late medieval period that can be obscured by a narrow concentration on the controversy surrounding the primacy.[55]

Turning from Dublin's cathedrals to its religious houses, the Cistercian abbey of St Mary the Virgin, Dublin, had succeeded in 1244 in supplanting the Augustinian priory of St Mary's, Louth, in its right to present the vicar to the parish church of St Finian, Drumcar (bar. Ardee), and continued to exercise and defend this right well into the fifteenth century, when it was questioned by the archbishops of Armagh.[56] In the thirteenth century the abbey had held at least 1,400 acres in Louth, but almost all of this land was alienated in the course of the next hundred years.[57] In like manner, the Augustinian abbey of St Thomas the Martyr appears to have shown little interest by the middle of the fourteenth century in grants made to it in Louth around 1200, but its responsibility for several churches in the barony of Ratoath and elsewhere in Meath was confirmed during a visitation of that diocese by Archbishop David Mág Oireachtaigh sometime between 1335 and 1345.[58] A visitation carried out by Archbishop Fitz Ralph in 1355 revealed that the bailiff of St Thomas's had allowed pigs to roam in the cemetery of the church at Donaghmore (bar. Ratoath), where they had exhumed human remains, while the church of Greenoge (bar. Ratoath), for which St Thomas's was also responsible, was in a

---

[52] *Reg. Fleming*, 164–5; *CPL 1404–15*, 281, 313–14.

[53] *Reg. Octaviani*, ii. 57, 89. Faunt's predecessor, also Thomas, died sometime between 1417 and 1425: *Original Letters*, 53–64; COA Rep. Records of the Exchequer, 1 Henry V–39 Henry VI, 19. He reached his majority in 1431: *Reg. Octaviani*, ii. 59–61, 89.

[54] *Reg. Fleming*, 86–8. Pyrroun had acted as a public notary for Milo Sweteman in the 1370s and was vicar of Dunboyne in 1400, at which time he was in Rome as proctor for the bishop of Meath. He ceased to be archdeacon of Armagh sometime after Jan. 1414: *Reg. Sweteman*, 13–15, 246–9; *RCH* 156 no. 4; *Reg. Fleming*, 244.

[55] *Reg. Mey*, 51–2

[56] *Reg. Fleming*, 239; *Reg. Swayne*, 93, 94; Smith, *Colonisation and Conquest*, 58–9.

[57] Colmcille Ó Conbhuí, 'The Lands of St Mary's Abbey, Dublin', *PRIA* 62 (1961–3), C, 69 (map), 70–5.

[58] *Reg. Sweteman*, 1–3; Smith, *Colonisation and Conquest*, 34–5.

state of disrepair and staffed by a chaplain who was illiterate and often drunk.[59] The abbey did, however, have some involvement in the affairs of Louth. In 1395, Pope Boniface IX provided John Sherbourne, a canon of St Thomas's, to the priory of Louth, but he resigned it two years later to return to St Thomas's as abbot.[60] The recorded indebtedness of Richard Verdon to the abbot of St Thomas's in 1380 reveals another link between Louth and this important Dublin house.[61]

The religious establishment in Dublin that proved most active in its dealings with Louth and its community was the hospital of St John of Jerusalem, Kilmainham—the priory of the Knights Hospitallers in Ireland. From the thirteenth century it held preceptories (subordinate communities and the estates that supported them) at Kilmainhambeg and Kilmainham Wood in the parts of Meath near Kells and Nobber that bordered on the territory of O'Reilly, and in 1312 was granted the extensive properties in Louth of the order of the Temple following its suppression.[62] These consisted of the manor of Cooley or Templetown along with the church of Carlingford (bar. Lower Dundalk); Kilsaran (bar. Ardee), to which were attached the fruits and tithes of eleven churches in the barony of Ardee; plots of land in Corlisbane and Dunany (bar. Ferrard); the vicarages of Port and Dunleer (bar. Ferrard); and a number of tenements in Drogheda.[63] The Hospitallers avoided conflict with the archbishop of Armagh by being careful not to challenge his right to institute the candidates they presented to these churches.[64] The archbishop, in turn, ensured that his superiority in this sphere was recognized as, for example, in 1411 when Nicholas Fleming confiscated the revenues of the church of St Mary, Carlingford, because the Hospitallers has allowed its chancel to fall into disrepair.[65] In similar fashion in 1435 Archbishop Swayne informed the prior of Kilmainham that he must present a new vicar to the church of Port on account of the deprivation of the previous incumbent, Richard Gaffney, by the archbishop for offences that included acts of adultery with one of his parishioners.[66] Swayne also held an inquisition into the patronage and vacancy of the church of St Catherine, Kildemock (bar. Ardee), in 1430. On being informed that its rector, Maurice Cussing, had resigned because of the poverty of the church Swayne ordered the

---

[59] *Reg. Sweteman*, 156–8.
[60] *CPL 1362–1404*, 525–6; Bodl Rawl MS B. 502, f. 97 (as referenced in Calendar of Irish Chancery Letters). The fragment of an Irish annal contained in Rawlinson B 488 contains an entry under the year 1396 which may refer to Sherborne's brief tenure of St Mary's, Louth: 'There was a foreign prior in Louth [*Lubha*]—an unusual event for it—and he died forthwith': *Misc. Ir. Annals*, 157.
[61] *RCH* 109 no. 85.
[62] Vanessa Ryan, 'The Archaeology of Medieval Rural Ecclesiastical Settlement in the Barony of Lower Dundalk, County Louth', Ph.D. thesis, University of Dublin, Trinity College (2009). I am grateful to Dr Simms for bringing this work to my attention.
[63] Smith, *Colonisation and Conquest*, 60, 130; D. Mac Iomhair, 'The Knights Templar in County Louth', *Seanchas Ardmhacha*, 4 (1960–1), 72–91; 'Documents Relating to the Suppression of the Templars in Ireland', ed. Gearóid Mac Niocaill, *Anal. Hib.* 24 (1967), 183–226; Gwynn and Hadcock, *Medieval Religious Houses Ireland*, 334–5, 337–8; *Reg. Kilmainham*, 3–4, 20–1, 23, 59–60, 86, 116, 130; *Reg. Octaviani*, ii. 54–5; *Reg. Fleming*, 256.
[64] *Reg. Sweteman*, 3–4, 225; *Reg. Fleming*, 173–4, 233–4; *Reg. Swayne*, 168.
[65] *Reg. Fleming*, 153–4.
[66] *Reg. Swayne*, 161; *Reg. Octaviani*, ii. 55–6.

prior of Kilmainham to augment its value or lose the right of presentation to the archbishop—a command that the prior appears to have obeyed.[67]

The prior in question, William Fitz Thomas, was one of six holders of that office who also served as chief governor of Ireland in the period 1330–1450.[68] Fulfilling their duties as the king's representative in Ireland might oblige these men to spend time in Louth, as in 1335 when Roger Outlaw journeyed through the county on his way to Ulster to fight 'English and Irish felons and enemies' and to parley with O'Neill, O'Reilly, and other northern chiefs.[69] In December 1336, Outlaw, again acting as deputy justiciar, held an inquisition at Ardee into the value of its manor.[70] John Archer witnessed letters as deputy justiciar at Drogheda in March and May 1348, while Thomas Butler, deputy lieutenant, convened a general council there in February 1412.[71] Butler also witnessed letters at Drogheda in November 1410 and March 1412, and at the town of Louth in May 1411.[72] Such excursions might also afford opportunities to visit properties belonging to the Hospitallers: it was at the order's manor of Kilsaran in September 1337 that Outlaw, in his capacity as deputy justiciar, appointed local commissioners to investigate breaches of a truce recently concluded with O'Hanlon.[73] Thomas Butler, while at Kells in September 1410, is likely to have visited the nearby Hospitaller preceptory of Kilmainhambeg.[74] His familiarity with Louth may also have encouraged him to submit a successful petition in 1415 to be awarded custody of two-thirds of the Irish estates of the family of Darcy of Knaith, which were in the king's hands on account of a minority. The manors of Louth, Castlering, and Ash (bar. Louth) made up the bulk of these estates.[75]

Religious houses located in places other than Dublin also had interests in Louth. The Augustinian abbey of St Mary's, Navan (co. Meath), held the manor and rectory of Smarmore (bar. Ardee), while the Cistercian abbey of Newry (co. Down) held land at Newtown Cooley and Irishgrange (bar. Lower Dundalk) and the Augustinian abbey of Sts Peter and Paul, Armagh, had property at the Curragh close to Dundalk.[76] In 1374, the possessions in Louth of Newry and Armagh were confiscated by the crown on the grounds that their abbots and convents 'were mere Irish and mix with the Irish and spend the issues and profits among the said Irish in their maintenance', and were granted to James Bellew.[77] Newry's rights to the rectory of the church of Newtown Cooley were confirmed by Archbishop Colton

---

[67] *Reg. Swayne*, 87; *Reg. Octaviani*, ii. 53, 73–5, 83–4.
[68] Roger Outlaw (1330–1, 1335, 1336–7, 1340–1); John Archer or Larcher (1347–8); William Tany (1373–4); Richard White (1386–8); Thomas Butler (1409–13); William Fitz Thomas (1422): *NHI* ix. 473–6; Wood, 'Chief Governors of Ireland', 225–34.
[69] *RCH* 41 nos. 21, 22; *IEP* 365, 378.
[70] *Inquisitions and Extents*, 160.
[71] TNA E 101/241/13; *RCH* 198 no. 26(c); 199 no. 60; *Reg. Fleming*, 203–4.
[72] BL Add MS 4790, f. 1; *RCH* 197 no. 14; 198 no. 19.
[73] *RCH* 42 no. 6.
[74] *RCH* 196 no. 69.
[75] *RCH* 211 no. 43.
[76] COA Rep. Records of the Exchequer, 1–10 Richard II, 493; Alan J. Bliss, 'The Inscribed Slates at Smarmore', *PRIA* 64 (1965–6), C, 38; Otway-Ruthven, 'Partition of the de Verdon Lands', 421; *Inquisitions and Extents*, 138; TNA C 47/10/20 no. 14.
[77] NLI MS 3, f. 122; COA Rep. Records of the Exchequer, 1–10 Richard II, 289, 365.

in 1390, but it did not regain its lands, which were said in 1394 to have been destroyed by O'Neill.[78] Niall Óc O'Neill also pleaded with Richard II in 1395 to confirm the title of Sts Peter and Paul, Armagh, to a carucate of land and a mill at the Curragh which they had held since before the conquest, but to no avail.[79] The only house from the island of Britain that held land in Louth—not including Drogheda, which will be considered in the following chapter—was the Augustinian abbey of Llanthony in Wales, which possessed the church of St John the Evangelist at Dunany (bar. Ferrard) and several hundred acres of arable land there, as well as land at Parsonstown, Cruisetown, and Killineer also in Ferrard.[80]

Substantial properties in Louth, in short, were held by a large number of religious houses located beyond its borders. These amounted to less in terms of total acreage, however, than the estates possessed by religious houses situated in Louth. The Cistercian abbey of Mellifont owned the manor of Collon (bar. Ferrard), and vigorously defended its right to have weirs on the river Boyne—rights, it asserted, that predated the English conquest.[81] Of the two Augustinian abbeys in the county, Sts Peter and Paul, Knock (bar. Louth), was poorly endowed, and its position on the western fringes of the settlement left it open to attacks from the Irish, such as that conducted by Magnus MacMahon 1428 in which the wheels of its mill were broken, its corn removed, and books, a missal, altar ornaments, and vessels stolen.[82] The nearby abbey of St Mary's, Louth, was also liable to attack by the MacMahons, but was a wealthier house, and when the abbot of Knock resigned and its canons fled for fear of the Irish in 1435, Louth was able to supply a canon, Patrick Ledwich, as Knock's new abbot.[83] Louth had possessions in more secure, eastern, parts of the county such as Philipstown, near Drogheda, as well as at Colpe in county Meath.[84] It also had the right of presentation to the vicarage of Termonfeckin, which ensured regular and for the most part cordial interaction with the archbishops of Armagh who usually resided either at Termonfeckin or their other Louth manor, Dromiskin.[85] The convent of nuns at St Mary's, Termonfeckin, which had lands both there and at Clogherhead and Callystown (bar. Ferrard), acknowledged the authority of the prior of Louth, as did the house of Inchmore (co. Longford).[86]

---

[78] *Reg. Fleming*, 225; COA Rep. Records of the Exchequer, 10–22 Richard II, 229; *RCH* 164 no. 170.

[79] *PKCI* 239–40; Curtis, *Richard II in Ireland*, 124–5, 133–4, 205–6, 213–14; *RCH* 186 no. 83.

[80] *Reg. Sweteman*, 61. For the dedication of Dunany church: *Reg. Octaviani*, ii. 93. Hogan, *Priory of Llanthony*, 217–18, 360–2, and map at 16. This map indicates possession by the Augustinian abbey of Llanthony in Gloucester of land north of Drogheda, but this appears to represent Killineer, which belonged to the abbey in Wales.

[81] TNA E 101/240/9; *Inquisitions and Extents*, 174; *RCH* 46 no. 114; 79 nos. 95, 118; 108 nos. 35–9; COA Rep. Records of the Exchequer, 10–22 Richard II, 165–6; *CPR 1399–1401*, 509–10; Colmcille (Ó Conbhuí), *The Story of Mellifont* (Dublin, 1958), 106–38.

[82] *RCH* 124 no. 59; 127 no. 210; *Reg. Swayne*, 93.

[83] *RCH* 258 no. 78. Ledwich had died by 1440: *Reg. Mey*, 34–5.

[84] *Reg. Octaviani*, ii. 487–8; BL Add MS 13597; Hogan, *Priory of Llanthony*, 381; Gwynn and Hadcock, *Medieval Religious Houses Ireland*, 185–6.

[85] *Reg. Sweteman*, 38, 116, 130, 197; *Reg. Fleming*, 240.

[86] *Reg. Swayne*, 183; *Rep. DKI* 44, 36; *CPL 1431–47*, 453; Gwynn and Hadcock, *Medieval Religious Houses Ireland*, 324; Kenny, *Anglo-Irish and Gaelic Women in Ireland*, 180–1.

The Augustinian canons known as the *Fratres Cruciferi* had hospitals with attached urban property in Drogheda and Dundalk, while their house at Ardee, dedicated to St John the Baptist, held considerable estates in the baronies of Ardee and Louth. These were confirmed to it in 1385, but it failed to have its claim to have the right of presentation to the parish church of Ardee recognized, and this remained with the lord of Ardee.[87] In conjunction with the abbey of St Mary's, Louth, it shared the right of presentation to the churches of Donaghmoyne and Ros (Carrickmacross) in the diocese of Clogher, which were in territory controlled by MacMahon. The importance of the Ardee house as a frontier institution was demonstrated in 1425 when it served as the venue for the meeting at which a treaty was concluded between that chief and the lieutenant, James Butler, earl of Ormond.[88] The landed wealth of the largest religious houses in Louth, and the role played by some of them in the defence of the settlement, was reflected in the summonses their abbots or priors might receive to attend parliament, and the service they might be called upon to offer as keepers of the peace.[89]

The most important ecclesiastical landowner in Louth was the archbishop of Armagh, who held the manors of Termonfeckin (bar. Ferrard) and Dromiskin (bar. Louth). In 1331, Archbishop Stephen Segrave had been briefly awarded custody of the manor of Ardee, vacant since the murder of John Bermingham, earl of Louth, in 1329, but the request by his successor, David Mág Oireachtaigh in *c*.1335 that the lordship of Ardee be awarded in perpetuity to the archbishops of Armagh 'because all their lands have been burned and destroyed by the Irish', came to nothing.[90] On the northern and western frontiers of the settlement in Louth the archbishops also claimed land at Newry (co. Down), Ivermongan (possibly Magoney, bar. Farney, co. Monaghan), and Iniskeen (bar. Farney).[91] Effective control over such places was difficult to establish, and the archbishops were content to grant their rights there to Louth settlers whom they wished to reward and patronize. In 1411, for instance, Archbishop Fleming granted Ivermongan and its tithes for forty-eight years to his chamberlain (*camerario nostro*), John Ruffus.[92] Milo Sweteman's rights in Iniskeen were contested by John Hadsor of Cappoge in the late 1360s, but the latter had failed to enforce his claim by the time of his death in 1385.[93] In 1375, Milo granted the manor to Roger Gernon, lord of Gernonstown

---

[87] Gwynn and Hadcock, *Medieval Religious Houses Ireland*, 210–13; *Christ Church Deeds*, 167, 186; *RCH* 196 no. 76; *Reg. Swayne*, 8; Bodl., MS Rawl. B. 502, f. 14; *Dowdall Deeds*, 174; *Reg. Octaviani*, ii. 57, 59–61, 89; Sayles, *Affairs*, 147–8; *CCR 1330–3*, 238–9; Aubrey Gwynn, 'Ardee in the Middle Ages', *CLAJ* 11 (1946), 88.

[88] *Reg. Fleming*, 151–3; *Handbook and Select Calendar…Ireland*, 222.

[89] Lynch, *View of the Legal Institutions*, 324; Betham, *Origin and History*, 322–3; *RCH* 265 no. 13 *PKCI* 305–8 (where St John's, Ardee, is mistakenly called St Peter's). Frame, 'Commissions of the Peace in Ireland', 21–3.

[90] TNA E 101/239/27; *Rep. DKI* 44, 38–9, 44–5; Connolly, 'Ancient Petitions', 87.

[91] TNA E 101/241/4; E 101/243/12; *Vetera Monumenta*, 295–6; *CPL 1342–62*, 398–9; Smith, *Colonisation and Conquest*, 91.

[92] *Reg. Fleming*, 176.

[93] *Reg. Sweteman*, 32–3, 35–6; *Dowdall Deeds*, 100; *CPR 1381–5*, 544; *RCH* 127 no. 201.

(now Castlebellingham, bar. Ardee), for five years in lieu of the annual pension that he had awarded to him, but in reality Iniskeen—some 12 kilometres west of Dundalk—was under the control of the MacMahons; a fact left unaltered by Archbishop Swayne's grant of it to Roger Gernon, lord of Killincoole (bar. Louth), in 1437.[94]

Of more value to the archbishops than these marcher properties were their estates in Meath. The manor of Kilmoon (bar. Skreen), for instance, contained a valuable fishery at Primatestown.[95] Archbishop Mág Oireachtaigh successfully defended the rights of his church to the manor of Nobber, close to Louth in co. Meath, which had been granted to Armagh in 1241 by Hugh Lacy.[96] In 1342 the deputy justiciar, John Morice, heard a case between the archbishop and Sir William London concerning the manor, and Richard Fitz Ralph and his successors were careful to have their rights there recognized.[97] Shortly before he died of plague in 1383, William London granted to Archbishop John Colton all his rights in the manor of Athboy (bar. Lune, co. Meath) and, before February 1399, Richard II supplemented this gift by donating to Armagh his rights of patronage in the parish church of St James.[98] Relations between the archbishops of Armagh and their suffragan bishops of Meath were not always easy, with rights of visitation a particular source of tension, and the frequency with which Archbishops Nicholas Fleming and John Swayne resided at Athboy in the first third of the fifteenth century may have had something to do with a desire to maintain a visible presence in the Meath diocese on the part of Armagh.[99]

Given the prominence of the Church in co. Louth as an owner of lands and benefices, it is no surprise that it played a major role in the development of settler society in the area.[100] It provided education and subsequent employment to young men from local families who might enjoy within its ranks long and varied careers that brought them into contact with a world much wider than their lay counterparts in Louth would ever experience.[101] While the early stages of learning for interested children were provided by local priests in the parish churches and chantries of Smarmore, Ardee, Dundalk, Drogheda, and elsewhere, the future for those destined for a clerical career and who wished to pursue their studies to a higher level

[94] *Reg. Sweteman*, 154; *Reg. Swayne*, 72, 100, 161, 171–2.
[95] *Rep. DKI 44*, 36; *Reg. Swayne*, 48, 49, 64; Griffith, 'Talbot–Ormond Struggle', 396–7.
[96] *Reg. Fleming*, 201–2.
[97] TNA KB 27/369 m. 64; *Reg. Sweteman*, 65–6, 81–2, 160, 244–5. Presentation to the church of Nobber rested with the bishop of Meath and was attached to the archdeaconry of Kells: *CPR 1377–81*, 555, 589; *CCR 1389–92*, 548; *CPL 1417–31*, 149; *Reg. Swayne*, 48.
[98] *A. Clon.* 309; *RCH* 193 no. 185; COA Rep. Records of the Exchequer, 10–22 Richard II, 142–6; *CPL 1396–1404*, 265.
[99] *Reg. Fleming*, 84, 178, 197–200, 205–7, 229–31, 257; *Reg. Swayne*, 52, 119. For Meath's resistance to Armagh's rights of visitation: *Reg. Octaviani*, ii. 485–6; *Reg. Sweteman*, 1–3, 226–7; *RCH* 62 no. 100; *Reg. Fleming*, 218–21. In 1434 Archbishop Swayne had a sentence of excommunication against the archdeacon and clergy of Meath for non-payment of procurations arising from a visitation read out at the high cross at Bothe St in Drogheda: *Reg. Mey*, 6–7, 62–3.
[100] For a useful comparison with north-west England see Bennett, *Community, Class and Careerism*, 134–61.
[101] Jefferies, *Priests and Prelates of Armagh*, 38–42.

lay beyond Louth and Ireland, at Oxford or Cambridge.[102] In an attempt to raise funds in June 1369, soon after his arrival as the king's lieutenant in Ireland, William Windsor, in the name of Edward III, ordered Milo Sweteman to sequester the benefices of priests from his province residing outside Ireland, and to transmit a list of the valuations of the benefices and the names of their holders to the Irish chancery. Milo had complied with regard to his own diocese by the middle of September, and appended the list of clergy to his reply to the king. It reported that from the deanery of Drogheda Andrew Waring, rector of the church of Beaulieu, and John Cusack, rector of Rath (= Rathdrumin, bar. Ferrard) had been given licence by the archbishop to study at Oxford; from the deanery of Ardee similar licence had been given to David Brakden, rector of Darver; and from the deanery of Dundalk James Staunton, vicar of St Nicholas's, Dundalk, was in Oxford with his permission.[103]

Windsor's intention was to profit from, but certainly not to end or curtail, the long-established practice by which clergy from places such as Louth travelled to England to further their education. Some of these students—such as Richard Fitz Ralph and John Prene—returned to serve at the highest levels in the archdiocese of Armagh after lengthy periods of study, whereas others remained in England.[104] Of the absent priests listed by Milo Sweteman in 1369, for instance, Adam Waring was still abroad in 1381 while John Cusack had returned to Rathdrumin before 1374, and was one of the two proctors for the clergy chosen by Archbishop Sweteman to represent him before the king in England in 1376.[105] In March 1365 Sweteman had given licence to the parson of Kilcurly (bar. Upper Dundalk), Richard Hopper, to study letters in London (*studio literarum Londoni*), but in September 1367 he ordered him to return to his cure before the end of the following February, even though the term of his release had not yet expired.[106] The parson of Stabannan, Thomas Brown, was given licence to study at Oxford in 1386, and appears not to have returned by the time of his death in 1389.[107] Not for the first time, succession to the church of Stabannan was contested by interested clerics from both England and Ireland, but by 1393 a winner had emerged in the person of the Irish-born John Whitehead.[108] In May of that year, Whitehead was licensed to be absent from Ireland for ten years but had

---

[102] Bliss, 'Inscribed Slates at Smarmore', 33–60. See also his comments in *Notes and Queries*, 212 (1967), 85. Murray, 'Ancient Chantries of Co. Louth', 181–208. For the suggestion that Richard Fitz Ralph received his earliest education at the Franciscan house in Dundalk: Walsh, *Fourteenth-Century Scholar and Primate*, 10–13.
[103] *Reg. Sweteman*, 58–62.
[104] For the sojourns of Nicholas Fleming and John Prene in England before they became archbishops, see above, 137–8.
[105] *RCH* 117 no. 69; COA Rep. Records of the Exchequer, 10–22 Richard II, 301; Clarke, 'William of Windsor in Ireland', 123. For those who remained in England: Virginia Davis, 'Irish Clergy in Late Medieval England', *IHS* 32 (2000), 145–60.
[106] *Reg. Sweteman*, 94, 227–8; *CPR 1364–7*, 133.
[107] *RCH* 127 nos. 228, 230; 136 no. 182; 143 no. 42.
[108] Sayles, 'Ecclesiastical Process and the Parsonage of Stabannon in 1351', 1–23; *CPR 1389–92*, 99, 109, 166, 167. For John's Irish birth: *CPR 1413–16*, 133. For his career see Ó Clabaigh, *Friars in Ireland*, 156–8.

returned to his cure by 1401, at which time his preaching against an indulgence in favour of the Dominicans at Drogheda attracted the ire of Pope Boniface IX.[109] Whitehead stood in better odour with his king, who granted his request in 1406 to found a perpetual chantry in his church, and in 1409 he was chosen by Archbishop Fleming as one of his proctors at the Council of Pisa.[110] He had returned to Ireland by June 1411, but in November of the following year was once more in England where he was permitted to remain until at least the end of 1414. He still held the rectory of Stabannan in 1415, but whether he ever visited Ireland again after 1412 is unclear.[111]

Some members of the clergy in Louth chose to study at the universities of Oxford or Cambridge, having already attained significant advancement in Ireland. Thomas Russell had served as vicar of St Peter's, Drogheda, for over a year when, in August 1410, he was permitted to study in England for five years while continuing to receive the fruits pertaining to his benefice.[112] He appears not to have returned to Ireland upon graduating as a Bachelor of Canon Law, but displayed great commitment to defending and extending his ecclesiastical interests both there and in England up to the time of his death at the papal court in 1429.[113] In 1413, he obtained a canonry in Dublin and between then and 1428 added to it the archdeaconry of Kells, to which was attached the vicarage of Nobber, and a canonry at Lincoln cathedral.[114] William Mowner was parson of the church of St Mary's, Mansfieldstown, in 1395 when Archbishop Colton secured licence for him to study at Oxford for four years.[115] As Bachelor of Canon and Civil Law he was appointed as his proctor in Rome in September 1405 by Colton's successor, Nicholas Fleming, and on his return to Ireland before February 1407 was assigned the role of president of the diocesan court.[116] He was with Archbishop Fleming at his manor of Termonfeckin on 22 August 1410 when the latter appointed John Swayne as one of his proctors at Rome, and continued to hold Mansfieldstown and serve as official of the archbishop's court until his death early in 1412.[117] Henry Logan, parson of Dromin (bar. Ardee), was licensed in 1414 to absent himself from Ireland for three years in order to study at Oxford and Cambridge, and graduated as a Bachelor of Civil and Canon Law.[118] He had returned to Ireland by March 1416, and put his legal expertise at the disposal of a succession of archbishops of Armagh for the following thirty-five years, serving

---

[109] COA Rep. Records of the Exchequer, 10–22 Richard II, 169; *CPR 1396–9*, 576; *CPL 1396–1404*, 432–3; Urban Flanagan, 'Papal Letters of the Fifteenth Century as a Source for Irish History', *PICHC* (1958), 11–15.
[110] *CPR 1405–8*, 178; *Reg. Fleming*, 64, 97–8; *RCH* 189 no. 2.
[111] *CPL 1404–15*, 291; *CPR 1413–6*, 133; *RCH* 202 no. 8; *Rotuli Selecti*, 44.
[112] *Reg. Fleming*, 110–11; *RCH* 192 no. 134; *CPR 1408–13*, 203.
[113] *CPL 1427–47*, 100.
[114] *De Annatis Hiberniae*, 3, 59–60; *RCH* 201 no. 2; *CPL 1417–31*, 199–200; *CPL 1427–47*, 58.
[115] *CPR 1391–6*, 645.
[116] COA Rep. Records of the Exchequer, Henry IV, 257; *Reg. Fleming*, 5–6, 15, 35–6; *CPL 1404–15*, 56. For a discussion of the significance of the court see *Reg. Octaviani*, i, iii–lx. For its operation in the province of Canterbury: Du Boulay, *Lordship of Canterbury*, 297–312.
[117] *Dowdall Deeds*, 151–2; *Reg. Fleming*, 64, 79–80, 130–2, 154–6, 168–70, 200–1.
[118] *RCH* 205 no. 59; *Reg. Swayne*, 122.

as president of the diocesan court and acting as one of Archbishop Mey's proctors at the Dublin parliament of October 1449.[119]

What this suggests is that in the administration of their diocese and province the archbishops of Armagh could call upon the services of educated men whose experience of the world stretched far beyond the shores of Ireland. In 1343, Archbishop Mág Oireachtaigh informed the pope that Roger Sampford, on whose behalf he successfully petitioned for a canonry at Armagh, had by that time already visited 'the Roman court'—that is, Avignon—in connection with diocesan business on six occasions.[120] He was there again between 1346 and 1348, successfully securing the pallium for Archbishop Fitz Ralph, and served thereafter in the diocese of Armagh, both as apostolic notary and as vicar of Termonfeckin.[121] Nor were the archbishops restricted in their search for capable officials to men of Irish birth. William Somerwell, who served as registrar of Armagh between 1429 and c.1458 and was also a canon of the diocese, was originally from Bristol and appears to have been related to another William Somerwell who acted briefly as archdeacon of Armagh in 1426. Somerwell was promoted to the order of deacon at St Peter's, Drogheda, in 1429 and was ordained a priest before May 1431 when he was instituted to the rectory of St Peter's, Rathdrumin.[122] In 1436, he was nominated by Archbishop Swayne, who was too ill to attend in person, to act as his proctor at a parliament summoned at Drogheda, and in June 1443 he recorded how Archbishop Prene, being ill and hoping for better health (*sperans se meliorem sanitatem*), arranged to be carried between two horses from Dromiskin to Termonfeckin, where he died two days later.[123]

The high calibre of administrative expertise at their disposal was especially helpful to the archbishops of Armagh when it came to choosing proctors to represent them at the parliaments convened outside of the province of Armagh that they refused to attend in person. They might select their representatives from among both the clergy and the laity, as did Milo Sweteman who in 1369 chose Master John Strode, rector of Stabannan, and John Clinton, lord of Drumcashel, as his proctors and attorneys at the Dublin parliament due to meet on 30 July of that year.[124] Strode had succeeded in establishing his position at Stabannan in 1355 after a lengthy struggle with a rival claimant, John Teeling, and went on to provide more than twenty-five years of counsel and service to his archbishop.[125] He acted once more as Archbishop Sweteman's proctor at a parliament at Dublin in April 1370, and in July 1373 witnessed the peace agreement concluded by the archbishop and the justiciar, Robert

[119] *Reg. Fleming*, 82; *Reg. Swayne*, 124–5, 175, 190, 195; *Reg. Mey*, 76–8, 89, 100–1; *Reg. Octaviani*, ii. 54–5.
[120] *CPL 1342–62*, 96, 100.
[121] Sayles, 'Ecclesiastical Process and the Parsonage of Stabannon', 13; *Reg. Sweteman*, 50–1.
[122] *Reg. Mey*, xliii–iv, 61–2; *Reg. Swayne*, 48, 56; *Reg. Octaviani*, ii. 88, 100–1; Watt, 'The Medieval Chapter of Armagh Cathedral', 236–7.
[123] *Reg. Swayne*, 165; *Reg. Mey*, 291–2.
[124] *Reg. Sweteman*, 41–2; *Parls. & Councils*, 26–7.
[125] Sayles, 'Ecclesiastical Process and the Parsonage of Stabannon', 1–23; BL Add MS 4790, ff. 27b–28. For his attendance on the archbishop: *Reg. Sweteman*, 31–2, 246–9. For his provision of counsel: *Reg. Sweteman*, 177.

Ashton, with Niall O'Neill and the Irish of Ulster.[126] Among the proctors selected by Archbishop Nicholas Fleming to represent him at the Dublin parliament of October 1409 was a later vicar of Stabannan, Thomas Hadsor, who held that church until his death in 1431.[127] He had already represented the clergy of Armagh at a council at Naas in June 1398 that granted a subsidy to the lieutenant, Roger Mortimer, and in 1402 had been elected as one of the assessors for the deanery of Dundalk of a subsidy granted by the clergy of Armagh to another lieutenant, Thomas of Lancaster.[128] Archbishop John Swayne's preferred clerical proctors included John Elliot, Bachelor of Laws and president of the diocesan court, who from 1430 was rector of St Columba's, Clonmore, and represented Swayne at parliaments convened at Dublin in 1435, 1436, and 1438.[129] James Leche, Bachelor of Laws, curator of wills in the deaneries of Ardee and Dundalk, and rector of Dunbin (bar. Upper Dundalk), was Archbishop John Mey's usual choice to act as proctor at parliament, attending sessions on his behalf at Dublin in 1446 and 1449, and at Naas in 1447.[130]

The archbishops of Armagh were summoned to parliament not only because of their high ecclesiastical office, but also because they were great temporal lords. Parliament provided an arena for the occasional expression of the political aspect of their lordship, but Louth was the location for its routine manifestation in the economic and social spheres. As substantial landowners in the county the archbishops required the services of a range of officials to administer their estates and maximize the revenues that might be collected from them. Some sense of the scale and complexity of what this entailed is conveyed in a letter patent issued by Archbishop Fleming in 1408. In it he announced the appointment of John Fleming of Mortoun (bar. Morgallion, co. Meath) and Richard White of Kilmoon (bar. Skreen, co. Meath) to supervise all his tenants throughout the diocese among the English (*inter Anglicos*), whether free tenants, farmers, or gavellers. The powers granted to the two men included the right to take possession of rents from tenants and receivers and to audit the accounts of seneschals, bailiffs, provosts, receivers, serjeants, and other servants of the archbishop. They might also supervise the workings of his courts and receive the amercements (financial penalties) imposed by these courts on his tenants.[131] In similar fashion, in November 1426 Archbishop Swayne appointed William Somerwell, archdeacon of Armagh, Walter Rowe and Peter Cham[b]er, his chaplains, as auditors for the manors of Dromiskin, Termonfeckin, and Kilmoon, the demesnes of Nobber, the new town of Chauncelton near Athboy, and his other lands and rents.[132]

---

[126] *Parls. & Councils*, 31–2; *Reg. Sweteman*, 14–15, 45.
[127] *Reg. Fleming*, 98–9, 143–4; *Reg. Swayne*, 93–4; *Reg. Octaviani*, ii. 57, 73–5, 89.
[128] RIA MS 12 D 10, 185; *RCH* 166 no. 253.
[129] *Reg. Swayne*, 151–2, 161–2, 178, *Reg. Mey*, 6–7, 62–3; *Reg. Octaviani*, ii. 73.
[130] *Reg. Swayne*, 193, 194–5; *Reg. Mey*, 7–8.
[131] *Reg. Fleming*, 76; Aubrey Gwynn, *The Medieval Province of Armagh 1470–1545* (Dundalk, 1946), 86–9. For the appointment by Sweteman of a receiver at Kilmoon in 1365: *Reg. Sweteman*, 170.
[132] *Reg. Swayne*, 48, 104.

An inquisition held before Archbishop Fitz Ralph at his vill of Nobber in 1351 provides some insight into the nature of the lordship exercised by the archbishops at manorial level. It revealed that by long-established custom the community of Nobber elected two of their number, of whom one was chosen by the archbishop or his seneschal to act as provost. The provost was responsible for levying the profits of the manor and accounted for them to the archbishop or his seneschal, with the serjeant of the vill also acting as the archbishop's serjeant.[133] In June 1427 Archbishop Swayne directed Peter Morgan, the receiver of moneys and rents due to him from his manor of Dromiskin, to deliver to William Swayne, his bailiff there, '12d for the labour of Simon Moule; 6d for that of Robert Moule; for fish, 2d; for shoes for Donald of the stable, 2d; for mowing the meadows next autumn, 20d; for the labour of the thatchers of houses to be done next, 3s 4d'.[134] Another glimpse into how an ecclesiastical lord in Louth might exercise his rights of lordship in practice is offered by the account roll of the priory of Holy Trinity, Dublin, which covers the period between 1337 and 1346. On Friday 21 November 1337 the prior and his party dined at Drogheda on bread, wine, ale, oysters, butter, cheese, and fish, before riding the 8 kilometres to the priory's manor of Drumshallon. There they remained until Sunday before returning to Drogheda in time for a dinner that included fowl sent from the manor. The seneschal of the priory in this period, John Comyn, was a frequent visitor to Louth, holding a session of the manor court of Drumshallon during Lent in 1345, and receiving money and provisions from its tenants during his sojourn there.[135]

With the responsibilities that accompanied their position as great spiritual and temporal lords came opportunities for the archbishops of Armagh to bestow patronage and demonstrate good lordship in Louth. Some holders of the office looked close to home for worthy recipients of their bounty. Richard Fitz Ralph, for instance, secured the rectory of Trim for his nephew and namesake in 1353, while in July 1378—soon after the return of the papacy to Rome—Archbishop Sweteman appointed as his proctor at the curia his nephew, Master Maurice Sweteman, Bachelor of Civil Law and rector of Kilcurly.[136] Maurice had returned to Ireland by May 1381, by which time he had been elevated to the position of archdeacon of Armagh, a dignity he was to hold for the next twenty years.[137] Robert Sweteman, who may also have been a member of the same family, began a long and successful ecclesiastical career in Louth in 1412 when he was ordained a priest at Dundalk. Three

---

[133] *Reg. Sweteman*, 244–5. For the appointment by Swayne of a seneschal at Termonfeckin in 1426: *Reg. Swayne*, 47; and at Kilmoon in 1431–2: *Reg. Sweteman*, 166–7.
[134] *Reg. Swayne*, 57.
[135] *Account Roll of Holy Trinity, Dublin*, 2, 42, 43, 93–5, 103–4, 109.
[136] *Reg. Sweteman*, xiii. 177, 252–4; Walsh, *Fourteenth-Century Scholar and Primate*, 14, 243–6, 315–18.
[137] Hogan, *Priory of Llanthony*, 360–2; *CPR 1389–92*, 265–6; TNA E 101/247/1; *De Annatis Hiberniae*, 2–3; *CPL 1417–31*, 559. William Morice had acted as archdeacon until at least 1369: *Reg. Sweteman*, 59–60, 225. Richard More, vicar of Termonfeckin, was appointed archdeacon in 1402 or shortly before, and held the office at his death in 1408: *Dowdall Deeds*, 132, 144; *RCH* 163 no. 138; COA Rep. Records of the Exchequer, Henry IV, 239; *Reg. Fleming*, 41, 42, 77–8, 140–2. Anthony Lynch, 'The Archdeacons of Armagh 1417–71', *CLAJ* 19 (1979), 218–26.

years later he was presented to the vicarage of Dunleer by its patron, the prior of Kilmainham, and held it until 1450 when he exchanged it for the rectory of Drakestown in Meath.[138] Patronage might also extend to relatives who were not in Holy Orders. It is likely that the William Swayne who served as bailiff of the archiepiscopal manor of Dromiskin in the 1420s was related to Archbishop John Swayne, who was a native of the diocese of Kildare. By 1436, John's sister, Joneta Swayne, and her husband, John White of Dublin, had taken up residence in Drogheda, within easy reach of the archbishop's manor of Termonfeckin.[139]

Those archbishops of Armagh in this period who originated in Meath—Nicholas Fleming, John Prene, and, possibly, John Mey—were members of well-established families in the area. The William Mey, priest of the diocese of Meath, who served as vicar of Kilcurly for at least twenty-six years up to the time of his death in 1428, and acted as a public notary during the same period, was probably related to John Mey, while Prene perhaps counted among his ancestors the John Prene who was seneschal of Drogheda in Meath in 1338.[140] The social background of Nicholas Fleming, who first appears in the records as vicar of Drumconrath (bar. Lower Slane) in 1381, was even more exalted, as he appears to have been a member of the family that provided the barons of Slane throughout the period.[141] In 1393, he and Thomas Fleming, baron of Slane, granted an annual pension to John Dowdall of Dundalk as a reward for the good service the latter had already provided and would render in the future.[142] As archbishop, Nicholas employed John Fleming of Mortoun—presumably a relative—as supervisor of his tenants and as a messenger to the bishop of Meath in 1408, but the initiation of legal proceedings against Nicholas by Thomas Fleming, baron of Slane, in 1410, in connection with the church of Rathdrumin, suggests that the archbishop put some distance between himself and the interests of his family.[143]

The archbishops of Armagh led busy, public, lives that allowed no concessions to a distinct, undisturbed, private sphere. Archbishop Fitz Ralph was awoken late one February evening in 1354 at his manor of Dromiskin to be told that the Hungarian pilgrim, George Grissaphan, who had returned from St Patrick's Purgatory, needed to see him in Dundalk immediately. In a subsequent missive to Grissaphan, Fitz Ralph described how 'on receipt of these letters we rose from our bed at midnight and that same Tuesday we came to Dundalk, performing a severer

---

[138] *Reg. Fleming*, 224–5, 256; *Reg. Octaviani*, ii. 54–5, 57, 73–5; *Reg. Mey*, 7–8, 191–3, 280–3, 299–303.

[139] *Reg. Swayne*, 57, 115, 165. Swayne was not an uncommon surname in Louth: *Reg Kilmainham*, 23 (Richard Swayne, 1330); Otway-Ruthven, 'Partition of the de Verdon Lands', 429 (Robert Swayne, 1332); *Dowdall Deeds*, 100 (Roger Swayne, 1372); *Dowdall Deeds*, 182 (Thomas Swayne, 1443); *CPR 1345–8*, 168 (William Swayne, 1346).

[140] *RCH* 166 no. 253; *Reg. Swayne*, 96; *Reg. Fleming*, 141–2. Mey's notarial mark is reproduced opposite the title page of *Reg. Fleming*. For John Prene: 'Ancient Deeds', 25. The William Prene 'layman of Armagh' who witnessed a deed at Termonfeckin in June 1439 was probably also a relative: *Reg. Swayne*, 181.

[141] *RCH* 109 no. 115; 130 no. 62; *Dowdall Deeds*, 122.

[142] *Dowdall Deeds*, 132.

[143] *Reg. Fleming*, 76, 80–2, 138.

journey than we have for a great time and we are much wearied this Wednesday by the travelling at our manor of Dromiskin'.[144] Fitz Ralph's successor, Milo Sweteman, was also in bed at Dromiskin in September 1367 when he was handed a letter from the dean of Armagh detailing the miseries endured by the church of Armagh and requesting the absolution from excommunication of O'Neill and O'Hanlon.[145] Not only slumber, but also ingestion might have to yield to pressure of business for the archbishop and his entourage. Sweteman was at the dinner table at Termonfeckin with one of his suffragan bishops and other companions sometime late in 1373 when news reached them that Thomas Verdon and others had broken into the church of Feld (Haynestown). They arose at once to investigate and were together at Termonfeckin the following day when a furious Verdon confronted the archbishop in his chapel.[146]

The archbishops conducted regular business in the halls of their manors. On 2 January 1370 Sweteman was in the hall at Dromiskin, surrounded by a large number of clergy and laymen of local importance, including Sir Thomas Verdon and the prior of St Leonard's, Dundalk, when a royal writ arrived summoning him to parliament. Sweteman replied that the writ, which had reached him after the ninth hour, had arrived too late to be acted upon immediately.[147] The more private room in the manorial residence, the chamber, was also the regular venue for the conduct of business by the archbishops. It was there, always in the presence of other members of the clergy, that the archbishops are recorded handing letters of safe conduct to messengers, receiving oaths of loyalty from servants and making payments to them, accepting the resignation of benefices, and dispensing clerical petitioners of their illegitimacy.[148]

As these examples remind us, the archbishops of Armagh, like all great lords, maintained large households and had around them advisers and friends who constituted the informal but important structure of support known as the *familia*.[149] For ecclesiastical lords the difference between family and *familia* may have been slight, and at his death at Termonfeckin in June 1443 John Prene perhaps drew comfort from the presence at his bed of 'diversi sui familiares'.[150] No doubt Richard Fitz Ralph was accompanied on his 10-kilometre night-time dash to Dundalk in February 1354 by some sleepy attendants, and when two months later he was permitted to come before the king and his council in England to pursue his affairs it was stipulated that he do so 'with a moderate household'.[151] Frequent travel was a defining feature of lordship, and their obligation to preach and to conduct regular visitations of the dioceses within their province meant that the archbishops of Armagh were regularly itinerant. During his first visit to

---

[144] Leslie, *St Patrick's Purgatory*, 52–4; Haren, 'Two Hungarian Pilgrims', 120–1.
[145] *Reg. Sweteman*, 205–6.
[146] *Reg. Sweteman*, 246–9. See above, 63–5.
[147] *Reg. Sweteman*, 42–3; *Parls. & Councils*, 29–30; *Reg. Swayne*, 165.
[148] *Reg. Sweteman*, 31–2, 98–9, 135–6, 206–7; *Reg. Fleming*, 15; *Reg. Swayne*, 181, 191–2.
[149] For household and *familia* see Davies, *Lords and Lordship*, 82–113.
[150] *Reg. Mey*, 291–2.
[151] *CCR 1349–54*, 537.

Ireland between April 1348 and the early summer of 1349, Archbishop Fitz Ralph delivered sermons at Dundalk, Louth, Ardee, Drogheda, and Mansfieldstown, while in September 1351 he preached at Coleraine, at the northern extreme of his province.[152] A detailed contemporary account of the visit undertaken in 1397 by Archbishop Colton to the vacant diocese of Derry reveals the size of the entourage that accompanied him on such journeys. The village of Cappagh (bar. Omagh, co. Tyrone) lacked sufficient buildings to house the primate and his retinue (*dominum Primatem et suam comitivam*), and seven horses were required to transport the possessions of the travelling party as it journeyed towards its destination. The archbishop was accompanied on his mission by numerous members of the clergy from both the Irish and English parts of his diocese and also by Thomas Talbot, Richard Bagot, and Richard White, his squires (*domicelli*).[153]

Service in the episcopal household was an important marker of social and political status for some settlers in county Louth, and was regarded as a significant indicator of their own powers of local patronage by the archbishops. Milo Sweteman distributed robes and pensions on an annual basis to members of his council and to his squires (*armigeri/domicelli*), and in 1368 was careful to describe John Clinton, lord of Drumcashel, and Robert Gilys as 'familiarem nostrum', when announcing their appointment as his proctors and attorneys at a parliament summoned at Dublin.[154] The institution of the household, however, did not circumscribe the powers of lordship of the archbishops: they frequently looked beyond this body when choosing proctors to represent them at parliament, and followed the same practice when seeking advice and support in executing their duties. It is unlikely that the Simon Gernon, *narrator* (legal advocate), to whom Milo Sweteman awarded a yearly pension of 20s in 1365 'for his faithful service and advice, past and future', was a member of his household, and the same is probably true of Nicholas Moynagh who in 1422 was granted an annual pension of 40s for similar service by Archbishop Swayne.[155]

In the same manner, for those laymen from Louth who accepted service in the episcopal household, the significance of this commitment might vary over time and in relation to other aspects of their careers. Our only record of Richard Clinton is as *domicellus* to Archbishop Sweteman in the late 1360s, but his kinsman, John Clinton, lord of Drumcashel, who was seneschal of the episcopal household in the same years, had previously served as sheriff and escheator of Louth in

---

[152] Alan J. Fletcher, *Late Medieval Preaching in Britain and Ireland: Texts, Studies, and Interpretations* (Turnhout, 2009), 259–61.

[153] *Acts of Colton*, 7, 14, 16, 18.

[154] *Reg. Sweteman*, 37–8, 89, 116–17, 194–5; *Parls. & Councils*, 25–6. Clinton had acted as Sweteman's proctor at the Kilkenny parliament of Feb. 1366 which passed the Statutes of Kilkenny: *Reg. Sweteman*, 113–14; *Parls. & Councils*, 22–3. He served in the same capacity at the Dublin parliament of July 1369: *Reg. Sweteman*, 41–2; *Parls. & Councils*, 26–7.

[155] *Reg. Sweteman*, 84–5. An earlier Master Simon Gernon was awarded a yearly pension of 100s by Archbishop Segrave in 1331: *CPR 1330–4*, 110. For Moynagh: *Reg. Swayne*, 37. He was still in receipt of his pension in 1444: *Reg. Swayne*, 191–2.

1355–6.¹⁵⁶ For some, membership of the episcopal household might continue for many years, and might involve an element of promotion: Richard White, who accompanied Archbishop Colton to Derry 1397, was first described as a squire of the archbishop in 1390.¹⁵⁷ In 1411, Archbishop Nicholas Fleming referred to him as 'our squire' (*nostro armigero*) and in the following year he held the title of marshal (*marascallus*) to the archbishop.¹⁵⁸ He retained this title in 1416 when Fleming appointed him as one of his proctors at a great council summoned at Naas, and he acted as administrator of the archbishop's goods upon his death later in the same year.¹⁵⁹ By 1419, he had been elevated to the position of seneschal, which in this context suggests leadership of the episcopal household as whole.¹⁶⁰

For the majority of those who served in the household of the archbishops of Armagh, however, the association was occasional rather than long-lasting and represented a welcome additional sign of prestige rather than a defining marker of social status. The two other squires who along with Richard White accompanied Archbishop Colton to Derry in 1397 are not subsequently mentioned in relation to the household, but went on to have important careers in Louth. Richard Bagot was lord of Carrickbaggot (bar. Ferrard) and claimed the right of presentation to the rectory of the church there.¹⁶¹ He appears to have studied law in England, was elected to parliament for Louth along with Bartholomew Verdon in 1420, served as a justice and keeper of the peace in the county in 1421, and in 1425 was one of those who witnessed the agreement between the lieutenant, James Butler, earl of Ormond, and Brian MacMahon at Ardee.¹⁶² The career of Thomas Talbot is less easy to analyse, as the records usually fail to distinguish between two contemporaries of that name, one from Louth and the other from Meath.¹⁶³ It is likely that the Thomas Talbot who accompanied Colton to Armagh hailed from Kiltallaght (bar. Ferrard) in Louth and was the same individual who had acted as translator in March 1395 for MacDonald and two O'Hanlons as they submitted to Richard II at Drogheda.¹⁶⁴ He remained close to Colton, who recommended his services as a translator to Ramon de Perellós as he set out to meet O'Neill in 1397, and late in 1400 was appointed as justice of the peace, commissioner of array, and sheriff of Louth.¹⁶⁵

---

¹⁵⁶ *Reg. Sweteman*, 116–17, 124, 194–5. Clinton stood as one of Archbishop Sweteman's pledges in a fine for trespass in 1374: COA Rep. Records of the Exchequer, 42–51 Edward III, 255. *RCH* 57 no. 109; TNA E 101/243/11, 12; *Inquisitions and Extents*, 185–6.
¹⁵⁷ *CFR 1383–91*, 316.
¹⁵⁸ *Reg. Fleming*, 187–8, 197–200. In 1449 Archbishop Mey apologized to the archbishop of Dublin for failing to send his *armiger*, Laurence Taaf, to join a hosting at Tallaght: *Reg. Mey*, 135–6.
¹⁵⁹ *Reg. Fleming*, 257–8; *Reg. Swayne*, 35–6. White had already served as the archbishop's proctor at two parliaments of 1409: *Reg. Fleming*, 98–9, 118.
¹⁶⁰ *Reg. Fleming*, 84.
¹⁶¹ *Reg. Fleming*, 79–80; *Dowdall Deeds*, 151–2, 153, 154, 160.
¹⁶² *Parls. & Councils*, 134–5, 151–2, 174–5, 177–8; *RCH* 217 no. 9, 221 no. 12; *Handbook and Select Calendar…Ireland*, 216–22; Brand, 'Irish Law Students', 165.
¹⁶³ Thomas Talbot of Meath was killed fighting against O'Toole in 1398: 'Henry Marleburrough's Chronicle of Ireland', 214; *CPR 1399–1401*, 227.
¹⁶⁴ Curtis, *Richard II in Ireland*, 58–60, 70–1, 149–52, 161. *RCH* 156 no. 36.
¹⁶⁵ Leslie, *St Patrick's Purgatory*, 22–4; Carpenter, 'Pilgrim from Catalonia/Aragon', 107–18. O'Neill had expressed his goodwill towards Talbot in a letter to Colton of 1395: Curtis, *Richard II in Ireland*, 143–4, 221–3. *RCH* 160 nos. 11, 18.

Our understanding of the nature of late medieval Ireland, and in particular of the power structures that prevailed among the settlers, is enhanced when appropriate weight is given to the crucial role of ecclesiastical lordship in contemporary society. In Louth the Church was the greatest landowner, and in the next chapter we will see that in the towns, as in the countryside, it wielded extensive economic power. The archbishop of Armagh—the most important ecclesiastic in Ireland—was also Louth's greatest local lord. His political standing and moral authority within the county were unchallenged, and he recognized no distinction between native and settler in the matter of saving souls. The impact of these realities on the development of settler society in the area was decisive: the fortunes of the settlers were inextricably bound to an institution that was international in character, possessed great wealth, exercised local power through the distribution of patronage, and wielded a determining influence in all aspects of everyday life. As a result, in all senses but the geographical, Louth was very far indeed from 'the ends of the world'.

6

The Towns

Louth was among the most heavily urbanized part of late medieval Ireland, containing within its small confines the walled and incorporated towns of Carlingford, Dundalk, Ardee, and Drogheda.[1] Central to the development and character of the towns, as to the county as a whole, was the Church, whether as landowner, dispenser of patronage, promoter of local commerce and international trade, or regulator of morals. The archbishops of Armagh had a residence in the part of Drogheda that lay north of the Boyne and sought to acquire custody of more property there from the crown as opportunities arose.[2] The parish church of Drogheda in Louth, St Peter's, which belonged to the Augustinian house of Llanthony in Wales, served as the centre of the archbishops' interests and activities in the town.[3] There they convened their law courts, held provincial councils and synods, presided over ordinations, and conducted the element of diocesan visitations of Armagh concerned with the deanery of Drogheda.[4] There also their archdeacons held their courts, and the diocesan curators of wills validated the testaments of the deceased.[5]

The church of St Peter's and its clergy received bequests for the purchase of altar ornaments from burgesses of Drogheda and other towns who wished to be buried within its precincts, and the archbishops of Armagh put pressure on the town authorities to pay for the gold cloth to be worn by the priests of St Peter's on their

---

[1] Avril Thomas, *The Walled Towns of Ireland*, 2 vols (Dublin, 1992). For late medieval Irish towns: Gearóid Mac Niocaill, 'Socio-Economic Problems of the Late Medieval Irish Town', in David Harkness and Mary O'Dowd (eds), *Historical Studies 13: The Town in Ireland* (Belfast, 1981), 7–22; Howard B. Clarke, 'Decolonization and the Dynamics of Urban Decline in Ireland, 1300–1500', in T. R. Slater (ed.), *Towns in Decline, A.D. 100–1600* (Aldershot, 2000), 157–92; Mac Niocaill, *Na Buirgéisí*, ii.

[2] *Reg. Swayne*, 57; TNA E 101/240/4; *PKCI* 87–8. The residence of the archbishops appears to have been that 'old palace within the graveyard of the church of St Peter', referred to in 1417: *Dowdall Deeds*, 162.

[3] *Reg. Sweteman*, 29; Hogan, *Priory of Llanthony*, 360–2, 371–9.

[4] For the archbishop's court: Sayles, 'Ecclesiastical Process and the Parsonage of Stabannon in 1351', 1–23; *Reg. Fleming*, 65–7, 71–3, 74–6; *Reg. Swayne*, 44, 66; *Reg. Mey*, 9–10, 10–11, 23–4, 24–5, 27–8, 31–2, 54, 63–4, 94–5, 99. For provincial councils and synods: *Reg. Octaviani*, ii. 485–6; *Reg. Fleming*, 143–4, 171–3, 179–81, 188–9; *Reg. Swayne*, 61–3, 73–7; Michael A. J. Burrows, 'Fifteenth-Century Irish Provincial Legislation and Pastoral Care', in W. J. Shiels and Diana Wood (eds), *Studies in Church History 25: The Churches, Ireland and the Irish* (Oxford, 1989), 55–67. For ordinations: *Reg. Fleming*, 231–2; *Reg. Swayne*, 54, 86–7, 116–17. For visitations: *Reg. Sweteman*, 161–2, 195–6, 209–11; *Reg. Fleming*, 34–5.

[5] For the archdeacons' court: Hogan, *Priory of Llanthony*, 360–2; *Reg. Fleming*, 110–11, 140–1, 141–2; *Reg. Octaviani*, ii. 59–61, 70. For testing of wills: *Dowdall Deeds*, 53–4; *Reg. Octaviani*, ii. 85.

copes.⁶ Archbishop Swayne joined with three clerks and seven burgesses of the town in successfully petitioning the Irish council in the late 1430s for permission to found a guild of St Anne in the chapel dedicated to that saint which he had annexed to St Peter's. The petitioners were permitted to enrol men and women to the fraternity, elect a master and two wardens each year, and have a common seal.⁷ The archbishops were also frequent visitors to the part of Drogheda south of the river Boyne. This lay in the diocese of Meath, and its parish church of St Mary's, held by the house of Llanthony in Gloucester, was used by the archbishops as one of the locations in which they convened the clergy of Meath when conducting visitations of that diocese.⁸ In the same manner as St Peter's on the north side of the Boyne, St Mary's was patronized by the burgesses of Drogheda in Meath. In 1418 the first mayor of the united town of Drogheda, William Symcock, and his wife, Agnes, paid for three new bells to be made for the church.⁹

Drogheda was not the only town in Louth in which the archbishops spent time. When conducting visitations of the diocese of Down they travelled there by sea from Carlingford, and when present in that town in the course of the visitation of their own diocese used its parish church of St Mary's as the venue for the conduct of business.¹⁰ They demonstrated particular interest in ensuring the collection of the valuable tithe of fish that was their due from a port that attracted fishermen from southern England and even Spain.¹¹ Dundalk was the birth-place of Archbishop Richard Fitz Ralph, and he is recorded as having preached in its parish church of St Nicholas's in 1348, 1351, 1355, and 1356.¹² Ordinations were carried out at St Nicholas's, and it served as the base for the archbishops—whose manor of Dromiskin lay only 10 kilometres to the south—when conducting visitations of the deanery of Dundalk.¹³ The links of the archbishops with Ardee were also strong. It was at the hospital of St John the Baptist that Archbishop Nicholas Fleming resided for almost two years from September 1405 as he awaited delivery of the papal bulls that would allow him to receive the temporalities of his archdiocese, and the parish church of the town, dedicated to St Mary, was frequently used by the archbishops in the discharge of their various responsibilities.¹⁴ There they

---

⁶ *Dowdall Deeds*, 53–4; *Reg. Fleming*, 137; *Reg. Mey*, 153, 193.

⁷ *Reg. Swayne*, 178–80; Eamon Duffy, *The Stripping of the Altars: Traditional Religion in England 1400–1580* (New Haven, 1992), 141–54.

⁸ *Reg. Sweteman*, 1–3, 156–8; *Reg. Fleming*, 120–4, 184–6, 213–15; *Reg. Swayne*, 73–7; *Reg. Mey*, 18–20, 205–6; *CPR 1338–40*, 431; *Reg. St John, Dublin*, 181–3; Hogan, *Priory of Llanthony*, 366–8. The advowson of this church was contested in the early 1330s by the crown, Mellifont, and Llanthony in Gloucester, with the English house emerging victorious: Colmcille (Ó Conbhuí), 'Cúis Dlí Idir Ab Agus Rí', *Seanchas Ardmhacha*, 4 (1960–1), 92–102. This article contains an edited version of TNA C 260/43/10. *CPR 1338–40*, 454; *CPR 1399–1401*, 173–4; Connolly, 'Ancient Petitions', 19; Hogan, *Priory of Llanthony*, 347–60; *CPR 1399–1401*, 173–4.

⁹ Mac Iomhair, 'Two Old Drogheda Chronicles', 94.

¹⁰ *Reg. Sweteman*, 177; *Reg. Fleming*, 153–4 226–7.

¹¹ *Reg. Swayne*, 86; *Handbook and Select Calendar…Ireland*, 170–1.

¹² Gywnn, 'Sermon-Diary of Richard Fitzralph', 13, 26, 28, 30. His remains were buried in the church: *Chartul. St Mary's, Dublin*, ii. 393.

¹³ *Reg. Sweteman*, 101–2, 103, 104–7, 176, 178–80, 184–6, 189, 197–8; *Reg. Fleming*, 34–5, 222–3; 224–5; *Reg. Mey*, 168–9.

¹⁴ *Reg. Fleming*, 5–6, 15–16, 38, 56–7, 74–6.

conducted ordinations, convened visitations of the deanery of Ardee, and assembled convocations of the clergy of those parts of their archdiocese under English control in order to decide the rate at which clerical subsidies granted to the king's representative in Ireland should be assessed.[15]

Relations between the archbishops and the town authorities in Louth were usually amicable, the most notable exception being the conflict that arose between Archbishop Fitz Ralph and the men of Drogheda in the 1350s. Drogheda had offered support to Fitz Ralph in his attempts to have the primacy of Armagh recognized in Dublin in 1349, but goodwill appears to have turned to hostility as the archbishop began to question the rights and privileges of the Franciscan order, which had an important friary in the town.[16] In 1353, Fitz Ralph laid Drogheda under an interdict, accusing its inhabitants of engaging in usury and avoiding the payment of tithes, and appears not to have revoked this sentence before his death.[17] This, however, did not prevent him holding a provincial council in the town in February 1355, as he had done in February 1352, and the business generated by the large number of individuals such meetings attracted no doubt encouraged the authorities in Drogheda to avoid any escalation of the conflict with their archbishop.[18] Provincial councils were also held at Drogheda by John Colton sometime before 1389, by Nicholas Fleming in October 1411, and by John Swayne in October 1427.[19]

The influence of the Church on the fortunes of the towns of Louth was not confined to the activities of the archbishops of Armagh. These urban centres contained not only parish churches, but also religious houses belonging to mendicant orders which were international in character and which played a crucial role in the development of urban identity throughout Christendom. When, in the middle of the fourteenth century, the inhabitants of Carlingford sought to raise the status and prosperity of their town their approach was two-pronged: in 1356, they secured royal permission for the establishment of a Dominican house on land granted by the community of the town and eleven of its wealthier inhabitants; two years later they encouraged their lord, Lionel, earl of Ulster, to obtain from his father, the king, the grant of a weekly market and annual fair in the town.[20] The small town

---

[15] *PKCI* 63–6; *Dowdall Deeds*, 101, 131, 164–5; COA Rep. Records of the Exchequer, 10–22 Richard II, 155–6; *Reg. Fleming*, 231–2, 241–2; *Reg. Swayne*, 164; *Reg. Sweteman*, 161–2, 195–6; *Reg. Swayne*, 188–9, 194, 195.
[16] *Reg. Octaviani*, ii. 478–9; Aubrey Gwynn, 'Richard Fitzralph, Archbishop of Armagh. Part VI', *Studies: An Irish Quarterly Review*, 25 (1936), 81–96.
[17] Walsh, *Fourteenth-Century Scholar and Primate*, 233–4, 298, 314–15, 322–5, 336–8, 341–6, 360–2, 416.
[18] Gwynn, 'Richard Fitzralph, Archbishop of Armagh. Part VI', 81. For the texts of the sermons preached by Fitz Ralph on these occasions: Aubrey Gwynn, 'Two Sermons of Primate Richard Fitzralph', *Archivium Hibernicum*, 14 (1949), 50–65. His comments on likely attendance at the councils are at 51.
[19] *Reg. Fleming*, 171–3, 179–81, 188–9; *Reg. Swayne*, 9–18, 61–3, 73–7, 123. For the provincial councils convened by Colton and Fleming: Aubrey Gwynn, 'Ireland and the English Nation at the Council of Constance', *PRIA* 45 (1939–40), C, 209–12.
[20] *CPI* 60. *Inquisitions and Extents*, 185–6; Arthur Curran, 'The Dominican Order in Carlingford and Dundalk', *CLAJ* 16 (1967), 143–5; Ó Clabaigh, *Friars in Ireland*, 43. At n. 67, Br Ó Clabaigh points out that the foundation date suggested in Gwynn and Hadcock, *Medieval Religious Houses*

of Ardee contained not only a hospital of Augustinian friars but also a Carmelite house dedicated to St Mary, while Dundalk was home to a house of the *Fratres Cruciferi* dedicated to St Leonard and also to a Franciscan friary.[21] In his will of September 1335, Richard Tanner of Dundalk chose to be buried at St Peter's, Drogheda, but left bequests to the parish church of Dundalk (St Nicholas) and the priests and clerks of the town, as well as to the house of the Friars Minor, and 'the sick of the house of St Leonard' there.[22] In 1419, Matthew Fleming requested in his will that he be buried in his father's grave at the chantry chapel of St Katherine in the church of St Nicholas, and left 6s 8d to every friar in Dundalk.[23] Drogheda was the site of the greatest number and variety of religious houses in medieval Louth. North of the river lay the Dominican friary of St Mary Magdalene, a Franciscan friary, two hospitals of the *Fratres Cruciferi*, one dedicated to St Laurence, the other to St Mary de Urso, and a house of Augustinian friars. To the south of the Boyne was another hospital of the *Fratres Cruciferi*, dedicated to St John the Baptist, the Carmelite house of St Mary the Virgin, and the hospital of St James, the history of which is obscure.[24]

The buildings in which the clergy of Louth's medieval towns lived and laboured were more substantial than the houses of the laity around them, and proved convenient venues for large assemblies of a religious or secular nature.[25] In 1370, the house of Augustinian friars in Drogheda hosted the general chapter of the order in Ireland, while in March 1395 Richard II accepted the submissions of Irish chiefs at the Dominican house at Drogheda, and the Franciscan house at Dundalk.[26] In Drogheda, the king also had a room set apart for himself at the house of Franciscans, where he perhaps resided.[27] The Franciscan chapter house in Drogheda was the venue for meetings of the Irish council in September 1423, October 1435, and March 1451.[28] With the exception of meetings at Trim in 1392 and Dunboyne in 1398, assemblies of the Irish settler community, whether labelled as general councils or parliaments, had never convened north of Dublin before 1412 when, for the first time, Drogheda was chosen as the venue for deliberation of an afforced

Ireland, 222, for this house of 1305 is incorrect. It is a mistake repeated in my *Colonisation and Conquest*, 60. The house at Carlingford was said in 1423 to be 'disfigured by age and the incursions of enemies and robbers': *CPL 1417–31*, 261.

[21] The convent of St Mary's, Ardee, should not to be confused with its parish church of the town, also dedicated to Our Lady: Gwynn and Hadcock, *Medieval Religious Houses Ireland*, 210, 286; *Dowdall Deeds*, 101; Diarmuid Mac Iomhair, 'The Carmelites in Ardee', *CLAJ* 20 (1983), 180–1; Peter O'Dwyer, 'The Carmelite Order in Pre-Reformation Ireland', *PICHC* (1968), 49–62; Harold O'Sullivan, 'The Franciscans in Dundalk', *Seanchas Ardmhacha*, 4 (1960–1), 34–6.

[22] *Dowdall Deeds*, 53–4.

[23] *Dowdall Deeds*, 163–4.

[24] Gwynn and Hadcock, *Medieval Religious Houses Ireland*, 211–12, 224, 247–8, 288, 298. For the location of these houses see the map in Bradley, 'Topography and Layout of Medieval Drogheda'. The house of St Mary also held property in Carlingford: *Dowdall Deeds*, 175–6.

[25] Ó Clabaigh, *Friars in Ireland*, 112–13.

[26] TNA E 101/245/3; Curtis, *Richard II in Ireland*, 58–9, 60, 68–9, 70–1, 97–8, 101–3, 105–7, 109–11, 116–18.

[27] Curtis, *Richard II in Ireland*, 85–90.

[28] Richardson and Sayles, *Irish Parliament*, 311–17; *RCH* 260 no. 26; *Reg. Mey*, 432–3.

council.[29] It was to be almost thirty years before the town was selected to host such a gathering again, but the parliament of November 1440 proved to be the first of at least six such meetings held there in the eleven years that followed.[30] The council chamber of Drogheda's Franciscan house, or the chapel of St John within the parish church of St Peter's, were the preferred venues for such assemblies, sessions of which could continue for several weeks.[31]

By putting its property at the disposal of the crown in this manner, the Church not only enabled the townsmen of Dundalk and, in particular, Drogheda to have contact with the most important political figures in the country, but also stimulated local economic activity associated with the business of government.[32] Irish treasurers' accounts reveal the purchase of 'chairs, bars, benches and other necessary items' for parliaments held at Drogheda in the early 1440s, and even more elaborate purchasing and transport arrangements were required in the middle of that decade when the Dublin exchequer temporarily relocated to the town.[33] The enrolled account of the Irish treasurer, Giles Thorndon, for the period March 1444–April 1446 details payments made for

> carts hired to carry the king's books from the city of Dublin to the town of Drogheda and back to Dublin... boards, timbers and *spyres* both large and small, ordered and for the places of the exchequer and receipt at Drogheda, and their carriage there; keeping and pasturing five cows for three days, with the wages of various carpenters and masons with their servants working on the making of the exchequer and receipt at Drogheda; a chest to hold the books of the exchequer bought there, with hooping and *heding* of pipes and one hogshead to hold the books of the exchequer and common bench; making of a chair of parliament (*cathedra parliamenti*) with nails bought for that purpose; bread, wine and wax bought for a friar celebrating divine service in the exchequer...

The contribution of the Church to economic activity in Drogheda and the other towns of Louth went far beyond simply allowing its buildings to be used by branches of royal government in Ireland. The Cistercian abbey of Furness in Cumbria and the Augustinian houses of Llanthony in Wales and Llanthony in Gloucester had significant landed interests in the hinterland of Drogheda and used the port of the town, in which they also owned property, as the point of export for the money and goods yielded by their Irish estates. Late in 1332, following an inquisition held by the Irish escheator, John Morice, in Drogheda, royal permission was given for the abbot and convent of Furness to receive from the house of Beaubec

---

[29] *NHI* ix. 593–8; *Reg. Fleming*, 203–4; *RCH* 198 nos. 19, 26(c) 30; 199 nos. 36, 60.
[30] *NHI* ix. 599–600.
[31] *RCH* 261 nos. 3, 5; 263 nos. 14, 15, 16; *COD* iii. 140–5; *PKCI* 305–8. The king's Irish council met in St John's chapel in Oct. 1442, *PKCI* 295–303.
[32] For a discussion of this topic in an English context: Masschaele, 'Town, Country, and Law'.
[33] *IEP* 579–80, 581. In 1332, the sheriff of Louth, John Gernon of Killincoole, was allowed £2 16s on his account, which he had paid to a merchant of Drogheda 'for a cloth of divers colours bought for king's use to cover both exchequers at Dublin, and for clipping, cutting and sewing the same': *Rep. DKI 43*, 53.

in Normandy its Irish estates, centred on the manor of Beybeg, south of Drogheda, as well as properties in that town and elsewhere in Meath, and a fishery on the Boyne.[34] In the two decades that followed, the abbey received additional grants of rent and property from Drogheda burgesses and its abbot visited the town in person as well as appointing prominent local men as his attorneys in Ireland.[35] The vigour with which Furness protected and sought to extend its new acquisitions in the Drogheda area in the 1330s brought it into conflict with the house of Llanthony in Wales, which had long-standing interests in the same location.[36]

That Furness continued to protect its rights in the area aggressively is suggested by the pardon which Edmund Mortimer, in his capacity as lord of Trim, found it necessary to issue to the abbot and his men in 1380 for their attack on Richard Preston of Beybeg, with whom the house had been in dispute since at least 1376.[37] Richard was a wealthy member of an important local family, but this did not prevent him being taken prisoner by the abbot's agents and having his property ransacked. His losses included not only his twenty-four plough beasts, eighty pigs, eleven oxen, ten sheep, and seven cows, as well as eighty acres of growing wheat and eighty acres of growing oats, but also his bedclothes, spoons, basin, tablecloths, and towels.[38] The shops and houses that it possessed in Drogheda provided Furness with welcome rental income, but it was the town's port facilities, and the ease with which the grain grown on its nearby estates could be transported to Cumbria as a result, that made it particularly important to the abbey.[39] This was especially the case in the decades after the first appearance of plague in England and Ireland in 1348: between 1355 and 1383 Furness received several exemptions from the general prohibition on the export of grain from Ireland, and was even permitted to purchase grain for export there to supplement the produce of its own lands. [40]

In transporting this grain it is likely that Furness's agents used the quay on the northern banks of the Boyne in Drogheda especially constructed by the house of Llanthony in Wales for the export of the crops, fish—and cash—derived from their manors in Louth and Meath.[41] The possession by the two Llanthony abbeys of various houses and shops in Drogheda, as well as their rights of presentation to the parish churches of St Peter's and St Mary's, ensured that the laymen and priests

---

[34] *Inquisitions and Extents*, 135; *CPR 1330–4*, 382; *CPR 1340–3*, 52–3; *CCR 1333–7*, 474–5.
[35] *Coucher Book of Furness Abbey*, ii/3. 726–7; 'Ancient Deeds', 25, 30; *CPR 1334–8*, 44, 224; *CPR 1338–40*, 16; *CPR 1340–3*, 128; *CPR 1374–7*, 13; *CPR 1350–4*, 101 *RCH* 45 no. 67.
[36] Atkinson and Brownhill (eds), *Coucher Book of Furness*, ii/3, nos. 6, 7. I am grateful to my Ph.D. student, Mr Paul Seage, for bringing this reference to my attention.
[37] 'Ancient Deeds', 25–6.
[38] 'Ancient Deeds', 29; *Gormanston Reg.* 61–2, 76. Richard was dead by Oct. 1384: *RCH* 120 no. 34; *Gormanston Reg.* 79–80.
[39] Hogan, *Priory of Llanthony*, 380–9; *CPR 1334–8*, 44, 224.
[40] *RCH* 62 nos. 105 and 106; 89 nos. 120 and 121; *Coucher Book of Furness Abbey* i, 184–5; *CPR 1381–5*, 329.
[41] In 1381, it was recorded that the proctors of Llanthony in Gloucester in Ireland sent £80 per annum to the house in England: Hogan, *Priory of Llanthony*, 360. *RCH* 130 no. 63; Bradley, 'Topography and Layout of Medieval Drogheda', 108, 111–12, 115.

they selected to discharge their secular and religious responsibilities there would figure prominently in the communal life of the town. The vicars of St Peter's, often referred to simply as vicars of Drogheda, held a place of particular significance. Richard Ross, vicar in the late 1360s, and William Faunt, who held the same position in the following decade, were close associates of Robert Preston and assisted him in the land transactions in the town that helped further his career at this time.[42] Nicholas Alexander, whose long clerical career from 1411 saw him serve successively in the parishes of Dromin, Dunbin, and Clonmore, was appointed vicar of St Peter's in 1430 and died in that post in 1454.[43] In 1420, he was elected as their proctor by the clergy of Armagh among the English to pay their contribution to a subsidy awarded to the lieutenant, James Butler, earl of Ormond, and thirty years later represented them at the Drogheda parliament summoned by Richard, duke of York.[44]

The interest of important members of the laity in the religious life of Drogheda extended beyond its parish churches and clergy. Nicholas Verdon chose to be buried at the Franciscan convent in the town in 1347, while in 1361-2 its Dominican house was the place of interment for Lady Joan Fleming and Lady Margaret Bermingham, the wife of Robert Preston.[45] The house of the *Fratres Cruciferi* dedicated to St Laurence also attracted secular patronage, as in 1335 when in his will Matthew Tanner of Dundalk left 40d to the anchorites enclosed in its church.[46] Archbishop Mey heard cases brought before his court in the same house in 1444 and a decade later dismissed its prior, Peter Clinton—who was probably a member of the important Louth and Meath family of that name—for neglecting his duties, including the care of the sick and needy, and for letting the house fall into disrepair.[47] Edward III appears to have taken an interest in the fortunes of the house of the *Fratres Cruciferi* located south of the Boyne, dedicated to St John the Baptist, granting it land in the vicinity of Drogheda in 1359 and 1361.[48] When William Symcock died in 1420, 'there was great moane made [in Drogheda] especially by the ffraternity of the Dominicans, the Minorites, and the Eremetes to whom the said William was a great benefactor'.[49]

The clergy of the other towns in Louth also played an important role in local economic and social affairs, both as participants in the land market and as recipients and disbursers of patronage. In 1372, John Styward, vicar of the parish church

---

[42] *Gormanston Reg.*, 20, 22, 24, 30, 49, 61–2; *Reg. Sweteman*, 60–2.
[43] *Reg. Fleming*, 82, 154–6, 168, 190, 197–200, 254–6; *Reg. Swayne*, 61–3, 83–4, 141–2, 162, 178–80; *Reg. Mey*, 6–7, 56, 62–3, 102–3, 153, 193, 430–1; *Reg. Octaviani*, ii. 73, 125–7.
[44] *Parls. & Councils*, 143–4, 153; *Reg. Swayne*, 196.
[45] *Clyn*, 240; *Chartul. St Mary's, Dublin*, ii. 395. For patronage of the friars by lesser lords in contemporary England: Coss, *Foundations of Gentry Life*, 151–63.
[46] *Dowdall Deeds*, 53–4.
[47] *Reg. Swayne*, 191; *Reg. Mey*, 191–3, 359–60.
[48] *CFR 1356–68*, 109; *Inquisitions and Extents*, 195–6.
[49] *Materials for the History of the Franciscan Province of Ireland*, ed. E. B. Fitzmaurice and A. G. Little (Manchester, 1920), 181.

of St Mary's of Ardee, was granted licence to receive from John Clinton of Drumcashel a gift of property in the town in return for celebrating masses 'for the souls of the king's progenitors and Simon Gernon, and of the king and the said John Clynton, after death'.[50] In 1381, Styward was one of three priests who enabled John Keppok to establish an entail on his inheritance by accepting enfeoffment of land worth £40 in Ardee before immediately regranting it to Keppok with reversion to his male heirs.[51] The right of presentation to the vicarage lay with the lord of Ardee and in periods of minority with the crown. In 1431, the king chose William Corre, vicar of Kildemock, to fill the vacant benefice, and during the more than forty years in which he subsequently held that position, Corre acted as vicar general of Armagh and represented its clergy at the Drogheda parliament of October 1450.[52] The hospital of St John the Baptist, a foundation of the *Fratres Cruciferi*, also played an important role in civic affairs in Ardee. In 1414, the provost, burgesses, and community of the town, who had earlier been awarded grants designed to allow them to strengthen its defences, were permitted to render their account not at the exchequer but at the court of either the archbishop of Armagh or prior of St John's.[53] That relations between the priory and the civic authorities were not always happy is revealed by a case of 1450 in which possession of a glebe in the town, and its associated liberties, was disputed by the parties, with victory being awarded to the hospital.[54]

In Dundalk, the hospital of the *Fratres Cruciferi*, dedicated to St Leonard, was in dispute with perhaps the town's most powerful resident, Peter Dowdall, in 1423, but in general it maintained good relations with its secular neighbours.[55] The right of presentation to the vicarage of the parish church of St Nicholas, Dundalk, alternated between the several patrons who had come into possession of rights of lordship in the town from the inheritors there of the original Verdon interest.[56] The attempts of John Bellew, lord of Roche, to oust John Taylor, who had been appointed by the Fleming barons of Slane, and replace him with Patrick Oweyn in 1414 and Thomas Hussey in 1418 failed, and he was no more successful in 1427 when, on Taylor's death, he nominated Hussey again for the post only for Archbishop Swayne to install Philip Norris as vicar on the grounds that the right of presentation lay not with Bellew but with John Blakeney, chief justice of the common bench.[57]

---

[50] *CPR 1389–92*, 419. This was probably the Simon Gernon of Ardee, *narrator*, who in 1365 was in receipt of a pension from Archbishop Milo Sweteman at the same time as Clinton served in the episcopal household: *Reg. Sweteman*, 84–5.

[51] BL Add MS 4790, ff. 27b–28; *PKCI* 63–6.

[52] *Reg. Swayne*, 138, 145–9, 164, 193, 196–7; *Reg. Mey*, 272–3; *Reg. Octaviani*, ii. 53, 57, 70, 73–5, 83–4, 86, 89, 450–2.

[53] *RCH* 203 no. 15.

[54] *Reg. Mey*, 280–3, 299–303. For the layout and development of medieval Ardee: John Bradley, 'Ardee: An Archaeological Study', *CLAJ* 20 (1984), 267–96.

[55] *Dowdall Deeds*, 167; *RCH* 170 no. 79.

[56] *RCH* 89 no. 106; *Dowdall Deeds*, 132.

[57] *Reg. Fleming*, 212; *CPL 1396–1404*, 571; *CPL 1417–31*, 73; *CPL 1427–47*, 468–9; *Reg. Swayne*, 60, 63, 163–4. Hussey had to settle for the vicarage of Mansfieldstown, which he held for twenty years after 1431, but did secure the position of dean of Ardee and Dundalk: *Reg. Swayne*, 66–8, 133–4, 188–9, 193, 194, 195; *Reg. Mey*, 191–3.

The Church was an integral part of the civil and economic life of the towns of medieval Louth, not least because its international character complemented and encouraged the development of those trading networks upon which these towns depended for their survival and prosperity. Both Dundalk and Carlingford had ports at which English ships are recorded as docking, and their merchants conducted sea trade with Ulster, but their facilities could not compete with those of Drogheda.[58] It was in a ship hired at Drogheda that two Dundalk merchants conveyed a consignment of hides to Antwerp in 1339, and at Drogheda that the Dundalk merchant, Richard Tanner, chose to be buried in 1335.[59] Drogheda conducted maritime commerce with other Irish ports such as Galway, Kinsale, and Waterford, and its ships played a prominent role in the trading life of Ulster.[60] In 1382, Thomas Rath and John Forster of Drogheda were granted licence to transport wheat, malt, and beans by sea to Ulster, and in 1389 and later the Drogheda merchant William Symcock was permitted to convey wine and ale there.[61] Ulster, in turn, provided the oxen and cows that merchants from Drogheda purchased, salted, and shipped home 'for the common profit of that town'.[62]

Drogheda's external trade was far-flung and faintly exotic, encompassing in the later fourteenth century commerce with ports as distant as Gdansk and Genoa. Geography, history, and market conditions, however, determined that for the most part its merchants traded with other components of the territories claimed by the English crown or held by its allies.[63] Like its later, British, version, the 'first English empire', was to a large extent a maritime enterprise, and Drogheda's location in one of its busiest stretches of water, the Irish Sea, ensured that the town's merchants participated fully in the economic life of north-west Europe.[64] The extent to which political considerations, and in particular England's wars with France and Scotland, determined the nature of this participation cannot be underestimated. It was 'to England and other parts of the king's friendship' that the mayor and burgesses of Drogheda in Louth were licensed in 1376 to ship 'wheat, oats, flesh, fish and other victuals, and... make their profit thereof'.[65] The king's 'friendship', however, was not a stable commodity. In the 1350s, Drogheda merchants made use of Spanish shipping to transport hides to Flanders without incident, but as the nature of relations with Castile changed so too did the pattern of trade. By the 1380s, special

---

[58] *RCH* 189 no. 3; *Dowdall Deeds*, 152–3. Wine was imported at Dundalk in 1349: TNA E 101/241/18. Paul Gosling, 'From Dún Delca to Dundalk: The Topography and Archaeology of a Medieval Frontier Town A.D. c.1187–1700', *CLAJ* 22 (1991), 317–20.

[59] *CCR 1339–41*, 334, 518; *Dowdall Deeds*, 44, 53–4; *Rep. DKI 44*, 51.

[60] *CCR 1339–41*, 624; *CPR 1401–5*, 86; *RCH* 179 no. 24; COA Rep. Records of the Exchequer, 1–10 Richard II, 373; *CPR 1374–1377*, 342; *RCH* 136 no. 189; *PKCI* 159–61.

[61] *RCH* 115 nos. 225 and 226; 142 no. 237; 176 no. 11; 181 no. 37.

[62] *RCH* 172 no. 12.

[63] *CPR 1381–5*, 500–1; *CCR 1392–6*, 34; Richard Britnell, *Britain and Ireland 1050–1530* (Oxford, 2004), 118–37.

[64] R. R. Davies, *The First English Empire: Power and Identities in the British Isles 1093–1343* (Oxford, 2000); Benjamin T. Hudson, 'The Changing Economy of the Irish Sea Province', in Brendan Smith (ed.), *Britain and Ireland 900–1300: Insular Responses to Medieval European Change* (Cambridge, 1999), 39–66; Wendy Childs and Timothy O'Neill, 'Overseas Trade', in *NHI* ii. 492–523.

[65] *CPR 1374–7*, 305.

licences had to be obtained to allow the export of grain from Drogheda to Spain, and complaints about the malign activities of Spanish ships in the vicinity of the town became common in the decades thereafter.[66] The Flemish trade changed in a similar manner. Hides destined for Flanders arrived in Drogheda from nearby inland towns such as Athboy, as well as from Ulster, and were transported from there to the Low Countries in Flemish ships as well as those from Drogheda. By 1400, however, this trade had gone into steep decline as economic policy followed political realignment in the Anglo-French hostilities.[67]

Ports in the French territories that lay under English suzerainty welcomed many ships and merchants from Drogheda. In 1364, Drogheda merchants successfully petitioned the crown for permission to conduct business in French ports other than Calais, and they subsequently attempted to bypass this town when engaging in trade in Picardy.[68] As part of Henry V's campaigns to integrate his northern French conquests into his domain, efforts were made to increase trading links between Drogheda and Brittany but from the mid-1430s, as the English position in France declined, the authorities in Drogheda were identifying Bretons as being among those 'enemies from the sea' who endangered the well-being of the town.[69] Drogheda's Gascon trade, consisting of the import of wine and export of grain, remained strong throughout the period. A Bordeaux merchant was recorded as selling wine at Drogheda in 1338, and at least one Drogheda merchant resided for a lengthy period in Bordeaux later in the century.[70] In 1393, Robert Preston entered into an indenture with the attorney and proctor of John Patristow concerning possession of three shops in Drogheda in Meath. John was unable to seal the indenture in person because he was 'at present resident in Bordeaux' and showed no inclination to return.[71]

It was in their dealings with Scotland that Drogheda's merchants demonstrated most clearly their capacity to align their entrepreneurial instincts with the political priorities of their king, being content to act as traders or raiders in the northern reaches of the Irish Sea as royal policy demanded. Just as the crown's Scottish ally in the region, John of the Isles, was awarded money from Drogheda's customs receipts and allowed to employ one of its merchants to provision his forces between 1336 and 1338, so in 1337 seven burgesses from the town were ordered to lead a force to the Isle of Man to expel a party of invading Scots loyal to David II.[72]

---

[66] *CCR 1349–54*, 578, 580; TNA E 101/246/3; *RCH* 137 no. 223; *Handbook and Select Calendar…Ireland*, 170–1; *CPR 1441–6*, 97, 132; Anthony Goodman, 'England and Iberia in the Middle Ages', in Michael Jones and Malcolm Vale (eds), *England and her Neighbours, 1066–1453: Essays in Honour of Pierre Chaplais* (London, 1989), 86–90.

[67] NAI, RC 8/21, 519–20; *CCR 1349–54*, 25–6; *CCR 1381–5*, 72, 73; *CPR 1381–5*, 500–1; *CCR 1389–92*, 258; COA Rep. Records of the Exchequer, 10–22 Richard II, 379; Timothy O'Neill, *Merchants and Mariners in Medieval Ireland* (Dublin, 1987), 77–83.

[68] *CCR 1364–9*, 8; *CCR 1389–92*, 195.

[69] *RCH* 213 no. 141; 257 nos. 3 and 68; NLI MS 4, f. 334.

[70] *Rep. DKI 45*, 45; *RCH* 118 no. 113; 137 no. 223; 198 no. 26(b); *CCR 1339–41*, 624; *CCR 1389–92*, 258; *Handbook and Select Calendar…Ireland*, 128; *CPR 1408–13*, 373; *CPR 1416–22*, 59.

[71] *Gormanston Reg.* 80–1.

[72] *RCH* 42 no. 7; *Rep. DKI 44*, 60; *CPR 1338–40*, 81.

A generous interpretation of the role played by another Drogheda merchant, Adam Serle, in a violent incident in the same stretch of sea in 1342 is that it was inspired by an excess of zeal on the king's behalf. With royal agreement the community of the Isle of Man had agreed to pay for a truce with the Scots, and the abbot of its Cistercian abbey of Rushen was among those who set off for Scotland with the money, horses, cows, and other goods promised as part of the agreement. The convoy of three ships was intercepted en route by Serle and fellow-merchants from Waterford and Ulster who took one vessel to Ireland, 'did their will' with its valuable cargo, and imprisoned the abbot.[73] In 1386, in circumstances reminiscent of a half-century before, one Drogheda merchant was permitted to transport wine to the Hebrides, while three others were ordered 'to sail upon the sea in order to capture' those Scots whose raids on the Irish coast were damaging the interests of the king.[74] In the first decade of the fifteenth century, the Drogheda men went a step further by attempting to establish a new industry derived from the unstable environment in which they traded. In the summer of 1405, 'the merchants of Drogheda entered Scotland and took pledges and preys', and in 1409 Janico Dartas was permitted to build a warship in the port.[75] No naval dockyard appears to have been founded at Drogheda, and complaints from its merchants about Scottish piracy continued throughout the fifteenth century, but the town had escaped assault from the sea and had shown itself to be a vital and vigorous component of the English economic and political order.[76]

The bulk of Drogheda's import and export trade was carried out with English and Welsh ports stretching from Furness in the north-west to London in the south-east, and many Drogheda ships destined for the continent stopped off in England as part of their commercial activities, or as a result of adverse weather conditions.[77] London attracted the interest of Louth men with capital to invest: in 1352, John Keppok gave Thomas Talbot of Malahide 10m 'to trade therewith for John's profit and to render account to him therefor at his pleasure, and to pay him the said £10 (*sic*) at SS. Simon and Jude next in London in the parish of St Bride, Fletestret'.[78] Although merchandise destined for Drogheda might embark from small western ports such as Milford in Pembrokeshire, the most important centre of commerce for Drogheda traders in England was Bristol.[79] It was there that Drogheda ships arrived carrying cargoes of hides, kippers, salmon, and other goods, and there also that Drogheda merchants might purchase produce displayed in the town by grocers from London.[80] Bristol merchants employed their equivalents in Drogheda as their attorneys in Ireland, and Bristol's role as a major trading centre with a wide

---

[73] *CCR 1341–3*, 655.   [74] *RCH* 127 no. 243; 136 no. 199.
[75] 'Henry Marleburrough's Chronicle of Ireland', 216; *RCH* 193 no. 184.
[76] *RCH* 201 no. 110; NLI MS 4, f. 334.
[77] *CCR 1341–43*, 697; *CCR 1381–5*, 72, 73; *CCR 1389–92*, 258.
[78] *CCR 1349–54*, 504–5.
[79] *RCH* 63 no. 137.
[80] TNA E 122/212/11; E 122/40/12; E 122/17/10; *CCR 1339–41*, 592; *Handbook and Select Calendar… Ireland*, 149.

commercial hinterland also accounts for the evidence of economic ties between Drogheda and certain towns in the southern Midlands of England.[81] Two Coventry men appointed Drogheda burgesses as their attorneys in Ireland in the 1370s, as did another merchant from the same town in 1438, while in 1381 a Drogheda burgess was one of two attorneys in Ireland chosen by Richard Spicer of Northampton.[82] The economic opportunities available in Drogheda were sufficient to encourage some merchants from England to relocate there. Walter Manning of Dartmouth resided in Drogheda in the early fifteenth century and conducted trade from there with Bordeaux and London.[83] William Walys (Walsh/Wallace) was Lancashire-born but a resident of Drogheda in the 1430s when his ship was rammed by a Dartmouth vessel off the Devon coast, while the continuing links of the Prestons of Drogheda and Meath to their ancestral home in north-west England encouraged other families from the Preston area, such as the Starkeys, to also acquire interests in Drogheda's hinterland.[84]

Most of the merchants from Louth who conducted business with England did so by means of short, frequent, trips across the Irish Sea. It was not unusual, however, for longer sojourns in England to be undertaken, and in some cases for this to result in a permanent relocation there. The grant of 1390–1 made at Daventry in Northamptonshire by John Everton of Rathdrumin and his son, William, to John's cousin, Walter, by which they released to him all rights in their lands at Rathdrumin, suggests a final cutting of already loosening ties with Ireland on the part of father and son.[85] Such finality may have been unusual, but the impression gleaned from this incident that at least some of those from Louth who spent lengthy periods in England were accompanied by family members is supported by other evidence. Joan, the wife of William Our of Drogheda, for instance, chose to stay in England when her husband, who had previously shipped 'wines, fish and other victuals' across the Irish Sea, died there in 1346.[86] When Stephen White of Drogheda sought permission to appoint attorneys in Ireland for two years before setting out for England in 1360 he did so both for himself and for his wife, Isabel.[87] Simon Keppok of Drogheda had been a significant figure in the town since the 1320s and a major exporter of grain to England in the early 1350s. On his death in 1354 his son and heir, John, was a minor living in England, which suggests that he had accompanied his father on what proved to be his final voyage across the Irish Sea.[88] The Dundalk man, William Skrene, who pursued a successful legal career in England in the decades around 1400, and who acquired the manor of

---

[81] *CPR 1385–89*, 370; Christopher Dyer and T. R. Slater, 'The Midlands', in David M. Palliser (ed.), *The Cambridge Urban History of Britain*, i. *640–1540* (Cambridge, 2000), 609–38.
[82] *CPR 1370–4*, 430; *CPR 1377–81*, 64, 588; *CPR 1436–41*, 222.
[83] *Handbook and Select Calendar…Ireland*, 128.
[84] *Handbook and Select Calendar…Ireland*, 123; *Gormanston Reg.* 41, 92; *RCH* 91 no. 80.
[85] *Dowdall Deeds*, 129. Neither John nor William appear in Irish records after this date: *Dowdall Deeds*, 117; *RCH* 136 no. 189.
[86] *CPR 1338–40*, 6; *CPR 1345–8*, 168.
[87] *CPR 1358–61*, 370.
[88] *Reg. Kilmainham*, 3–4; *Inquisitions and Extents*, 136–7; *RCH* 42 no. 15; *CPR 1350–4*, 192, 235; *CPR 1354–8*, 25.

Great Finborough in Suffolk and land at Terling in Essex, as well as property in Kent, Cambridgeshire, and Hertfordshire, brought some of his kin with him to England, but also maintained contact with a sister, Christine, who remained in Ireland.[89]

In such cases, it was assumed that those from Ireland granted leave to come to England would return there upon completion of their business. The attempts made in advance of Richard II's first expedition to Ireland in 1394 to force people of Irish birth living in England to move back across the Irish Sea revealed that such an assumption had often been misplaced. Among those granted special licence to remain in England upon payment of a fine in July and August of that year were several individuals with surnames that suggest a Louth/Meath origin, such as Nicholas Verdon of Bristol, tailor, John Clinton, chaplain, John Neterville of Dagenhale (Dagnall, Buckinghamshire), Henry Gernon, and Barnabas Plunket.[90] Archbishop John Swayne's complaint to an unnamed English or colonial lord in the late 1420s that 'the housbonde pepill [of Ireland]...be gone out of the londe within fewe yeris into Englonde and into odir contreys that in good faith as I suppose there is mo gone oute of the londe of the kyngis lege pepyll then be in' was intended to startle, but was also grounded in personal observation. As one who lived on the manors of Dromiskin, Termonfeckin, and Athboy, and who spent a great deal of time in Drogheda, Swayne was in a stronger position than most to offer considered reflection on patterns of migration across the Irish Sea.[91] Legislation passed in the English parliament in the second and third decades of the fifteenth century provided for the forcible repatriation of Irish-born inhabitants of England on the grounds that they were inclined towards criminal behaviour.[92] It is possible that the legislators had in mind incidents such as that which occurred in Exeter in 1389, when Stephen Teeling of Drogheda and five other 'felons and clerks' escaped from the prison of the bishop of Exeter. After killing its warden and porter, and mortally wounding another servant in the process, they proceeded to ransack the episcopal palace.[93]

Merchants were among the groups excluded from English parliamentary provisions designed to force Irish-born subjects of the crown to leave England. Although the buying and selling of goods was the primary motivation for such men to cross the Irish

[89] Paul Brand, 'An Irishman in Westminster Hall: William Skrene of Dundalk, King's Serjeant at Law (c.1358–c.1420)', *The Irish Jurist*, 31 (1996), 255–65.

[90] *CPR 1391–6*, 455, 457, 460, 461, 462, 463; Jim Bolton, 'Irish Migration to England in the Late Middle Ages', *IHS* 32 (2000), 1–21; Cosgrove, *Late Medieval Ireland*, 18–20. For the Irish in Bristol: Peter Fleming, 'Identity and Belonging: Irish and Welsh in Fifteenth-Century Bristol', in Linda Clark (ed.), *The Fifteenth Century*, vii. *Conflicts, Consequences and the Crown in the Late Middle Ages* (Woodbridge, 2007), 175–93.

[91] *Reg. Swayne*, 107–8. Justices were appointed in Meath in 1390 to identify shipowners who, contrary to proclamation, had carried labourers from Ireland: *RCH* 146 no. 214. In 1420 John Bonefaunt paid part of a fine imposed upon him sometime before for carrying six labourers as well as corn from Drogheda 'to foreign parts, contrary to the statute': TNA E 101/247/8.

[92] *Statutes of the Realm*, ii. 173, 214, 221. Ralph A. Griffiths, 'Crossing the Frontiers of the English Realm in the Fifteenth Century', in Pryce and Watts, *Power and Identity in the Middle Ages*, 211–25; Ruddick, 'Ethnic Identity and Political Language', 15–31.

[93] *CPR 1389–92*, 103.

Sea, they might also have other reasons for doing so. It appears to have been in connection with the affairs of his exalted relative, Richard Fitz Ralph, for instance, that John Rauf spent a year in England in 1333 and two years from 1345 and again from 1351.[94] In the ten years before 1412, 'the king's service' or 'the king's business', rather than trade, were frequently cited as the reasons why senior figures in the borough administration of Drogheda travelled to England. William Peacock of Drogheda, 'a person of good repute and a victim of malice', crossed the Irish Sea in the king's service in 1403 and 1405.[95] Peter Chapman, one of the bailiffs of Drogheda, appointed a deputy in the town before embarking for England in April 1404, as did the mayor of Drogheda in Louth, Richard White, when he made the same journey in October 1405.[96] It is likely that these men were still in England in the following spring when they were joined by two more prominent burgesses, Robert Sexton and Simon Mole.[97] In February 1412, 'the king's business' was again specified as the reason why John Ryver, one of the bailiffs of Drogheda in Meath, intended to set out for England.[98] The nature of the 'business' which required the presence in England of such important men was revealed on 15 December 1412, when 'Robert Ball came to Drogheda with a charter of union'.[99]

The charter Ball carried had been issued by Henry IV at Westminster on 1 November and provided for the union of the towns of Drogheda on either side of the Boyne into a single town and county to be governed by a mayor and two sheriffs chosen by the community.[100] The reasons given for this constitutional change included the harm caused by the existing arrangements to Drogheda's trading fortunes, and the dissension and debates (*dissensiones et debate*) that they had given rise to among its inhabitants. What little evidence there is for such rancour should be approached with caution. A Dominican friar of the town, Philip Bennett, is credited with preaching a sermon on the feast of Corpus Christi 1412 at St Peter's church that ended the 'dissensions…bloodshed and murder' that had arisen between the townsmen on either side of the river, and that encouraged them instead to petition the king successfully for the unification of Drogheda.[101] In the absence of any other trace in the records of trans-pontine violence, and given the frequency of contact with the crown of important burgesses 'on the king's business' in the years before 1412, it is best to regard talk of 'dissension' as part of a collusive strategy intended to provide the crown with a pretext to order a radical restructuring of the constitutional position of an important town.[102] It was probably more than coincidence

---

[94] *CPR 1330–4*, 432; *CPR 1345–8*, 10; *CPR 1350–4*, 101; Walsh, *Fourteenth-Century Scholar and Primate*, 13–14, 252–3.
[95] *PKCI* 225–6; *RCH* 174 no. 92; 177 no. 4; 180 no. 4.
[96] *RCH* 178 no. 5; 181 no. 7. It is not clear if England was the destination of Nicholas White, bailiff of Drogheda, who appointed a deputy before going 'overseas' in Oct. 1405: *RCH* 181 no. 8.
[97] *RCH* 182 nos. 60 and 63.
[98] *RCH* 198 no. 25.
[99] Mac Iomhair, 'Two Old Drogheda Chronicles', 94.
[100] For the text of the charter, Mac Niocaill, *Na Buirgéisí*, i. 200–10. COA Rep. Records of the Exchequer, Henry IV, 466, 469.
[101] Ó Clabaigh, *Friars in Ireland*, 293–4.
[102] For similar considerations that prevailed when Bristol was elevated to the status of a county in Aug. 1373, see Liddy, *War Politics and Finance*, 190–212. Both towns straddled diocesan borders.

that the decision to unify the town came in the same year as Edmund Mortimer, whose ancestors had pursued claims to lordship in Drogheda in Meath, reached his majority.[103] The new dispensation appears to have been welcomed with enthusiasm in Drogheda, and represented the fruits of at least ten years of lobbying at the highest levels in England by its leading men.

Securing the charter of union of 1412 was but the latest, if by far the most significant, demonstration by Drogheda's rulers of their political skills. In the midst of their bitter dispute with Archbishop Fitz Ralph in the early 1350s, which had led to the town being placed under interdict, its burgesses found ingenious ways to place pressure on the primate to relax his censures.[104] In November 1353, a Hungarian pilgrim, George Grissaphan, sought out Fitz Ralph to obtain his permission to enter St Patrick's Purgatory on Lough Derg. The likelihood that it was at the episcopal manor of Termonfeckin, near Drogheda, or in the town itself, that George's wish was granted is strengthened by evidence that suggests that the pilgrim was also in contact at this time with some of Drogheda's leading advocates. When, in February 1354, George reported to Fitz Ralph the visionary messages he had received while in the Purgatory, he included one transmitted by the Archangel Michael that must have made uncomfortable listening for the archbishop. This concerned the 'absolution of a certain great city of the archdiocese, which the said primate was unjustly interdicting and excommunicating: not perhaps from malice and injustice, as it seemed, but because he thought the city had not paid him his due and was unwilling to do so'.[105] The incident must have left Fitz Ralph wondering either at the power of the intercessory prayers offered by the folk of Drogheda, or at the temerity of the townsmen in turning the head of the suggestible and youthful stranger who had fallen briefly among them.

Less than two decades later, Drogheda's leaders found their political skills put to a much sterner test when they confronted William Windsor over his financial demands. Windsor had reason to suspect soon after his arrival in Ireland in July 1369 that Drogheda was not contributing as fully as it was required to do to his coffers. He was granted the proceeds of the New Custom in Dublin, Drogheda, and counties Meath, Kildare, and Louth in that year, and the early proceeds of this tax must have aroused his suspicions. For the period from 8 August 1369 to 21 January 1370, the city of Dublin offered over £40 and Carlingford £8, whereas Drogheda yielded £11. The figures for the next period of account, up to 20 May, were even more startling: whereas the city of Dublin provided over £18, and Carlingford over £11, Drogheda offered less than £8.[106] If later accusations were to be believed, Windsor's response to such disappointing returns was to impound the ships of Drogheda merchants in other Irish ports and keep for himself the proceeds of the goods therein which he sold.[107] This was but the start: the traumas endured

---

[103] Buldorini, 'Drogheda as a Case Study of Anglo-Norman Town Foundation', 328.
[104] For the interdict see Buldorini, 'Drogheda as a Case Study of Anglo-Norman Town Foundation', 264–70.
[105] Walsh, *Fourteenth-Century Scholar and Primate*, 308–15; Leslie, *St Patrick's Purgatory*, 19–20.
[106] RIA MS 12 D 10, 171.
[107] See above, 55. Clarke, 'William of Windsor in Ireland', 116–19.

by the community of Drogheda at the hands of Windsor up to the time of his final departure from Ireland in June 1376—the insistence that influential individuals serve in arms in person in Munster or pay heavy fines to be exempted from so doing; the summoning of numerous parliaments in distant places; the coercion of representatives at these gatherings to agree to heavy taxation; the imprisonment of those who refused to do so; the requirement to send elected representatives to England—have been discussed in a previous chapter. When the storm had passed it was difficult to discern what Drogheda had gained from its resistance. It meekly paid to Windsor's successors the moneys it had sought to withhold from him, and was deprived even of the satisfaction of witnessing an inglorious end to the career of its enemy.[108]

It is arguable, however, that the lengthy nature of its dispute with the chief governor, and the involvement of the crown in its course, had important positive consequences for at least some of those who held power in late fourteenth-century Drogheda. If the political acuity of this group was already refined by 1368 it was honed still further in the decade that followed, and if Drogheda already had extensive mercantile ties with England to these were now added political contacts at the highest level. That the dispute with Windsor provided opportunities for personal advancement—as well as the dangers of imprisonment and financial ruin—for some members of the Drogheda elite can be demonstrated with reference to the careers of a selection of those targeted by the chief governor for rough treatment during his first period in office, which ended in the spring of 1372. Richard Mole was among the Drogheda burgesses to whom a writ was sent in February 1370 ordering attendance on the governor at Limerick, and who considered it worthwhile paying a fine—in this case £20—to avoid doing so.[109] By 1377, however, Mole, who in the 1350s had been a major exporter of wheat to England, was acting as collector of customs in Drogheda, and between then and his death in 1401, served on occasion as a justice of novel disseisin and collector of a grant made to the king, and continued to accumulate property both in Drogheda and its hinterland.[110] John Ashwell, seneschal of Drogheda in Meath, and John Stameen, who had held that position in 1366, were arrested at the Dublin parliament of April 1370 and detained until they agreed to grant a subsidy to Windsor from the town.[111] In 1384, Stameen was granted custody of the manor of Ricetown (bar. Lower Slane, co. Meath), which was in the king's hand, while Ashwell's career also blossomed in the same period.[112] He acquired custody of land in Platin, near Drogheda, from the crown in 1385 and in the following year was elected mayor of the Drogheda staple, having previously served as controller of the customs of the town.[113]

---

[108] See above, chapter 2.

[109] Clarke, 'William of Windsor in Ireland', 117, 118.

[110] *CPR 1350–4*, 235; COA Rep. Records of the Exchequer, 42–51 Edward III, 406; *Dowdall Deeds*, 106, 108–9, 114, 132; COA Rep. Records of the Exchequer, 1–10 Richard II, 342–3, 486, 493; RCH 133 no. 111; 139 no. 93; 162 no. 80.

[111] Clarke, 'William of Windsor in Ireland', 119; *Gormanston Reg.* 61–2.

[112] *Dowdall Deeds*, 118–20, 128; RCH 122 no. 10. For Ricetown see Clare, *On the Edge of the Pale*.

[113] RCH 123 no. 27; 135 no. 167; 141 no. 196; *CPR 1381–5*, 49.

In the same year as his election, 1386, Ashwell was also one of three Drogheda burgesses entrusted by the crown with the task of taking to the seas to capture the Scottish raiders who had caused damage along the Irish coast.[114] Ashwell's contacts with Scotland were already of long standing: eleven years earlier he and John Stameen were two of three burgesses from the town granted licence to sell bread and ale to the Lord of the Isles, who was then in alliance with the English, and whose men were permitted to bring their galleys to Drogheda for purposes of trade.[115] The third burgess granted a licence on this occasion, William Symcock, seneschal of Drogheda in Meath, enjoyed a remarkable career that spanned the four decades separating the strife of the Windsor era from the triumph of the establishment of the united county of Drogheda on 1 November 1412.[116] William first appears in our records in the list of Drogheda men summoned by Windsor in February 1372 to attend a great council in Dublin; a list that also included Simon Mole and John Ashwell.[117] As Symcock is not a surname that appears in Drogheda records before this date it is likely that William had migrated to there from England or from another town in Ireland sometime earlier, and by 1372 he was already an important figure in the town. He was not in the forefront of those from Drogheda who confronted Windsor, but his appearance as a guarantor for John Ashwell, who was one of the twenty-three individuals required by the governor to pay for charters of peace on account of their 'contempt and trespass' in November 1373, suggests his support for the resistance to the governor offered by the men of Drogheda.[118]

The popularity of Symcock's stance secured his election for the first time as seneschal of Drogheda in Meath in 1374, and his efforts to repair the bridge over the Boyne while in office led to the cancellation by the Windsor government of a debt of 46s 8d owed by the town at the exchequer.[119] He was nominated as one of his Irish attorneys by the abbot of Furness in October 1374, and secured temporary release from his post as seneschal in May 1375 in order to allow him to prosecute his business interests in Munster.[120] He next appears in the records in 1384, acquiring property in the part of Drogheda north of the Boyne and a windmill in the Louth countryside, and in the following year increased his rural interests substantially by securing a grant from the crown of custody of the manor of Ardcath (bar. Upper Duleek, co. Meath).[121] In 1386, again acting as seneschal of Drogheda in Meath, Symcock was given licence to go to England, and appears at this time to have attracted the favourable attention of Richard II who, through the deputies of Robert de Vere, marquis of Dublin and duke of Ireland, granted to him a fishery

---

[114] *RCH* 127 no. 243.
[115] *RCH* 96 no. 218.
[116] For Symcock's career and the 1412 grant, see Buldorini, 'Drogheda as a Case Study of Anglo-Norman Town Foundation', 325–38.
[117] Betham, *Origin and History*, 314.
[118] COA Rep. Records of the Exchequer, 42–51 Edward III, 117.
[119] *RCH* 89 no. 109.
[120] *CPR 1374–1377*, 13; *RCH* 97 no. 239.
[121] COA Rep. Records of the Exchequer, 1–10 Richard II, 428, 499; *RCH* 124 no. 45.

on the river Bann in Ulster and licence in December 1386 to transport wine to the Hebrides 'and to do there as he wishes'.[122]

Two months later, Symcock's trading ambitions received a further boost when he was permitted to transport wheat from Drogheda to Gascony or Spain, and it was probably the wine carried back to Ireland as part of such enterprises that he was permitted to sell in Ulster in March 1389.[123] William is absent from our records from this date until March 1400, when he was again granted custody of Ardcath. One of his mainpernors on this occasion was John Symcock, who was possibly his son or brother, and who since the 1380s had claimed property in the marches of Louth at Serlestown and Pepperstown north of Ardee.[124] Symcock was licensed to carry wheat to Bordeaux 'in aid of the lieges there' in February 1412, but most of his energies in the 1400s appear to have been directed towards extending and protecting his commercial interests in Ulster.[125] He received licences to transport wine and ale there in 1403 and 1405, and in 1409 was among those appointed in Drogheda to facilitate the building of a warship in the town by arresting the masons needed to complete its construction. The ship, under the command of Janico Dartas, was intended to clear the north Irish Sea of enemy Scottish shipping—a feat which would clearly have benefited Symcock's trading ventures.[126]

William Symcock's career reached a fitting climax when he was elected as the first mayor of the newly united town and shire of Drogheda in late 1412 or 1413. On his death in 1420, 'there was great moane made' in the town, and he was fondly remembered by the inhabitants of Drogheda as one who 'well and honourably governed the same'.[127] He stands as one of the most successful urban politicians not only of late medieval Ireland, but of the English world in general. While a recorded career of almost half a century that embraced the establishment of extensive domestic and foreign trading networks, lengthy periods of civic office-holding, election to parliament, the forging of ties with powerful individuals in both Ireland and England, and the accumulation of both urban and rural property, marks Symcock out as an individual of unique energy and ability, there were others among his contemporaries in the towns of Louth who emulated at least some of his achievements. Robert Sexton was among those Drogheda merchants who in May 1370 saw goods they had already purchased being impounded at Dalkey by agents of Windsor and sold for his profit, and who in November 1373 was forced to pay a fine by the chief governor for his 'contempt and trespass'.[128] By 1406 he was receiving licence to travel to England 'on the king's business', and in 1422 he served as mayor of Drogheda.[129]

---

[122] *RCH* 125 no. 138; 133 no. 84; 135 nos. 162 and 172; 136 no. 199.
[123] *RCH* 137 no. 223; 142 no. 237.
[124] *RCH* 159 no. 6; COA Rep. Records of the Exchequer, 10–22 Richard II, 232.
[125] *RCH* 198 no. 26(b).
[126] *RCH* 176 no. 11; 181 no. 37; 193 no. 184.
[127] *Christ Church Deeds*, 186–7; Mac Iomhair, 'Two Old Drogheda Chronicles', 94; FitzMaurice and Little, *Materials for the History of the Franciscan Province*, 181.
[128] Clarke, 'William of Windsor in Ireland', 118; COA Rep. Records of the Exchequer, 42–51 Edward III, 114–17.
[129] *RCH* 182 no. 60; 214 no. 12; *Rotuli Selecti*, 51; *Parls. & Councils*, 152; NAI, RC 8/39, 218.

The rise of the Prestons from migrant merchants in Drogheda around 1300 to lords of Gormanston within two generations has been discussed in previous chapters, but it should be remembered that members of the family continued to exploit the opportunities for personal advancement offered by Drogheda long after their more exalted relatives joined the country set. One such was William Preston, who was elected as one of Drogheda's two sheriffs in 1421, the year after Symcock's death.[130] By this time Preston had already made an advantageous marriage to a daughter of Sir Edward Perrers, and been granted a substantial yearly rent of £20 from the estates in Duleek, Kells, and Dundalk of Thomas Cruys, to whom part of the original Verdon lands in Louth and Meath had descended.[131] He served as a collector of customs in Drogheda in 1427, and in the following decade became more involved in overseas trade.[132] In 1435, he was among a small number of Drogheda merchants licensed on two occasions to carry large quantities of salt, iron, and other merchandise in ten ships from Brittany, and later in the decade acted as one of the attorneys in Ireland of a Coventry merchant, Thomas Wildegryce.[133]

As these examples suggest, those who thrived in late medieval Drogheda were either already possessed of interests outside the town in counties Meath and Louth or acquired them as part of their advancement.[134] John Ash, merchant of Drogheda, who served as one of the attorneys of Richard Spicer of Northampton in 1381, and who appeared in the court of staple in Bristol before its mayor, William Canynge (d.1396), in 1386, held property including a watermill at Lucystown (now Castletowncooley, bar. Lower Dundalk) on the Cooley peninsula, and with his wife, Petronilla, also had land in Kildemock in the barony of Ardee.[135] Thomas Skinner, burgess of Drogheda, who on his death in *c*.1410 left money for the purchase of ornaments for the high altar of his parish church of St Peter's, had been among the seven burgesses forced by William Windsor to attend him in Kilkenny in May 1371 and pay money demanded of the town before being allowed to return home.[136] In 1376, he acted as one of the attorneys of the abbot of Furness in a dispute concerning the rights of the abbey in Beybeg, and in the 1380s acquired custody of the manor of Ricetown in Meath.[137] A contemporary of Skinner's in Drogheda, Walter Taylor, who was among those burgesses fined for contempt and trespass by Windsor in November 1373, held property in the town and barony of

---

[130] TNA E 101/247/15.
[131] 'Henry Marleburrough's Chronicle of Ireland', 218. William's wedding took place on the same day as that of two of the daughters of his cousin, Christopher Preston. For a family tree see *Gormanston Reg.*, xi. *Dowdall Deeds*, 157; *RCH* 239 no. 115.
[132] TNA E 101/248/1.
[133] *RCH* 257 nos. 3 and 68; *CPR 1436–41*, 222.
[134] For the case of Robert Babe, see above, 66–7.
[135] *CPR 1377–81*, 588; *Handbook and Select Calendar…Ireland*, 149; *Dowdall Deeds*, 144, 155–6; COA Rep. Records of the Exchequer, Henry IV, 216; *Christ Church Deeds*, 182, 183.
[136] *Reg. Fleming*, 136–7; Clarke, 'William of Windsor in Ireland', 117.
[137] 'Ancient Deeds', 29–30; *RCH* 112 no. 121; 139 no. 83; *Dowdall Deeds*, 118–20, 122–4, 124, 125; *PKCI* 48; *CPR 1396–9*, 206.

Ardee with his wife, Margery, up to the time of his death in 1407.[138] It was also the case that property in Drogheda was seen as desirable by men of standing in the countryside.[139] The archbishops of Armagh were not the only important figures in Louth also to have residences in Drogheda. The Verdon family held property there, and Nicholas Verdon chose to be buried in the town in 1347.[140] James White, one of the murderers of the sheriff, John Dowdall, in 1402 and later seneschal of Ulster, had a house on West Street in Drogheda in Louth, which was confiscated with the rest of his interests in 1403 on account of his crime.[141]

The possession of property beyond the walls of their town was even more prevalent among the burgesses of Dundalk than of Drogheda, and the former were also more likely than the latter to hold public office in county Louth. Matthew Tanner was associated in Dundalk with the powerful Dowdall family from the 1360s and in the same decade acquired property north of the town at Raskeagh and Ballymascanlan.[142] In February 1372, he was among those to receive a personal summons to the great council convened at Dublin by William Windsor, and served as sheriff of Louth in 1379–80.[143] Tanner increased his stake in the marches north of Dundalk in 1385 when he was granted the manor of Faughart, adjacent to Raskeagh, by Robert Kerdiff, while at the same time continuing to acquire property in Dundalk.[144] In 1390, he was appointed, along with his fellow Dundalk man, Geoffrey White, as keeper of the peace and commissioner of array for county Louth, and in 1396 established an entail by which he endowed his son and heir, also Matthew, with all his property in Louth.[145] Matthew junior followed in the footsteps of his father, serving as justice of the peace for Louth in 1412, and combining that role with the position of sheriff of the county in 1420.[146]

Among those with whom Matthew Tanner had property dealings in Dundalk in the 1410s and 1420s was Peter Dowdall, who built upon a long tradition of family involvement in the town to emerge as one of its most important and successful inhabitants in the first half of the fifteenth century.[147] Peter was the first head of the Dundalk branch of the Dowdall family in five generations stretching back to the 1300s not to serve as sheriff of Louth. His preference for advancing his position by increasing his landowning in the Dundalk region and forging alliances with other prominent individuals with interests there paid dividends. He required a pardon for unspecified trespasses in 1407, the same year in which John Ash of Drogheda granted him his

---

[138] COA Rep. Records of the Exchequer, 42–51 Edward III, 114–17; *Christ Church Deeds*, 167, 168, 170, 182; *RCH* 105 no. 108.

[139] As was property in Newcastle by the gentry of 14th-cent. Tynedale: Holford and Stringer, *Border Liberties and Loyalties*, 337.

[140] NAI RC 8/22, 609–10; *Clyn*, 240.

[141] See above, 97–101; *RCH* 174 no. 86.

[142] *CPR 1364–7*, 190; *Dowdall Deeds*, 93, 95, 96, 97, 106.

[143] COA Rep. Records of the Exchequer, 1–10 Richard II, 92, 150, 177.

[144] *Dowdall Deeds*, 112–13, 117–18, 120, 121, 122.

[145] *RCH* 147 no. 242; *Dowdall Deeds*, 128–9, 135.

[146] *RCH* 201 no. 123; 217 no. 15; TNA E 101/247/8 and 15; *Dowdall Deeds*, 167. Tanner was dead by July 1444: *Dowdall Deeds*, 183.

[147] *Dowdall Deeds*, 157, 168–9.

watermill at Castletowncooley.¹⁴⁸ On 31 December 1408 he entered into an indenture with Janico Dartas, discussed above, by which he received custody of the latter's castles of Greencastle and Carlingford in return for an annual payment of £18 and the promise to ride with Dartas against his enemies anywhere in Ulster, Louth, or Meath.¹⁴⁹ His fortune was secured in July 1410 when his widowed mother, Matilda Gernon, bound herself to pay him the remarkable sum of 4,000m, and he came into possession of her estate, which included property in Ardee, on her death sometime before September 1419.¹⁵⁰ In September 1416 Matthew Fleming, who died soon afterwards, granted Peter Dowdall all his possessions in Louth. Fleming, who was possibly related to Dowdall and who was already a figure of some note in the town in the 1390s, had enhanced his position in Dundalk by his marriage before 1407 to Agnes, the widow of Walter Kerisley, a member of another important family in the town.¹⁵¹ Dowdall was at Ardee in June 1417 where 'in the garden of the dwelling of John Glyssot, notary' he took possession of a deed sealed by Thomas Wotton, burgess of Ardee, by which Wotton granted him his estate in Dundalk, and in 1419 he was granted all his property in the vicinities of Carlingford and Dundalk by Thomas Leynagh.¹⁵² He was probably responsible for the construction of 'Dowdall's castle'—the first tower house in Dundalk noted in surviving records—which is mentioned in a deed of 1443, and which was located close to the parish church of St Nicholas.¹⁵³

Dowdall's wealth and ingenuity had not escaped the notice of his social superiors in Ireland, and sometime before 1420 he had become a retainer of James Butler, earl of Ormond.¹⁵⁴ This association led to Peter's imprisonment by Ormond's rival, John Talbot, and Dowdall appears subsequently to have avoided entanglement in high politics in Ireland. Over the next three decades he continued to acquire interests in Dundalk ranging from rabbit warrens to a stone castle, and added properties at Ardee, Roche, and Carlingford to his estate.¹⁵⁵ Secure possession of the mill at Castletowncooley proved difficult to achieve, requiring Peter to have notarial instruments drawn up at Carlingford and Haggardstown (bar. Upper Dundalk) in 1439 and Drogheda in 1449. These instruments contained statements from elderly witnesses to the effect that the mill had belonged to Peter's father, John, and that grain milled there had been taken on horseback to Dundalk for John's use, and following his death to Greencastle for Peter's use. The mill, however, had been burnt by O'Neill, and rebuilt by John Hasse, and Dowdall had failed to regain possession of it by the time of his death in 1449.¹⁵⁶

---

¹⁴⁸ *RCH* 187 no. 26; *Dowdall Deeds*, 144.
¹⁴⁹ *Dowdall Deeds*, 152–3.
¹⁵⁰ *Dowdall Deeds*, 154, 157, 164–5.
¹⁵¹ *Dowdall Deeds*, 126, 141, 145, 155, 163–4; *RCH* 171 nos. 109, 110; COA Rep. Records of the Exchequer, 10–22 Richard II, 239. For the Dowdall–Fleming connection: Clare, *On the Edge of the Pale*, 37.
¹⁵² *Dowdall Deeds*, 161–2, 164, 166.
¹⁵³ Gosling, 'From Dún Delca to Dundalk', 301.
¹⁵⁴ Griffith, 'Talbot–Ormond Struggle', 394–5; see above, 112–14.
¹⁵⁵ *Dowdall Deeds*, 169, 171, 172, 173–4, 175–6, 181–3.
¹⁵⁶ *Dowdall Deeds*, xv, 177–8, 179–80, 185–6.

Peter Dowdall's long and successful career had features distinct from those of many of the other notable townsmen discussed in this chapter. Apart from serving briefly as collector of debts owed to the bailiffs and commons (*communitates*) of Dundalk in 1439 he held no public office in either his native town or county.[157] He appears never to have travelled to England and, aside from executing his duties as constable of Greencastle in county Down, is not recorded as having strayed beyond the confines of county Louth. It is possible to regard him as a man of narrow interests and ambitions—a personification of the shrinking world of English Ireland in the first half of the fifteenth century. Perhaps: but it can also be argued that it was always more likely that foreign trade and travel would be integral to fortunes amassed in Drogheda than in Dundalk, and that a disinclination towards office-holding and extensive travel did not prevent Dowdall enjoying the patronage of such important men as Janico Dartas and James Butler, earl of Ormond. If the physical reach of English authority in Ireland was contracting, then it was also being experienced more intensely in those parts of the lordship, such as the towns of county Louth, where it was still effective. Why should Peter Dowdall travel in search of power, when power was prepared to travel in search of him?

The visit of Richard II to Drogheda and Dundalk in 1395, and the increase in the number of occasions on which Drogheda was chosen as a venue for parliament after 1400, have been discussed above. William Windsor had found it possible to disrupt the lives of the ruling elite in Drogheda in the early 1370s without ever setting foot there, but he was unusual among the king's representatives in late medieval Ireland in failing to visit the town.[158] Until the late fourteenth century the presence of senior crown officials in other towns in Louth was a rare occurrence, and for Carlingford this remained the case throughout the rest of the Middle Ages. In August 1342 the escheator, John Morice, and the treasurer, Hugh Burgh, held inquisitions at Carlingford into the value of the estate of the late Maud, countess of Lancaster, and a royal service was proclaimed there by the justiciar, Alexander Balscot, bishop of Meath, in 1388.[159] Thomas of Lancaster's decision to land at the town on his return to Ireland as lieutenant in August 1408, however, set no precedent, and Carlingford continued to have little direct contact with senior personnel in the Dublin administration.[160]

By contrast, Ardee, which had not played host to a chief governor in the fourteenth century, was frequently visited by senior officials after 1400. Thomas of Lancaster's government spent most of December 1402 in the town, dealing with the aftermath of the murder of John Dowdall, sheriff of Louth, and it returned there in September 1403.[161] John Stanley, the lieutenant, celebrated Christmas at Ardee in 1413, and died there on 18 January 1414. He was the first of two chief

---

[157] *Dowdall Deeds*, 180.
[158] Connolly, 'Pleas Held Before the Chief Governor', 103–31.
[159] TNA C 47/10/20 no. 14; COA Rep. Records of the Exchequer, 10–22 Richard II, 98.
[160] Nicholls, 'Late Medieval Irish Annals', 98.
[161] See above, 98–9; *RCH*, 171 nos. 82, 83; NAI KB 1/3, m. 27d.

governors to expire in the town in the space of forty years, with James Butler, earl of Ormond, ending his life there in August 1452.[162] Between these two dates Ardee played host to the chief governor and other senior officials frequently, if irregularly. John Talbot conducted business there in September, October, and December 1415, while James Butler, earl of Ormond, appointed keepers of the peace for Louth in the town in July 1420.[163] In July 1423, 'the commons of Louth' assembled at Ardee before the justiciar, Richard Talbot, and the chief justice, Stephen Bray, to relay their security concerns and grant a subsidy for their defence.[164] Ormond spent some weeks at Ardee before and after sealing the indenture with MacMahon there on 12 May 1425, and between then and his death visited the town in his capacity as chief governor at least twice, in May 1441 and January 1451.[165]

The experience of Dundalk was akin to that of Ardee. When the town was threatened with assault by the Irish in 1355 the justiciar, Thomas Rokeby, ordered Archbishop Fitz Ralph to deal with the matter, and the most senior official to visit Dundalk in these years was the escheator, John Pembroke, who held an inquisition there in June 1360 into the value of the estate of the late Elizabeth Verdon, the widow of Bartholomew Burghersh.[166] The proximity of the town to lands that lay within the earldom of Ulster in part explains why Edmund Mortimer, earl of March and Ulster, and Irish lieutenant, visited Dundalk in February 1381, and its proximity to the lands of O'Neill enhanced its importance in the eyes of the government in the disturbed years that followed.[167] The justiciar, John Stanley, was there in January 1390 to conduct negotiations about the fate of O'Neill hostages captured the previous year, and the lieutenant, James Butler, earl of Ormond, arranged to meet O'Neill in the town in 1421.[168] The indentures entered into with O'Neill by Butler in July 1425, John Talbot in December 1446, and Richard, duke of York, in July 1449 were all sealed at Dundalk.[169]

The towns of late medieval Louth were crucial to the development of society in the county as a whole. In the same manner as the Church, they functioned as a bridge between the region and the rest of the world, while simultaneously helping to ensure that the settlement survived the frontier environment in which it operated. The role of the towns in maintaining the security of the English settlement in Louth and adjacent parts of Meath was appreciated by contemporaries.[170] In 1435, the phrase 'the key of the county' was used to describe both

---

[162] Nicholls, 'Late Medieval Irish Annals', 92, 98; Mac Iomhair, 'Two Old Drogheda Chronicles', 94; *RCH* 202 nos. 6, 7; 203 nos. 14, 15.
[163] *RCH* 211 nos. 56, 57, 67; 212 nos. 76, 109; 213 nos. 120, 121, 124; 217 no. 15.
[164] *RCH* 230 no. 120.
[165] *RCH* 227 nos. 30, 31; 237 no. 71; 264 no. 32; 266 no. 21; *Handbook and Select Calendar… Ireland*, 216–22; *Reg. Swayne*, 184.
[166] *RCH* 62 no. 100; *Inquisitions and Extents*, 195; *CFR 1356–68*, 131.
[167] *RCH* 108 no. 52; *Dowdall Deeds*, 109.
[168] *RCH* 144 no. 100; *CPR 1389–1392*, 275; *AFM* iv. 851.
[169] *Handbook and Select Calendar… Ireland*, 222–3, 226; *CPR 1446–52*, 63; *Reg. Mey*, 176, 178.
[170] For a town in England that played a similar role: Henry Summerson, *Medieval Carlisle: The City and the Borders from the Late Eleventh to the Mid Sixteenth Centuries*, 2 vols (Kendal, 1993).

Nobber and Drumconrath in government grants designed to improve the defences of these small boroughs, and two years later was used again in reference to Ardee.[171] How the towns of Louth adapted to frontier conditions will be considered in the next chapter.

---

[171] *RCH* 258 no. 92; Lynch, *View of the Legal Institutions*, 197; NAI Ferguson Coll. iii. 152. The priory of Fore was described as 'the key of the march there' in 1423: *RCH* 229 no. 96. Greencastle was said to be the key to the parts of Ulster in which it lay in 1382: TNA E 101/246/3.

7

The Marches

The marchlands of late medieval Ireland were characterized by a violence that was sporadic and an instability that was permanent and insidious. Their existence had an impact on wider society that stretched far beyond any vague geographical boundaries assigned to them by contemporaries and later historians. In Louth and Meath, the consequences of the marches were felt not only in the countryside but also in the towns. In 1425, eighty inhabitants of Nobber were taken captive by MacMahon, and in 1434 the O'Neills attempted to burn the town.[1] In 1410, the bailiffs and community of Carlingford and the surrounding lordship of Cooley asserted that their lands had 'often been burned and devastated' by the Scots and Irish.[2] The report of the constable of Carlingford castle following a Scottish naval raid in 1388 to the effect that the area was 'burned and wasted' supports their claim, and in 1423 the town's Dominican priory was said to be 'disfigured by age and the incursions of enemies and robbers'.[3] Only the intervention of Archbishop Richard Fitz Ralph preserved Dundalk from O'Neill attack in 1355, but the town was not so fortunate in 1374, 1392, 1399, 1423, 1434, and 1444, when it endured Irish raids.[4] Acceptance by the townsmen of the likelihood of attack was reflected in the grant of a house in Dundalk made in 1442. The property was to be returned to the grantor after a term of years in the same good condition in which it was granted 'unless burned by the rebels, the king's enemies, or by accidental fire'.[5]

It is not necessary to minimize the dangers presented to the towns of Louth and Meath by the proximity of the marches to also acknowledge that their inhabitants sought to use such dangers to their own advantage. The closest Drogheda came to experiencing an Irish raid in this period was in 1429 when 'many husbandmen with their sons and servants were slayne at Duleek', 7 kilometres south-west of the town, by O'Connor Faly.[6] The absence of onslaughts by the enemy did not deter the town authorities from employing the rhetoric of the frontier in order to extract concessions from the crown. The statement by the burgesses of Drogheda in Louth

---

[1] *Handbook and Select Calendar... Ireland*, 216–22; *Reg. Swayne*, 42; *AFM* iv. 899; *AU* iii. 133.
[2] *RCH* 196 no. 75.
[3] Otway-Ruthven, *History of Medieval Ireland*, 321; *RCH* 143 no. 28; *CPL 1417–31*, 261.
[4] *Dowdall Deeds*, 103; *RCH* 62 no. 100; *AFM* iv. 723, 725, 765, 767, 859, 899; Mac Firbis, *Annals*, 205. Dundalk men had been among those killed in the MacMahon raid of 1346: *Clyn*, 238.
[5] *Dowdall Deeds*, 183.
[6] Mac Iomhair, 'Two Old Drogheda Chronicles', 91.

in November 1358 that they lived in a place 'situated by the march of the king's Irish enemies by which all the neighbouring country is defended against invasions of the enemies' went unchallenged, and encouraged Edward III to grant to them valuable trading concessions that were to last for twelve years.[7] In the spring of 1364 the king issued an even more favourable charter to the burgesses of Drogheda

> in consideration of the services of the said burgesses and their ancestors to the king and his forefathers, and especially for the defence of their town and the neighbouring parts not without cost and pains against attacks of the Irish and other the king's enemies, striving to invade the lands of the king and of his lieges in Ireland, and to rob and destroy his people there.[8]

In 1386, on account of 'the damages and losses endured by the mayor and commons of Drogheda both by sea and by land in resisting our divers enemies up to now, and the help it has always given to relieve the faithful men of adjacent places', a fine of 20m was waived by the crown.[9] In 1437 the town authorities were exonerated from paying the annual fee-farm of the town, worth 100m, 'because so much of the land around the city has been destroyed by the Irish enemies, by the Scots and Bretons and other enemies from the sea', and this concession was renewed in 1442.[10]

If Drogheda was situated at some distance from the marches, Ardee could hardly have been closer to them. While the town also avoided direct attack after 1316, its proximity to lands controlled by the king's enemies lent a particular urgency to its requests for aid from the crown. It was to help better resist 'our Irish enemies in the march adjacent to the town' that the king in 1376 granted to the provost and commune of Ardee trading concessions designed to enable them to strengthen the town walls.[11] The 'malice of the king's Irish enemies' was offered as the reason for the renewal of this grant on more favourable terms in 1400 and 1414.[12] Carlingford and Dundalk, which did experience Irish raids, also sought aid from the crown on account of the threats they faced as marcher towns. In March 1410, the community of Carlingford was granted its request that the collection of all exactions from it be suspended until its lord, Edmund Mortimer, earl of March, reached his majority.[13] In 1369, John Crophull, Simon Fleming, and John Bellew, who held the Verdon manor and town of Dundalk, sought allowance of the dues they owed on the grounds that most of the lands concerned were occupied by Brian MacMahon and O'Hanlon.[14] The town was incorporated in the reign of Richard II, and in

---

[7] *CPR 1358–61*, 114.
[8] *CCR 1364–9*, 8; Buldorini, 'Drogheda as a Case Study of Anglo-Norman Town Foundation', 257–61. For the text of the charter: Mac Niocaill, *Na Buirgéisí*, i. 195–200.
[9] *CPI* 83.
[10] NLI MS 4, f. 334; *CPR 1441–6*, 97, 132.
[11] *CPI* 73, 77.
[12] *RCH* 203 no. 15.
[13] *RCH* 196 no. 75. Mortimer was declared of age in June 1413: Griffiths, 'Mortimer, Edmund (V)'.
[14] COA Rep. Records of the Exchequer, 42–51 Edward III, 34.

June 1412 its bailiffs and commons received licence to take customs from items being sold there for eighteen years in order to enable the strengthening of the town walls.[15]

The townsmen of Louth not only sought to exploit the marches to gain concessions from the king, but also attempted to benefit from them commercially. During Richard II's first expedition to Ireland in 1394–5 the Leinster chief Feidlimid O'Toole (Ó Tuathail) sought the king's permission to trade peacefully at the fair at Ballymore Eustace (co. Kildare), arguing that 'I shall [thereby] be able to sustain my life and that of my people, for without buying and selling I can in no way live'.[16] Evidence of the desire of the settlers in the marches of Louth and Meath to benefit from the same reality is not hard to find. In February 1405, the crown granted special licence to Thomas Bath 'to treat and communicate with, and sell to and buy from, Irish enemies and rebels upon his march in co. Meath'.[17] A more systematic approach was taken to regulating this trade in February 1412 when, for the 'preservation of that town and in relief of the inhabitants of the neighbouring parts', Thomas Fleming, baron of Slane, was granted permission to hold a market and fair at his borough of Drumconrath, which had been repeatedly burnt by the Irish.[18] In the indenture sealed by the lieutenant, James Butler, earl of Ormond, and Brian MacMahon and his brothers at Ardee in 1425 it was agreed that any men of the MacMahons who sought food and victuals among the English must do so only in the towns of Louth, Dundalk, and Ardee, which they must enter and exit 'by the public highway' (*per vias puplicas*). That Irish traders purchased more than food and drink in the towns is suggested by MacMahon's ability to hand over to Ormond 'six woven English cloths' as part of the same agreement.[19] Niall Óc O'Neill had informed Richard II in 1395 that his men were forced to pay a toll of 1d for each horse in their possession when entering Dundalk, presumably in pursuit of trade, and in July 1423 a licence was issued to John Singleton, merchant of Dundalk, permitting him to sell to the Irish and Scots at Lough Foyle and Lough Swilly (co. Donegal) all goods with the exception of horses and arms, 'both in time of war and of peace; notwithstanding any statutes'.[20]

In conjunction with such initiatives to encourage and regulate trade on the marches, attempts were made to disrupt unlicensed commerce. A petition of the settlers to the crown in 1366 complained that Irish traders who had purchased charters of English franchise were now 'among the richest merchants in Ireland' (*les queux sunt deveus les plus riches marchaunz dirland*) and asserted that these men sought to use their economic power to help their fellow Irishmen. Legislation was passed in 1431 to prohibit settler merchants trading in Irish towns, which, in the

---

[15] *RCH* 200 no. 87; COA Rep. Records of the Exchequer, Henry IV, 407; Mac Niocaill, *Na Buirgéisí*, i. 210–14.
[16] Curtis, *Richard II in Ireland*, 125–6, 206–8.
[17] *RCH* 180 no. 6.
[18] *RCH* 198 no. 30.
[19] *Handbook and Select Calendar...Ireland*, 221.
[20] Curtis, *Richard II in Ireland*, 132–3, 212–13; *RCH* 227 no. 39.

context of the marches of Louth and Meath, was directed against the O'Reilly town of Cavan.[21] In 1337, an investigation was ordered into the supply of victuals to felons who sought to disturb the peace agreed between the English of Louth and O'Hanlon, while in 1385 the order was given 'to arrest and take all victuals from the parts of Louth near the lands of Neel Oneel and other rebels, carried there contrary to the proclamation'.[22] In 1394, the sheriff and keepers of the peace in Louth were commanded to proclaim and have observed an ordinance prohibiting the sale 'to any Irishman not abiding among our lieges any corn, malt, bread, wine, ale, salt, iron, horses, armour or any other necessaries whatsoever', and two years later a commission of local men was established in the county 'to inquire who took corn and horses, arms, bread, wine, etc. to Neal ONeele, Philip MacMahon or Philip McGynnisa or others, Scottish or Irish'.[23]

The towns of late medieval Louth and Meath not only survived the marches; to some extent they relied upon them for their well-being. The claim by the men of Drogheda in 1358 that their town was 'situated by the march' appears problematic only if the all-encompassing nature of the marches is underestimated. The marches had a geographical meaning, but they had other features that transcended territorial boundaries in this small region. The towns of Louth were English foundations; their walls, towers, gates, fairs, and markets spoke to a purpose and identity that distinguished them from the countryside around them, whether that countryside was peopled predominantly by fellow-settlers or by hostile Irish families. But the towns depended upon the countryside both for the produce that was consumed and traded within their walls, and for the men and women who replenished their populations. From the outset the towns welcomed not only migrants from England, but also individuals and families from nearby manors who wished to partake of the opportunities offered by urban life. Among these were men and women of Irish origin, and the reaction to their presence on the part of the settlers was one reason why the concerns of the marches were also the concerns of the towns. This reaction was not universally hostile. It was certainly possible for Irishmen to succeed in the towns: in 1404, for instance, Philip Ofynan, 'burgess of the town of Drogheda', was granted licence to transport wheat to Kinsale.[24] In 1358, the Dundalk burgess John Rathcoul—whose surname reveals the migration of his own ancestors at some earlier time from a settlement in the barony of Ardee—was content to take

---

[21] Sayles, *Affairs*, 224–6; *Stat. Ire., Hen. VI*, 42; Cherry, 'Indigenous and Colonial Urbanization of Cavan Town', 87–8; Patrick J. Duffy, 'The Nature of the Medieval Frontier in Ireland', *Studia Hibernica*, 22 and 23 (1982–3), 33–5; Katharine Simms, 'References to Landscape and Economy in Irish Bardic Poetry', in Howard B. Clarke, Jacinta Prunty, and Mark Hennessy (eds), *Surveying Ireland's Past: Multidisciplinary Essays in Honour of Anngret Simms* (Dublin, 2004), 145–68.
[22] *RCH* 42 no. 6; COA Rep. Records of the Exchequer, 1–10 Richard II, 495. In 1375 attempts were made to stop unlicensed trade with Scotland: COA Rep. Records of the Exchequer, 42–51 Edward III, 159, 175.
[23] *Stat. Ire., John–Hen. V*, 498 n. 1, 499; COA Rep. Records of the Exchequer, 10–22 Richard II, 396. Philip Magennis is not mentioned in other records, and his name may appear in error in the transcript of the original. I am grateful to Dr Simms for comment on this point.
[24] *RCH* 179 no. 24.

on as his apprentice Nicholas O Molghallyn, whom he agreed to train 'in the merchant's art'.[25]

The terms of O Molghallyn's apprenticeship have been cited as an example of the discrimination suffered by the Irish in the towns, since they appear less favourable than those offered seven years earlier by another merchant of Dundalk, John Kerisley, when he engaged an apprentice of settler stock, John Ellis.[26] While a sample of two apprenticeship agreements is too small an evidence base from which to draw such a conclusion—it is just as possible that the terms offered by Kereseley were unusually easy and that Rathcoul's arrangements were standard—other contemporary evidence does support the idea that the Irish were unfairly treated in at least some aspects of town life. In sermons he preached at Drogheda in March 1349, December 1352, and February and June 1355, and at Dundalk in April 1356, Archbishop Richard Fitz Ralph criticized the townsmen on a number of grounds, some of which concerned their attitude towards the Irish. Irishmen and women, he said, had been hindered from making their wills freely, while 'those of a certain nation'—by which he appears to have meant the Irish—had been excluded from membership of the town guilds in Drogheda.[27] When discussing in the course of these sermons the acts of violence against the Irish and the theft of their property perpetrated by the townsmen, Fitz Ralph on more than one occasion used an arresting phrase. It would not suffice for the perpetrators of these deeds, he pronounced in December 1352, to soothe their consciences by suggesting that they were loyal subjects who had acted according to the 'law of the march' (*lex marchie*). In April 1356, in like manner, he told the men of Dundalk to abandon their argument that in behaving in this way they were merely acting as their ancestors had always done, and were 'following march law' (*sequentes legem marchie*). In fact, he argued, they were following 'march law and the law of the devil' (*legem marchie sive dyaboli*).[28]

Fitz Ralph's sermons suggest that marcher attitudes dominated the thinking of the urban settlers in Louth in relation to their Irish neighbours. The archbishop was not given to understatement and it is possible that his remarks reflect tensions particular to the years in which they were made, but other evidence can be found that lends some support to his assertions. In 1406, the crown seized property in Drogheda belonging to Thomas Walsh on the grounds that his name was really Thomas O'Kelly, and that as an Irishman he was not entitled to hold land in fee.

---

[25] *Dowdall Deeds*, 86–7.
[26] *Dowdall Deeds*, 82; Gwynn, 'Anglo-Irish Church Life', 20–1; Walsh, *Fourteenth-Century Scholar and Primate*, 342–3.
[27] *et sunt multi testamenta hibernicorum et eciam mulierum contra statutum domini regis et dei iusticiam cohibentes*: Gwynn, 'Two Sermons', 65; Gwynn, 'Sermon Diary'; Walsh, *Fourteenth-Century Scholar and Primate*, 341–2.
[28] Gwynn, 'Anglo-Irish Church Life', 18–20; Walsh, *Fourteenth-Century Scholar and Primate*, 285–90, 325–45.

In response,

> Thomas asserted that he has the name of Thomas Walsh and was born at Trim, co. Meath, and that his father was Roger Walsh and his grandfather was Milo Walsh; and that he is an Englishman of English birth, and that his ancestors had the surname Walsh and were Englishmen, and that he is not Thomas Okelly, an Irishman of the Okelles.[29]

His argument was upheld and it may be the case that his difficulties arose as a result of his status as a recent migrant to the town. It remains the case, however, that an unidentified fellow townsman had sought to deprive him of his property on the basis that he was an Irishman. Archbishop Fitz Ralph would have sympathized, since one element of the attack upon him by his enemies in Dublin in the course of the primacy controversy concerned his family background and identity. It was no wonder Fitz Ralph sought to put the church of Dublin under the subjection of himself and the king's Irish enemies, asserted a petition sent by his detractors to the council in England in 1350, 'since his family was for the most part Irish' (*qad soun lineage pur la greindre partie Irreys*).[30]

The trading activities of the townsmen with the Irish beyond their walls was marked by a distinct element of contempt for their customers. In November 1402, three Drogheda merchants were licensed to buy provisions in Ulster for the town and in return to transport there 'six tuns of old wine not for sale among the English', while in December 1405 the future mayor of the town, William Symcock, was permitted to take to Lough Foyle in Ulster 'two tuns of old wine, which is not suitable for sale among the English'.[31] Two, however, could play at that game. It clearly galled the settlers that the supporters of MacMahon billeted upon them in 1402 refused 'such food and drink as the poor commons use themselves'.[32] The tract on the rights of MacMahon, which possibly dates from the second quarter of the fifteenth century, dwells exultantly on the victuals that the English of Louth were supposedly forced to yield to the Irish. Feidlimid 'of the wine' MacMahon, reports the tract, 'was so called because he would not accept anything but wine instead of malt', from the settlers.[33]

If some aspects of life in the towns of medieval Louth were conditioned by marcher thinking, the same was at least as true in the countryside. Occasional attempts to disinherit individuals on the basis of supposed Irish rather than English origin were not confined to urban centres. An inquisition was convened at Drogheda in 1384 to determine if Adam Norris, who held land in Rathdrumin by right of his wife, was in fact Irish and should therefore lose his property. The jurors concluded that he was of English stock, and noted that members of the family were 'free tenants in divers places' in the county.[34] In 1443, John Feld and his wife, Margery, succeeded in regaining possession of land at Stonehouse (bar. Ferrard) that had been seized by the crown as a result of an inquisition that

---

[29] COA Rep. Records of the Exchequer, Henry IV, 194. [30] Sayles, *Affairs*, 194.
[31] *RCH* 172 no. 12; 181 no. 37.
[32] *Proceedings and Ordinances*, ii. 49–50.
[33] Pender, 'A Tract on MacMahon's Prerogatives', 254–5.
[34] *Dowdall Deeds*, 117.

erroneously concluded that the land had once 'belonged to William McKegan, an Irishman'.³⁵

Such incidents in both town and country should be viewed in the context of a more general willingness on the part of the settlers to disinherit their friends, neighbours, and especially relatives, on the basis of the supposed illegitimate birth of the existing occupier. A petition to the English council from Meath dating from the reign of Henry IV provides one example of the practice:

> Joan, wife of Geoffrey Cusak asks the king to order his lieutenant in Ireland to send Geoffrey before the king in England so that right can be done to him. John Sugley and Robert Curles asserted that Geoffrey was a bastard son of Thomas Cusak, ousted him from his lands and imprisoned him in Trim castle.³⁶

In similar fashion, in 1417 Thomas Wotton, burgess of Ardee, granted land in Dundalk to Peter Dowdall on the basis that it belonged to him and not to its current occupant, Walter Wotton, who was a bastard.³⁷ Disputes among the settlers on the marches about property might even result in bloodshed. In the 1360s George Teeling was convicted of murdering his nephew, Walter, 'for his heritage', which consisted of land in the Louth/Meath border area between Crowmartin and Siddan worth 100m per annum. Walter was the son of George's elder brother, and was referred to as the 'captain of his nation'.³⁸ The Teelings, it would appear, had adopted the practice recently instituted among settler families in the marches of south Dublin of identifying a leader who would represent them in their dealings both with their Irish enemies and with the Dublin administration.³⁹

The application by the government of the term 'captain of his nation' to Irish lords in the same period should not automatically lead to the conclusion that marcher settler families such as the Teelings had begun to align their inheritance practices with those of their Irish neighbours. The succession by Walter Teeling to his father's estate involved no deviation from standard English rules concerning the transmission of property, though George's resort to violence to gain his 'heritage' might have been inspired by observation on his part of the way in which such matters were handled by families such as the MacMahons and O'Neills. This is not to suggest that the settlers in this part of Ireland eschewed manipulation of the rules of inheritance, but rather to observe that they were able to do so by legitimate means, as their frequent recourse to the device of entail demonstrates.⁴⁰ The entail was not a direct consequence of marcher conditions, and still less a borrowing from Irish customs, but its popularity in Louth and Meath suggests that it was seen as useful in the maintenance of settler interests in a frontier world.

---

³⁵ BL Add MS 43769, ff. 60, 61.
³⁶ Connolly, 'Ancient Petitions' (TNA SC 8/181/9012).
³⁷ *Dowdall Deeds*, 161–2. Sir John Dowdall, son of the sheriff murdered in 1402, and his wife, Elizabeth Stokes, brought a case of bastardy against Laurence Netterville and Alice Stokes before the episcopal courts of Meath and Armagh in 1454: *Reg. Mey*, 374–5.
³⁸ Clarke, 'William of Windsor in Ireland', 84, 98–9, 107, 116.
³⁹ Smith, 'Lordship in the British Isles', 157; Christopher Maginn, 'English Marcher Lordships in South Dublin in the late Middle Ages', *IHS* 34 (2004–5), 113–36.
⁴⁰ See above, 10–11.

That Irish customs associated with the marches had the capacity to penetrate deep into Louth and adjacent parts of Meath is suggested by an incident from 1384. The sheriff of Meath, Thomas Chambers, reported that he had arrayed and provisioned a force of knights to support him in resisting O'Neill, but had not been compensated for the 25m he had paid them for six weeks of their services. The word he used to describe this payment, 'twerestell', represents only a slight deviation from the original Irish *tuarastal*, which by this period had the meaning of wages paid to fighting men.[41] Another native custom identified as current in the heart of the settlement was the 'creaght', or large-scale and destructive movement of cattle.[42] In 1427, Archbishop John Swayne complained that Sir Nicholas Taaf, and John and Roger Gernon, had entered his wood near the episcopal manor of Dromiskin, some 3 kilometres from the coast, with 'their men and also *kyriaghtys*'. There they had cut down and removed his trees, and 'consumed his lands and pastures with their animals'.[43] The practice was sufficiently common, and viewed as sufficiently pernicious, to warrant specific prohibition at the Dublin parliament of 1430, but in 1432 Brian MacMahon was permitted to bring his creaghts into Louth on account of the dangers he faced as an ally of the settlers.[44]

In 1420, the clergy of Armagh among the English had willingly agreed to pay a subsidy of over £9 to the lieutenant, James Butler, earl of Ormond, for having defended the king's lieges 'and for ending the extortion called "coignes" (*et distruccionem et extorcionem que dicuntur "coignes"*)'.[45] The Irish custom *coinnmheadh* referred to here involved the exaction of free lodging and provisions from the general populace for the lord's soldiers and servants, and sometimes also for his horses and dogs.[46] Archbishop Fleming had fulminated against the practice in 1411, and it is clear that it was deployed in Louth both by local lords and by visiting chief governors from at least the late fourteenth century.[47] In 1378, Archbishop Milo Sweteman wrote to commiserate with the prior of Ardee, whose house had been 'reduced to poverty by the numbers of officers of the king quartered upon it', and in 1422 the abbot of Mellifont complained that purveyors and royal officers had extorted £40 from the tenants on his lands in Louth and Meath.[48] MacMahon and his men were billeted on the county by the government in 1402, and in 1433 a similar arrangement saw the Ulster chief MacQuillin and his men being 'entertained' (*do choinnmídh*) by the inhabitants of Louth after they were expelled from their lands by O'Neill.[49]

Other legislation passed in the parliament of 1430 adds to the impression that the influence of the marches permeated the settlements in Louth and Meath in their entirety. Already in 1428 it had been agreed in parliament that a £10 subsidy would be paid to any liege in Louth who would build a castle or tower in the county within the following five years, and in 1430 this was extended to include

---

[41] *RCH* 120 no. 30; Simms, *From Kings to Warlords*, 178. [42] See above, 126.
[43] *Reg. Swayne*, 68. [44] *Stat. Ire., Hen. VI*, 35, 37; *AFM* iv. 891.
[45] *Parls. & Councils*, 143–4. [46] Simms, *From Kings to Warlords*, 173.
[47] *Reg. Swayne*, 18. [48] *Reg. Sweteman*, 251–2; *Proceedings and Ordinances*, ii. 50.
[49] *AFM* iv. 894–5.

Dublin, Meath, and Kildare, with a new time-frame of ten years for completion of the fortifications.[50] A petition of 1431 from the commons of Louth declared that the county could not be defended 'unless certain castles and fortresses be made in the marches', and a liberal definition of 'marches' was understood by those who sought a remedy for this situation. While some of the tower houses that were built as a result of these initiatives were located in the countryside on the fringes of the settlement, many were also constructed in the towns and in rural parts of Louth near the east coast that had never been subject to Irish raids. Some of those who built these towers were no doubt motivated in part by the desire to improve the standard of their accommodation at subsidized cost. But the high density of tower houses also spoke to the security concerns that the marches occasioned for Louth as a whole.[51]

The 1430 statute condemning creaghts contained a second Irish loan-word: creaghts, it ordained, were not to be driven from the marches into the maghery (= *machaire*, a plain) of the land of peace. The Irish names for the flat, fertile, lands around Dundalk (*Machaire-Conaille*), Louth and Ardee (*Machaire-Oirghiall*), and Nobber (*Machaire-Gaileang*) had clearly come to be deployed also by the settlers in reference to these places.[52] Niall O'Neill even used the word *Conaille* to refer to Dundalk when writing to Richard II in April 1395, in the expectation that its meaning would be made clear to him.[53] If Irish loan-words were considered appropriate for inclusion in a document as formal as a parliamentary statute, it is no surprise that they also appear in less formal writings relating to late medieval Louth. The complaints of the settlers about the consequences of the decision to billet MacMahon and his followers on them in 1402 included the charge that the Irish had brought with them into the county 'their caifs and their children' (*lours caifs norys et lour enfauntz*) who proceeded to spy upon them.[54] The word 'caif', which can be translated as concubine or prostitute, had previously been employed in an enactment passed by a provincial council summoned by Archbishop Milo Sweteman which sought to eradicate concubinage in the province of Armagh.[55]

It would appear that the settlers in Louth had a particular affection for Irish words that denigrated native women. In 1441, the court of Archbishop John Mey, which dealt with cases of defamation, heard of how Elena Oweyn of Termonfeckin

---

[50] *Stat. Ire., Hen. VI*, 17, 33, 35.
[51] *Stat. Ire., Hen. VI*, 45, 47; Victor M. Buckley and P. David Sweetman, *Archaeological Survey of County Louth* (Dublin, 1991), 301–60.
[52] For examples of the use of these words: *Reg. Octaviani*, ii. 487–8; *AC* 463, 465; *AFM* iii. 549; *AFM* iv. 859, 879, 893, 895, 899. For discussion see the works of Steven G. Ellis, esp. *Reform and Revival: English Government in Ireland 1470–1534* (Woodbridge, 1986), 50–2, and *The Pale and the Far North: Government and Society in Two Early Tudor Borderlands* (Galway, 1988).
[53] Curtis, *Richard II in Ireland*, 124–5, 205–6.
[54] *Proceedings and Ordinances*, ii. 50.
[55] *Acts of Colton*, xvii, note c; *Reg. Swayne*, 11. The word derives from *coibhche*, which by this time had come to mean a payment to a woman entering into a relationship of concubinage: Katharine Simms, 'The Contents of Later Commentaries on Brehon Law Tracts', *Ériu*, 49 (1998), 23–40, esp. 26 n. 12. I am most grateful to Dr Simms for guidance on this point.

had verbally abused her neighbours, Geffyn Oloucheran and his wife Agnes Rogan.[56] She had accused the husband of being a thief before calling the wife, to her face, a 'foule oold caylagh, trate [trot or mare] and heigge [hag]'.[57] The Irish word 'caylagh' (*cailleach*) means old woman, hag, or witch. Elena Oweyn's outburst provides an insight into the extent to which the marches influenced daily life in medieval Louth as a whole, and not only on account of her vocabulary. The surnames of the targets of her abuse, Oloucheran (Ó Lúchaireáin/O'Loughran) and O'Rogan (Ó Rudacáin), are of Ulster origin, and their appearance among the inhabitants of Termonfeckin, a few kilometres north of Drogheda, in the middle of the fifteenth century testifies to a degree of Irish migration deep into Louth. An appreciation of the different backgrounds of both these families, and the probable routes by which they came to reside in Louth, reveals some key features of this process of migration.

Agnes O'Rogan's ancestors were minor secular lords in south Armagh. In 1346, Auly and Petrus O'Rogan were accepted into the king's peace and allowed to settle with their adherents in the Dundalk region, close to their original homeland.[58] In 1361 and 1391 more members of the family were granted the king's peace, and in 1434, William Rogan was among those from Louth who proved their readiness to fight against the Irish before Archbishop Swayne at Mellifont.[59] How Agnes and William O'Rogan were related is unknown, but the circumstances of their appearances in the records of the 1430s and 1440s suggest movement from the borders of Louth to its heartland over the course of the previous century, and a readiness on the part of the family to integrate fully into settler society. Louth was the destination for members of several other Irish secular families from south Ulster that had, in the manner of the O'Rogans, suffered a loss of status as a result of the English conquest and the rise of the O'Neills. The family of O'Hanratty (Ó hAnrachtaig) continued to hold some of its ancestral lands at Machaire Mucnamha in east Monaghan from the Burgh family into the early fourteenth century, but a century later its leading members were canons in the cathedral chapters of Armagh and Clogher.[60] The movement into Louth of some members of the family is confirmed by the presence of Margaret O'Hanratty in Stabannan in 1427.[61]

Members of more successful Ulster families were also to be found in late medieval Louth. The family of MacGilroy (Mac Gilla Ruad) originated in Fermanagh, but by the early fifteenth century was also present in south Down.[62] The Richard

---

[56] The case is discussed in Art Cosgrove, 'The Armagh Registers: An Under-Explored Source for Late Medieval Ireland', *Peritia*, 6–7 (1987–8), 307–20 at 316. See also Anne (Sparky) Booker, 'After the "Middle Nation": The English of Ireland, Gaelicisation, and Identity in the "Four Loyal Shires" of Ireland in the Fifteenth and Sixteenth Centuries', Ph.D. thesis, University of Dublin, Trinity College (2011), ch. 4: 'The Irish Language in the Four Loyal Shires'. I am grateful to Dr Booker for making her thesis available to me.
[57] *Reg. Mey*, 73–4.
[58] *RCH* 50 no. 70.
[59] TNA E 101/244/4; *RCH* 148 no. 55; *Reg. Swayne*, 145–9.
[60] *AFM* iv. 861 863; *Inquisitions and Extents*, 137; TNA C 47/10/20 no. 14; *CPL 1417–31*, 405; *CPL 1427–47*, 70–1; *Reg. Swayne*, 73–7, 126–8; *Reg. Octaviani*, ii. 69.
[61] *Reg. Swayne*, 55.
[62] *AFM* iv. 795; *Reg. Swayne*, 114.

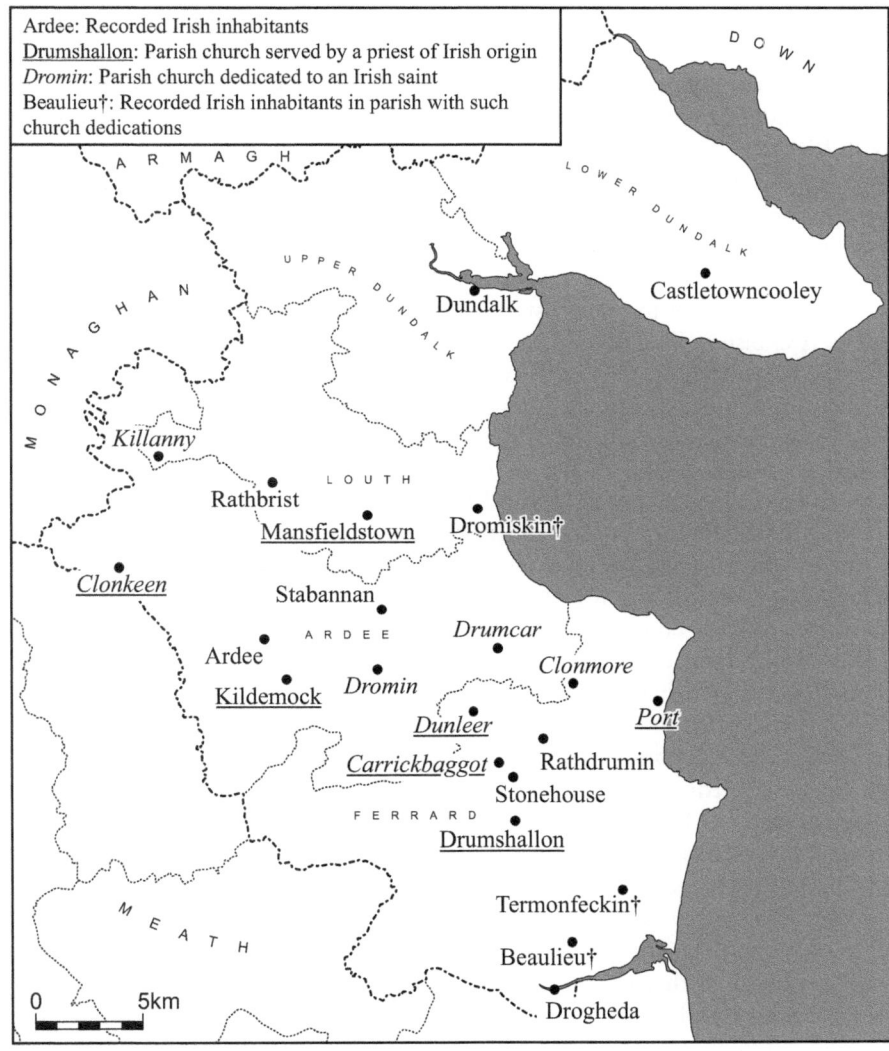

Map 5. The Irish in Louth

MacGilroy who in the 1440s testified regarding the ownership of a mill on the Cooley peninsula, in his capacity as Peter Dowdall's miller there, was probably a member of this family who had made the short journey south into Louth.[63] Walter Mckyllamura of Beaulieu, who features in a case of perjury in 1444, may have been related to the MacGilmore family which threatened the English settlement in Down in the early fifteenth century.[64] John O'Kane was sufficiently wealthy to

---

[63] *Dowdall Deeds*, 181, 185–6.
[64] 'Lord Chancellor Gerrard's Notes on his Report on Ireland', 207–8; *Reg. Mey*, 90–1; *Reg. Swayne*, 82; *Misc. Ir. Annals*, 173.

stand as one of the mainpernors of John Taaf when he received custody of two-thirds of the manor of Louth in July 1427.⁶⁵ His surname reveals him to have been a member of the important Derry family whose leader in 1395 described himself as 'your friend' in a letter he wrote to Archbishop Colton asking for his intercession with Richard II.⁶⁶

A significant number of the Irish who moved to Louth served as clergy in the county, even if the families from which they sprang had not held hereditary clerical positions in Ulster. The O'Hamill (Ó hAdmaill) family claimed kinship with the O'Neills, but lost its estates in south Tyrone and Armagh in the twelfth century and over time came to serve instead as hereditary poets to the O'Hanlons.⁶⁷ In 1436, Archbishop Swayne instituted a member of this family, John O'Hamill, as vicar of Kildemock on the Louth–Meath borders.⁶⁸ The O'Hanlon patrons of the O'Hamills frequently attacked Louth, but also sought refuge there when pressurized by greater Irish families in Ulster.⁶⁹ That some members of the family established a permanent base in the county is demonstrated by the case of William O'Hanlon, chaplain, who paid 6s 8d for a charter of English liberty at Ardee in 1451.⁷⁰ Master Philip MacGowan (Mac Gabann, also anglicized as 'Smith'), who witnessed the oath of fealty taken by the bishop of Raphoe to Archbishop Nicholas Fleming at Dromiskin in March 1416, was a member of a family originating on the Cavan–Meath borders that had provided Archbishop Milo Sweteman with a receiver of his rents in Armagh in the 1360s.⁷¹ Lay members of the family resided at Colpe, near Drogheda, in 1408, and at Rathdrumin and Ardee in 1431.⁷²

Individuals with links to the hereditary clerical families of Ulster also settled in Louth. The ancestors of Geffyn O'Loughran, Agnes O'Rogan's husband, for instance, were hereditary priests from Donaghmore in county Tyrone.⁷³ Since at least the episcopate of Milo Sweteman (1361–80), the archbishops of Armagh had called upon their services in running the part of their diocese that lay among the Irish, and the numerous letters to members of the family drawn up at the episcopal manor of Termonfeckin testify to the close links that existed between the archbishops and the O'Loughrans.⁷⁴ The services of Master Thomas O'Loughran, dean of Tullaghoge, were availed of with particular frequency by Archbishop John Colton.⁷⁵ It was Thomas who translated into English the submissions to Richard II of Niall Óc O'Neill at Drogheda and of Aed MacMahon at Dundalk in March 1395, and he also accompanied Colton on his visit to the vacant diocese of Derry in 1397.⁷⁶ Christian O'Loughran, who was later to serve as dean of Airthir, was entertained by

---

⁶⁵ *RCH* 241 no. 18.   ⁶⁶ Curtis, *Richard II in Ireland*, 142–3, 220–1.   ⁶⁷ *AC* 347.
⁶⁸ *Reg. Swayne*, 168.   ⁶⁹ See above, chapter 4.   ⁷⁰ *RCH* 266 no. 21.
⁷¹ *Reg. Fleming*, 82; *Reg. Sweteman*, 223–4.
⁷² Hogan, *Priory of Llanthony*, 380; *Reg. Octaviani*, ii. 54–5, 57.
⁷³ Katharine Simms, 'Frontiers in the Irish Church: Regional and Cultural', in Terry Barry, Robin Frame, and Katharine Simms (eds), *Colony and Frontier in Medieval Ireland: Essays Presented to J. F. Lydon* (London, 1995), 181. Geoffrey O'Loughran was a canon of Armagh cathedral at his death in Aug. 1366: *Reg. Sweteman*, 118–19.
⁷⁴ *Reg. Sweteman*, 214–15; *Reg. Swayne*, 121; *Reg. Octaviani*, ii. 84, 95.
⁷⁵ For Thomas's career: Watt, 'Medieval Chapter of Armagh Cathedral', 230–2.
⁷⁶ Curtis, *Richard II in Ireland*, 68–9, 97–8, 159–60, 184–5; *Acts of Colton*, 12, 28, 48, 59.

Archbishop Swayne at his residence in Drogheda in 1427, and it is likely that it was with the permission of one of the archbishops of Armagh that members of the O'Loughran family were allowed to settle on the episcopal manor of Termonfeckin at some point before Geffyn's appearance there in 1441.[77]

Geffyn O'Loughran did not pursue a clerical career in Louth, unlike another Irishman with links to the hereditary Irish clerical class, John Keenan (Ó Cianáin). Keenan, who served as a public notary for Archbishop Sweteman and proctor for the canons of Derry in the 1360s, came from a family that provided many priests in its home territory of Fermanagh, including the abbot of the Augustinian house of Lisgoole, who died in 1345.[78] In the early fifteenth century, members of the Keenan family were living at Stabannan and Rathbrist (bar. Louth), while English law was granted in 1426 to John Keenan, chaplain.[79] A member of the clerical O'Mulholland (Ó Maelchallainn) family from Derry, who were hereditary keepers of the bell of St Patrick, was vicar of Dunleer in 1450.[80] Native bishops of dioceses within the province of Armagh may also have used their influence to introduce members of their families into Louth— as did settler archbishops of Armagh such as Milo Sweteman and John Swayne.[81] The William Brady (Mac Brádaig or Ó Brádaig) who owed £40 to the late Matthew Fleming of Dundalk in 1418 was probably related to Nicholas Brady, bishop of Kilmore, from 1395 to 1421.[82] Matilda MacCormack (Mac Carmaic) of Drogheda, who features in the records of a divorce case from the 1450s, was possibly a member of the family that provided several bishops of Raphoe in the late medieval period, while Thomas O'Corkeran (Ó Corcráin), who served as a witness in divorce proceedings at the episcopal court at Dromiskin in 1436, may have come from the same family as John O'Corkeran, bishop of Clogher between 1373 and 1389.[83]

It is clear that some parishes in Louth were more likely to be served by Irish priests than were others. Thomas Condlagh (Ó Congalaig = Connelly) was presented to the vicarage of Kildemock by the prior of the hospital of St John of Jerusalem in Dublin in the late 1360s and in 1370 was appointed to collect from the clergy of Ardee their portion of the subsidy granted in parliament to William Windsor.[84] In 1411 another priest of Irish origin, Patrick Okoyn (Ó Cadain), was presented to the same church, holding it until his death in 1428 while, as we have seen, the vicar presented to Kildemock in 1436 was John O'Hamill.[85] Clonkeen,

---

[77] *Reg. Swayne*, 57; *Reg. Octaviani*, ii. 95. For communication between the archbishop of Armagh and their officials in the Irish parts of their diocese see Anthony Lynch, 'Religion in Late Medieval Ireland', *Archivium Hibernicum*, 36 (1981), 3–15.

[78] *AFM* iii. 585; *Reg. Sweteman*, 38, 48–50, 67–73, 89, 101–2, 118–19, 181–4, 186–8, 199–201, 206–7, 209–11; Canice Mooney, 'The Church in Gaelic Ireland: 13th to 15th Centuries', in Patrick J. Corish (ed.), *A History of Irish Catholicism* (Dublin, 1969), ii/5. 24.

[79] *Reg. Swayne*, 37, 45, 55; *RCH* 195 no. 30.

[80] Simms, 'Frontiers in the Irish Church', 184.

[81] See above, 153–4.

[82] *Reg. Fleming*, 74–6, 100–1; *Dowdall Deeds*, 163; *NHI* ix. 288.

[83] *Reg. Mey*, 348–9; *NHI* ix. 274, 287; *Reg. Fleming*, 82, 188–9; *Reg. Swayne*, 165–6.

[84] *Reg. Sweteman*, 63–6, 225.

[85] *Reg. Fleming*, 112, 161–2, 173–4; *Reg. Swayne*, 56, 87. The Gyllarevyth Oconne who lived at Carlingford in 1439 was possibly a member of the same family as Patrick Okoyn: *Dowdall Deeds*, 177–8.

close to lands of the MacMahons, also had several Irish priests in this period. The Richard Conlan (Ó Congalain), vicar of Clonkeen (bar. Ardee), who died in 1433, was probably related to the Cormac Okonnolan who acted on behalf of Archbishop Swayne in business relating to the diocese of Clogher in 1430.[86] In 1449, Archbishop Mey collated William Omeghan (? Ó Mithidéin) to the vicarage of Clonkeen, which had fallen vacant on the death of its previous, Irish, incumbent, Simon Olowan (Ó Luain).[87]

While Irish clergy certainly appear as vicars of parishes on the fringes of the English settlement in Louth, it is also the case that some of these parishes, such as Kane, Kilcurly, and Barronstown, to the north and west of Dundalk, were staffed by priests with settler backgrounds throughout this period.[88] Furthermore, even parishes such as Kildemock and Clonkeen, which were often served by Irish priests, also had clergy of settler stock appointed as their vicars on occasion.[89] What is equally noticeable is that Irish priests served in parishes in Louth far from the marches. The rector of Carrickbaggot, 8 kilometres north of Drogheda, Bartholomew Mulchan (? Ó Maelcháine = Mulqueen), was provided to that church in 1408 by its patron, Sir Richard Bagot, and held it until at least 1433.[90] Matthew Mcheugh was parish chaplain of Drumshallon, adjacent to Carrickbaggot, in 1431, while in 1451 the vicar of Mansfieldstown, some 8 kilometres from the coast, was Nicholas Omurry.[91] The archbishops of Armagh also employed Irish priests to help them administer the part of their diocese that lay among the English. Master Philip McKewyn (? Mac Eoin), clerk of the diocese of Armagh, placed his legal expertise at the service of Archbishops Swayne and Prene, and for twenty years from the mid-1420s was frequently in their attendance at Dromiskin, Termonfeckin, and Drogheda. He was allowed to purchase a grant of English law in 1423 on account of his good work as a negotiator with the Irish, but does not appear to have held a parish in Louth.[92]

Irishmen were also present in the religious houses of late medieval Louth and adjacent parts of Meath, sometimes holding senior positions in these foundations. Richard, abbot of Knock, was granted English law in 1385, while the prior of the same house in the late 1440s was John Mulghan, who was presumably related to Bartholomew Mulchan, vicar of Carrickbaggot, and who had previously been a canon at the house of St Mary's, Louth.[93] In 1391, English law was granted to the

---

[86] *Reg. Octaviani*, ii. 69, 73–5, 97.
[87] *Reg. Mey*, 151–2.
[88] Kane: *Reg. Sweteman*, 151; *RCH* 109 no. 115; *CPL 1417–31*, 73; *Reg. Swayne*, 156–60. Kilcurly: *Reg. Sweteman*, 252–4; *RCH* 166 no. 253; *Reg. Swayne*, 96. Barronstown: *Reg. Sweteman*, 123; *Reg. Fleming*, 101–2, 143–4; *Reg. Swayne*, 155.
[89] Clonkeen: *Reg. Octaviani*, ii. 73–5, 97. Kildemock: *Reg. Swayne*, 87.
[90] *Reg. Fleming*, 79–80, 110–11; *Dowdall Deeds*, 151–2; *Reg. Octaviani*, ii. 54–5; *Reg. Swayne*, 142–4.
[91] *Reg. Octaviani*, ii. 54–5; *Reg. Mey*, 272–3.
[92] *RCH* 226 no. 76(a); *Reg. Swayne*, 154–5, 156–60, 183, 191–2; *Reg. Mey*, 9–11, 27–8, 54, 76–8, 388–9.
[93] *RCH* 124 no. 59; *Reg. Mey*, 34–5.

newly elected prior of Louth, Patrick McGonnes, who may have been related to the powerful Magennis family of south Down, while in 1423 a similar grant was made to the abbot of Kells, John O'Reilly, a member of the ruling family of Breifne, who was encouraged to bring his relatives to peace.[94] William, prior of St Mary's abbey, Louth, in 1385 was granted English law, and in 1402 the abbot of Mellifont, who appears to have been of settler stock, was obliged to pay a fine of 50m for having allowed Irish monks to be professed in the abbey.[95] As was the case with parochial cures, however, senior positions in religious houses in Louth did not come to be held exclusively by clerics of Irish origin in this period. Geoffrey Broun, abbot of Knock, died in 1411; James Locard (Lockhart) resigned from the same post in 1435; while John Mulghan succeeded another settler in the abbacy, Patrick Ledwich.[96] At St Mary's, Louth, John Schorbrun (Sherbourne) from the house of St Thomas's, Dublin, was appointed prior in 1395.[97]

Nor would it be necessarily correct to assume that all Irish clergy in late medieval Louth were recent migrants or descendants thereof. The grants of English law to Richard, abbot of Knock, and William, prior of Louth, in 1385 stressed that their 'ancestors were born among the English and were faithfully at the king's allegiance'.[98] The Irish element in the Church of Louth was not an import: settlers were accustomed to the presence of native clergy in their parishes, just as they accepted as entirely natural the dedication of so many parish churches in the county to Irish saints. These were located throughout Louth and included the churches of St Fintan or Finnian (Fintán, Finn, or Finnán) in Dromin and Drumcar; St Columba (Colum Cille) in Clonmore, Port, and Carrickbaggot; Sts Brethany and Frethany (Báetán and Furodrán) in Dunleer; St Aidan (Áedán) and St Medoc (M'Áedóc) in Clonkeen, and St Ultan (Ultán) in Killanny.[99] The extent to which the settlers were at ease with this situation is demonstrated by the decision of John Plunket in the early fourteenth century to dedicate the new parish church he was permitted to found and construct on his manor of Beaulieu, close to Drogheda, to St Brigit (Brigid).[100] The parish churches of the episcopal manors of Termonfeckin and Dromiskin were dedicated to St Fechin and St Ronan respectively, and it was with a sympathetic eye on the nature of church dedications and popular devotion in the county that Archbishop Nicholas Fleming ordained in a provincial council

---

[94] *RCH* 147 no. 1; 227 no. 49.
[95] *RCH* 124 no. 56; 163 no. 120; Gearóid Mac Niocaill, *Na Manaigh Liatha in Éirinn, 1142–c. 1600* (Cló Morainn, 1959), 166–7. It is possible that William was prior of St Mary's, Louth, in 1371 when Brian MacMahon, who had attacked the settlement many times in the course of his career, was buried there: *AU* ii. 557.
[96] *Reg. Fleming*, 127–8, 164–5; *RCH* 258 no. 78; *Reg. Mey*, 34–5.
[97] *CPL 1362–1404*, 525–6.
[98] *RCH* 124 nos. 56 and 59.
[99] Dromin and Drumcar: TNA E 101/242/13; TNA C 47/10/19 no. 14; *Reg. Fleming*, 190; *Reg. Swayne*, 93; Clonmore and Port: *PKCI* 240–1; *Reg. Octaviani*, ii. 54–5; L. P. Murray (Lorcán P. Ua Muireadhaig), 'St Columba in Louth', *CLAJ* 2 (1911), 337–46; Dunleer: *Reg. Fleming*, 254–5; Clonkeen and Killanny: *Reg. Octaviani*, ii. 97; Smith, *Colonisation and Conquest*, 58. Now essential to this topic is Pádraig Ó Riain, *A Dictionary of Irish Saints* (Dublin, 2011).
[100] Brand, 'Formation of a Parish', 271; TNA E 101/247/15.

Table 3. Parish church dedications in late medieval Louth

Ardee	St Mary
Beaulieu	St Brigit
Carlingford	St Mary
Carrickbaggot	St Columba
Castletown	St John the Baptist
Clonkeen	St Aidan and St Medoc
Clonmore	St Columba
Darver	St Michael
Drogheda in Louth	St Peter
Drogheda in Meath	St Mary
Dromin	St Fintan or Finnian
Dromiskin	St Ronan
Drumcar	St Fintan or Finnian
Drumshallon	St Mary
Dunany	St John the Evangelist
Dunbin	St Mary
Dundalk	St Nicholas
Dunleer	Sts Brethany and Frethany
Feld/Haynestown	St Nicholas
Kildemock	St Catherine the Virgin
Killanny	St Ultan
Mansfieldstown	St Mary
Port	St Columba
Rathdrumin	St Peter
Stabannan	St Nicholas
Termonfeckin	St Fechin

held in 1411 that the feast days of Sts Patrick, Brigit, Columba, Fechin, and Ronan be celebrated throughout the province of Armagh.[101]

It is probable that native Irish clergy originating from outside of the county staffed parishes and religious houses in Louth in increasing numbers from the middle of the fourteenth century onwards. Clyn reported that before the end of 1348 the first onset of plague had taken the lives of twenty-five of the Franciscan community at Drogheda, and the impact of the disease also lay behind the permission granted by the papacy to Archbishop Fitz Ralph in 1351 to dispense sixty men of their illegitimacy so that they might be ordained as priests.[102] While the ideal of celibacy was never abandoned by the entirety of the clergy of Gaelic Ireland, and enjoyed a renewal from the middle of the fifteenth century in territories such as those of the MacMahons in Monaghan, it remained the case that many native clerics had 'wives' and that many of the male children of such unions became priests in adulthood.[103] There is limited evidence of such practices spreading into Louth in the wake of the arrival of native clergy from beyond the county. Richard Gaffney

---

[101] *Reg. Swayne*, 13. For the dating of this council: Burrows, 'Provincial Legislation', 58–61.
[102] *Clyn*, 246, 250; *CPL 1342–62*, 387; Kelly, *History of the Black Death in Ireland*, 109–30.
[103] Simms, 'Frontiers in the Irish Church'; Simms, *Medieval Gaelic Sources*, 86–7.

(Ó Gomna), who was ordained by Archbishop Swayne in 1426, was deprived of the vicarage of Port by the same prelate in 1435 on account of his adultery with a female parishioner, but is unclear whether this was a lasting union.[104] The careers of Bartholomew Mulchan, rector of Carrickbaggot, and John Mulghan, abbot of Knock, have been mentioned, and a contemporary of John's, Master Richard Mulghan, was vicar of Kilmoon in Meath in the 1440s.[105] It is not possible to be certain that these men were related, nor to identify which, if any of them, was the father of the Thomas Omulchan, 'son of priest and unmarried woman', who was dispensed from his illegitimacy by Archbishop Swayne at Dromiskin in 1427.[106] Thomas's background was similar to that of an earlier cleric of Irish origin whose family originated in Louth and Meath, Ralph O'Kelly. Ralph's father was the Carmelite theologian, David Ó Buge, and his mother was the wife of the Drogheda merchant, William O'Kelly. Ralph, who was also a Carmelite, was provided to the archbishopric of Cashel in January 1346, and visited his home town of Drogheda in April of that year.[107]

It is important to note in this context that failure to observe celibacy among the clergy in Louth was not confined to the Irish—indeed the evidence points to a quite different scenario. It is not clear whether John Kendy, canon of St Mary's, Louth, and 'son of a priest religious and a married woman', was of settler or native stock. He was dispensed of his illegitimacy in 1392 and provided by the pope to the abbacy of Bangor.[108] John Penbroke, clerk of the diocese of Meath, was certainly not of Irish origin. He was the son of a priest and an unmarried woman, and by 1442 had 'obtained a chantry in St Nicholas in the Shambles, London'.[109] In 1426 Henry Saundyr or Sander, vicar of the church of Dromiskin, where the archbishops of Armagh had one of their two manors in Louth, required absolution for having kept a concubine, while Richard White, who succeeded Richard Mulchan as rector of Kilmoon, was deprived of his cure in the late 1440s for failing to dismiss his concubine.[110] The future bishop of Meath, William Hadsor, required dispensation in the 1420s from his illegitimate birth before commencing his ecclesiastical career, though it is stated that his father was a married man.[111]

---

[104] MacLysaght, *Irish Families*, 153; *Reg. Swayne*, 44, 142–4, 161; *Reg. Octaviani*, ii. 55–6, 88.
[105] Griffith, 'Talbot–Ormond Struggle', 396–7; Mooney, 'Church in Gaelic Ireland', 56–60.
[106] *Reg. Swayne*, 83–4.
[107] B. H. Blacker, 'Ó Ceallaigh, Ralph (d. 1361)', rev. Philomena Connolly, *Oxford Dictionary of National Biography* (Oxford, 2004). 'Ancient Deeds', 22–3; *NHI* ix. 290, 315. Ralph died in 1361. The dates of his episcopate match very closely those of his contemporary, and fellow native of Louth, Richard Fitz Ralph, archbishop of Armagh 1346–60.
[108] *CPL 1362–1404*, 434.
[109] *CPL 1431–47*, 246–7.
[110] *Reg. Swayne*, 48. Sander's long recorded career, stretching from the 1390s to the 1440s, also involved him in acquiring the manor of Killincoole and the right of presentation to its church: *Dowdall Deeds*, 135–6, 136–7, 182; *RCH* 188 no. 47; COA Rep. Records of the Exchequer, 1 Henry V–39 Henry VI, 4–5, 9; *Reg. Swayne*, 47, 68, 152, 162–3; *Reg. Octaviani*, ii. 57. *Reg. Mey*, 130–1. Beyond Louth, the bishop of Down and prior of its cathedral both kept concubines in the 1430s, leading Archbishop Mey to launch a campaign against the practice in the late 1440s: *Reg. Swayne*, 150–1; *Reg. Mey*, 47–9, 188–9.
[111] *De Annatis Hiberniae*, 2–3, 19; *CPL 1417–1431*, 498, 559; *CPL 1427–1447*, 181; *Reg. Swayne*, 49, 150, 193–4; Lynch, 'Archdeacons of Armagh', 219–20. Hadsor served as keeper of the peace for Louth and Meath in 1431: *RCH* 251 no. 9.

The approach to monastic discipline at the Cistercian house of Mellifont in the early fifteenth century appears to have been relaxed: in 1427 Laurence Roche, a monk of the house, and 'son of a Cistercian monk and an unmarried woman', was permitted to receive Holy Orders, having earlier being dispensed from his illegitimacy.[112] In 1439, at Dromiskin, Archbishop Swayne dispensed from his illegitimacy Henry Awell, clerk, 'being born of a priest, a professed Cistercian monk, and a married woman', and three years later Henry, who by then was a monk of Mellifont, was ordained a priest.[113] It is possible that Henry's father was William Avel 'monk of Mellifont' who was ordained in 1412, and who may have been a member of a family with property in Drogheda.[114] It should be noted, however, that any perceived laxness of monastic discipline at Mellifont did not deter wealthy laymen from seeking burial in its church, as the will of William Gory from 1430 makes clear.[115] It can also be observed that if there was a decline in observance of celibacy among the clergy of late medieval Louth, it was not because an increasing number of them were of Irish origin.

The presence among the clergy of late medieval Louth of individuals drawn from both the native and settler communities mirrored the linguistic profile of the county, and some priests were able to speak both vernacular languages.[116] Thomas O'Loughran, dean of Tullaghoge, translated the submissions of O'Neill and Mac-Mahon to Richard II into English at Drogheda in 1395, while Archbishop John Mey was accompanied on a visit to Ardglass in Down in 1449 by John Mckasshyn, *juris perito* and interpreter.[117] The papal grant of 1406 by which John Posswyk was appointed to the church of St Columba's, Clonmore, noted that 'John, whose parents were English, says that he understands the tongue spoken by the parishioners, and can speak it intelligibly'.[118] This would appear to indicate that the language of the parishioners of Clonmore, some 15 kilometres north of Drogheda and 4 kilometres from the coast, was Irish, and that John was conversant in that language.[119] Whether John's flock also spoke English is impossible to determine, but it is clear that English was the common vernacular of the inhabitants of Termonfeckin, 8 kilometres south of Clonmore, thirty-five years later. Elena Oweyn may have included an Irish word in the abuse she hurled at her neighbours

---

[112] *CPL 1417–1431*, 513. John White, clerk, of Armagh diocese, who was allowed to become a priest in 1439, was 'the son of a Cistercian abbot, a priest, and an unmarried woman'. A Mellifont connection is not made explicit: *CPL 1431–47*, 33 (Ó Conbhuí), *Story of Mellifont*, 117–26.

[113] *Reg. Swayne*, 181, 186–7.

[114] *Reg. Fleming*, 140–2, 224–5; COA Rep. Records of the Exchequer, 10–22 Richard II, 194; *Dowdall Deeds*, 134.

[115] *Reg. Octaviani*, ii. 84–5.

[116] For language use in late medieval Ireland: Alan Bliss, 'Language and Literature', in James Lydon (ed.), *The English in Medieval Ireland* (Dublin, 1984), 27–45.

[117] See above, 82–4; *Reg. Mey*, 135, 210–11.

[118] *CPL 1404–15*, 88, 120; Booker, 'After the "Middle Nation"', 19; Harvey, *English in Rome*, 166–7.

[119] In 1400 the pope ordered that John Taaf be deprived of his rectory of Castlerickard, south of Trim, if it was found that he 'does not understand well nor speak intelligibly the language (*ydioma*) commonly spoken by the greater part of his parishioners': *CPL 1396–1404*, 449.

there in 1441, but she vented her spleen in English and expected her audience, Geffyn Oloucheran and his wife Agnes Rogan, to understand the entirety of her tirade, regardless of their Irish origins.[120] Her use of the same term of abuse—caylagh/heigge—in both the Irish and English languages in a single short sentence may even suggest that she did not know the meaning of the Irish word. Closer to the marches, the form of the English words inscribed on slates at the chantry school of Smarmore, 5 kilometres south-west of Ardee, in the early fifteenth century conforms to what is known of how the language was spoken in Ireland at the time. Furthermore, the grammatical errors that appear on the Latin-inscribed slates unearthed at the same site result from a tendency to translate too literally from the English language.[121]

To draw attention to the continued, extensive, use of the English language in late medieval Louth, and to note the absence of any clear link between laxness with regard to clerical celibacy and the presence of native clergy in the county, is not to dispute the increasing 'Irishness' of the area. It is rather to suggest that the impact of this reality upon settler society was more complex than some contemporary sources and later commentaries might indicate, and involved a degree of anglicization of the Irish who lived in Louth. In 1427 Archbishop John Swayne wrote to the vicar of St Ronan's church, Dromiskin, in connection with an attack that had been carried out on the episcopal manor there. The recipient of the letter, Henry Saundyr, had two years earlier been chastized by Swayne for keeping a concubine. The letter told how the archbishop had been informed that three prominent local settlers, Sir Nicholas Taaf, John Gernon, and Roger Gernon of Drummoghan, 'and their men and also *Kyriaghtys*', had plundered his property.[122] Which elements of this story about an act of lawlessness that occurred some distance from the marches of Louth, contained in a letter sent to a sexually incontinent priest, can we identify as 'Irish', and which as 'English'? Which spoke to cultural borrowing and which to impulses towards self-gratification that were ever-present and knew no communal boundaries? The layering over centuries of native and settler customs, and the continued dynamic interaction between the two, preclude any easy unpicking of the texture of life in late medieval Louth.

That such considerations apply to the county as a whole has implications for a discussion of the particular situation of the marches. These had no definite geographical parameters and contemporaries referred to them with a lack of precision that was entirely appropriate to their nature.[123] The Irish petition of June 1346, which referred to 'la primaci de Ardemagh qest en la plus fort marche de tout la terre' displayed a more flexible understanding of the term than is found in royal

---

[120] See above, 191–2.
[121] Bliss, 'Inscribed Slates at Smarmore', 35–7, 40, 45–60.
[122] *Reg. Swayne*, 48, 68.
[123] For the marches of Louth as 'a vague entity', see Patrick J. Duffy, 'Geographical Perspectives on the Borderlands', in Raymond Gillespie and Harold O'Sullivan (eds), *The Borderlands: Essays on the History of the Ulster-Leinster Border* (Belfast, 1989), 5–22, at 6.

edicts of the same period.[124] In 1344, Edward III ordered the justiciar to hold an inquisition to determine what lands had been granted in the past

> for the defence of the marches between the English and the Irish, and what lands were laid waste by the Irish and occupied by them and for how long, sending that inquisition to the king without delay, as the king is informed that divers lands were so granted and the tenants thereof have not made any defence upon the marches for a long time, wherefore the men who used to dwell there have withdrawn, and the lands of the marches are occupied by the Irish.[125]

In similar vein, the ordinance made for the estate of Ireland in 1357 asserted that

> [t]he marches near the enemy have been laid waste by hostile invasions, the marchers being slain and plundered and their dwellings horribly burnt. And others have been compelled to desert their proper homes, some of them flying to the enemy and others to strange places. And divers parts of the said marches being thus desolate and deserted have been occupied by the enemy.[126]

In this view, the marches were lands adjacent to Irish-controlled territories—or 'between the English and the Irish'—and were inhabited by a particular group of loyal lieges, the marchers, who either had been or might be violently expelled and replaced by the Irish. Determining which places were in the marches and which were not was no simple matter. The inhabitants of Carlingford and Drumconrath in petitions dating from 1410 and 1412 respectively claimed that their settlements were 'in the frontier of the marches' (*in frontura marchie*), by which they wished to indicate those parts of the marches closest to the Irish enemy.[127] In 1422 the inhabitants of the town of Louth avoided the word 'march' altogether, saying simply that their town 'was situated between [or among]' (*sita est inter*) the English and the MacMahons, and had been so badly burnt by the latter that they had been forced to flee in terror.[128] Irish enemies were said to inhabit 'the march adjacent to the town' of Ardee in 1376 but the town of Roche was at the same time identified as being 'situated in the march'.[129] The manor of Crowmartin was described as being 'in the marches' of Meath and Louth in 1402, while in the following year the manor of Raskeagh was described as 'lying in the marches of Dundalk near Onell, Magennis and Ohannelan, Irish enemies, and utterly devastated by them'.[130] It was 'in the marches of Dundalk' that Niall Óc O'Neill arranged to meet Archbishop John Colton in March 1395, and in the following month he wrote to Richard II

---

[124] Sayles, *Affairs*, 186. [125] *CCR 1343–6*, 375.
[126] *Statutes of the Realm*, i. 357–64.
[127] *RCH* 196 no. 75; 198 no. 30. In 1441 Thomas Feld was paid £10 by the exchequer 'for service in the frontier of the march (*in fronturis march*') in defence and preservation of the king's lieges against the Irish enemies and English rebels': *RCH* 263 no. 17. The same phrase was used in relation to Ardee in 1437: NAI Ferguson Coll. iii. 152.
[128] *RCH* 180 no. 13.
[129] *CPI* 73, 77.
[130] *RCH* 163 no. 135; 174 no. 107. In 1366 Archbishop Sweteman had been prepared to meet O'Hanlon at the chapel of Newry, *juxta Rathskeagh*, and did not mention it as being in the march: *Reg. Sweteman*, 131.

from 'near the marches of Dundalk' to express his fears about an imminent attack by Roger Mortimer.[131] The town of Dundalk itself was said by its inhabitants to be 'in the marches near the Irish enemies' in 1412.[132]

No set of objective criteria existed by which it could be determined whether or not a settlement lay 'in the marches', and nor was it a clear-cut matter to identify with whom authority lay in these areas.[133] Archbishop Sweteman arranged to meet Philip O'Reilly, king of Breifne, 'in some march of your country (*in aliqua marchia terre vestre*) beyond Kilmainham Beg' in the summer of 1366, while manors south of Dundalk were said to be 'situated in the marches of McMaghon' in 1421.[134] On the other hand, Niall Mór O'Neill was careful to refer to 'your marches of Dundalk' (*marchias vestras de Dundalk*) when writing to Richard II in January 1395, and asked him to confirm a grant of land he had made there to the Augustinian abbey of Sts Peter and Paul, Armagh.[135] Archbishop Sweteman clearly believed that the march of Kells was under settler control when in July 1366 he ordered the bishop of Meath to have minor Irish lords (*reguli*) of his diocese, who were under excommunication, meet him there in order to receive absolution.[136] That this situation pertained in the middle of the fifteenth century is confirmed by the observation of the Flemish pilgrim, Gilbert Lannoy, in 1430 that Kells was 'an ill-walled town still belonging to the king of England, seated on the frontier of the wild Irish'.[137]

Some semblance of English control of certain marches was acknowledged by the different parties who came to agreements concerning Irish migration into these areas. In 1346, the sheriff of Louth and two prominent settlers were appointed to hold an inquisition to determine 'whether it would be to the profit and advantage of the K. and the men of the march of the parts of Dundalk to receive into the king's peace Auly Orogan and Petrus Orogan, Irishmen, with their adherents'.[138] In 1395, Muirchertach Magennis requested the permission of Richard II to bring his men and goods into the marches for fear of O'Neill and Edmund Savage, and in 1410 a licence was provided to two O'Reillys and their men to inhabit the marches of Kells.[139] The repeated attempts by the government to regulate MacMahon settlement around the royal manor of Donaghmoyne in the barony of Farney, 12 kilometres north-west of the town of Louth, assumed an air of unreality from at least the early fourteenth century as it became clear that little could be done to deflect the determination of the Irish to permanently inhabit and control this territory.[140] In 1360 John Clinton, who had been granted the manor for life in 1332, said that it had been destroyed and

---

[131] Curtis, *Richard II in Ireland*, 124–5, 126–7, 205–6, 208.   [132] *RCH* 200 no. 87.
[133] Brendan Smith, 'Keeping the Peace', in James Lydon (ed.), *Law and Disorder in Thirteenth-Century Ireland: The Dublin Parliament of 1297* (Dublin, 1997), 57–65.
[134] *Reg. Sweteman*, 55; *RCH* 252 no. 31.
[135] Curtis, *Richard II in Ireland*, 124–5, 131–2, 133–4, 205–6, 211–12, 213–14.
[136] *Reg. Sweteman*, 54.
[137] Leslie, *St Patrick's Purgatory*, 39.
[138] *RCH* 50 no. 70.
[139] Curtis, *Richard II in Ireland*, 219–20; *RCH* 196 no. 69.
[140] Smith, *Colonisation and Conquest*, 83–8.

wasted by the local Irish for longer than anyone could remember, and it was said to be 'then in the hands of the king's Irish rebels' when granted to Roger Gernon in 1371.[141] The lordship of Farney was granted to several different settlers in the first half of the fifteenth century, but the territory remained in the hands of the MacMahons, whose effective control was officially recognized on more than one occasion.[142] In 1445 Rudraige MacMahon, who enjoyed good relations with the settlers, was induced to petition for the keeping of the lordship from the crown for fifty years for an annual rent of £10. The acknowledgement in the charter granting this petition that up to that moment 'the king has received nothing therefrom by the space of twenty-two years and more' came close to an honest and accurate assessment of the real balance of power in this part of the marches.[143]

Life in the marches, as portrayed in our surviving sources, was harsh, and the belief among the settlers who lived there that the particular challenges they faced were not recognized by the government added to their woes. In 1342, a lengthy set of petitions sent to the crown from Ireland included the following complaint:

> Likewise, sire, although there be in every march of your said land of Ireland, enough and more of the Irish enemies to trouble your English people, who have not power to stop them, save the grace of God, which maintains them, sire; still more do the extortions and oppressions of your officers trouble them than does the war with the said Irish; for, sire, when your officers are in the counties for the purpose of holding pleas, they amerce those who dwell in the march heavily, without having regard to their misfortune.[144]

Their misfortune—compounded but not caused by the government—was to live close to Irish enemies who sought to extract resources from them either by force or by the threat of force. Amidst the numerous, generalized, reports of raids in the marches that involved killings, burnings, and robbery, it is possible to identify more specific strategies employed by the Irish to attain their ends. The targeting of particular components of the economic infrastructure of the settlement was one such strategy. Weirs and fisheries were to be found on many manors throughout the county, and played a particularly important role on the estates of the Cistercian abbey of Mellifont and the archbishops of Armagh.[145] In 1371, Archbishop Milo Sweteman's tenants at Iniskeen, which felt the same pressure from the MacMahons as did nearby Donaghmoyne, took the dangerous step of wounding one of MacMahon's men who had damaged the stream and fishery of the manor.[146]

Even more likely to be targeted for destruction than the fisheries were the mills of Louth and Meath, without which the manorial economy of the region could not

---

[141] *CFR 1327–37*, 329; *CFR 1337–47*, 66, 228; TNA E 101/241/1; NAI 999/184/18; NAI RC 8/28, 256–8; *CPR 1374–7*, 340.
[142] *RCH* 165 no. 232. Text from NAI Lodge MS 17, 15; *RCH* 187 no. 12; 194 no. 5; 204 no. 22; TNA E 101/248/11; *Handbook and Select Calendar... Ireland*, 220.
[143] *CPR 1441–6*, 343.
[144] *Stat. Ire., John–Hen. V*, 361.
[145] *RCH* 46 no. 114; 79 nos. 95, 118;108 nos. 35–9; 242 nos. 26, 27; COA Rep. Records of the Exchequer, 10–22 Richard II, 165–6; Otway-Ruthven, 'Partition of the de Verdon Lands', 421–36; *Reg. Fleming*, 242–4; *Reg. Swayne*, 54, 64; *Dowdall Deeds*, 88–9; *Inquisitions and Extents*, 195; *CPR 1330–4*, 382; *CPR 1399–1401*, 509–10.
[146] *Reg. Sweteman*, 211–12.

function.¹⁴⁷ In 1352–3, it was reported that the mill of the town of Kells had been burnt to the ground by the Irish, while in the 1420s O'Neill burnt the mill of Castletowncooley, which belonged to Peter Dowdall.¹⁴⁸ The account of an attack by an associate of MacMahon on the estate of the abbey of Sts Peter and Paul at Knock in 1428 suggests a deliberate attempt to do permanent damage to the economy of the house. The attackers 'burnt a grange belonging to the abbey and broke a mill and its wheels and devoured various meadows with their animals'.¹⁴⁹ Even where mills survived, they seemed destined to become museum pieces in the scenario described by Archbishop Swayne in the late 1420s. In bemoaning the general lawlessness of the country he noted that in 'the northsyde of the contre', by which he appears to have meant Meath and Louth, the king's enemies had burnt many towns and slain and imprisoned many men. He dwelt especially on the sufferings of 'the pore housbondmen that have nothing to liw by bot [but] hare [their] housbondrye hare corne is brent [burnt] and they have noʒt [nothing to] sowe and be noʒt of pouer [powerless] to by corne and so they be undo for evyre'.¹⁵⁰

If a manor in the marches of Louth and Meath could be crippled by the destruction of its mill, it also faced ruin if those who laboured on it were prevented from working. Not only did O'Neill burn Dowdall's mill, he also took the miller, Richard McGilroy, hostage.¹⁵¹ The large-scale abduction of settler tenantry was not uncommon. In 1412, 'O'Connor did great mischief in Meath and took 160 Englishmen'.¹⁵² The peace agreement reached by the lieutenant, James Butler, earl of Ormond, with Brian MacMahon and his brothers in 1425 revealed that as well as burning Nobber the Irish had also taken more than eighty of its inhabitants prisoner, while in 1429 Archbishop Swayne complained that Irish enemies, including the sons of Magennis, had attacked a manor of his near Athboy and carried away its free tenants and their animals.¹⁵³ More typical of marcher abductions was the taking of prominent local individuals such as the three named settlers from Ricetown, near Nobber, whose release was negotiated in the MacMahon–Ormond agreement in 1425.¹⁵⁴ Nobber suffered another loss later in 1425 when John Weston, chaplain of the town, was abducted one night by four Irish enemies.¹⁵⁵ In 1346, Hugh Golding, who, 'with others of his surname and household (*cum aliis de cognomine et familia suis*)', had been captured and imprisoned by O'Reilly, was permitted by the Dublin government to pay a ransom for his release.¹⁵⁶

It was common practice to allow one captive to go free in order to raise the ransom money that would result in the liberation of other hostages, and the archbishops of

---

¹⁴⁷ For a recent, remarkable, insight into the agricultural economy of rural Dublin, which shared many of the features of that of Louth, see Murphy and Potterton, *Dublin Region in the Middle Ages*. For Louth: James F. Lydon, 'The Mills of Ardee in 1304', *CLAJ* 19 (1980), 259–63.
¹⁴⁸ *Handbook and Select Calendar... Ireland*, 304–6; *Dowdall Deeds*, 177–8.
¹⁴⁹ *Reg. Swayne*, 93.
¹⁵⁰ *Reg. Swayne*, 110.
¹⁵¹ *Dowdall Deeds*, 181.
¹⁵² 'Henry Marleburrough's Chronicle of Ireland', 218.
¹⁵³ *Handbook and Select Calendar... Ireland*, 217; *Reg. Swayne*, 119.
¹⁵⁴ *Handbook and Select Calendar... Ireland*, 217.
¹⁵⁵ *Reg. Swayne*, 42.   ¹⁵⁶ *RCH* 50 no. 105.

Armagh might be called upon to help in the raising of the funds. In 1427 Archbishop Swayne ordered his clergy to encourage their parishioners, in return for an indulgence of forty days, to assist Nicholas Chamberlain to 'raise the ransom he is obliged to pay to Irish enemies who had taken him prisoner and compelled him to leave hostages as pledge'.[157] Three years later, Swayne offered the same reward to those who helped Stephen Thorleston of Siddan who, 'at the time of the burning of his house', was captured and detained by Rudraige MacMahon and his men, and was obliged to pay 14m for his release, 'which he cannot pay without help of charity of God's faithful'.[158] An entry in the roll of the proceedings of the Irish council of 1393 provides another insight into the role played by the Church in the matter of hostage-taking. Two years earlier John Colton, archbishop of Armagh, and Alexander Balscot, bishop of Meath and justiciar of Ireland, had persuaded George Teeling to hand over his son to O'Reilly as security for a payment of 84m promised to the Irish lord on condition that he withdraw his forces from the settlement. A subsidy to raise this sum was agreed upon by the laity and clergy of Meath, but contributors proved tardy and Teeling, fearing for the well-being of his son, was forced to borrow £25 from the Irish exchequer. In time the exchequer sought to recoup this loan by confiscating Teeling's property, but Colton succeeded in having this process halted.[159]

The marches were contested by and shared between natives and settlers, and the targeting of the economy, property, and person of the enemy, and the taking of hostages from them, were aspects of marcher warfare that were as likely to be practised by the English as they were by the Irish. The settlers gloated in a letter to the king in 1417 of how John Talbot had attacked MacMahon and had

> burnte and destroyed one of his chiefe places, with all his townes and corne aboute, and wounded and killed a greate multitude of his people, until he must of force yealde himself to your peace and deliver divers English prisoners without ransome, which he and his people have taken.[160]

In the summer of 1421 it was the turn of James Butler, earl of Ormond, to ravage Airgialla. Over three days his forces destroyed MacMahon's 'stronge newe castell, his townes, his fayre toures, and his stronge plaases', and slew many of his people. After briefly returning to Ardee they entered Airgialla again to burn more of Mac-Mahon's corn.[161] A rare insight into the impact of such policies on Irish women is provided by an indulgence granted by Archbishop Swayne in 1427. In it he remitted forty days' penance to anyone who would 'help the bearer, Moyre Nakanary, of Armagh diocese, who has been beggared by depredation by the royal power'.[162]

Just as the Irish were content to take humble settler tenants captive, so the English did not confine the collection of hostages from among the Irish to members of aristocratic families such as the O'Neills, MacMahons, O'Reillys, and Magennises. In 1429, John White of Carlingford 'caused the wife of Mcarcennaydy, tenant of

---

[157] *Reg. Swayne*, 61.   [158] *Reg. Swayne*, 124.
[159] *PKCI* 192–6; Watt, 'John Colton', 202.
[160] *Original Letters*, 57–8.
[161] *Three Prose Versions of the Secreta Secretorum*, 203–4.   [162] *Reg. Swayne*, 68.

Master John McGylkaway, the archbishop's farmer, to be imprisoned for the debts of Arthur McGunissa, captain of his nation, and detained her until she should pay him 10s.', while in 1435 it was in pursuit of debts owed by another Magennis that Peter Dowdall and two other Dundalk settlers took horses from a priest from county Down, M. Ohannon, and imprisoned his servant. In both cases Archbishop Swayne ordered the settlers to desist.[163] Dowdall was no stranger to the taking of hostages— in 1408 he had entered into an indenture with Janico Dartas which included the provision that the profits gleaned from the ransom of enemy prisoners captured by Peter 'by fortune of war' be shared equally between the two men.[164]

Shared approaches to warfare on the marches were accompanied by common ideas about the making of peace.[165] A case recorded on the Irish plea roll from 1377–8 gives a sense of the formalized nature of dispute-settlement on the marches of Louth.[166] John Nysene was accused of having killed Lavertagh Obryn, a man of MacMahon, who was then in the king's peace, and was tried in the king's court. John argued that MacMahon was not a liege subject of the king, but had merely conformed to the king's peace for a certain period, and that as a result he was not guilty of murder. Further, he said, the custom in county Louth from time out of mind between the English and the Irish was that if an Englishman killed an Irishman who was in the king's peace he should be held to account locally. Accordingly, he continued, the marchers of the county had satisfied MacMahon and did not wish the court to interfere with local custom. James Penkiston, representing the king, insisted that John was guilty, but the latter was acquitted when evidence confirming the custom of which he had spoken was produced and examined by the jury.[167]

In considering dispute-settlement on the marches, and the extent to which local custom was preferred to common law procedure, it is important to remember that extra-curial arbitration was also employed to end conflicts in Louth that did not involve warfare between natives and settlers.[168] The episcopal court was particularly keen to encourage contending parties to enter arbitration as revealed, for example, in a letter of Archbishop Swayne to Peter Chambre, chaplain of St Feighin's,

[163] *Reg. Swayne*, 118, 158–9.
[164] *Dowdall Deeds*, 152–3.
[165] Robin Frame, 'War and Peace', 221–39; W. R. Jones, 'Violence, Criminality, and Culture Disjunction on the Anglo-Irish Frontier: The Example of Armagh, 1350–1550', *Criminal Justice History*, 1 (1980), 29–47.
[166] Cambridge UL Add MS 7107. The late Dr Philomena Connolly provided me with a transcript of this document.
[167] 'Et dicit quod usus et consuetudo in comitatu Loueth predicta a tempore quo non currit memoria inter anglicos et hibernicos talis est quod si aliquis anglicus aliquem hibernicum ad pacem domini regis existentem occiderit calumpniari debet per dominum regem seu aliquem alium de morte huiusmodi occisi. Et dicit quod marceriores illius comitatus satisfecerunt dicto Ech' Mcmahon, capitaneo dicti Lavertagh, pro morte eiusdem et non intendit quod curia nic ipsum inde contra usus et consuetudines predicta inquietare velit. Et Jacobus Penkeston qui etc. pro rege dicit quod felonie eum interfecit. Juratum monstravit specialem materiam in veredicto suo et affirmavit usum et consuetudinem predicta et satisfactionem factam. Ideo quietus est.'
[168] Crooks, 'Factions, Feuds and Noble Power', 450–1; Edward Powell, 'Arbitration and the Law in England in the Late Middle Ages', *TRHS* 5th ser. 33 (1983), 49–67; Cynthia J. Neville, 'Arbitration and Anglo-Scottish Border Law in the Later Middle Ages', in Michael Prestwich (ed.), *Liberties and Identities in the Medieval British Isles* (Woodbridge, 2008), 37–55; Llinos Beverley Smith, 'Disputes and Settlements in Medieval Wales: The Role of Arbitration', *EHR* 106 (1991), 835–60.

Termonfeckin, from September 1432. Peter was to admonish John Rykard to pay William Barron 6s, as judged by John Adyn and John Overton, and Robert Saunder and Richard Geoffrey of Termonfeckin, 'elected as friendly compositors of a dispute between Barron and Rykard over an acre of corn'.[169] The same procedure and principle were applied by the archbishops of Armagh in their dealings with the Irish who threatened their estates. In October 1371, Archbishop Sweteman wrote to John and William Brisbon acknowledging that they had been elected as arbitrators and friendly compositors by Magnus (Maurice) MacMahon (*Et vos idem Mauricius ex parte sua elegit in arbitros seu amicabiles compositores*), who was in dispute with the archbishop about an attack on one of his men at the episcopal manor of Iniskeen.[170]

It is possible that the Church led the way in encouraging the development of peace-keeping institutions on the marches capable of gaining the confidence of both Irish enemies and loyal English lieges. The former were always likely to be less inspired by parleys and treaties (*tractatus*) initiated by the crown, the declared aim of which was 'to restore them to the peace by force'.[171] The government may have been following the example of the Church in devising, instead, peace agreements in which natives and settlers elected or nominated named individuals whose role it was to arbitrate in disputes that arose between them. The indenture entered into by Brian MacMahon and James Butler, earl of Ormond, in 1425, provided for the election of arbitrators by the English of Louth and Meath on the one hand and by MacMahon on the other, who, within a fortnight of a crime having been perpetrated, would reach a judgment on culpability and identify pledges for the guilty party whose goods could be confiscated until restitution had been made.[172]

Attempts to bring peace to the marches extended beyond formal treaties and involved the cultivation of family ties between natives and settlers. It was 'because therefrom probably peace will be strengthened between the English and the Irish' that in 1427 Archbishop Swayne asked the pope to allow the marriage of Rudraige MacMahon and Alice White to proceed.[173] Two female members of the Betagh family of the Meath/Louth borders—itself of Irish origin, as suggested by the surname, *biatach*, the original meaning of which in Irish was 'food provider' or tenant farmer—were fostered with neighbouring Irish families, including the O'Reillys, between 1389 and 1406, with the permission of the government, while a third was sponsored at baptism by an Irish lord.[174] In 1410 James White was licensed to have his sons and daughter fostered with any branch of the O'Neills, 'Irish enemies in the marches of Ulster and co. Louth, and [with] any other enemies, and also to make compaternity between himself and the said enemies for the king's profit'.[175] Nor was the traffic in fostering all in one direction: in 1405 Thomas Bath was permitted 'to treat and communicate with, and sell to and buy from, Irish enemies and rebels upon his march in co. Meath, and also to foster their boys (*necnon pueros ipsorum nutrire*)'.[176]

---

[169] *Reg. Swayne*, 139. For other examples: *Reg. Mey*, 82, 90–1.   [170] *Reg. Sweteman*, 212.
[171] *RCH* 170 no. 56; 209 no. 192.   [172] *Handbook and Select Calendar… Ireland*, 217.
[173] *Reg. Swayne*, 45–6.   [174] *RCH* 146 no. 187; 180 no. 5; 182 no. 72.
[175] *RCH* 196 no. 82.
[176] *RCH* 180 no. 6. It is possible that this was the Thomas Bath who was archdeacon of Meath and rector of St Columba's, Kells, in the same period: *CPR 1396–9*, 359; *Reg. Fleming*, 102–4.

Prominent settlers who sought royal permission to enter into alliances of marriage and fosterage with the Irish enemies were among that cohort known to contemporaries as 'the marchers'. The case of John Nysene from 1377–8 shows that the term was used by the settlers to describe themselves, and it was regularly applied to them by their Irish neighbours and foes. In January 1395 Niall Mór O'Neill expressed the hope that Richard II would offer him justice 'against the English marchers (*Anglicos marchiales*)', while two months later his son informed the king that he had sustained 'many injuries from the marchers of Uriel (*marchiales Uriel*)'.[177] As such complaints suggest, willingness on the part of Louth settlers to engage fully on a cultural level with their Irish neighbours did not imply any lack of readiness to confront them when necessary or opportune. John Brisbon, the 'friendly compositor' employed by MacMahon in 1371, for instance, served as a keeper of the peace in Louth in 1382.[178] Important local men were among those who translated from Irish the submissions of the native lords to Richard II at Drogheda and Dundalk in 1395, yet a glance at the backgrounds of these individuals suggests that bilingualism was no indicator of divided or multiple political loyalties. Stephen Gernon, 'interpreter, of the diocese of Armagh', had served as a keeper of the peace in Louth in 1386, and in 1394 was granted custody of the lands of Newry abbey in the Cooley peninsula, which had been confiscated because the abbot of the house was Irish.[179] He was joined in the task of interpreting by Thomas Talbot who two years later put his language skills at the disposal of Ramon de Perellós as he set out to meet O'Neill en route to St Patrick's Purgatory, and also accompanied Archbishop Colton on his visit to the diocese of Derry.[180] Talbot held important O'Neill hostages in 1393 and served as sheriff and keeper of the peace in Louth in the early 1400s.[181] Another of the interpreters, John Bocombe (? Butcombe, Somerset), whose son, Richard, was to become bishop of Leighlin in 1400, held land in the barony of Slane.[182] With his immediate lord, Thomas Fleming, baron of Slane, he had been permitted to treat with Irish enemies in 1386, and in 1390 was responsible for the safe-keeping of important O'Neill hostages in Trim castle.[183]

Those settlers who were prepared to act as arbitrators on behalf of Irish lords—as John and William Brisbon had been in 1371 for MacMahon—can with confidence be numbered among 'the marchers of Louth', as can those who witnessed the numerous peace treaties drawn up between the settlers and the natives in this period. The heads of the families of Verdon, Dowdall, White, and Gernon, acted

---

[177] Curtis, *Richard II in Ireland*, 129–32, 210–12. Magnus O'Kane informed the king sometime after Mar. 1395 that any evil he had done to the marchers (*marchialibus*) was in retaliation for their attacks on him: Curtis, *Richard II in Ireland*, 142–3, 220–1.

[178] Frame, 'Commissions of the Peace', 21.

[179] Curtis, *Richard II in Ireland*, 70, 102–3, 160, 188–9; *RCH* 135 no. 165; COA Rep. Records of the Exchequer, 10–22 Richard II, 229.

[180] Curtis, *Richard II in Ireland*, 58–60, 70–1, 149–52, 161; *Acts of Colton*, 12–15; Leslie, *St Patrick's Purgatory*, 22–4.

[181] *RCH* 160 nos. 11 and 18.

[182] Curtis, *Richard II in Ireland*, 101–2, 116–18, 187–8, 199–201; Clare, *On the Edge of the Pale*, 36–7; *NHI* ix. 316; *Dowdall Deeds*, 139, 140.

[183] *RCH* 127 no. 224; 'Lord Chancellor Gerrard's Notes on his Report on Ireland', 214.

as witnesses to the indentures made with Niall Mór O'Neill in 1373 and Brian MacMahon in 1425. Among the other witnesses to the latter agreement were members of the families of Bellew, Hadsor, Taaf, Clinton, and Bagot.[184] These were men whose landed interests in Louth and Meath were not confined to the marches of these counties, and whose political connections and ambitions might extend beyond Ireland itself into England and continental Europe. But it was the marches that absorbed the bulk of their energies and the marches that endowed them with a special and advantageous identity as they moved within this larger, English, world. The permanence of this situation was taken for granted by contemporaries. They were not to know that settler identity in Louth would eventually be destroyed not by the spread of the marches, but by their disappearance.

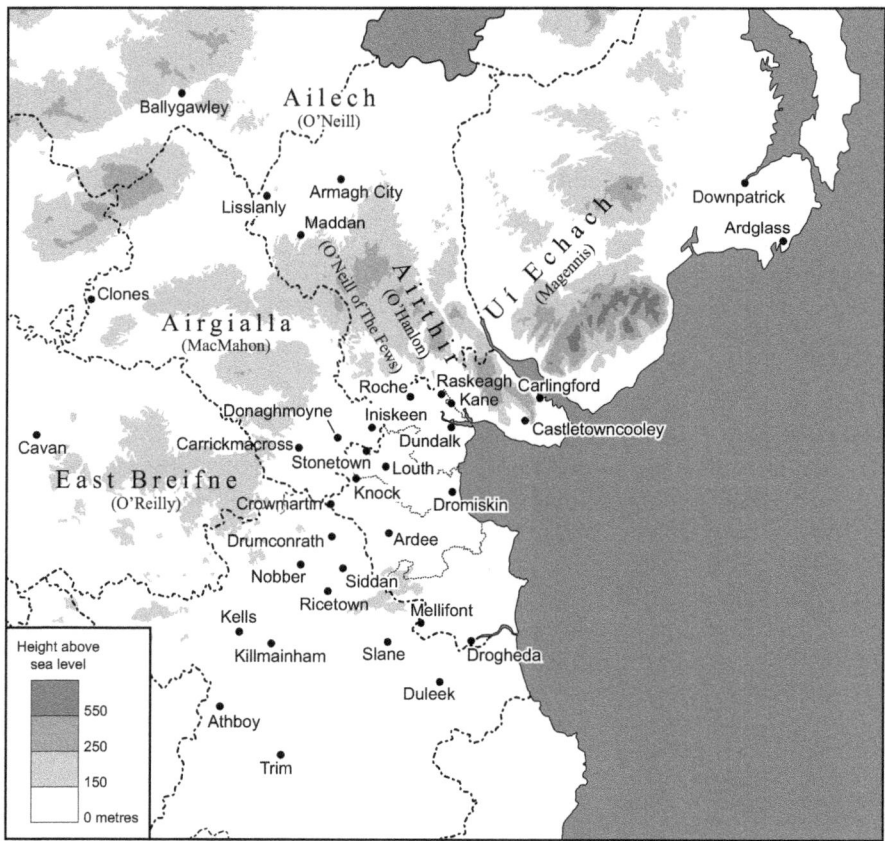

Map 6. The marches of Louth and Meath and neighbouring Irish lordships

[184] *Reg. Sweteman*, 15, 212; *Handbook and Select Calendar... Ireland*, 221–2.

Conclusion

This study of settler society in late medieval Louth has focused in particular on two aspects of its development: first, the influence upon it of its frontier location and, second, its relationship with the larger English world of which it was part. The period between 1330 and 1450 did not witness any decisive break with the past in these matters, but did see the appearance of new challenges and new responses to them that give this era a distinctive character. Beneath the surface of continuity, the community underwent profound change in this century and a quarter. The fact that the physical location and extent of the marches were approximately the same in 1450 as they had been in 1330, for instance, was the result not of inertia, but of an interminable process of assault and resistance that also changed the character of the contending parties. The Bellew lords of Roche and Dundalk had managed by the middle of the fifteenth century to make a reality of their claims to land around Ballybinaby on the border of Armagh, but succeeded in doing so only after decades of conflict with the Irish of south Ulster, represented most recently by the O'Neills of the Fews.[1] Further south, the absentee family of Darcy of Knaith retained ownership of the manors of Louth, Castlering, and Ash until 1465 when they were purchased by Thomas Talbot of Malahide. Before that, in 1425, custody of half of the three manors had been acquired by the local lord, John Taaf, who in the same year witnessed the agreement between the lieutenant and the MacMahons at Ardee, and who already held the marcher manor of Clonkeen.[2] Nor were the small changes in the boundaries and political allegiances of the marches that did occur in this period all in favour of the settlers. West of Castlering, the MacMahons succeeded in incorporating Stonetown, which lay within county Louth, into their lordship of Farney in the middle of the fifteenth century, and held it until 1581.[3]

To have lost so little land to their Irish foes represented a considerable achievement on the part of the settlers, and could not have been accomplished had important families with land in more peaceful parts of Louth not been willing to accept the challenges of frontier conditions. A narrow focus on acres held and lost, however, runs the risk of obscuring what marcher lordship meant for the both the Irish

---

[1] Harold O'Sullivan, 'Dynamics of Regional Development: Processes of Assimilation and Division in the Marchland of South-East Ulster in Late Medieval and Early Modern Ireland', in Ciaran Brady and Jane Ohlmeyer (eds), *British Interventions in Early Modern Ireland* (Cambridge, 2005), 51–3; Ó Fiaich, 'O'Neills of the Fews', 3.
[2] COA Rep. Records of the Exchequer, 1 Henry V–39 Henry VI, 11; *Rotuli Selecti*, 86; *Reg. Octaviani*, ii. 97.
[3] Nicholls, *Gaelic and Gaelicised Ireland*, 149; O'Sullivan, 'March of South-East Ulster', 58–60.

and the settlers. While new territory was always welcome, it was control of men and the exaction of payment from them—tributary lordship—that both sides sought to achieve in the late Middle Ages. This explains why the innumerable burnings and ransackings of English settlements ranging in size from the tiny Iniskeen to the substantial Dundalk, did not also involve the permanent expulsion from them of their existing inhabitants. It also explains why no amount of razing of their 'strong places' by colonial chief governors ever led to the departure of the O'Reillys or MacMahons from their lordships. As the case of the MacQuillins suggested, the uprooting of lesser Irish septs in Ulster was more likely to be accomplished by their great Irish overlords than by the representatives of the crown.[4]

The Irish lords of south Ulster regarded Louth in much the same way as the eleventh-century Christian rules of Iberia had viewed the Muslim territories on their borders. Louth was a Taifa state, the *parias* (revenues) of which were most easily skimmed by O'Neill or MacMahon while the county remained under settler control.[5] In the 1430s Magnus MacMahon—that Mr Kurtz of medieval Monaghan—might dot the heads of his defeated settler enemies around the perimeter of his 'strong place' at Carrickmacross, and Eógan O'Reilly might commission bloodcurdling poems about what lay in store for the English, but such native lords would have been at a loss had they ever found themselves in actual possession of the towns of Ardee or Drumconrath. 'The Rights of MacMahon' of the mid-fifteenth century gloated over the quantities of grain, malt, and cloth that the settlers of Louth were forced to hand over in recognition of the overlordship of the Irish chief; it had nothing to say about any requirement on their part to relinquish their lands. In the 1330s the MacMahons acknowledged that they owed rent for their lands to the Verdons—in 1441 James Verdon was one of those who collected from his fellow settlers in Louth the £20 they had agreed to pay to Brian MacMahon to guarantee his goodwill.[6]

The primacy of tributary lordship in the eyes of the contending parties on the marches explains why the bonnacht of Ulster—enforced provision and maintenance of billeted mercenaries—featured so regularly in the peace agreements drawn up between the Irish and the English authorities. In the early 1330s the O'Neills, O'Hanlons, and MacMahons still acknowledged some responsibility to sustain troops in the service of the earls of Ulster; a century later it was the English of Louth who were providing food and lodging for the men of MacQuillin, who had been driven from Ulster by O'Neill.[7] In August 1388 Edmund London, constable of Carlingford castle, accepted royal appointment as 'constable of the bonnacht', but the honorific status of this post was shown less than two years later when Niall O'Neill agreed to return the bonnacht to Roger Mortimer, earl of March and Ulster, a promise he reiterated in person to Richard II in 1395.[8] In 1425 the MacMahons

---

[4] See above, 212.
[5] For Taifa states and *parias*: Angus MacKay, *Spain in the Middle Ages: From Frontier to Empire, 1000–1500* (Basingstoke, 1977), 15–22.
[6] Otway-Ruthven, 'Partition of the de Verdon Lands', 421–36; NLI, MS 2689, ff. 143–4.
[7] *Inquisitions and Extents*, 155; *CPR 1385–9*, 308.
[8] *RCH* 138 nos. 43, 44, and 45; 147 no. 240; Curtis, *Richard II in Ireland*, 85–90, 173–9.

agreed to fulfil their obligations with regard to the bonnacht to the heir of Edmund Mortimer, and this promise was repeated by Eógan O'Neill in 1446.[9]

The English understood as well as did the Irish that territorial conquest or the expulsion of the other people from their lands were out of the question, and sought instead to have acknowledged by their enemies those rights of lordship that involved practical manifestations of power.[10] Thus, while it is possible to identify certain periods in which pressure from the Irish on Louth was particularly intense (the mid-1340s, the mid-1370s, the late 1380s and the 1390s, the mid-1410s to the mid-1430s), it would be a mistake to imagine that the settlement was ever in danger of total and final collapse—even if that was how its spokesmen, such as Archbishop John Swayne, chose to portray the situation. Hostage-taking, castle-building, and the forging of political and marriage alliances with some of the Irish were not undertaken by the settlers as last throws of the dice but represented, instead, the necessary means to the end of greater security in a frontier environment. In good times they took tribute; in bad times they paid tribute; at no time did they face extinction.

The frontier was imagined to be permanent by the settlers, the natives, and the crown, and could be invoked as an excuse for behaviour that might in other circumstances not have been tolerated. In 1368 Archbishop Milo Sweteman spared himself an unwelcome journey to London to discuss the cross-bearing controversy with the archbishop of Dublin by convincing Edward III that he needed to defend the marches of his archdiocese against the king's Irish enemies in person.[11] In 1374 the sheriff of Louth, John Dowdall, was excused financial penalties imposed upon him for his failure to account at the exchequer when he explained that he had been occupied with defending the marches of Louth against Magennis and negotiating with O'Neill in the company of the justiciar.[12] Two years later a jury found that Walter Cusack, the seneschal of the liberty of Trim, could not have attended the Kilkenny parliament of June 1375 as required because at the time he was defending the marches of west Meath from attacks by the Irish.[13] In September 1443 the Churchmen to whom the spiritual revenues of the vacant archbishopric of Armagh had been entrusted explained that they would be unable to attend the forthcoming great council at Naas 'on account of the immense war with them, which they are compelled to resist in proportion to their strength'.[14] In 1381 forty-two tenants of the manor of Haggardstown, south of Dundalk, which was then in the king's hands, had a year of their rent remitted upon pleading that the burning of their 'houses, corn and moveable goods' made it impossible for them to remain there and pay their rent.[15]

It was clear to some contemporaries that the dangers posed to the settlement in Louth by the Irish of south Ulster were heightened at times by the actions of

---

[9] *Handbook and Select Calendar...Ireland*, 216–17, 226; Simms, 'Ulster Revolt of 1404', 147, 150.
[10] 'It is true, of course, that the conquest was never completed, and that in many respects it went into reverse in the late medieval period. But there is no sign that its completion in a territorial sense was ever on the crown's agenda': Frame, 'English Political Culture', 1.
[11] Sayles, *Affairs*, 227–8. [12] *Dowdall Deeds*, 103; *RCH* 86 no. 46.
[13] *Parls. & Councils*, 71–3. [14] *Reg. Swayne*, 190.
[15] *RCH* 108 no. 33.

the settlers themselves. In 1436 Sir Nicholas Taaf, Thomas Verdon, John Gernon, and others incurred heavy financial penalties from the Dublin government for conducting an unauthorized cattle raid in the territory of O'Reilly.[16] Their Christian duty, and their role as major landowners in the marches, encouraged the archbishops of Armagh in particular to urge restraint on the settlers in Louth. In a sermon preached at Dundalk during Lent in 1356 Archbishop Richard Fitz Ralph complained that his attempts to prevent O'Neill attacking the town in the previous year had been hampered by the willingness of the settlers to make war on their own initiative and to commit acts of theft and arson against the Irish.[17] In 1373 Archbishop Milo Sweteman admitted to 'knowing certainly (*scientes pro certo*) that some of the English are culpable', when pleading with an Irish lord to remain at peace, and the peace agreement he helped forge between the settlers of Louth and the Irish of Ulster in the same year required both peoples to keep peace with the other.[18] He reinforced his message in a provincial council which required

> under pain of excommunication, each suffragan bishop...to labour to reform, hold and preserve peace between the English and the Irish of Armagh province according to his power and preach peace between the same and compel all subjects by ecclesiastical censure to hold the peace. Any sower of discord between said English and Irish to be not only suspended from pontificals, but by the very fact excommunicated.[19]

In 1377 a contemporary of Milo's, John O'Corkeran, bishop of Clogher, whose diocese bordered Louth, complained to the king that he had been ejected from his see 'by the mere Irish and the evil English' (*puri hibernici et mali anglici*).[20]

The archbishops of Armagh were happy to have native Irish clergy in their households in Louth, and when Archbishop Colton travelled to Derry in 1397 his party included several Irish Churchmen.[21] Among these was the abbot of the Augustinian house of Sts Peter and Paul, Armagh, whose lands in Louth had been confiscated sometime before 1375 on the grounds that he 'is Irish and dwelling with them in time of peace and time of war' (*est Irrois et demourant oveque eux sibien en temps du pees comme en temps de guerre*).[22] There were limits, however, to the extent to which the archbishops were prepared to regard their Irish clergy in the same way as they viewed those of settler stock. While they were content to send them as their proctors to the papal curia, they were not willing to allow them to act in a similar capacity at parliaments held in Ireland.[23] In April 1409 Archbishop Nicholas Fleming, in returning to chancery the name of the proctor chosen by the clergy of Armagh among the English to represent them at a forthcoming parliament, noted that the parliamentary summons could not conveniently be delivered

---

[16] *RCH* 260 no. 34.   [17] Gwynn, 'Anglo-Irish Church Life', 19.
[18] *Reg. Sweteman*, 14–15, 244.   [19] *Reg. Swayne*, 11–12.
[20] Sayles, *Affairs*, 241.   [21] *Acts of Colton*, 12–15.
[22] *RCH* 91 no. 39; *PKCI* 239–40.
[23] *Reg. Sweteman*, 121, 122–3, 132, 136–7; *Reg. Fleming*, 137–8. Sweteman appears to have been the last medieval archbishop of Armagh to employ Irishmen as his proctors at the curia.

to the dean and chapter of the diocese at Armagh. Nor had such summonses been delivered to them in the past, he continued, since they 'are mere Irish and dwell among the Irish' (*quod decanus et capitulum sunt meri Hibernici et inter Hibernicos conversantes*).²⁴ Archbishop John Swayne expanded upon the theme in similar circumstances in 1431 by adding that it was not appropriate that the secrets of the king's council in Ireland be revealed to such people.²⁵

As part of his submission to Richard II in 1395 John MacMahon agreed to attend parliament when summoned, but nothing more was heard of such a possibility, and the idea that parliament was not an institution suitable for the Irish to attend remained unchallenged.²⁶ Behind such thinking lay the assumption, fully shared by senior Churchmen, that the Irish were not only ungoverned but also ungovernable. In 1353 Archbishop Fitz Ralph warned a Hungarian pilgrim who was about to journey to St Patrick's Purgatory in the diocese of Clogher that 'it lay among a people lacking rule' (*inter homines minus domitos situatur*).²⁷ Almost half a century later in 1397 Roger Mortimer, earl of March, issued a similar warning to the Catalan pilgrim, Ramon de Perellós, in Dublin, informing him that to reach the Purgatory he would have to travel through the lands of 'a savage, ungoverned people whom no man could trust'.²⁸ Mortimer had in mind the lands of Niall Mór and Niall Óc O'Neill, with whom he had clashed bitterly since his first appearance in Ireland as an adult in 1394.

O'Neill was to tell Ramon in 1397 that the customs of the Irish were better than those of any other Christian people 'and more advantageous than any others in the whole world', and had already made clear that Mortimer's disdain for him was heartily reciprocated.²⁹ In 1391 Mortimer had charged that, since his release from captivity, the younger O'Neill had shown no concern for the hostages handed over as surety for his good behaviour.³⁰ Perhaps it was this slight on his natural affections that prompted O'Neill in his correspondence with Richard II in 1395 to dwell on the dangers faced by Mortimer's prisoners in his castle of Trim. He pleaded for the release of his son from captivity in Trim, arguing that otherwise the boy would die—as other prisoners had done—of neglect or torture.³¹ O'Neill's low opinion of the treatment of prisoners at Trim appears to have been justified. Two noble MacMurrough captives died in the castle in suspicious circumstances before May 1363; in 1383 a Magennis hostage died there of plague; and the same fate befell an O'Reilly in 1447.³² It may be the case that those captives from Louth who

---

²⁴ *Reg. Fleming*, 118.   ²⁵ *Reg. Swayne*, 52–3.
²⁶ Curtis, *Richard II in Ireland*, 102–3, 188–9.
²⁷ Haren, 'Two Hungarian Pilgrims', 120–1. In 1346 the chapter of the diocese of Achonry (Sligo, Mayo, and part of Roscommon) informed the pope that 'the ungovernable character of the Irish' made it necessary to dissolve the union of their diocese with that of Tuam: *CPL 1342–62*, 227.
²⁸ Carpenter, 'Pilgrim from Catalonia/Aragon', 108.
²⁹ Carpenter, 'Pilgrim from Catalonia/Aragon', 111.
³⁰ Sayles, *Affairs*, 261–2.
³¹ Curtis, *Richard II in Ireland*, 133–6, 213–16.
³² *CPR 1361–4*, 368; *A. Clon.* 308; *AFM* iv. 953. Ormond's indenture with O'Neill in 1446, which involved the handing over by the latter of his son as a hostage, included the provision: 'If this hostage dies in custody, the lieutenant will be able to choose the next eldest son to replace him': *Handbook and Select Calendar…Ireland*, 222–3.

in 1432 found themselves surrounded by the impaled heads of their former friends, neighbours, and relatives at MacMahon's fortress at Carrickmacross, or the sixty settler prisoners from Meath upon whom O'Connor Faly placed fetters on the floor of his house in 1423, fared no worse than those Irish captives incarcerated in Trim castle in the same period.[33]

This raw frontier environment shaped how the settlers in Louth viewed their relationship with the crown and its representatives in Ireland. By the middle of the fifteenth century they had proved their loyalty as royal lieges with their blood over many generations, and had developed a clear and uncompromising idea of how they should be governed.[34] Central to this idea was the belief that more government was not the same as good government. Their views were forcefully stated in a petition presented to the Dublin parliament of 1431:

> Also, for as much as the commons of the counties of Meath, Dublin, Kildare and Louth complain that whereas the chancery and the chief place of our lord the king, for the greater part, and his common place and his exchequer are continually in the said parts, by which courts all the lieges of the same parts can sufficiently have justice done them by common law; nevertheless divers commissioners of our lord the king from day to day are appointed in said counties, by whom the lieges of our lord the king of the same counties are too excessively vexed, harassed, aggrieved and impoverished (*trop excessiuement vexez, trauaillez, greuez et enpoueryz*).[35]

Resentment towards the operation of special commissions was but one manifestation of a more general distaste for aspects of government that can be detected among members of the settler elite in Louth in the late Middle Ages. Perhaps because of the disruption it might cause to their business activities, some townsmen were anxious to avoid participation in the operation of local justice and government. In 1334 the English chancery issued an '[e]xemption for life of Matthew de Baa [Bath] of Drogheda from being put on assizes, juries or recognisances, and from appointment as mayor, escheator, coroner or other bailiff or minister of the king against his will'.[36] John White, burgess of Dundalk, received a similar licence in 1348, as did John Walsh, burgess of Drogheda, in 1386.[37] That such attitudes were not confined to the towns is suggested by the grants of exemption from service issued to John Gernon of Killincoole before 1345, to Robert Clinton in 1366, and to William More of Barmeath (upon payment of 6s 8d) in 1407.[38] Unsurprisingly, in the ten years following the murder of John Dowdall, sheriff of Louth, in 1402

---

[33] *AC* 463.
[34] The sharp reminder delivered by Henry VI's council to Edmund Mortimer, earl of March, in Jan. 1424 of his responsibilities as lieutenant of Ireland directed him 'to consider…the agreements he has made for the governance of the said land and ensure as quickly as possible that the king's loyal lieges be kept safe and protected from the king's Irish rebels, so that they may live in peace and tranquillity': *Handbook and Select Calendar…Ireland*, 190 (TNA E 28/43/52).
[35] *Stat. Ire., Hen. VI*, 43.
[36] *CPR 1330–4*, 417.
[37] *CPR 1348–50*, 57; *RCH* 126 no. 192.
[38] NLI MS G[enealogical] O[ffice] 191, 153; NAI RC 8/29, 179; *RCH* 188 no. 51. More had served as one of the collectors in the barony of Ferrard of a subsidy granted by the community of Louth in 1400 to resist Niall O'Neill: *RCH* 158 no. 119; 159 no. 7.

Table 4. Succession to Irish lordships adjacent to Louth

	O'Neill	
Henry son of Brian of Clandeboy	1325	dep. 1345
Aed Mór son of Domnall	1345	1364
Niall Mór son of Aed Mór	1364	abd. 1397
Niall Óc son of Niall Mór	1397	1403
Brian son of Niall Óc	1403	1404
Domnall son of Henry	1404	1432 (contested)
Eógan son of Niall Óc	1404	abd. 1455 (contested)
	MacMahon	
John	1331	1342
Aed son of Ralph	1342	1344
Murcad Óc	1344	1344
Magnus	1344	1357
Philip son of Ralph	1357	1362
Brian Mór son of Aed	1362	1371 (contested)
Niall son of Murcad	1365	1368 (contested)
Philip Ruad son of Brian	1371	1403
Ardgal son of Brian	1403	1416
Brian son of Ardgal	1416	1442
Rudraige son of Ardgal	1442	1446
Aed Ruad son of Rudraige	1446	1453
	Magennis	
Muirchertach	?	1349
Art son of Muirchertach	1360	1383 (imprisoned from 1380)
Muirchertach Óc son of Muirchertach	1380(?)	1399
Rudraige son of Art	1399	1401
Aed son of Art	1407	1424
Rudraige son of Aed	1424	1426
Art son of Aed	1427	1449
	O'Reilly	
Richard son of Gilla Ísa	1330	1349
Cú Connacht son of Gilla Ísa	1349	abd. 1365
Philip son of Gilla Ísa	1365	1384
Magnus son of Cú Connacht	1369	dep. 1369
Thomas Mór son of Mahon	1384	1392
John son of Philip	1392	1400
Mael Morda son of Cú Connacht	1403	1411
Richard son of Thomas Mór	1411	1418
Eógan son of John	1418	1449
John son of Eógan	1449	1460 (contested)
Fergal son of Thomas Mór	1449	dep. 1450

by a number of the most important settlers in the county, it proved difficult to find men willing to take up the post of sheriff.[39] When the barons of the exchequer decided in September 1406 that William Stokes, seneschal of the abbot of Mellifont,

---

[39] In contemporary England 'the office of sheriff was one which men contended to avoid as much as to assume': Harriss, 'Dimensions of Politics', 6.

should be made sheriff of Louth he produced a royal grant dating from June 1405 excusing him from office-holding.[40] In 1408 the commons of Louth elected Nicholas Muriel as their sheriff, and in 1410 chose Roger Gernon. In both instances the individuals concerned produced royal letters patent granting them liberty for life from taking up office.[41] Gernon had secured his letter in May 1403, eight months after John Dowdall's murder.[42] In May 1411 John Clinton of Drumcashel produced at the king's bench in Dublin a letter patent of Henry IV, obtained through the intercession of Thomas Butler, deputy lieutenant of Ireland, declaring him free for life from serving on juries and from office-holding.[43]

Linked to some extent to such reluctance to participate in the operation of royal justice and government was the widespread desire in late medieval Louth to avoid the obligation to take up knighthood.[44] Richard Taaf of Braganstown served as sheriff of Louth in 1336–7 and 1341–2, and as collector of a parliamentary subsidy in Meath in 1347, but refused to accept knighthood. In 1347 he received a royal pardon for this trespass and licence for life to avoid becoming a knight.[45] In 1384 another Louth man, John Napton, was permitted to decline the obligation to become a knight against his will at the request of Sir Robert Preston and other councillors.[46] In 1389 Richard II made a determined effort to increase the number of knights in Louth and Meath, only to have his efforts thwarted by local juries. Of the eighteen men identified by the crown as required to accept the obligation of knighthood, sixteen were found by inquisitions to have land worth less per annum than the £40 threshold required to become a knight.[47]

The complaint of the commons of Louth, Meath, Dublin, and Kildare in 1431 about being overgoverned spoke to an uncomfortable reality: as the geographical reach of English authority in Ireland contracted, it came to be felt more intensely in those areas still within its purview.[48] While this resulted in more frequent and substantial demands upon the limited financial resources of the settlers in Louth, it is difficult to see the rising profile of the county in the eyes of the government as pernicious to its inhabitants in all regards. Whereas in the 1370s William Windsor had used his power to issue summonses to attend parliaments in distant and remote locations as a weapon against his enemies in the county, the increased frequency with which the assembly met in Drogheda in the fifteenth century brought not only more short-term economic activity to the town, but also easier access to

---

[40] COA Rep. Records of the Exchequer, Henry IV, 197–8.
[41] COA Rep. Records of the Exchequer, Henry IV, 285.
[42] COA Rep. Records of the Exchequer, Henry IV, 334.
[43] BL Add MS 4790, f. 1.
[44] For discussion of this theme in an English context see Carpenter, *Locality and Polity*, 66–7, 82–8. Knighthood in Ireland is a neglected topic. For useful insights by Bernadette Williams see *Clyn*, 106–10.
[45] TNA E 101/241/10; *Rep. DKI 54*, 53; *CPR 1345–8*, 547; *CCR 1346–9*, 565.
[46] *RCH* 119 no. 9; COA Rep. Records of the Exchequer, 1–10 Richard II, 434.
[47] See above, 87.
[48] 'The Yorkist kings...contemplated an English land [in Ireland] limited to the counties around Dublin, the ports of the south coast, and (more doubtfully) some southern lordships, whose social complexion was at best hybrid': Robin Frame, 'Kingdoms and Dominions at War and Peace', in Ralph Griffiths (ed.), *The Fourteenth and Fifteenth Centuries* (Oxford, 2003), 149–80, quote at 179.

patronage and power for the local elite. Windsor and other fourteenth-century chief governors failed even to visit Louth: their fifteenth-century successors were frequently present in the county.[49]

Nor could many counties in England situated at some remove from London boast between 1360 and 1450 of having played host to a king of England (Richard II), two sons of kings (Lionel of Antwerp and Thomas of Lancaster), and the father of a future king (Richard, duke of York).[50] The settlers of Louth may not have had much time for the lawyers and bureaucrats upon whom royal government depended, but their craving for the presence in their midst of a *bone chiefteyn suffisant* knew no bounds. The Mortimer name exerted a particular fascination, and the muscular and uncritical support afforded by the settlers to Edmund and Roger Mortimer as they stampeded around their earldom of Ulster in the late fourteenth century exposed the political naïveté of the settlers. They suffered grievously at the hands of the O'Neills and their allies as each Mortimer campaign ended in the failure and death of its leader, but did nothing to prevent the cycle of folly repeating itself. So detached from reality was it possible for those involved in these proceedings to become that when in the summer of 1449 Richard, duke of York, the inheritor of the Mortimer lands and titles, received yet another set of submissions from the Ulster Irish, one of his supporters even claimed that 'with the myght of Jesus or twelmonth come an end ye wildest Yrishman in Yrland shall be swore English'.[51]

Less exalted than the earls of March and Ulster, but more reliable as guarantors of the fortunes of the settlers, were the earls of Ormond. The more frequent employment by the crown of the earls as chief governors of Ireland coincided with the rise of Louth to a position of greater prominence in the eyes of the Dublin government as its hold on more distant parts of the country weakened. The third earl revived ancient Butler claims to land in the county in the 1390s, and his son and successor, James Butler, fourth earl of Ormond, campaigned frequently in Louth, eventually dying at Ardee in 1452.[52] The precedent set by the earls of Ormond of increased involvement in Louth was to be followed by their successors and rivals for power among the settler nobility: by the end of the fifteenth century the earls of Kildare had founded a chantry in the parish church of Dundalk, St Nicholas's, and acquired Dungooley on the northern fringes of the county.[53]

Louth was a very different place in 1450 than it had been in 1330, not least because in this period the composition of its population had undergone considerable change. At best we catch fleeting glimpses of this process in our surviving records. In January 1402 Janico Dartas and John Teeling were given permission to receive Irish tenants on their manor of Crowmartin 'for the relief of the lieges of those marches', which suggests that the area was underpopulated.[54] The impression

---

[49] See above, Part I.
[50] Henry of Monmouth, the future Henry V, and his brother, Humphrey, appear to have remained at Trim during their brief sojourn in Ireland in the custody of Richard II in 1399.
[51] Curtis, 'Richard, duke of York', 168.
[52] Crooks, 'Factions, Feuds and Noble Power', 442–6.
[53] Lyons, *Church and Society*, 86; O'Sullivan, 'March of South-East Ulster', 59–60, 152.
[54] *RCH* 163 no. 135.

that settler tenants were abandoning their holdings is supported by the comment of Archbishop John Swayne in the late 1420s that

> ...the housbonde pepill for the meschefe and governaunces aforsaide be gone out of the londe within fewe yeris into Englonde and into odir contreys that in good faith as I suppos there is mo (more) gone oute of the londe of the Kyngis lege pepyll then be in.[55]

It must not be imagined, however, that the Irish tenants who replaced the settlers in the marches of Louth represented some fifth column of native power, imbued with a mission to destroy the settlement. In 1375 Archbishop Milo Sweteman wrote to Niall Mór O'Neill informing him that, because of repeated attacks upon them by O'Neill's sons, the archbishop's tenants intended to surrender their lands.[56] If they carried out this threat it is possible that they were able to start new lives on the manors in Louth from which settler tenants were at the same time migrating. Once there, they may have been joined by native peasants from the lands of the O'Neills, O'Hanlons, and MacMahons, eager to escape a system of lordship designed to strip them of resources so that the poets who despised them and galloglass who intimidated them might live in comfort.[57] The 1402 grant to Dartas and Teeling specified that 'traitors' among the Irish were not be accepted as tenants, and it should not be concluded that a growth in the proportion of the population of late medieval Louth that was of Irish origin and spoke the Irish language in itself weakened the ties that bound the county to the English crown and the English world.

Towards the end of the period with which this study is concerned the 'poor commons of the little county of Louth' wrote to their king to complain about their treatment at the hands both of their Irish enemies and of the servants of the crown.[58] They had good reason to feel aggrieved, and understood that it was by bringing their plight in its starkest detail to the attention of their lord that they might receive redress.[59] It was not to their advantage to try to present a balanced view of their situation, nor were they expected to do so. The new belfry tower constructed at the Franciscan friary at Dundalk in *c.*1400, the new churches built on his Meath manors of Dunsany and Rathmore by Christopher Plunket before 1445, and the welter of new tower houses that sprang up in the same period in both town and country, spoke to a degree of economic vitality and revival that would feature in no petition from the poor commons of Louth.[60] It is for later historians to point out that the settlers of Louth had not been broken by the traumas of this period, and were at least as assured in their identity as representatives of English civilization in a conquered country at its end as they had been at its beginning.

---

[55] *Reg. Swayne*, 108.   [56] *Reg. Sweteman*, 140.
[57] Simms, 'References to Landscape and Economy', 149–51.
[58] *Proceedings and Ordinances*, ii. 49–50.
[59] Gwilym Dodd, *Justice and Grace: Private Petitioning and the English Parliament in the Late Middle Ages* (Oxford, 2007), 254–66.
[60] Harold G. Leask, *Irish Churches and Monastic Buildings*, iii. *Medieval Gothic: The Last Phase* (Dundalk, 1960), 14, 16, 22; Helen M. Roe, *Medieval Fonts of Meath* (Navan, 1968), 9, 54; Steven G. Ellis, *Ireland in the Age of the Tudors, 1447–1603: English Expansion and the End of Gaelic Rule* (Harlow, 1998), 38–9.

Bibliography

MANUSCRIPT SOURCES

Ireland

Dublin

National Library
NLI D Ormond Deeds
NLI MS 2, 3, 4 *Collectanea de Rebus Hibernica*, compiled by Walter Harris, ii, iii, iv
NLI MS 2689 Canon Leslie Collection: Typescript Copy of Bishop Reeves's Calendar of Primate Prene's Register
NLI MS G[enealogical] O[ffice] 191 Extracts from Plea Rolls 1 Edward I–19 Edward III

National Archives
NAI Ex 1 Memoranda Rolls (Originals)
NAI Ex 2 Memoranda Rolls (Calendars)
NAI Ferguson Coll. iii J. F. Ferguson's Collection from the Irish memoranda rolls, iii
NAI KB 1/3 Justiciary Rolls
NAI Lodge Ms 17 John Lodge: ancient commissions, Irish chiefs (articles with) denizations, general pardons
NAI M 999 Calendar of Pipe Rolls, 1356–7
NAI MS 1121 Bellew Deeds
NAI RC 8 Record Commissioners' Calendar of Memoranda Rolls

Royal Irish Academy
RIA MS 12 D 10 Extracts from Memoranda Rolls

Trinity College Dublin
TCD MS 1747 Report of searches respecting the office of the clerk of the common pleas of the Ex. of Ire., made by order of the Commissioners on the Public Records, 1816
TCD MS 3411 O'Reilly MSS

United Kingdom

London

British Library
BL Add Charter 7041 Charter relating to Drumshallon, 1372
BL Add Charter 13597 Escheator's account, Louth and Meath, 1341–3
BL Add MS 4790 Abstracts from estreat rolls, common pleas, 13 Henry IV
BL Add MS 4797 Milles Collection, vol. 44
BL Add MS 4798 Milles Collection, vol. 45
BL Add MS 6041 List of Mortimer muniments
BL Add MS 23693 Lodge manuscripts
BL Add MS 43769 Delafield manuscript
BL Cotton Titus B xi, 26 Cotton manuscripts

BL Egerton Charter 7228 Indenture between Walter Brugge and John Maryman, 1375
BL Egerton MS 75 Abstracts of Irish patent, close, and mixed rolls, Edward I–James I
BL Landsdowne MS 315 A transcript of the Rotulus Hiberniae of 1 Ed. III. to 12 Edw. III, with an index, 1327–38

The National Archives
TNA C 1 Court of Chancery: Six Clerks' Office: Early Proceedings, Richard II–Philip and Mary
TNA C 47 Chancery Miscellanea
TNA C 59/14 Extracts of Charters and Patents Relating to Ireland. [Grants of Crown Lands and Rents and Remissions of Debts in Ireland, 19 Edw II–12 Edw III]
TNA C 143 Inquisitions Ad Quod Damnum: Henry III–Richard III
TNA C 260 Chancery Files (Recorda)
TNA DL 25 Duchy of Lancaster: Deeds
TNA DL 27 Duchy of Lancaster: Deeds (Fine Seals)
TNA E 28 Treasury of Receipt: Council and Privy Seal Records
TNA E 30 Treasury of Receipt: Diplomatic Documents
TNA E 101 King's Remembrancer: Accounts Various
TNA E 122 Customs Accounts
TNA E 210 King's Remembrancer: Ancient Deeds
TNA E 352 Pipe Office: Chancellor's Rolls
TNA E 368 Memoranda Rolls, Lord Treasurer's Remembrancer
TNA KB 27 *Coram Rege* Rolls
TNA SC 6 Ministers' and Receivers' Accounts
TNA SC 8 Ancient Petitions

College of Arms
Betham. Repertory to Records of the Exchequer, i. 42 Edward III–51 Edward III
Betham. Repertory to Records of the Exchequer, ii. 1 Richard II to 10 Richard II
Betham. Repertory to Records of the Exchequer, iii. 10 Richard II to 22 Richard II
Betham. Repertory to Records of the Exchequer, iv. Henry IV
Betham. Repertory to Records of the Exchequer, v. I Henry V–39 Henry VI

PRINTED WORKS

Account Roll of the Priory of the Holy Trinity, Dublin, 1337–1346, ed. J. Mills (Dublin, 1891).
Acts of Archbishop Colton in his Metropolitical Visitation of the Diocese of Derry, ed. William Reeves. Irish Archaeological Society (Dublin, 1850).
Aithdioghluim Dána: A Miscellany of Irish Bardic Poetry, Historical and Religious, including the Historical Poems of the Duanaire in the Yellow Book of Lecan, ed. and tr. Lambert McKenna SJ, 2 vols. Irish Texts Society (Dublin, 1939–40).
Anglo-Norman Letters and Petitions from All Souls Ms 182, ed. M. Dominica Legge (Oxford, 1941).
Annála Ríoghachta Éireann: Annals of the Kingdom of Ireland by the Four Masters from the Earliest Period to the Year 1616, ed. and tr. John O'Donovan, 7 vols (Dublin, 1851; 3rd edition, 1990).
Annála Uladh, Annals of Ulster, ed. W. M. Hennessy and B. Mac Carthy, 4 vols (Dublin 1887–1901; 2nd edn, 1998).
The Annals of Clonmacnoise, ed. D. Murphy (Dublin, 1896; repr. Llanerch, 1983).
The Annals of Ireland by Friar John Clyn, ed. Bernadette Williams (Dublin, 2007).

The Annals of Ireland by Friar John Clyn and Thady Dowling, ed. Richard Butler (Dublin, 1849).
'Annals of Ireland from the Year 1443 to 1468 Translated from the Irish by Dudley Firbissse, or as he is More Usually Called, Duald Mac Firbis, for Sir James Ware, in the Year 1666', ed. John O'Donovan, in *Miscellany of the Irish Archaeological Society*, i (Dublin, 1846), 198–302.
'The Annals of Nenagh', ed. Dermot F. Gleeson, *Anal. Hib.* 12 (1943), 157–64.
The Armburgh Papers, ed. Christine Carpenter (Woodbridge, 1998).
Calendar of Archbishop Alen's Register, c.1172–1534, ed. Charles Mac Neill. Royal Society of Antiquaries of Ireland (Dublin, 1950).
Calendar of the Carew Manuscripts Preserved in the Archiepiscopal Library at Lambeth, 1515–74, ed. J. S. Brewer and W. Bullen, 6 vols (London, 1867–73).
Calendar of Close Rolls (London, 1892–).
Calendar of Documents Relating to Ireland, ed. H. S. Sweetman, 5 vols (London, 1875–86).
'Calendar of Documents Relating to Medieval Ireland in the Series of Ancient Deeds in the National Archives of the United Kingdom', ed. Paul Dryburgh and Brendan Smith, *Anal. Hib.* 39 (2006), 1–61.
Calendar of Entries in the Papal Registers Relating to Great Britain and Ireland: Papal Letters (London, 1893–).
Calendar of Fine Rolls (London, 1911–).
Calendar of the Gormanston Register, ed. James Mills and M. J. McEnery (Dublin, 1916).
Calendar of Justiciary Rolls, 3 vols (Dublin, 1905–).
Calendar of Ormond Deeds, 1172–1603, ed. Edmund Curtis, 6 vols. Irish Manuscripts Commission (Dublin, 1932–43).
Calendar of Patent Rolls (London, 1891–).
Chartae, Privilegia, et Immunitates (London, 1889).
Chartularies of St Mary's Abbey, Dublin… and Annals of Ireland, 1162–1370, ed. J. T. Gilbert, 2 vols. Rolls Series (London, 1884–6).
Christ Church Deeds, ed. M. J. McEnery and Raymond Refaussé (Dublin, 2001).
'Cíos MacMathghamhna', ed. Seósamh Ó Dufaigh, *Clogher Record*, 4 (1962), 125–34.
A Collection of all the Wills, Now Known to Be Extant, of the Kings and Queens of England, Princes and Princesses of Wales, and every Branch of the Blood Royal, from the Reign of William the Conqueror, to that of Henry the Seventh Exclusive: With Explanatory Notes and a Glossary, ed. J. Nichols (London, 1780).
The Coucher Book of Furness Abbey, ed. J. C. Atkinson and J. Brownhill, 3 vols. Chetham Society (Manchester, 1886–1916).
De Annatis Hiberniae: A Calendar of the First Fruits' Fees Levied on Papal Appointments to Benefices in Ireland A.D. 1400 to 1535, ed. M. A. Costello OP (Dundalk, 1909).
Documents on the Affairs of Ireland before the King's Council, ed. G. O. Sayles. Irish Manuscripts Commission (Dublin, 1979).
'Documents Relating to the Suppression of the Templars in Ireland', ed. Gearóid Mac Niocaill, *Anal. Hib.* 24 (1967), 183–226.
Dowdall Deeds, ed. C. McNeill and A. J. Otway-Ruthven. Irish Manuscripts Commission (Dublin, 1960).
Foedera, Conventiones, Litterae et cuiuscunque Generis Acta Publica, ed. Thomas Rymer, 20 vols (London, 1704–35).
Handbook and Select Calendar of Sources for Medieval Ireland in the National Archives of the United Kingdom, ed. Paul Dryburgh and Brendan Smith. The National Archives (Dublin, 2005).

'Henry Marleburrough's Chronicle of Ireland', in *The Historie of Ireland*, ed. Meredith Hanmer, Edmund Campion, and Edmund Spencer (Dublin, 1633).
Inquisitions and Extents of Medieval Ireland, ed. Paul Dryburgh and Brendan Smith. List and Index Society, 320 (Kew, 2007).
The Irish Cartularies of Llanthony Prima and Secunda, ed. Eric St John Brooks. Irish Manuscripts Commission (Dublin, 1953).
Irish Exchequer Payments, 1270–1446, ed. Philomena Connolly. Irish Manuscripts Commission (Dublin, 1998).
'Irish Materials in the Class of Ancient Petitions (SC 8) in the Public Record Office, London', ed. Philomena Connolly, *Anal. Hib.* 34 (1987), 1–106.
Jacobi Grace, Kilkenniensis, Annales Hiberniae, ed. Richard Butler (Dublin, 1842).
Jean Creton, 'Metrical History of the Deposition of King Richard the Second', ed. J. Webb, *Archaeologia*, 20 (1824), 13–239.
Kingsford's Stonor Letters and Papers, 1290–1483, ed. Christine Carpenter (Cambridge, 1996).
'Late Medieval Irish Annals: Two Fragments', ed. Kenneth Nicholls, *Peritia*, 2 (1983), 87–102.
'List of Irish Material in the Class of Chancery Files (Recorda) (C. 260) Public Record Office, London', ed. Philomena Connolly, *Anal. Hib.* 31 (1984), 3–18.
'Lord Chancellor Gerrard's Notes on his Report on Ireland', ed. C. McNeill, *Anal. Hib.* 2 (1931), 93–291.
Materials for the History of the Franciscan Province of Ireland, ed. E. B. Fitzmaurice and A. G. Little (Manchester, 1920).
Miscellaneous Irish Annals (AD 1114–1447), ed. Séamus Ó hInnse (Dublin, 1947).
Original Letters Illustrative of English History, including Numerous Royal Letters, ed. H. Ellis, 2nd ser., 4 vols (London, 1827).
Parliaments and Councils of Mediaeval Ireland, i, ed. H. G. Richardson and G. O. Sayles. Irish Manuscripts Commission (Dublin, 1947).
The Parliament Rolls of Medieval England, 1275–1504, ed. Chris Given-Wilson (gen. ed.) et al., 16 vols (Woodbridge, 2005).
The Plumpton Letters and Papers, ed. Joan Kirby (Cambridge, 1996).
'Private Indentures for Life Service in Peace and War, 1278–1476', ed. Michael Jones and Simon Walker, *Camden Miscellany*, 32 (1994), 5–190.
Proceedings and Ordinances of the Privy Council of England, ed. N. H. Nicolas, 7 vols (London, 1834–7).
'The Register of Clogher', ed. Kenneth Nicholls, *Clogher Record*, 7 (1971–2), 361–431.
Register of the Hospital of St John the Baptist Without the Newgate, Dublin, ed. E. St John Brooks. Irish Manuscripts Commission (Dublin, 1936).
The Register of John Swayne, Archbishop of Armagh and Primate of Ireland 1418–1439, ed. D. A. Chart (Belfast, 1935).
The Register of Milo Sweteman, Archbishop of Armagh 1361–1380, ed. Brendan Smith. Irish Manuscripts Commission (Dublin, 1996).
The Register of Nicholas Fleming, Archbishop of Armagh 1404–1416, ed. Brendan Smith. Irish Manuscripts Commission (Dublin, 2003).
Registrum de Kilmainham, ed. C. McNeill. Irish Manuscripts Commission (Dublin, 1932).
Registrum Johannis Mey: The Register of John Mey Archbishop of Armagh, 1443–1456, ed. W. G. H. Quigley and E. F. D. Roberts (Belfast, 1972).

Registrum Octaviani, alias Liber Niger: The Register of Octavian de Palatio, Archbishop of Armagh 1478–1513, ed. Mario Alberto Sughi, 2 vols. Irish Manuscripts Commission (Dublin, 1999).
Reports of the Commissioners Appointed by His Majesty to Execute the Measures Recommended in an Address of the House of Commons Respecting the Public Records of Ireland; with Supplement and Appendixes, 3 vols (London, 1815–25), i, rep. 1–5 (1811–15).
Reports of the Deputy Keeper of the Public Records of Ireland (Dublin, 1869–).
A Roll of the Proceedings of the King's Council in Ireland for a Portion of the Sixteenth Year of the Reign of Richard the Second, A.D. 1392–93, ed. James Greaves (London, 1877).
Rotuli Selecti ad Res Anglicas et Hibernicas Spectantes, ex Archivis in Domo Capitulari Westmonasteriensi, Deprompti, ed. Joseph Hunter (London, 1834).
Rotulorum Patentium et Clausorum Cancellariae Hiberniae Calendarium, ed. E. Tresham. Irish Record Commission (Dublin, 1828).
Royal and Historical Letters during the Reign of Henry IV, ed. F. C. Hingeston (London, 1860).
Select Cases in the Court of King's Bench, vii. *Richard II, Henry IV and Henry V*, ed. G. O. Sayles. Selden Society (London, 1971).
Statute Rolls of the Parliament of Ireland, Reign of King Henry VI, ed. Henry F. Berry (Dublin, 1910).
Statutes of the Realm, ed. A. Luders, T. E. Tomlins, and J. Raithby, 11 vols (London, 1810–28).
Statutes and Ordinances and Acts of the Parliament of Ireland, King John to Henry V, ed. Henry F. Berry (Dublin, 1907).
Three Prose Versions of the Secreta Secretorum, ed. Robert Steele. English Text Society (London, 1898).
'Two Old Drogheda Chronicles', ed. Diarmuid Mac Iomhair, *CLAJ* 15 (1961), 88–95.
Vetera Monumenta Hibernorum et Scotorum Historiam Illustrantia, ed. A. Theiner (Rome, 1864).

SECONDARY WORKS

Abulafia, David, Franklin, Michael, and Rubin, Miri (eds), *Church and City 1000–1500: Essays in Honour of Christopher Brooke* (Cambridge, 1992).
Acheson, Eric, *A Gentry Community: Leicestershire in the Fifteenth Century, c.1422–c.1485* (Cambridge, 1992).
—— 'Ferrers Family (*per. c.*1240–1445)', *Oxford Dictionary of National Biography* (Oxford, 2004; online edn, Jan. 2008).
Appleby, John C., and Dalton, Paul (eds), *Government, Religion and Society in Northern England 1000–1700* (Stroud, 1997).
Archer, Rowena E., ' "How ladies... who live on their manors ought to manage their households and estates": Women as Landholders and Administrators in the Later Middle Ages', in P. J. P. Goldberg (ed.), *Women in Medieval English Society* (Stroud, 1997), 149–81.
Ayton, Andrew, and Preston, Sir Philip, *The Battle of Crécy, 1346* (Woodbridge, 2005).
Bailey, Mark, *Medieval Suffolk: An Economic and Social History 1200–1500* (Woodbridge, 2007).
Bannerman, John, W. M., 'The Lordship of the Isles', in Jennifer M. Brown (ed.), *Scottish Society in the Fifteenth Century* (New York, 1977), 209–40.

Barry, Terry, 'The Last Frontier: Defence and Settlement in Late Medieval Ireland', in Terry Barry, Robin Frame, and Katharine Simms (eds), *Colony and Frontier in Medieval Ireland: Essays Presented to J. F. Lydon* (London, 1995), 217–28.

Barry, Terry, Frame, Robin, and Simms, Katharine (eds), *Colony and Frontier in Medieval Ireland: Essays Presented to J. F. Lydon* (London, 1995).

Bartlett, Robert, and Mackay, Angus (eds), *Medieval Frontier Societies* (Oxford, 1989).

Bartlett, Thomas, and Jeffery, Keith (eds), *A Military History of Ireland* (Cambridge, 1996).

Bennett, Michael J., *Community, Class and Careerism: Cheshire and Lancashire Society in the Age of Sir Gawain and the Green Knight* (Cambridge, 1983).

—— *Richard II and the Revolution of 1399* (Stroud, 1999).

—— 'Richard II and the Wider Realm', in Anthony Goodman and James L. Gillespie (eds), *Richard II and the Art of Kingship* (Oxford, 1999), 187–204.

Betham, William, *The Origin and History of the Constitution of England and of the Early Parliaments of Ireland* (Dublin, 1834).

Biancalana, Joseph, *The Fee Tail and the Common Recovery in Medieval England, 1176–1502* (Cambridge, 2001).

Biggs, Douglas, 'The Reign of Henry IV: The Revolution of 1399 and the Establishment of the Lancastrian Regime', in Nigel Saul (ed.), *Fourteenth Century England I* (Woodbridge, 2000), 195–210.

—— *Three Armies in Britain: The Irish Campaign of Richard II and the Usurpation of Henry IV, 1397–1399* (Leiden, 2006).

Blacker, B. H., 'Ó Ceallaigh, Ralph (d. 1361)', rev. Philomena Connolly, *Oxford Dictionary of National Biography* (Oxford, 2004).

Bliss, Alan J., 'The Inscribed Slates at Smarmore', *PRIA* 64 (1965–6), C, 33–60.

—— 'Comment', *Notes and Queries*, 212 (1967), 85.

—— 'Language and Literature', in James Lydon (ed.), *The English in Medieval Ireland* (Dublin, 1984), 27–45.

Boardman, Stephen, *The Early Stewart Kings: Robert II and Robert III, 1371–1406* (East Linton, 1996).

—— 'Robert III (d. 1406)', *Oxford Dictionary of National Biography* (Oxford, 2004).

Bolton, Jim, 'Irish Migration to England in the Late Middle Ages', *IHS* 32 (2000), 1–21.

—— '"The World Turned Upside Down": Plague as an Agent of Economic and Social Change', in Mark Ormrod and Phillip Lindley (eds), *The Black Death in England* (Donington, 2003), 17–78.

Bonney, Margaret, *Lordship and the Urban Community: Durham and its Overlords, 1250–1540* (Cambridge, 1990).

Booker, Anne (Sparky), 'After the "Middle Nation": The English of Ireland, Gaelicisation, and Identity in the "Four Loyal Shires" of Ireland in the Fifteenth and Sixteenth Centuries', Ph.D. thesis, University of Dublin, Trinity College (2011).

Booth, Paul H. W., *The Financial Administration of the Lordship and County of Chester, 1272–1377* (Manchester, 1981).

Bradley, John, 'The Topography and Layout of Medieval Drogheda', *CLAJ* 19 (1978), 98–127.

—— 'Ardee: An Archaeological Study', *CLAJ* 20 (1984), 267–96.

—— (ed.), *Settlement and Society in Medieval Ireland: Studies Presented to F. X. Martin O.S.A.*, ed. John Bradley (Kilkenny, 1988).

Brand, Paul, 'King, Church and Property: Mortmain in the Lordship of Ireland', *Peritia*, 3 (1984), 481–502.

—— 'The Formation of a Parish Church: The Case of Beaulieu, County Louth', in John Bradley (ed.), *Settlement and Society in Medieval Ireland: Studies Presented to F. X. Martin O.S.A.* (Kilkenny, 1988).
—— 'The Birth and Early Development of a Colonial Judiciary: The Judges of the Lordship of Ireland, 1210–1377', in W. N. Osborough (ed.), *Explorations in Law and History: Irish Legal History Discourses, 1988–1994* (Dublin, 1995), 1–48.
—— 'An Irishman in Westminster Hall: William Skrene of Dundalk, King's Serjeant at Law (*c*.1358–*c*.1420)', *The Irish Jurist*, 31 (1996), 255–65.
—— 'Irish Law Students and Lawyers in Late Medieval England', *IHS* 32 (2000), 161–73.
Breen, Colin, *The Gaelic Lordship of the O'Sullivan Beare* (Dublin, 2005).
Britnell, Richard (ed.), *The Winchester Pipe Rolls and Medieval English Society* (Woodbridge, 2003).
—— *Britain and Ireland 1050–1530* (Oxford, 2004).
—— 'English Agricultural Output and Prices, 1350–1450: National Trends and Regional Divergences', in Ben Dodds and Richard Britnell (eds), *Agriculture and Rural Society After the Black Death: Common Themes and Regional Variations* (Hatfield, 2008), 20–39.
Britnell, R. H., and Pollard, A. J. (eds), *The McFarlane Legacy: Studies in Late Medieval Politics and Society* (Stroud, 1995).
Bromwich, Rachel, 'The Earlier *Cywyddwyr*: Poets Contemporary with Dafydd ap Gwilym', in A. O. H. Jarman and Gwilym Rees Hughes (eds), *A Guide to Welsh Literature, 1282-c.1550*, rev. Daffyd Johnston (Cardiff, 1997), 126–49.
Brown, Jennifer M. (ed.), *Scottish Society in the Fifteenth Century* (New York, 1977).
Brown, Michael, and Tanner, Roland (eds), *Scottish Kingship, 1306–1542: Essays in Honour of Norman Macdougall* (Edinburgh, 2008).
Buldorini, Chiara, 'Drogheda as a Case Study of Anglo-Norman Town Foundation in Ireland, 1194–1412', 2 vols, Ph.D. thesis, University of Dublin, Trinity College (2009).
Burns, Charles, 'Papal Letters of Clement VII of Avignon (1378–94) Relating to Ireland and England', *Collectanea Hibernica*, 24 (1982), 7–44.
Burrows, Michael A. J., 'Fifteenth-Century Irish Provincial Legislation and Pastoral Care', in W J. Shiels and Diana Wood (eds), *Studies in Church History 25: The Churches, Ireland and the Irish* (Oxford, 1989), 55–67.
Carpenter, Christine, *Locality and Polity: A Study of Warwickshire Landed Society, 1401–1499* (Cambridge, 1992).
—— 'Gentry and Community in Medieval England', *Journal of British Studies*, 33 (1994), 340–80.
—— 'England: The Nobility and the Gentry', in S. H. Rigby (ed.), *A Companion to Britain in the Later Middle Ages* (Oxford, 2003), 261–82.
Carpenter, D. M., 'The Pilgrim from Catalonia/Aragon: Ramon de Perellós, 1397', in Michael Haren and Yolande de Pontfarcy (eds), *The Medieval Pilgrimage to St Patrick's Purgatory: Lough Derg and the European Tradition*. Clogher Historical Society (Enniskillen, 1988), 99–119.
Castor, Helen, *The King, the Crown, and the Duchy of Lancaster: Public Authority and Private Power, 1399–1461* (Oxford, 2000).
Cherry, Jonathan, 'The Indigenous and Colonial Urbanization of Cavan Town, *c*.1300–*c*.1641', in Brendan Scott (ed.), *Culture and Society in Early Modern Breifne/Cavan* (Dublin, 2009), 85–105.

Cheyette, Frederic L., 'Georges Duby's *Mâconnais* After Fifty Years: Reading it Then and Now', *Journal of Medieval History*, 28 (2002), 291–317.

Clare, Linda, *On the Edge of the Pale: The Rise and Decline of an Anglo-Irish Community in County Meath, 1170–1530* (Dublin, 2006).

—— 'Continuity and Change in North-East Meath, 1400–1540', *Ríocht na Midhe*, 18 (2007), 108–31.

Clark, Linda (ed.), *The Fifteenth Century VI: Identity and Insurgency in the Late Middle Ages* (Woodbridge, 2006)

—— (ed.), *The Fifteenth Century VII: Conflicts, Consequences and the Crown in the Late Middle Ages* (Woodbridge, 2007).

Clarke, Howard B., 'Decolonization and the Dynamics of Urban Decline in Ireland, 1300–1500', in T. R. Slater (ed.), *Towns in Decline, A.D. 100–1600* (Aldershot, 2000), 157–92.

—— Prunty, Jacinta, and Hennessy, Mark (eds), *Surveying Ireland's Past: Multidisciplinary Essays in Honour of Anngret Simms* (Dublin, 2004).

Clarke, John P., 'Notes on the Devolution of Title to the Manors of Louth, Castlering and Ash, County Louth', *CLAJ* 21 (1987), 257–73.

Clarke, Maude V., 'William of Windsor in Ireland, 1369–1376', *PRIA* 41 (1932–34), C, 55–130.

Collins, Hugh, *The Order of the Garter, 1348–1461: Chivalry and Politics in Late Medieval England* (Oxford, 2000).

Connolly, Philomena, 'Lionel of Clarence and Ireland, 1361–1366', Ph.D. thesis, University of Dublin, Trinity College (1977).

—— 'The Financing of English Expeditions to Ireland, 1361–1376', in James Lydon (ed.), *England and Ireland in the Later Middle Ages: Essays in Honour of Jocelyn Otway-Ruthven* (Dublin, 1981), 104–21.

—— 'Pleas Held Before the Chief Governor of Ireland, 1308–76', *The Irish Jurist*, 18 (1983), 101–31.

—— 'The Proceedings against John de Burnham, Treasurer of Ireland, 1343–49', in Terry Barry, Robin Frame, and Katharine Simms (eds), *Colony and Frontier in Medieval Ireland: Essays Presented to J. F. Lydon* (London, 1995), 57–74.

—— *Medieval Record Sources* (Dublin, 2002).

—— 'Windsor, William, Baron Windsor (1322x8–1384)', *Oxford Dictionary of National Biography* (Oxford, 2004).

Corish, Patrick J. (ed.), *A History of Irish Catholicism*, ii (Dublin, 1968–9).

Cosgrove, Art, *Late Medieval Ireland, 1370–1541* (Dublin, 1981).

—— (ed.), *A New History of Ireland II: Medieval Ireland, 1169–1534* (Oxford, 1987).

—— 'The Armagh Registers: An Under-Explored Source for Late Medieval Ireland', *Peritia*, 6–7 (1987–8), 307–20.

—— 'Consent, Consummation and Indissolubility: Some Evidence from Mediaeval Ecclesiastical Courts', *Downside Review* (Apr. 1991), 94–104.

Coss, Peter, *The Lady in Medieval England, 1100–1500* (Stroud, 1998).

—— *The Foundations of Gentry Life: The Multons of Frampton and their World, 1270–1370* (Oxford, 2010).

Coward, Barry, *The Stanleys, Lords Stanley and Earls of Derby 1385–1672: The Origins, Wealth and Power of a Landowning Family* (Manchester, 1983).

Crooks, Peter, '"Hobbes", "Dogs" and Politics in the Ireland of Lionel of Antwerp', *Haskins Society Journal*, 16 (2005), 117–48.

—— 'The Background to the Arrest of the Fifth Earl of Kildare and Sir Christopher Preston in 1418: A Missing Membrane', *Anal. Hib.* 40 (2007), 1–15.

—— 'Factions, Feuds and Noble Power in the Lordship of Ireland, c.1356–1496', *IHS* 35 (2007), 425–54.

—— 'Factionalism and Noble Power in English Ireland, c.1361–1463'. Ph.D. thesis, University of Dublin, Trinity College (2007).

—— (ed.), *Government, War and Society in Medieval Ireland: Essays by Edmund Curtis, A. J. Otway-Ruthven and James Lydon* (Dublin, 2008).

—— 'Negotiating Authority in a Colonial Capital: Dublin and the Windsor Crisis, 1369–78', in Seán Duffy (ed.), *Medieval Dublin IX* (Dublin, 2009), 131–51.

—— 'Representation and Dissent: "Parliamentarianism" and the Structure of Politics in Colonial Ireland c.1370–1420', *EHR* 125 (2010), 1–34.

—— 'State of the Union: Perspectives on English Imperialism in the Late Middle Ages', *Past and Present*, 212 (2011), 1–40.

Curran, Arthur, 'The Dominican Order in Carlingford and Dundalk', *CLAJ* 16 (1967), 143–60.

Curtis, Edmund, *Richard II in Ireland, 1394–5, and the Submissions of the Irish Chiefs* (Oxford, 1927).

—— 'Unpublished Letters from Richard II in Ireland, 1394–5', *PRIA* 37 (1927), C, 276–303.

—— 'Janico Dartas, Richard the Second's "Gascon Squire": His Career in Ireland, 1394–1426', *Journal of the Royal Society of Antiquaries of Ireland*, 7th ser. 3 (1933), 182–205.

—— 'Richard, Duke of York, as Viceroy of Ireland, 1447–1460: With Unpublished Materials for his Relations with the Native Chiefs', in Peter Crooks (ed.), *Government, War and Society in Medieval Ireland: Essays by Edmund Curtis, A. J. Otway-Ruthven and James Lydon* (Dublin, 2008), 232–59.

Dalton, John, *The History of Drogheda with its Environs; and an Introductory Memoir of the Dublin and Drogheda Railway*, 2 vols (Dublin, 1844).

Davies, R. R., *Lordship and Society in the March of Wales, 1282–1400* (Oxford, 1978).

—— (ed.), *The British Isles, 1100–1500: Comparisons, Contrasts and Connections* (Edinburgh, 1988).

—— *The Age of Conquest: Wales 1063–1415* (Oxford, 1991), 408. First published as *Conquest, Coexistence and Change: Wales 1063–1415* (Oxford, 1987).

—— *The Revolt of Owain Glyn Dŵr* (Oxford, 1995).

—— *The First English Empire: Power and Identities in the British Isles 1093–1343* (Oxford, 2000).

—— 'Mortimer, Roger (VII), Fourth Earl of March and Sixth Earl of Ulster (1374–1398)', *Oxford Dictionary of National Biography* (Oxford, 2004; online edn, Jan. 2008).

—— *Lords and Lordship in the British Isles in the Late Middle Ages*, ed. Brendan Smith (Oxford, 2009).

Davis, Virginia, 'Irish Clergy in Late Medieval England', *IHS* 32 (2000), 145–60.

Dodd, Gwilym, *Justice and Grace: Private Petitioning and the English Parliament in the Late Middle Ages* (Oxford, 2007).

—— and Biggs, Douglas (eds), *Henry IV: The Establishment of the Regime, 1399–1406* (Woodbridge, 2003).

—— and Musson, Anthony (eds), *The Reign of Edward II: New Perspectives* (Woodbridge, 2006).

Dodds, Ben, and Britnell, Richard (eds), *Agriculture and Rural Society After the Black Death: Common Themes and Regional Variations* (Hatfield, 2008).

—— and Liddy, Christian D. (eds), *Commercial Activity, Markets and Entrepreneurs in the Middle Ages: Essays in Honour of Richard Britnell* (Woodbridge, 2011).

Dolan, T. P., 'Yonge, James (*fl.* 1405–1434)', *Oxford Dictionary of National Biography* (Oxford, 2004).

Doran, Linda, and Lyttleton, James (eds), *Lordship in Medieval Ireland: Image and Reality* (Dublin, 2007).

Dryburgh, Paul, 'The Last Refuge of a Scoundrel? Edward II and Ireland, 1321–7', in Gwilym Dodd and Anthony Musson (eds), *The Reign of Edward II: New Perspectives* (Woodbridge, 2006), 119–39.

—— 'Roger Mortimer and the Governance of Ireland, 1317–20', in Brendan Smith (ed.), *Ireland and the English World in the Late Middle Ages: Essays in Honour of Robin Frame* (Basingstoke, 2009), 89–102.

Du Boulay, F. R. H., *The Lordship of Canterbury: An Essay on Medieval Society* (London, 1966).

Duby, Georges, *La Société aux XIe et XIIe siècles dans la région mâconnaise* (Paris, 1953).

Dudley Edwards, R., 'Conflict of Papal and Royal Jurisdictions in Fifteenth-Century Ireland', *PICHC* (1960), 3–9.

Duffy, Eamon, *The Stripping of the Altars: Traditional Religion in England 1400–1580* (New Haven, 1992).

Duffy, Patrick J., 'The Nature of the Medieval Frontier in Ireland', *Studia Hibernica*, 22 and 23 (1982–3), 21–38.

—— 'Geographical Perspectives on the Borderlands', in Raymond Gillespie and Harold O'Sullivan (eds), *The Borderlands: Essays on the History of the Ulster–Leinster Border* (Belfast, 1989), 5–22.

—— Edwards, David, and FitzPatrick, Elizabeth (eds), *Gaelic Ireland c.1250–c.1650: Land, Lordship and Settlement* (Dublin, 2001).

Duffy, Seán (ed.), *The World of the Galloglass: Kings, Warlords and Warriors in Ireland and Scotland, 1200–1600* (Dublin, 2007).

—— (ed.), *Medieval Dublin IX* (Dublin, 2009).

—— (ed.), *Princes, Prelates and Poets: Essays in Honour of Katharine Simms* (Dublin, 2013).

Dunn, Alistair, 'Richard II and the Mortimer Inheritance', in Chris Given-Wilson (ed.), *Fourteenth Century England II* (Woodbridge, 2002), 159–70.

—— *The Politics of Magnate Power: England and Wales, 1389–1413* (Oxford, 2003).

Dyer, Christopher, and Slater, T. R., 'The Midlands', in *The Cambridge Urban History of Britain, Volume I, 640–1540*, ed. David M. Palliser (Cambridge, 2000), 609–38.

—— Coss, Peter, and Wickham, Chris (eds), *Rodney Hilton's Middle Ages: An Exploration of Historical Themes* (Oxford, 2007).

Edwards, David, *The Ormond Lordship in County Kilkenny, 1515–1642: The Rise and Fall of Butler Feudal Power* (Dublin, 2003).

Ellis, Steven G., 'Ioncam na hÉireann, 1384–1534', *Studia Hibernica*, 22 and 23 (1982–3), 39–49,

—— *Reform and Revival: English Government in Ireland 1470–1534* (Woodbridge, 1986).

—— *The Pale and the Far North: Government and Society in Two Early Tudor Borderlands* (Galway, 1988).

—— *Ireland in the Age of the Tudors, 1447–1603: English Expansion and the End of Gaelic Rule* (Harlow, 1998).

Empey, C. A., 'Butler, James, Third Earl of Ormond (*c.*1360–1405)', *Oxford Dictionary of National Biography* (Oxford, 2004).

—— and Simms, Katharine, 'The Ordinances of the White Earl and the Problem of Coign in the Later Middle Ages', *PRIA* 75 (1975), C, 161–87.

Flanagan, Marie Therese, 'St Mary's Abbey, Louth, and the Introduction of the Arrouaisian Observance into Ireland', *Clogher Record*, 10 (1980), 223–34.

Flanagan, Urban, 'Papal Letters of the Fifteenth Century as a Source for Irish History', *PICHC* (1958), 11–15.

Fleming, Peter, 'Identity and Belonging: Irish and Welsh in Fifteenth-Century Bristol', in Linda Clark (ed.), *The Fifteenth Century VII: Conflicts, Consequences and the Crown in the Late Middle Ages* (Woodbridge, 2007), 175–93.

—— 'The Landed Elite, 1300–1500', in Sheila Sweetinburgh (ed.), *Later Medieval Kent, 1220–1540* (Woodbridge, 2010), 209–33.

Fletcher, Alan J., *Late Medieval Preaching in Britain and Ireland: Texts, Studies, and Interpretations* (Turnhout, 2009).

Fletcher, Christopher, *Richard II: Manhood, Youth, and Politics, 1377–99* (Oxford, 2008).

Fowler, Kenneth A., *The King's Lieutenant: Henry of Grosmont, First Duke of Lancaster 1310–1361* (London, 1969).

Frame, Robin, 'The Justiciarship of Ralph Ufford: Warfare and Politics in Fourteenth-Century Ireland', *Studia Hibernica*, 13 (1973), 7–47.

—— *Colonial Ireland, 1169–1369* (Dublin, 1981; 2nd edn, 2012).

—— *English Lordship in Ireland, 1318–1361* (Oxford, 1982).

—— *The Political Development of the British Isles 1100–1400* (Oxford, 1990; 2nd edn, 1995).

—— 'Commissions of the Peace in Ireland, 1302–1461', *Anal. Hib.* 35 (1992), 3–43.

—— 'Two Kings in Leinster: the Crown and the MicMhurchadha in the Fourteenth Century', in Terry Barry, Robin Frame, and Katharine Simms (eds), *Colony and Frontier in Medieval Ireland: Essays Presented to J. F. Lydon* (London, 1995), 155–75.

—— 'The Defence of the English Lordship, 1250–1450', in Thomas Bartlett and Keith Jeffery (eds), *A Military History of Ireland* (Cambridge, 1996), 76–98.

—— 'Thomas Rokeby, Sheriff of Yorkshire, Justiciar of Ireland', *Peritia*, 10 (1996), 274–96.

—— *Ireland and Britain, 1170–1450* (London, 1998).

—— 'King Henry III and Ireland: The Shaping of a Peripheral Lordship', in his *Ireland and Britain*, 31–57.

—— 'English Policies and Anglo-Irish Attitudes in the Crisis of 1341–42', in his *Ireland and Britain*, 113–29.

—— 'War and Peace in the Medieval Lordship of Ireland', in his *Ireland and Britain*, 221–39.

—— 'English Officials and Irish Chiefs in the Fourteenth Century', in his *Ireland and Britain*, 249–77.

—— 'Military Service in the Lordship of Ireland, 1290–1360: Institutions and Society on the Anglo-Gaelic Frontier', in his *Ireland and Britain*, 279–99.

—— 'The Judicial Powers of the Medieval Irish Keepers of the Peace', in his *Ireland and Britain, 1170–1450* (London, 1998), 301–17.

—— 'English Political Culture in Later Medieval Ireland', *History Review*, 13 (2002), 1–11.

—— 'Kingdoms and Dominions at War and Peace', in Ralph Griffiths (ed.), *The Fourteenth and Fifteenth Centuries* (Oxford, 2003), 149–80.

—— 'St Amand, Almaric, third Baron St Amand (1314–1381)', *Oxford Dictionary of National Biography* (Oxford, 2004; online edn, Jan. 2008).

—— 'Morice, Sir John (d. 1362)', *Oxford Dictionary of National Biography* (Oxford, 2004; online edn, Jan. 2008).

Frame, Robin, 'Exporting State and Nation: Being English in Medieval Ireland', in Len Scales and Oliver Zimmer (eds), *Power and the Nation in European History* (Cambridge, 2005), 143–65.

—— 'The Wider World', in Rosemary Horrox and W. Mark Ormrod (eds), *A Social History of England 1200–1500* (Cambridge, 2006), 435–53.

—— 'Lordship Beyond the Pale: Munster in the Late Middle Ages', in Roger Stalley (ed.), *Limerick and South-West Ireland: Medieval Art and Architecture..* British Archaeological Association Conference Transactions, 34 (Leeds, 2011), 5–18.

Gilbert, J. T., *History of the Viceroys of Ireland* (Dublin, 1865).

Gillespie, James L., 'Holland, Thomas, Sixth Earl of Kent and Duke of Surrey (*c.*1374–1400)', *Oxford Dictionary of National Biography* (Oxford, 2004; online edn, Oct. 2008).

Gillespie, Raymond, and O'Sullivan, Harold (eds), *The Borderlands: Essays on the History of the Ulster–Leinster Border* (Belfast, 1989).

Given-Wilson, Chris, *The Royal Household and the King's Affinity: Service, Politics and Finance in England 1360–1413* (New Haven, 1986).

—— *The English Nobility in the Late Middle Ages* (London, 1996).

—— (ed.), *Fourteenth Century England II* (Woodbridge, 2002).

—— and Bériac, Françoise, 'Edward III's Prisoners of War: The Battle of Poitiers and its Context', *EHR* 116 (2001), 802–33.

Goddard, Richard, Langdon, John, and Müller, Miriam (eds), *Survival and Discord in Medieval Society: Essays in Honour of Christopher Dyer* (Turnhout, 2010).

Goldberg, P. J. P., *Women in Medieval English Society* (Stroud, 1997).

Goodman, Anthony, *John of Gaunt: The Exercise of Princely Power in Fourteenth-Century Europe* (Harlow, 1992).

—— 'England and Iberia in the Middle Ages', in Michael Jones and Malcolm Vale (eds), *England and her Neighbours, 1066–1453: Essays in Honour of Pierre Chaplais* (London, 1989), 73–96.

—— 'Kingship and Government', in Ralph Griffiths (ed.), *The Fourteenth and Fifteenth Centuries* (Oxford, 2003), 183–215.

—— 'Holt, Sir John (*d.* 1418/19)', *Oxford Dictionary of National Biography* (Oxford, 2004; online edn, May 2011).

—— and Gillespie, James L., *Richard II and the Art of Kingship* (Oxford, 1999).

—— and Tuck, Anothony (eds), *War and Border Societies in the Middle Ages* (London, 1992).

Gosling, Paul, 'From Dún Delca to Dundalk: The Topography and Archaeology of a Medieval Frontier Town A.D. c.1187–1700', *CLAJ* 22 (1991), 225–353.

Grant, Alexander, 'Scotland's "Celtic Fringe" in the Late Middle Ages: The MacDonald Lords of the Isles and the Kingdom of Scotland', in R. R. Davies (ed.), *The British Isles, 1100–1500: Comparisons, Contrasts and Connections* (Edinburgh, 1988), 118–41.

Green, David, *The Battle of Poitiers, 1356* (Stroud, 2002).

—— *Edward the Black Prince: Power in Medieval Europe* (Harlow, 2007).

—— 'Lordship and Principality: Colonial Policy in Ireland and Aquitaine in the 1360s', *Journal of British Studies*, 47 (2008), 3–29.

Griffith, Margaret C., 'The Talbot–Ormond Struggle for Control of the Anglo-Irish Government, 1414–47', *IHS* 2 (1941), 376–97.

Griffiths, Ralph (ed.), *The Fourteenth and Fifteenth Centuries* (Oxford, 2003).

—— 'Mortimer, Edmund (V), Fifth Earl of March and Seventh Earl of Ulster (1391–1425)', *Oxford Dictionary of National Biography* (Oxford, 2004; online edn, Jan. 2008).

—— 'Crossing the Frontiers of the English Realm in the Fifteenth Century', in Huw Pryce and John Watts (eds), *Power and Identity in the Middle Ages: Essays in Honour of Rees Davies* (Oxford, 2007), 211–25.

Gundacker, Jay, 'Absolutions and Acts of Disobedience: Excommunication and Society in Fourteenth-Century Armagh', *Traditio*, 64 (2009), 183–212.

Gwynn, Aubrey, SJ, 'Richard FitzRalph, Archbishop of Armagh', *Studies: An Irish Quarterly Review*, 22 (1933), 389–405.

—— 'The Black Death in Ireland', *Studies: An Irish Quarterly Review*, 24 (1935), 25–42.

—— 'Richard Fitzralph, Archbishop of Armagh: Part VI', *Studies: An Irish Quarterly Review*, 25 (1936), 81–96.

—— 'The Sermon-Diary of Richard Fitzralph, Archbishop of Armagh', *PRIA* 44 (1937–8), C, 1–57.

—— 'Ireland and the English Nation at the Council of Constance', *PRIA* 45 (1939–40), C, 183–233.

—— 'Ardee in the Middle Ages', *CLAJ* 11 (1946), 77–89.

—— *The Medieval Province of Armagh 1470–1545* (Dundalk, 1946).

—— 'Two Sermons of Primate Richard Fitzralph', *Archivium Hibernicum*, 14 (1949), 50–65.

—— 'Anglo-Irish Church Life: Fourteenth and Fifteenth Centuries', in Patrick J. Corish (ed.), *A History of Irish Catholicism* (Dublin, 1968), ii/4.

—— and Hadcock, R. Neville, *Medieval Religious Houses Ireland* (London, 1970; repr. Dublin, 1988).

Hagger, Mark S., *The Fortunes of a Norman Family: The de Verduns in England, Ireland and Wales, 1066–1316* (Dublin, 2001).

Harbison, S., 'William of Windsor, the Court Party and the Administration of Ireland', in James Lydon (ed.), *England and Ireland in the Later Middle Ages: Essays in Honour of Jocelyn Otway-Ruthven* (Dublin, 1981), 153–74.

Haren, Michael, 'Two Hungarian Pilgrims', in Michael Haren and Yolande de Pontfarcy (eds), *The Medieval Pilgrimage to St Patrick's Purgatory: Lough Derg and the European Tradition*. Clogher Historical Society (Enniskillen, 1988), 120–68.

—— and de Pontfarcy, Yolande (eds), *The Medieval Pilgrimage to St Patrick's Purgatory: Lough Derg and the European Tradition*. Clogher Historical Society (Enniskillen, 1988).

Harkness, David, and O'Dowd, Mary (eds), *Historical Studies 13: The Town in Ireland* (Belfast, 1981).

Harper-Bill, Christopher, 'The English Church and English Religion After the Black Death', in Mark Ormrod and Phillip Lindley (eds), *The Black Death in England* (Donington, 2003), 79–123.

—— (ed.), *Medieval East Anglia* (Woodbridge, 2005).

Harriss, Gerald L., *King, Parliament and Public Finance in Medieval England to 1369* (Oxford, 1975).

—— 'Political Society and the Growth of Government in Late Medieval England', *Past and Present*, 138 (1993), 28–57.

—— 'The Dimensions of Politics', in R. H. Britnell and A. J. Pollard (eds), *The McFarlane Legacy: Studies in Late Medieval Politics and Society* (Stroud, 1995), 1–20.

—— *Shaping the Nation: England 1360–1461* (Oxford, 2005).

Hartland, Beth, 'Absenteeism: The Chronology of a Concept', in Björn Weiler, Janet Burton, Phillipp Schofield, and Karen Stöber (eds), *Thirteenth Century England XI* (Woodbridge, 2007), 215–29.

—— 'Policies, Priorities and Principles: The King, the Anglo-Irish and English Justiciars in the Fourteenth Century', in Brendan Smith (ed.), *Ireland and the English World in the Late Middle Ages: Essays in Honour of Robin Frame* (Basingstoke, 2009), 130–40.

Harvey, Barbara, *Westminster Abbey and its Estates in the Middle Ages* (Oxford, 1977).
Harvey, Margaret, *The English in Rome 1362–1420: Portrait of an Expatriate Community* (Cambridge, 1999).
Hilton, Rodney H., *A Medieval Society: The West Midlands at the End of the Thirteenth Century* (Cambridge, 1966, 2nd edn. 1983).
Hogan, Arlene, *The Priory of Llanthony Prima and Secunda in Ireland, 1172–1541: Lands, Patronage and Politics* (Dublin, 2008).
Hogan, James, 'The Irish Law of Kingship, with Special Reference to Ailech and Cenél Eoghain', *PRIA* 40 (1931–2), C, 186–254.
—— 'Miscellanea of the Chancery, London', *Anal. Hib.* 1 (1934), 179–219.
Holford, M. L., and Stringer, K. J. (eds), *Border Liberties and Loyalties: North-East England, c.1200–c.1400* (Edinburgh, 2010).
Holmes, George A., *The Estates of the Higher Nobility in XIV Century England* (Cambridge, 1957).
—— *The Good Parliament* (Oxford, 1975).
Hudson, Benjamin T., 'The Changing Economy of the Irish Sea Province', in Brendan Smith (ed.), *Britain and Ireland 900–1300: Insular Responses to Medieval European Change* (Cambridge, 1999), 39–66.
Hudson, John, *The Formation of the English Common Law: Law and Society in England from the Norman Conquest to Magna Carta* (Harlow, 1996).
Jarman, A. O. H., and Hughes, Gwilym Rees (eds), *A Guide to Welsh Literature, 1282–c.1550*, rev. Daffyd Johnston (Cardiff, 1997).
Jefferies, Henry A., *Priests and Prelates of Armagh in the Age of Reformations, 1518–1558* (Dublin, 1997).
—— (ed.), *History of the Diocese of Clogher* (Dublin, 2005).
Johnston, Dorothy, 'Richard II and the Submission of Gaelic Ireland', *IHS* 22 (1980), 1–20.
—— 'The Interim Years: Richard II and Ireland, 1395–1399', in James Lydon (ed.), *England and Ireland in the Later Middle Ages: Essays in Honour of Jocelyn Otway-Ruthven* (Dublin, 1981), 175–95.
—— 'Richard II's Departure from Ireland, July 1399', *EHR* 98 (1983), 785–805.
—— 'Chief Governors and Treasurers of Ireland in the Reign of Richard II', in Terry Barry, Robin Frame, and Katharine Simms (eds), *Colony and Frontier in Medieval Ireland: Essays Presented to J. F. Lydon* (London, 1995), 97–115.
—— 'Colton, John (d. 1404)', *Oxford Dictionary of National Biography* (Oxford, 2004; online edn, Jan. 2008).
Jones, Michael, 'Ashton, Sir Robert (d. 1384)', *Oxford Dictionary of National Biography* (Oxford, 2004; online edn, Jan. 2008).
—— and Vale, Malcolm (eds), *England and her Neighbours, 1066–1453: Essays in Honour of Pierre Chaplais* (London, 1989).
Jones, W. R., 'Violence, Criminality, and Cultural Disjunction on the Anglo-Irish Frontier: The Example of Armagh, 1350–1550', *Criminal Justice History*, 1 (1980), 29–47.
Kelly, Maria, *A History of the Black Death in Ireland* (Stroud, 2001).
Kenny, Gillian, 'The Power of Dower: The Importance of Dower in the Lives of Medieval Women in Ireland', in Christine Meek and Catherine Lawless (eds), *Studies on Medieval and Early Modern Women* (Dublin, 2003), 59–74.
—— *Anglo-Irish and Gaelic Women in Ireland, c.1170–1540* (Dublin, 2007).
Larson, P. L., *Conflict and Compromise in the Late Medieval Countryside: Lords and Peasants in Durham, 1349–1400* (London, 2006).
Leask, Harold G., *Irish Churches and Monastic Buildings*, iii. *Medieval Gothic: The Last Phase* (Dundalk, 1960).

Lee, John S., 'Grain Shortages in Late Medieval Towns', in Ben Dodds and Christian D. Liddy (eds), *Commercial Activity, Markets and Entrepreneurs in the Middle Ages: Essays in Honour of Richard Britnell* (Woodbridge, 2011), 63–80.
Leland, John L., 'Bealknap, Sir Robert (*d.* 1401)', *Oxford Dictionary of National Biography* (Oxford, 2004; online edn, May 2011).
Leslie, James B., *History of Kilsaran* (Dundalk, 1908).
—— 'The Clinton Family in County Louth', *CLAJ* 2 (1911), 398–412.
Leslie, Shane, *St Patrick's Purgatory* (London, 1932).
Liddy, Christian, *War Politics and Finance in Late Medieval English Towns: Bristol, York and the Crown, 1350–1400* (Woodbridge, 2005).
—— and Britnell, Richard H. (eds), *North-East England in the Later Middle Ages* (Woodbridge, 2005).
Lydon, James, 'William of Windsor and the Irish Parliament', *EHR* 80 (1965), 252–67.
—— *The Lordship of Ireland in the Middle Ages* (Dublin, 1972; new edn, 2003).
—— *Ireland in the Later Middle Ages* (Dublin, 1973).
—— 'The Braganstown Massacre, 1329', *CLAJ* 19 (1977), 5–16.
—— 'The Mills of Ardee in 1304', *CLAJ* 19 (1980), 259–63.
—— (ed.), *England and Ireland in the Later Middle Ages: Essays in Honour of Jocelyn Otway-Ruthven* (Dublin, 1981).
—— (ed.), *The English in Medieval Ireland* (Dublin, 1984).
—— 'The Middle Nation', in Lydon (ed.), *The English in Medieval Ireland*, 1–26.
—— (ed.), *Law and Disorder in Thirteenth-Century Ireland: The Dublin Parliament of 1297* (Dublin, 1997).
—— 'Richard II's Expeditions to Ireland', in Peter Crooks (ed.), *Government, War and Society in Medieval Ireland: Essays by Edmund Curtis, A. J. Otway-Ruthven and James Lydon* (Dublin, 2008), 216–31.
Lynch, Anthony, 'The Archdeacons of Armagh 1417–71', *CLAJ* 19 (1979), 218–26.
—— 'Religion in Late Medieval Ireland', *Archivium Hibernicum*, 36 (1981), 3–15.
Lynch, William, *A View of the Legal Institutions, Honorary Hereditary Offices, and Feudal Baronies, Established in Ireland during the Reign of Henry the Second* (London, 1830).
Lyons, Mary Ann, *Church and Society in County Kildare, c.1470–1547* (Dublin, 2000).
McCormack, Anthony M., *The Earldom of Desmond, 1463–1583: The Decline and Crisis of a Feudal Lordship* (Dublin, 2005).
Macdonald, Alistair J., 'Douglas, Sir William, Lord of Nithsdale (*c.*1360–1391)', *Oxford Dictionary of National Biography* (Oxford, 2004).
McFarlane, K. B., *The Nobility of Later Medieval England* (Oxford, 1973).
McGrath, Thomas, and Nolan, William (eds), *Carlow: History and Society* (Dublin, 2008).
Mac Iomhair, Diarmuid, 'The Knights Templar in County Louth', *Seanchas Ardmhacha*, 4 (1960–1), 72–91.
—— 'The Carmelites in Ardee', *CLAJ* 20 (1983), 180–9.
MacLysaght, Edward, *Irish Families: Their Names, Arms and Origins* (Dublin, 1957).
Mac Niocaill, Gearóid, *Na Manaigh Liatha in Éirinn, 1142–c.1600* (Cló Morainn, 1959).
—— *Na Buirgéisí, XII–XV Aois*, 2 vols (Dublin, 1964).
—— 'Socio-Economic Problems of the Late Medieval Irish Town', in David Harkness and Mary O'Dowd (eds), *Historical Studies 13: The Town in Ireland* (Belfast, 1981), 7–22.
Maddern, Philippa C., *Violence and Social Order: East Anglia 1422–1442* (Oxford, 1992).
Maginn, Christopher, *'Civilizing' Gaelic Leinster: The Extension of Tudor Rule in the O'Byrne and O'Toole Lordships* (Dublin, 2005).

Maginn, Christopher,'English Marcher Lordships in South Dublin in the late Middle Ages', *IHS* 34 (2004–5), 113–36.

Masschaele, James, 'Town, Country, and Law: Royal Courts and Regional Mobility in Medieval England, *c.*1200–*c.*1400', in Richard Goddard, John Langdon, and Miriam Müller (eds), *Survival and Discord in Medieval Society: Essays in Honour of Christopher Dyer* (Turnhout, 2010), 127–44.

Matthew, H. D. G., and Harrison, Brian (eds), *Oxford Dictionary of National Biography* (Oxford, 2004): <http://www.oxforddnb.com>.

Matthew, Elizabeth, 'The Financing of the Lordship of Ireland under Henry V and Henry VI', in Tony Pollard (ed.), *Property and Politics: Essays in Later Medieval English History* (Gloucester, 1984), 97–115.

—— 'Butler, James, Fourth Earl of Ormond (1390–1452)', *Oxford Dictionary of National Biography* (Oxford, 2004; online edn, Jan. 2008).

—— 'Talbot, Richard (*d.* 1449)', *Oxford Dictionary of National Biography* (Oxford, 2004; online edn, Jan. 2008).

—— 'Henry V and the Proposal for an Irish Crusade', in Brendan Smith (ed.), *Ireland and the English World in the Late Middle Ages: Essays in Honour of Robin Frame* (Basingstoke, 2009), 161–75.

Meek, Christine, and Lawless, Catherine (eds), *Studies on Medieval and Early Modern Women* (Dublin, 2003).

Mercer, Malcolm, 'Exchequer Malpractice in Late Medieval Ireland: A Petition from Christopher Fleming, Lord Slane, 1438', *IHS* 36 (2009), 407–17.

Moody, T. W., Martin, F. X., and Byrne, F. J. (eds), *A New History of Ireland IX: Maps, Genealogies, Lists* (Oxford, 1989).

Mooney, Canice 'The Church in Gaelic Ireland 13th to 15th Centuries', in Patrick J. Corish (ed.), *A History of Irish Catholicism* (Dublin, 1969), ii/5.

Morgan, Philip, *War and Society in Medieval Cheshire, 1277–1403* (Manchester, 1987).

—— 'The Ranks of Society', in Ralph Griffiths (ed.), *The Fourteenth and Fifteenth Centuries* (Oxford, 2003), 59–85.

Mortimer, Ian, *The Greatest Traitor: The Life of Sir Roger Mortimer, Ist Earl of March, Ruler of England 1327–1330* (London, 2003).

Moynes, James, 'The Prestons of Gormanston, *c.*1300–1532: An Anglo-Irish Gentry Family', *Ríocht na Midhe*, 14 (2003), 26–55.

Murphy, Margaret, and Potterton, Michael, *The Dublin Region in the Middle Ages: Settlement, Land-Use and Economy* (Dublin, 2010).

Murray, L. P. (Lorcán P. Ua Muireadhaig), 'St Columba in Louth', *CLAJ* 2 (1911), 337–46.

—— 'The Ancient Chantries of Co. Louth', *CLAJ* 9 (1939), 181–208.

Musson, Anthony, and Ormrod, W. M., *The Evolution of English Justice: Law, Politics and Society in the Fourteenth Century* (Basingstoke, 1999).

Neville, Cynthia J., *Violence, Custom and Law: The Anglo-Scottish Border Lands in the Later Middle Ages* (Edinburgh, 1998).

—— 'Arbitration and Anglo-Scottish Border Law in the Later Middle Ages', in Michael Prestwich (ed.), *Liberties and Identities in the Medieval British Isles* (Woodbridge, 2008), 37–55.

Nicholls, Kenneth, *Gaelic and Gaelicised Ireland in the Middle Ages* (Dublin, 1972).

—— 'Anglo-French Ireland and After', *Peritia*, 1 (1982), 370–403.

—— 'Scottish Mercenary Kindreds in Ireland, 1250–1600', in Seán Duffy (ed.), *The World of the Galloglass: Kings, Warlords and Warriors in Ireland and Scotland, 1200–1600* (Dublin, 2007), 86–105.

Nicholson, Ranald, 'An Irish Expedition to Scotland in 1335', *IHS* 13 (1963), 197–211.
O'Byrne, Emmett, *War, Politics and the Irish of Leinster, 1156–1606* (Dublin, 2003).
—— '"A Divided Loyalty": The MacMurroughs, the Irish of Leinster and the Crown of England 1340–1420', in Thomas McGrath and William Nolan (eds), *Carlow: History and Society* (Dublin, 2008), 273–306.
Ó Clabaigh, Colmán, OSB, *The Friars in Ireland, 1224–1540* (Dublin, 2012).
[Ó Conbhuí], Colmcille, OCSO, *The Story of Mellifont* (Dublin, 1958).
—— 'Cúis Dlí Idir Ab Agus Rí', *Seanchas Ardmhacha*, 4 (1960–1), 92–102.
—— 'The Lands of St Mary's Abbey, Dublin, *PRIA* 62 (1961–3), C, 21–86.
O'Dwyer, Peter, 'The Carmelite Order in Pre-Reformation Ireland', *PICHC* (1968), 49–62.
Ó Fiaich, Tomás, 'The O'Neills of the Fews', *Seanchas Ardmhacha*, 7 (1973), 1–64.
—— 'The Primacy in the Irish Church', *Seanchas Ardmhacha*, 21 (2006), 1–23.
Ó Floinn, Raghnall, 'Two Medieval Seals from County Louth', *CLAJ* 22 (1992), 387–94.
O'Neill, Timothy, *Merchants and Mariners in Medieval Ireland* (Dublin, 1987).
Ó Riain, Pádraig, *A Dictionary of Irish Saints* (Dublin, 2011).
Ormrod, W. Mark, 'Edward III and his Family', *Journal of British Studies*, 26 (1987), 398–422.
—— *The Reign of Edward III: Crown and Political Society in England, 1327–1377* (New Haven, 1990).
—— *Political Life in Medieval England, 1300–1450* (Basingstoke, 1995).
—— 'Darcy, Sir John (*b.* before 1284, *d.* 1347)', *Oxford Dictionary of National Biography* (Oxford, 2004; online edn, Jan. 2008).
—— 'Lionel, Duke of Clarence (1338–1368)', *Oxford Dictionary of National Biography* (Oxford, 2004; online edn, Jan. 2008).
—— 'The Trials of Alice Perrers', *Speculum*, 83 (2008), 366–96.
—— *Edward III* (New Haven, 2011).
—— and Lindley, Phillip (eds), *The Black Death in England* (Donington, 2003).
Orpen, G. H. *Ireland under the Normans*, 4 vols (Dublin, 1911–20; repr. as a single volume with an introduction by Seán Duffy, Dublin, 2005).
—— 'The Site of Castle Blathach', *Journal of the Royal Society of Antiquaries of Ireland*, 6th ser. 4/2 (June 1914), 167–70.
Osborough, W. N. (ed.), *Explorations in Law and History: Irish Legal History Discourses, 1988–1994* (Dublin, 1995).
O'Sullivan, Harold, 'The Franciscans in Dundalk', *Seanchas Ardmhacha*, 4 (1960–1), 33–71.
—— 'The March of South-East Ulster in the Fifteenth and Sixteenth Centuries: A Period of Change', in Raymond Gillespie and Harold O'Sullivan (eds), *The Borderlands: Essays on the History of the Ulster–Leinster Border* (Belfast, 1989), 55–79.
—— 'Dynamics of Regional Development: Processes of Assimilation and Division in the Marchland of South-East Ulster in Late Medieval and Early Modern Ireland', in Ciaran Brady and Jane Ohlmeyer (eds), *British Interventions in Early Modern Ireland* (Cambridge, 2005), 49–72.
Otway-Ruthven, A. J., 'Ireland in the 1350s: Sir Thomas Rokeby and his Successors', *Journal of the Royal Society of Antiquaries of Ireland*, 97 (1967), 47–59.
—— *A History of Medieval Ireland* (London, 1968).
—— 'The Partition of the de Verdon Lands in Ireland in 1332', *PRIA* 66 (1968), C, 401–55.
—— 'The Background to the Arrest of Sir Christopher Preston in 1418', *Anal. Hib.* 29 (1980), 71–94.

Otway-Ruthven, A. J., 'The Chief Governors of Medieval Ireland', in Peter Crooks (ed.), *Government, War and Society in Medieval Ireland: Essays by Edmund Curtis, A. J. Otway-Ruthven and James Lydon* (Dublin, 2008), 79–89.

—— 'Royal Service in Ireland', in Peter Crooks (ed.), *Government, War and Society in Medieval Ireland: Essays by Edmund Curtis, A. J. Otway-Ruthven and James Lydon* (Dublin, 2008), 169–76.

Palliser, David M. (ed.), *The Cambridge Urban History of Britain*, i. *640–1540* (Cambridge, 2000).

Palmer, Robert C., *The County Courts of Medieval England, 1150–1350* (Princeton, 1982).

Payling, Simon, *Political Society in Lancastrian England: The Greater Gentry in Nottinghamshire* (Oxford, 1991).

—— 'Social Mobility, Demographic Change, and Landed Society in Late Medieval England', *Economic History Review*, 45 (1992), 51–73.

Pender, Séamus, 'A Tract on MacMahon's Prerogatives', *Études Celtiques*, 1 (1936), 248–60.

Penman, Michael, 'David II (1329–1371)', in Michael Brown and Roland Tanner (eds), *Scottish Kingship, 1306–1542: Essays in Honour of Norman Macdougall* (Edinburgh, 2008), 49–71.

Phillips, [J. R. S]eymour, *Edward II* (New Haven, 2010).

—— 'The Anglo-Norman Nobility', in James Lydon (ed.), *The English in Medieval Ireland* (Dublin, 1984), 87–104.

Pollard, Anthony J., *John Talbot and the War in France, 1427–1453* (London, 1983).

—— (ed.), *Property and Politics: Essays in Later Medieval English History* (Gloucester, 1984).

—— 'Talbot, John, First Earl of Shrewsbury and First Earl of Waterford (c.1387–1453)', *Oxford Dictionary of National Biography* (Oxford, 2004; online edn, Oct. 2008).

Potterton, Michael, *Medieval Trim: History and Archaeology* (Dublin, 2005).

Powell, Edward, 'Arbitration and the Law in England in the Late Middle Ages', *TRHS* 5th ser. 33 (1983), 49–67.

—— *Kingship, Law and Society: Criminal Justice in the Reign of Henry V* (Oxford, 1989).

Prestwich, Michael, *Plantagenet England, 1225–1360* (Oxford, 2005).

Pryce, Huw, 'Robert Rees Davies, 1938–2005', *Proceedings of the British Academy*, 161 (2009), 135–55.

Radulescu, Raluca, and Truelove, Alison (eds), *Gentry Culture in Late Medieval England* (Manchester, 2005).

Rawcliffe, Carole, *The Staffords: Earls of Stafford and Dukes of Buckingham 1394–1521* (Cambridge, 1978).

Richardson, H. G., and Sayles, G. O., *The Administration of Ireland, 1172–1377*. Irish Manuscripts Commission (Dublin, 1963).

—— and —— 'Irish Revenue, 1278–1384', *PRIA* 62 (1961–3), C, 87–100.

—— and —— *The Irish Parliament in the Middle Ages* (Philadelphia, 1964).

Richmond, Colin, *The Paston Family in the Fifteenth Century: The First Phase* (Cambridge, 1990).

—— *The Paston Family in the Fifteenth Century: Fastolf's Will* (Cambridge, 1996).

—— *The Paston Family in the Fifteenth Century: Endings* (Manchester, 2000).

Rigby, Steven H. (ed.), *A Companion to Britain in the Later Middle Ages* (Oxford, 2003).

Roe, Helen M., *Medieval Fonts of Meath* (Navan, 1968).

Rogers, Clifford J., *War Cruel and Sharp: English Strategy under Edward III, 1327–1360* (Woodbridge, 2000).

Ronan, M. V., 'Some Medieval Documents', *Journal of the Royal Society of Antiquaries of Ireland*, 67 (1937), 229–41.
Ruddick, Andrea C., 'Ethnic Identity and Political Language in the King of England's Dominions: A Fourteenth-Century Perspective', in Linda Clark (ed.), *The Fifteenth Century VI: Identity and Insurgency in the Late Middle Ages* (Woodbridge, 2006), 15–31.
—— 'Gascony and the Limits of Medieval British Isles History', in Brendan Smith (ed.), *Ireland and the English World in the Late Middle Ages: Essays in Honour of Robin Frame* (Basingstoke, 2009), 68–88.
Ryan, Vanessa, 'The Archaeology of Medieval Rural Ecclesiastical Settlement in the Barony of Lower Dundalk, County Louth', Ph.D. thesis, University of Dublin, Trinity College (2009).
Saul, Nigel, *Knights and Esquires: The Gloucestershire Gentry in the Fourteenth Century* (Oxford, 1981).
—— *Scenes from Provincial Life: Knightly Families in Sussex, 1280–1400* (Oxford, 1986).
—— *Richard II* (New Haven, 1997).
—— (ed.), *Fourteenth Century England I* (Woodbridge, 2000).
—— *Death, Art and Memory in Medieval England: The Cobham Family and their Monuments 1300–1500* (Oxford, 2001).
Sayles, G. O., 'Ecclesiastical Process and the Parsonage of Stabannon in 1351: A Study of the Medieval Irish Church in Action', *PRIA* 55 (1952), C, 1–23.
Scales, Len, and Zimmer, Oliver (eds), *Power and the Nation in European History* (Cambridge, 2005).
Scott, A. B., 'Latin Learning and Literature in Ireland, 1169–1500', *NHI* i. 934–95.
Scott, Brendan (ed.), *Culture and Society in Early Modern Breifne/Cavan* (Dublin, 2009).
Shiels, W. J., and Wood, Diana (eds), *Studies in Church History 25: The Churches, Ireland and the Irish* (Oxford, 1989).
Shirley, E. P., *The History of the County of Monaghan* (London, 1879).
Simms, Katharine, 'The Archbishops of Armagh and the O'Neills 1347–1471', *IHS* 19 (1974), 38–55.
—— 'The O Hanlons, the O Neills and the Anglo-Normans in Thirteenth-Century Armagh', *Seanchas Ardmhacha*, 9 (1978), 70–94.
—— 'The O Reillys and the Kingdom of East Breifne', *Breifne*, 5 (1976–81), 305–19.
—— '"The King's Friend": O'Neill, the Crown and the Earldom of Ulster', in James Lydon (ed.), *England and Ireland in the Later Middle Ages: Essays in Honour of Jocelyn Otway-Ruthven* (Dublin, 1981), 214–36.
—— 'Nomadry in Medieval Ireland: The Origins of the Creaght or *Caoraigheacht*', *Peritia*, 5 (1986), 379–91.
—— *From Kings to Warlords: The Changing Political Structure of Gaelic Ireland in the Later Middle Ages* (Woodbridge, 1987, repr. 2000).
—— 'Bards and Barons: The Anglo-Irish Aristocracy and the Native Culture', in Robert Bartlett and Angus Mackay (eds), *Medieval Frontier Societies* (Oxford, 1989), 177–97.
—— 'Frontiers in the Irish Church: Regional and Cultural', in Terry Barry, Robin Frame, and Katharine Simms (eds), *Colony and Frontier in Medieval Ireland: Essays Presented to J. F. Lydon* (London, 1995), 178–200.
—— 'Gaelic Warfare in the Middle Ages', in Thomas Bartlett and Keith Jeffery (eds), *A Military History of Ireland* (Cambridge, 1996), 99–115.
—— 'The Contents of Later Commentaries on Brehon Law Tracts', *Ériu*, 49 (1998), 23–40.
—— 'The Dating of Two Poems on Ulster Chieftains', in Alfred P. Smyth (ed.), *Seanchas: Studies in Early and Medieval Irish Archaeology, History and Literature in Honour of Francis J. Byrne* (Dublin, 2000), 381–6.

Simms, Katharine, 'Native Sources for Gaelic Settlement: The House Poems', in Patrick J. Duffy, David Edwards, and Elizabeth FitzPatrick (eds), *Gaelic Ireland c.1250–c.1650: Land, Lordship and Settlement* (Dublin, 2001), 246–67.

—— 'References to Landscape and Economy in Irish Bardic Poetry', in Howard B. Clarke, Jacinta Prunty, and Mark Hennessy (eds), *Surveying Ireland's Past: Multidisciplinary Essays in Honour of Anngret Simms* (Dublin, 2004), 145–68.

—— *Medieval Gaelic Sources* (Dublin, 2009).

—— 'The Ulster Revolt of 1404: An Anti-Lancastrian Dimension?', in Brendan Smith (ed.), *Ireland and the English World in the Late Middle Ages: Essays in Honour of Robin Frame* (Basingstoke, 2009), 141–60.

Slater, T. R. (ed.), *Towns in Decline, A.D. 100–1600* (Aldershot, 2000).

Smith, Brendan, 'The Medieval Border: Anglo-Irish and Gaelic Irish in Late Thirteenth and Early Fourteenth Century Uriel', in Raymond Gillespie and Harold O'Sullivan (eds), *The Borderlands: Essays on the History of the Ulster-Leinster Border* (Belfast, 1989), 41–53.

—— 'A County Community in Early Fourteenth-Century Ireland: The Case of Louth', *EHR* 108 (1993), 561–88.

—— 'Tenure and Locality in North Leinster in the Early Thirteenth Century', in Terry Barry, Robin Frame, and Katharine Simms (eds), *Colony and Frontier in Medieval Ireland: Essays Presented to J. F. Lydon* (London, 1995), 29–40.

—— 'Lionel of Clarence and the English of Meath', *Peritia*, 10 (1996), 297–302.

—— 'Keeping the Peace', in James Lydon (ed.), *Law and Disorder in Thirteenth-Century Ireland: The Dublin Parliament of 1297* (Dublin, 1997), 57–65.

—— *Colonisation and Conquest in Medieval Ireland: The English in Louth, 1170–1330* (Cambridge, 1999).

—— (ed.), *Britain and Ireland 900–1300: Insular Responses to Medieval European Change* (Cambridge, 1999).

—— 'Swayne, John (d. 1439x42)', *Oxford Dictionary of National Biography* (Oxford, 2004).

—— 'Lordship in the British Isles, c.1320–c.1360: The Ebb Tide of the English Empire?', in Huw Pryce and John Watts (eds), *Power and Identity in the Middle Ages: Essays in Honour of Rees Davies* (Oxford, 2007), 153–63.

—— (ed.), *Ireland and the English World in the Late Middle Ages: Essays in Honour of Robin Frame* (Basingstoke, 2009).

—— 'Late Medieval Ireland and the English Connection: Waterford and Bristol, ca. 1360–1460', *Journal of British Studies*, 50 (2011), 546–65.

—— 'The Murder of John Dowdall, Sheriff of Louth, 1402', in Seán Duffy (ed.), *Princes, Prelates and Poets: Essays in Honour of Katharine Simms* (Dublin, 2013).

Smith, Llinos Beverley, 'Disputes and Settlements in Medieval Wales: The Role of Arbitration', *EHR* 106 (1991), 835–60.

Smyth, Alfred P. (ed.), *Seanchas: Studies in Early and Medieval Irish Archaeology, History and Literature in Honour of Francis J. Byrne* (Dublin, 2000).

Stalley, Roger, 'Sailing to Santiago: The Medieval Pilgrimage to Santiago de Compostela and its Artistic Influence in Ireland', in John Bradley (ed.), *Settlement and Society in Medieval Ireland: Studies Presented to F. X. Martin O.S.A.* (Kilkenny, 1988), 397–420.

—— (ed.), *Limerick and South-West Ireland: Medieval Art and Architecture*. British Archaeological Association Conference Transactions, 34 (Leeds, 2011).

Summerson, Henry, *Medieval Carlisle: The City and the Borders from the Late Eleventh to the Mid Sixteenth Centuries*, 2 vols (Kendal, 1993).
—— 'Clifford, Roger, Fifth Baron Clifford (1333–1389)', *Oxford Dictionary of National Biography* (Oxford, 2004; online edn, Jan. 2008).
Sweetinburgh, Sheila (ed.), *Later Medieval Kent, 1220–1540* (Woodbridge, 2010).
Thomas, Avril, *The Walled Towns of Ireland*, 2 vols (Dublin 1992).
Thornton, Tim, 'Scotland and the Isle of Man, *c*.1400–1625: Noble Power and Royal Presumption in the Northern Irish sea Province', *SHR* 78 (1998), 1–30.
Tuck, Anthony, 'Anglo-Irish Relations, 1382–1393', *PRIA* 69 (1970), C, 15–31.
—— *Crown and Nobility, 1272–1461* (Oxford, 1986).
—— 'Neville, John, Fifth Baron Neville (*c*.1330–1388)', *Oxford Dictionary of National Biography* (Oxford, 2004; online edn, Jan. 2008).
Verduyn, Anthony, 'Darcy Family (*per. c*.1284–1488)', *Oxford Dictionary of National Biography* (Oxford, 2004).
Verstraten, Freya, 'Images of Gaelic Lordship in Ireland, *c*.1200-*c*.1400', in Linda Doran and James Lyttleton (eds), *Lordship in Medieval Ireland: Image and Reality* (Dublin, 2007), 47–74.
Walker, Simon, *The Lancastrian Affinity, 1361–1399* (Oxford, 1990).
—— 'Janico Dartasso: Chivalry, Nationality and the Man-at-Arms', *History*, 84 (1999), 31–51.
Walsh, Katherine, *A Fourteenth-Century Scholar and Primate: Richard FitzRalph in Oxford, Avignon and Armagh* (Oxford, 1981).
—— 'The Roman Career of John Swayne, Archbishop of Armagh 1418–1439: Plans for an Irish Hospice in Rome', *Seanchas Ardmhacha*, 11 (1983–4), 1–21.
—— 'Fitzralph, Richard (*b.* before 1300, *d.* 1360)', *Oxford Dictionary of National Biography* (Oxford, 2004; online edn, May 2010).
—— '… *in Finibus Mundi*: The Late Medieval Pilgrims to St Patrick's Purgatory, Lough Derg, and the European Dimension of the Diocese of Clogher', in Henry A. Jefferies (ed.), *History of the Diocese of Clogher* (Dublin, 2005), 41–69.
Ward, Jennifer, C., *English Noblewomen in the Later Middle Ages* (Harlow, 1992).
Watt, John A., 'John Colton, Justiciar of Ireland (1382) and Archbishop of Armagh (1383–1404)', in James Lydon (ed.), *England and Ireland in the Later Middle Ages: Essays in Honour of Jocelyn Otway-Ruthven* (Dublin, 1981), 196–213.
—— '*Ecclesia inter Anglicos et inter Hibernicos*: Confrontation and Coexistence in the Medieval Diocese of Armagh', in James Lydon (ed.), *The English in Medieval Ireland* (Dublin, 1984), 46–64.
—— 'The Anglo-Irish Colony under Strain, 1327–99', in Art Cosgrove (ed.), *A New History of Ireland II: Medieval Ireland, 1169–1534* (Oxford, 1987), 352–96.
—— 'The Church and the Two Nations in Late Medieval Armagh', in W J. Shiels and Diana Wood (eds), *Studies in Church History 25: The Churches, Ireland and the Irish* (Oxford, 1989), 37–54.
—— 'The Medieval Chapter of Armagh Cathedral', in David Abulafia, Michael Franklin, and Miri Rubin (eds), *Church and City 1000–1500: Essays in Honour of Christopher Brooke* (Cambridge, 1992), 219–45.
Waugh, Scott L., *The Lordship of England: Royal Wardships and Marriages in English Society and Politics, 1217–1327* (Princeton, 1988).

Weiler, Björn, Burton, Janet, and Schofield, Phillipp (eds), *Thirteenth Century England XI* (Woodbridge, 2007).
Wood, Herbert, 'The Office of Chief Governor of Ireland, 1172–1509', *PRIA* 36 (1921–4), C, 206–38.
—— 'The Muniments of Edmund de Mortimer, Third Earl of March, Concerning his Liberty of Trim', *PRIA* 40 (1932), C, 312–55.
Wright, Susan M., *The Derbyshire Gentry in the Fifteenth Century* (Chesterfield, 1983).

Index

Abergavenny 5 n. 21
Absenteeism:
   absentee lords 34–5, 39, 47, 49, 50, 61–2,
      74, 211
Achonry 215 n. 27
Adare 57, 60, 66
Adultery 51, 144, 199
Advowsons, *see* Presentation, rights of
Adultery 51, 144, 199
Adyn(e), John 70, 208
Aghyre 9
Airgialla 22, 30, 32, 44, 45, 52, 76–7, 84, 95,
      111, 118, 126, 128, 206
Airthir/Erthir 30, 139, 194
Ale 153, 167, 175, 176, 186
Alexander, Nicholas 165
Alton 98, 111 n. 30
Anchorites 165
Antrim 31, 45, 84, 104, 126
Antwerp 37, 167
Aragon 135
Archer, John, prior of Kilmainham,
   justiciar 145
Archers 57, 77 n. 6, 88 n. 82, 126–7, 139
Ardcath 175–6
Ardee 13, 34, 101, 148, 156, 159, 179, 191,
   194, 201
   presence in of chief governor 96–9, 105,
      110–11, 118–19, 180–1, 206,
      211, 219
   barony of 95, 144, 177–8, 186
   Carmelite house of St Mary 161–2
   deanery of 149, 152, 161, 166 n. 57, 195
   lords of, *see* Faunt family
   manor of 9, 37, 39, 68, 145
   marches of, defence of 121–2, 125, 128,
      138, 157, 182, 184–5, 202, 212
   parish church of St Mary 166
      vicarage of 9, 166
   priory/hopital of St John the Baptist (*Fratres
      Cruciferi*) 9, 13, 122, 147, 160, 190
Ardglass 200
Armagh:
   abbey of Sts Peter and Paul 145–6, 203, 214
   archbishops of 20, 52, 54, 83, 129, 135–42,
      148, 150–2, 155–61, 178, 194–5,
      204, 206, 208, 214
      Colton, John (1383–1404) 68, 77, 82,
         88, 137–8, 140–1, 143, 145, 148,
         157, 161, 194, 206, 214
      Fitz Ralph, Richard (1346–60) 40, 42–3,
         137, 148, 149, 151, 153, 154–7,
         161, 199 n. 107, 214

Fleming, Nicholas (1404–16) 108, 137–9,
   141, 142–3, 144, 147, 152, 154,
   157, 190, 194, 214–15
Mág Oireachtaigh, David (1334–46) 137,
   140, 147, 151
Mey, John (1443–56) 123 n. 113, 130,
   138–9, 141, 152, 154, 191–2
Prene, John (1439–43) 137, 141, 149,
   154, 156
Segrave, Stephen (1324–33) 137, 147
Suerbeer, Albrecht (1240–6) 142
Swayne, John (1414–39) 116, 121, 122,
   123, 125, 137–8, 144, 152, 154,
   161, 195, 206
Sweteman, Milo (1361–80) 41, 45, 48,
   61, 71, 80, 137, 149, 151, 190–1,
   194, 204, 208, 214
   dispute with Dublin over primacy
      140, 142
   dispute with Thomas Verdon 9, 64
   patronage dispensed by 68, 147–8,
      153, 155, 195
   archdeacon of, *see* Pyrroun, Willam; Ragg,
      Richard; Sweteman, Maurice
   cathedral chapter of 192, 194 n. 73
   chancellor of 53
   city of 52, 78, 82, 83, 85, 109, 126, 127
   clergy of 165, 190
   county 32, 53, 111, 113, 120, 129, 135,
      137–9, 194, 211
   court of 189 n. 37, 191–2
   dean of 52, 53, 215
   diocese of 5, 7, 36, 135, 136, 209, 213
   official of 52, 131
   province of 41, 127, 135, 139, 191, 195,
      198, 214
   registrars/registers of 8, 44, 51, 151
   vicar general of, *see* Corre family
Arundel, earl of 111
Ash 80, 145, 211
Ash:
   John 177, 178
   Petronilla 177
Ashton, Robert, justiciar 53, 59, 64, 66–7,
   151–2
Ashwell, John, seneschal of Drogheda in
   Meath 13, 57, 174–5
Assizes 13–14, 38, 74, 216
Athboy 148, 152, 168, 171, 205
Athlone 71
Aubrey, John, O.P., bishop of Ardagh
   (1373–4?) 64 n. 83
Audley, James, sheriff of Louth 12, 14

Augustinian Order 5, 6, 12, 43, 52, 71, 89, 119, 128, 143, 145–7, 159, 162, 163, 195, 203, 214
Avignon 42–3, 77 n. 9, 137, 151
Awell/Avel, Henry, O. Cist. 200
  William, O. Cist. 200

Babe family 11, 12, 13, 36, 128
  John, sheriff 10, 12, 18, 101
  Robert 14, 60, 66–7, 69
  Thomas 14, 18
Bacon family 50 n. 159
  John, serjeant of Meath 33
Bagot family 11, 12, 210
  Richard, K.P., M.P. 10, 14, 156, 157, 196
Ball, Robert 172
Balliol, Edward 31
Ballybinaby 211
Ballydoyle, parliament of (June 1371) 58, 59–60, 72
Ballygawley 31
Ballymascanlan 178
Ballymore Eustace 185
Balregan 100
Balscot, Alexander, bishop of Meath (1386–1400), justiciar 139, 180, 206
Bangor, abbey of 199
Bann, river 45, 71, 176
Barmeath 5 n. 20, 216
Barron, William 208
Barronstown 10, 196
Bastardy, *see* Illegitimacy (bastardy)
Bath, Matthew 27 n. 14, 216
  Thomas 185, 208
Bealknap, Robert 89
Beans 167
Beaubec 38, 163–3; *see also* Beybeg
Beaulieu 8, 9, 10, 18, 149, 193, 197
Bedford, duke of 112
Bedfordshire 37
Belgard 99 n. 160
Bellew family 5 n. 20, 11, 12, 127, 210, 211
  James 64, 145
  John (father, son, and grandson), M.Ps., sheriffs, K.Ps. 10, 12, 14, 48, 65, 80 n. 32, 86–7, 95, 98, 122
    acquisition of Dundalk and Roche 8, 9, 13, 18, 47, 61, 100, 130, 166, 184
    involvement in Talbot–Ormond dispute 114–17
Bellewstown 114
Bellurgan 100
Bennett, Philip, O.P. 172
Berde, Roger 48
Berlystoun [Marlay] 9
Bermingham family of Carbury 39, 66
Bermingham, James 66
  John, earl of Louth, justiciar (d.1329) 25, 34, 37, 62, 68 n. 116, 147

John, justice of the king's bench 73
Margaret, wife of Robert Preston (d.1361) 39, 66, 165
Matilda, sister of John Bermingham, wife of Nicholas Verdon 35, 63
Matilda, daughter of John Bermingham, wife of Arnold le Poer 35 n. 66, 39 n. 90
Walter (d.1350), justiciar 39
Betagh family 109, 128 n. 146, 208
Beybeg [Beaubec, co. Meath] 38, 164, 177
Bicknor, Alexander, archbishop of Dublin 140 n. 36
'Black rent' 121–2
Black Prince, *see* Edward the Black Prince
Blakeney, John, chief justice of the common bench 166
Blount, William (d.1337) 34
Bocombe, family 10, 11, 18
  Anne 19
  John 209
  Richard, bishop of Leighlin (1400–19) 209
Bonefaunt, John 171 n. 91
Boniface IX, pope 144, 150
Bonnacht [*buannacht*] 82–3, 122, 129, 130, 212–13
Bordeaux 20, 37, 168, 170, 176
Bothwell 102
Boyne, river 22, 38, 65 n. 94, 66, 89–90, 127, 136, 146, 159–60, 162, 164, 165, 172, 175
Brady, *see* MacBrady
Brakden, David 149
Braganstown 5 n. 20, 14, 18, 25, 68 n. 116, 218
Bray 139
Bray, Stephen, chief justice 58, 72, 89 n. 89, 98, 99, 105, 181
Bread 153, 163, 175, 186
Breifne, east 30, 51, 85, 95, 107, 122, 197, 203
Brent, John 136
Breton, Richard 67
Brisbon, John, K.P. 209
  William 208, 209
Bristol 20, 37, 41, 53, 93, 151, 169–70, 171, 172 n. 102, 177
Britain 5, 146
British Isles 4, 20 n. 101, 46
Brittany, Bretons 80, 168, 177, 184
Brittstown [Brettonstown, bar. Upper Slane] 39
Bromley, William, treasurer 44
Bromwich, John, justiciar 13
Brook, William 129
Broun, Geoffrey, abbot of Knock (d.1411) 197
Brown, Thomas 149
Bruce invasion 25–6, 29, 32, 47
Bruce, Edward (d.1318) 25
  Robert, *see* Robert I, king of Scotland
Brugge, Walter 70–3, 79
Bruisyard 36

Burgh family 36, 192
  Elizabeth (d.1363), countess of Ulster, wife of Lionel of Antwerp 28, 31, 43, 46
  Hugh, treasurer 180
  Joan 34
  John (d.1313) 28, 35
  Matilda 31, 34 n. 60
  Richard, earl of Ulster (d.1326) 28
  Richard, esquire of Richard II 89, 102
  William, earl of Ulster (d.1333) 28, 30–1, 35, 50, 70, 72
Burghersh, Bartholomew (d.1355) 29, 34, 66 n. 100, 181
  Elizabeth 34
  Henry, bishop of London (d.1340) 29
Burley, Thomas, chancellor 49, 66
Burri, John 40
Butler family 219
  James, second earl of Ormond (d.1382) 69
  James, third earl of Ormond (d.1405) 81, 86 n. 77, 101, 113, 115, 219
  James, fourth earl of Ormond, lieutenant (d.1453) 7, 11, 21, 110, 136 nn. 3 and 6, 165, 179–80, 190, 219
    dispute with John Talbot 112–17
    presence in Louth 117–18, 121–3, 128–9, 141, 147, 157, 181, 185, 205, 206, 208, 219
  James, earl of Wiltshire and fifth earl of Ormond (d.1461) 139
  Katherine, wife of Thomas Fleming, baron of Slane 113 n. 48
  Thomas, prior of Kilmainham, deputy lieutenant, half-brother of fourth earl 8, 110, 113–15, 145, 218
  Thomas, brother of third earl 89, 113
Butter 153
Bysset, Marjorie 104

Cadell, Robert 87
Caeraigecht, see 'Creaght'
'Caifs' 191
Calais 20, 33, 168
Callystown 146
Cambridge, University of 137, 149–50
Cambridgeshire 171
Campbell, Alexander 102
Canterbury, archbishops and archbishopric of 142, 150 n. 116
Canynge, William, mayor of Bristol (d.1396) 177
Cappagh 156
Cappoge 14, 17, 68, 98, 108, 116, 147
'Captain of his nation' 55, 108, 129, 189, 207; see also Magennis [Mac Aengusa] family; O'Reilly [Ó Raigillig] family; Teeling family
Carbury 39, 66

Carlingford 35, 41, 46, 104, 113, 144, 159–61, 167, 173, 195 n. 85, 198, 206
  attacks on by Irish and Scots; royal service at 76–9, 102, 111, 118 n. 78, 119 n. 87, 126, 183–4, 202
  castle of 79, 97, 103, 112, 124, 179–80, 212
  Dominican friary 72, 119 n. 87
  presence in of governor and officials 70, 72, 99, 180
Carlisle, William, second baron of the exchequer 61
Carlow 49 n. 157, 58–9, 86
Carmarthen 41
Carrickbaggot 10, 157, 196–9
Carrickfergus 70 n. 136, 77, 100, 101, 125
Carrickmacross 126, 128, 147, 212, 216
Carts 163
Cashel 58
  archbishop of 139; see also O'Kelly, Ralph O. Carm
Castile 167
Castleblaney 118 n. 80
Castledermot, parliament at (March 1390) 78 n. 18
Castlelumny 11, 17
Castlerickard 200 n. 119
Castlering 80, 145, 211
Castletown 80 n. 30, 198
Castletowncooley [Lucystown] 131, 177, 179, 205
Castles, building, maintenance, and destruction of 103–4, 123, 124–5, 190–1, 213
Cattle, cows, herds 71, 81, 82 n. 45, 126, 163, 164, 167, 169; see also Hides
Cattle raiding 66, 108, 127, 190, 214; see also 'Creaght'
Cavan 30, 123, 136, 186, 194
'Caylagh' [*cailleach*] 192, 201
Chamber/Chambre/Chambers, Peter 207
  Thomas, sheriff of Meath 77, 190
Chamberlain, Nicholas 206
Channel Islands 29
Chantries 148, 150, 162, 199, 201, 219
Chapman family 18
  Peter 172
Charlton, John, justiciar 140
Chauncelton 152
Cheese 153
Cheshire 2, 92 n. 117, 101 n. 169
Chichester, bishop of 88
Cinque Ports 29
Cistercian Order 6, 12, 38, 39, 43, 88, 143, 145, 146, 163, 169, 200, 204
Clane 113 n. 48
Clare family 39, 69
Clare, Elizabeth (d.1360) 28–9, 35–6, 40, 43, 47
  Gilbert, earl of Gloucester (d.1314) 28
Clement VI, pope 42

Clement VII, antipope 77 n. 9
Clifford, Roger (d.1389) 39
Clinton family 5 n. 20, 11, 12, 115, 127, 128, 210
  Gerald, sheriff, K.P. 11, 15, 17
  Hugh, sheriff 15
  John [several], sheriff, K.P. 11, 14, 15, 17, 30, 62, 80 n. 32, 203
  John of Cappoge, sheriff, K.P. 14, 17, 98, 108, 116
  John of Drumcashel 8, 114, 151, 156, 157 n. 156, 166, 218
  John, chaplain 171
  Peter 165
  Richard 156
  Robert, sheriff, K.P. 14, 16, 79,
  Robert 33–4, 54, 216
  Robert Jr 34 n. 57
  Simon 34 n. 57
  Thomas 14, 34 n. 57
Clogher, city and diocese of 40, 147, 196, 215
  bishop of, *see* Mac Cathasaigh, Matthew; O'Corkeran (Ó Corcráin), John
  chapter of 192
  Register of 40, 135
Clogherhead 146
Clonee 48, 54
Clonegall 49 n. 157
Clones, abbey of Sts Peter and Paul 128
Clongall 49 n. 157
Clonkeen 9, 195–6, 197, 198, 211
Clonmacnoise 48, 82
Clonmel 46 n. 137
Clonmore 63, 64, 152, 164, 197, 198, 200
Cogan, Anne 18
'Coign' 190
Coleraine 71, 100, 156
Collon 33, 146
Colpe 146, 194
Colton, John, archbishop of Armagh, *see* Armagh: archbishops of
Comyn, John 153
  William 67 n. 107
Concubinage 191, 197, 199 n. 110, 201
Condlagh (Ó Congalaig = Connelly), Thomas 195
Conlan/okonnolan (Ó Congalain), Cormac 196
  Richard 196
Connacht 52, 69, 85, 87, 89, 110, 119
Constance 137
Conway 93
Cooley 30, 70, 72, 90, 103, 104 n. 187, 131, 144, 177, 193, 209
  Irish raids on 78–9, 126, 183
Cork 4, 41, 59, 71, 88 n. 85
Corlisbane 144
Cornwall 46
Corre family 127

William 166
Cottenham, James 90
Courtenay, Philip, lieutenant 77
Coventry 170, 177
  parliament, November 1404 102
Cranley, Thomas, archbishop of Dublin (1397–1417) 110, 141, 143
'Creaght' 126, 190–1
Crécy 33, 34
Crophull, John (d.1383) 13, 34, 61, 184
Crowmartin 56, 103, 128, 189, 202, 219
Cruisetown 146
Cruys, family 12, 18, 127
  Henry, K.P. 17
  John, sheriff 13, 16, 18, 78
  John of Merrion 65
  Mahon 11
  Thomas 177
Culmullin 41
Cumbria 38, 163, 164
Curles, Robert 189
Curragh, near Dundalk 145, 146
Cusack family 13
  Joan 18–19
  Geoffrey 189
  John, sheriff 12, 15, 49, 89 n. 89
  John (d.1370), baron of Culmullin 41
  John, rector of Rathdrumin 149
  Luke 19
  Peter 11
  Thomas 94
  Walter 13, 19, 47, 48, 51, 54, 65, 68–70, 73, 213
Cusackstown 65
Cussing, Maurice 144

Dagnall, Buckinghamshire 171
Dagworth, Nicholas 60–1, 69, 89 n. 89
Dalby, Walter, treasurer 49
Dalkey 55, 60, 102, 111, 176
Damory, Roger (d.1322) 28, 35 n. 64
Dantsey, Edward, bishop of Meath (1412–30) 120
Darcy family 34, 145, 211
  Elizabeth (d.1390), daughter of John, wife of James Bulter, second earl of Ormond 113 n. 48
  John of Knaith, justiciar (d.1347) 29–31, 34, 36, 37, 62, 80, 113 n. 49
  John *le fitz* (d.1356) 39
  John of Knaith (d.1411) 81
  John of Platin, sheriff of Meath, K.P. (d.1415) 17, 78, 79, 80, 81 n. 36, 89, 94, 98–100
  Philip of Knaith (d.1399) 80–1
  Roger, escheator 39
  William 34
  William, son of John (d.1418) 110, 115
Dardiz, John 111

Dartas, Janico, K.P. 17, 93–4, 98, 108–10, 112–13, 115, 123–4, 169, 176, 179–80, 207, 219–20
   acquisition of property in Louth/Meath 100, 102–5
   dispute with John Talbot 110, 115
Dartmouth 170
Dartree 126
Darver 10, 18, 67, 149, 198
Daventry 170
David II, king of Scotland (1329–71) 31, 168
Dedications of churches 197–8
Delvin, baron of 125
Derbyshire 2
Derry 45, 84, 156–7, 184–5, 209, 214
Desmond, earls of 39
   Maurice fitz Thomas (d.1356) 29
   Gerald fitz Maurice (d.1398) 49, 56, 69 n. 124
Desmond, earldom of 39
Devon 46, 170
Dominican order 39 n. 94, 72, 82, 83, 88, 108 n. 4, 119 n. 87, 150, 161–2, 165, 172, 183
Donaghmore (co. Meath) 143
Donaghmore, (co. Tyrone) 194
Donaghmoyne 34, 62–3, 121, 129, 147, 203–4
Donegal 43, 71, 119, 128, 185
Dongan, John, bishop of Sodor and Man, bishop of Down 104
Douglas, earl of 102
   Sir William, lord of Nithsdale 76
Dover 29
Dover, Robert 60
Dowdall family and records 5, 6, 10, 11, 12, 14, 18, 113, 178, 209
Dowdall, Joan 99
   John [several], sheriff, K.P. M.P. 10, 13, 15, 16–17, 53–4, 64, 89, 112–13, 114, 122, 154, 213
   John, of Newtown, sheriff of Louth (d.1402) 19, 96–103, 105, 108 n. 10, 119, 123, 178, 180, 216–17
   John, son of John of Newtown 189 n. 37
   Peter 104, 112–15, 125–6, 129, 131, 166, 178–80, 189, 193, 205, 207
   Richard 18 n. 86
   Walter [several], sheriff 9, 10, 13, 14, 15
   William 15
Down, diocese and bishop of 8, 122, 123 n. 113, 160, 199 n. 110; *see also* Dongan
Downpatrick 46 n. 137, 54, 70–3, 100
Drakestown 154
Drogheda 7, 20, 21, 28, 30, 34, 35, 36, 37–9, 46, 55, 78–9, 93–4, 101, 104, 110, 113, 119, 125, 135, 148, 153–4, 159–82, 200, 218
   burgesses, mayors, seneschals of, *see* Ash,
   John; Ashwell, John; Brent, John; Frombold, John; Mole, Richard; Ofynan, Philip; Preston: Richard, Roger, William; Roth, William; Skinner, Thomas; Stanley, John; Sexton, Robert; Symcock, William; Walsh, John; White: Nicholas, Robert, Stephen
   archbishops of Armagh and 138, n. 16, 139–42, 156, 159–61, 187, 195–6
   deanery of 149
   Dominican friary of St Mary Magdalane 39 n. 94, 82, 88, 150, 162
   Franciscan friary 83, 120, 162, 165
   Irish in 187–8, 199
   military role 11, 29, 31, 57, 76, 101–2, 126, 168–9, 183–4
   plague in 40–2, 198–9
   presence of chief governor in 26, 53, 70, 74, 78, 81, 99, 117–18, 128, n. 148, 130–1, 140, 145
   Richard II in 71, 82–9, 157, 180, 194, 200, 209
   St Laurence 162
   St Mary d'Urso 11 n. 63, 162
   St James's hospital (Meath) 136, 162
   St John the Baptist (Meath) 162
   St Mary's (Meath) 162
   St Mary the Virgin (Meath, Carmelite) 162
   St Nicholas's (Meath) 89
   St Peter's, and chapel there of St John and guild of St Anne 150, 151, 159–60, 162, 165, 177
   king's Irish council, meetings in:
     1391: 79 n. 23
     1393: 81
     1423: 120, 138 n. 18, 139
     1429: 140 n. 31
     1436: 140
     1442: 163 n. 31
     1443: 140
     general council 1412: 114
     general council October 1442: 163 n. 31
     great council 1444: 14
     parliament 1440: 163
     parliament October 1450: 166
     parliament March 1451: 141
   unification and elevation to status of county 172–3
   William Windsor and 51–69, 173–5, 180
Dromin 150, 165, 197, 198
Dromiskin 64, 72, 146, 147, 151–5, 160, 171, 190, 194–201
Drumcar 9, 143, 197, 198
Drumcashel 8, 114, 151, 156, 166, 218
Drumconrath 125, 128, 154, 182, 185, 202, 212
Drummoghan 201

Drumshallon 142, 153, 196, 198
Dublin, city of 4–6, 13, 20, 21, 30, 32, 36–7,
    40, 41, 43, 49, 56, 59, 61, 63, 70,
    73, 76–9, 83–4, 88–9, 98, 102, 118,
    119 n. 89, 122, 140, 161–3, 173,
    180, 205, 214, 215, 219
  archbishop of, *see* Bicknor, Alexander;
    Cranley, Thomas; Tregury, Michael;
    Talbot, Richard
  castle 28, 101, 121
  cathedrals, Christ Church 142
    St Patrick's 68, 140, 143, 153
  county of 27, 33, 58, 80, 93, 189, 191
  Holy Trinity, priory 142, 153
  marquis of, *see* Vere, Robert
  parliament at:
    1368: 156
    July–August 1369: 56, 151
    April 1370: 14, 57, 62, 151, 174
    April 1372: 67
    November 1380: 71
    September 1402: 96
    October 1409: 141, 152
    January 1417: 112
    June and December 1420: 14
    November 1428: 124
    May 1430: 124, 190
    November 1431: 216
    March 1435: 152
    1436: 152
    1438: 152
    March 1438: 152
    March 1446: 152
    October 1449: 151, 152
    great council 1372: 14, 175, 178
    great council 1375: 14
  province of 140–2, 188
  St John of Jerusalem, Kilmainham,
    hospital 113, 144–5, 195
  St Mary the Virgin 9, 143
  St Thomas the Martyr 143–4, 197
Duleek 35, 38, 125, 177, 183
Dullard, Bartholomew 64 n. 83
Dumbarton 29
Dunany 144, 146, 198
Dunbin 152, 165, 198
Dunboyne 143 n. 54, 162
Dundalk 12, 29–30, 71–2, 89, 92, 96, 113–14,
    117, 122–3, 138, 148, 153, 159–82,
    189, 191, 220
  barony of 13
  deanery of 149, 152
  Franciscan friary 88, 162, 220
  lord/lordship of 8, 61, 114, 177, 211
  marches of 32, 83, 84, 100, 178, 192, 202–3
  St Katherine's chantry chapel 167
  St Leonard's priory 100, 122, 155, 162, 166
  St Nicholas's 9, 149, 162, 166, 198, 219
  Richard Fitz Ralph and 42–3, 149 n. 102,
    154, 155–6, 160, 183, 187, 214
  Richard II and 84, 87–8, 180, 194, 209
  warfare and 44–5, 53–4, 77–80, 86, 107,
    118–19, 125, 127–30, 181, 184,
    207, 212
  see also Brook, William; Dowdall: John, Peter,
    Walter; Fleming, Matthew; Kerisley:
    John, Walter; Skreen/Skrene: Thomas,
    William; Tanner: John, Matthew,
    Richard, Walter; White: Geoffrey,
    James, John
Dundrennan 39
Dungooley 80, 219
Dunleer 96, 144, 154, 195, 197, 198
Dunsany 220
Dysart 66 n. 100

East Anglia 2, 6 n. 31
Edward III (1327–77) 11–12, 25–6, 29–32,
    34, 36–7, 42–3, 46–7, 49, 54 n. 15,
    56, 58–9, 63, 80, 88, 140, 142, 149,
    165, 184, 202, 213
Edward IV (1461–70, 1471–83) 131
Edward the Black Prince 67
Elliot, John 152
Ellis, John 187
England 2–6, 10, 20–1, 25, 33–6, 47, 50,
    55–6, 59, 69, 74, 76, 103, 105–6,
    112–14, 120, 125, 127, 135–6, 142,
    188–9, 210, 219
  English language 136, 191–2, 200–1
  English law/liberty, grants of 119, 194–7
  Louth/Meath men in 37–9, 42–3, 46, 49,
    61–3, 67–8, 72, 80–1, 86–90, 93,
    97, 98–101, 136 n. 7, 138–9,
    149–50, 157, 172–3, 175–6
  migration to 125, 170–1, 174–5
  trade with 37–8, 41–2, 60, 66, 160, 164–5,
    167–70
  Verdon family and 18, 27–9, 63, 92, 115, 123
Enfeoffment to use, entail 10–11, 65 n. 90,
    166, 178, 189
Epworth, William, baron of the exchequer 63
Everton, John 170
  Walter 170
  William 170
Exchequer, Irish 5 n. 22, 6–8, 10, 26, 28,
    38 n. 85, 58–9, 78, 89, 138, 163,
    166, 175, 202 n. 127, 206, 213, 216
  barons, chamberlains of 217; *see also*
    Epworth, William; Holywood,
    Robert; Keppok, John; Rede,
    Richard; Stanihurst, Henry
  White Book of 113
Excommunication 45, 48, 51–2, 108, 123 n.
    113, 148 n. 99, 155, 173, 203, 214
Executors, *see* Wills
Exeter 20, 41
  bishop of 171; *see also* Grandison, John

Exeter, Richard, son of Richard 67 n. 107
  Walter, sheriff 12, 15

Falconer, of archbishop of Armagh 108
Farney 62, 95, 108, 109, 118, 121–2, 124, 129, 203–4, 211
Faughart 25, 178
Faunt family 9
  Thomas 9, 143
  William 165
Feld [Haynestown] 9, 64, 155, 198
Feld family 36
  John 188
  Margery 188
  Thomas 202 n. 127
Ferrard 62, 96, 146, 216 n. 38
Ferrers, Henry (d.1343) 29
  Henry, husband of Joan Tuyt 48, 54, 69, 73
  Ralph 48 n. 151
  William 47
Fír Manach 45
Fish, fishermen, fisheries, fishing 41, 60, 88, 102, 148, 153, 160, 164, 167, 170, 175, 204; see also Weirs
Fitz Hugh, Nicholas 60
Fitz John, John 57
Fitz Ralph, Richard, archbishop of Armagh, see Armagh: archbishops of
Fitz Ralph, Richard, rector of Trim 153
Fitz Rery, Robert 131
Fitz Thomas, William, prior of Kilmainham, justiciar 144–5
Flagellants 40
Flanders, Flemings 167–8, 203
Fleming family 113, 166
  Christopher, baron of Slane 19, 94–5, 111, 125
  David 91
  Elizabeth 95
  Joan 165
  John of Mortoun 152, 154
  Matthew of Dundalk, K.P. 17, 112, 162, 195
  Nicholas, archbishop of Armaghee, see Armagh: Archbishops of
  Simon (d.1370), baron of Slane 41, 46–7, 49, 66, 184
  Stephen 66
  Thomas, K.P., baron of Slane 17, 66, 77, 79, 94–5, 100, 113, 115, 154, 179, 185, 209
Fore 99 n. 160, 111, 182 n. 171
Forster, John 167
France, French 1, 4, 33, 34, 36, 43, 50, 106, 110, 123, 135, 167–8
Franciscan Order 30, 31 n. 37, 36, 40, 83–4, 88, 120, 141, 149 n. 102, 161–3, 165, 198, 220
French language 8

Frombold, John, mayor of Drogheda in Uriel 58–9
Furness, Cistercian house of 38, 42, 163–4, 169, 175, 177
Furnival family 61, 114
  Joan 34
  Thomas (d.1339) 34, 35
  William of Sheffield 47, 111 n. 30, 114
  see also Talbot, John; Neville, Thomas

Gaffney (Ó Gomna), Richard 144, 198
Galloglass 31–2, 52–3, 82–4, 108, 121, 220
Galway 167
Gaol, see Prison/imprisonment
Gaol delivery, see Assizes
Garter, Order of 29
Gascony, Gascon 67, 168, 176
Gaulstown [Fingalstown, bar. Lower Duleek] 38
Gaydon, Isabella 18, 19
Gdansk 167
Geneville:
  Joan, wife of Roger Mortimer 25, 26
  Simon 49
Genoa 167
Geoffrey, Richard 208
Gerald fitz Maurice, earl of Kildare, see Kildare, earls of: Gerald fitz Maurice
Gerald fitz Maurice, earl of Desmond, justiciar, see Desmond, earls of: Gerald fitz Maurice
Gernon family 10, 11, 12, 13, 18, 20, 98, 209
  Adam 13
  Barnaby 19
  Henry, sheriff 16, 171
  Hugh 36
  Isabella 18 n. 86
  John [Several], sheriff 14, 15, 16, 36, 201, 214
  John, chief justice of common bench 37, 68 n. 117
  John of Killincoole, sheriff 11, 163 n. 33, 216
  Katharine 19
  Matilda 112, 179
  Nicholas 35–6, 56 n. 27, 63, 66
  Richard, sheriff 15
  Robert, K.P. 17
  Roger 11, 13, 17, 36, 95, 124, 190, 204
  Roger of Drummoghan 201
  Roger of Gernonstown [several], sheriff, K.P. M.P. 8, 9, 14, 18, 57, 62, 63, 69, 116, 147
  Roger of Killincoole 148
  Roger of Rathbrist 14
  Simon 36, 156, 166
  Stephen, K.P. 17, 79 n. 28, 97–101, 103, 209
  Thomas of Killincoole 97, 99 n. 160
Gernonstown [Castlebellingham] 8, 9, 116, 147

Gilbertstown 9
Gilys, Robert 156
Glasgow 29, 102
Glenluce, abbot of 102
Glens of Antrim 104
Gloucester, duke of, *see* Thomas,
    duke of Gloucester
Gloucestershire 2
Glyn Dŵr, Owain 98, 101
Glyssot, John 179
Golding:
  Hugh 44, 205
  Thomas 89
Goodman, Thomas 13
Gormanston 47, 65, 68, 177
Gory, William 200
Gouvernance of Prynces 118
Grain (corn, oats, wheat) 39, 41–2, 50, 66–7,
    70, 77 n. 5, 101–3, 111, 118, 146,
    164, 167–8, 170, 171 n. 91, 174,
    176, 179, 186, 205–6,
    208, 212–13
Granaries 77
Grandison, John, bishop of Exeter
    (1327–69) 41
Great Finborough, Suffolk 171
Greencastle 45, 78, 80, 97, 100, 102–4, 112,
    124, 179–80, 182 n. 171
Grissaphan, George 154, 173
Greenoge 143
Guilds:
  St Anne, Drogheda 160, 187
Gurney, John 65, 66 n. 102

Hadsor family 10, 11, 12, 18, 210
  John [several], sheriff, K.P. 11, 12, 14, 17
  John of Cappoge, K.P. 17, 147
  Milo, sheriff, K.P. 16, 17
  Peter, sheriff 15
  Reginald, K.P. 13, 17, 97, 100, 103
  Thomas 152
  William, bishop of Meath, K.P. 12, 17, 199
Haggardstown 77 n. 5, 179, 213
Hall, James 136
Hampshire 20
Hartort, Joan (d.1397?) 18, 19, 64
Hasse, John 179
Hauberge:
  Adam 28
  Benedict, sheriff 15, 27–8
  Hugh 56 n. 27, 67
  Philip 96 n. 142
Hebrides 76, 169, 176
Henry IV [Bolingbroke] (1399–1413) 91–4,
    96, 97–9, 101–2, 105–7, 138, 141,
    172, 189, 218
Henry V [Monmouth] (1413–22) 91, 98, 101,
    110, 112, 168, 219 n. 50
Henry VI (1422–61, 1470–1) 119, 216 n. 34

Henry, duke of Lancaster (d.1361) 18, 35, 63
Heresy, heretical conduct 53, 64
Heyne, John 13
Hides 55, 167–9
Heyroun, Robert 13
Holland
  Eleanor, countess of March and Ulster
    (d.1405) 86 n. 77, 103
  Thomas, duke of Surrey, lieutenant 90, 93
Holt, John 89
Holy Land 136
Holywood:
  Christopher 110
  Nesta 55
  Robert, chief baron of the exchequer 47, 55,
    61–2, 64, 66, 68–9
Homildon Hill 101
Hopper, Richard 149
Horses 45, 80, 81, 88, 111, 151, 169, 179,
    185–6, 190, 207
Hospitallers 114 n. 53
Hostages/hostage-taking 44, 66, 78, 81–2, 84,
    86, 90–1, 93, 107 n. 1, 108, 109, 117,
    121–2, 126, 181, 205–7, 209, 213,
    215; *see also* Prison/imprisonment;
    Ransom
Howth (Ireland) 70, 72, 130
Howth:
  Nicholas 8
  Peter 18–19, 65
Humbleton, John 89, 94, 113
Humphrey, son of Henry IV 91, 219 n. 50
Hungary 43, 135
Husee, Mark (d.1346) 34
Hussey family 49, 105 n. 194
  John, baron of Galtrim 48, 49
  Matthew, baron of Galtrim, sheriff of Meath
    (d.1418) 108 n. 4
  Thomas 166
Hyde:
  James, M.P. 47–8, 49 n. 157, 54, 57, 72, 86
  Walter 37, 86

Illegitimacy (bastardy) 19, 40, 64, 155, 189,
    198–200
Incest 51
Inchmore 146
Iniskeen 41, 63, 147–8, 204, 208, 212
Inquisitions 9–10, 26, 30, 38, 40, 79, 87, 105,
    144–5, 153, 163, 188, 202–3, 218
  concerning William Windsor 55–9, 66–7
  post mortem 27 n. 14, 72, 180, 181
Iolo Goch 85
Ireland:
  duke of, *see* Vere, Robert
  Great Seal of, *see* Seal
Irish, accusations of Irish birth 187–9
  in Louth 186–7, 195–201, 208, 220
Irishgrange 145

Irish Sea 20, 35, 37–8, 41, 76, 101–2, 135,
    167–8, 170–2, 176
Iron 177, 186
Isabella, queen of England (d.1358) 25
Italy 43, 135
Ivermongan 147

James, son of Robert III, king of Scotland 104
Jenkinstown 99
John of Gaunt, duke of Lancaster (d.1399) 88
John of the Isles (John del Ontyles), see
    MacDonald [Mac Domnaill] family
Jordan, Isabella 19

Kane 196
Keenan (Ó Cianáin), John 195
Keeper/justice of the peace (K.P.) 12, 17
Kells 27, 30, 35, 38, 40, 44, 70 n. 135, 71, 79,
    82 n. 49, 99, 103, 118, 205
  archdeaconry of 148 n. 97, 150, 177,
    208 n. 176
  march of 203
  St Mary's, abbey and abbot of 119, 122,
    128 n. 146, 135–6, 144, 145, 197
Kendy, John, abbot of Bangor 199
Kent 2, 20, 171
Keppok family 10, 11, 13
  John 68 n. 116
  John, chief justice of the justiciar's bench,
    chief governor 37, 54, 55, 68, 69,
    166, 169
  John, son of Simon 170
  Simon 170
Kerdiff, Robert 178
Kerisley:
  Agnes 179
  John 187
  Walter 179
Kilcurly 149, 153, 154, 196
Kildare 33, 39, 58, 66, 77, 124, 154, 173, 191,
    216, 218
Kildare, earls of 34, 219
  Maurice fitz Thomas (d.1390) 29, 34, 49, 69
  Gerald fitz Maurice (d.1432) 85,
    113 n. 48, 114
Kildemock 144, 166, 177, 194, 195–6, 198
Kilkenny 40, 44, 57–8, 60, 63 n. 75, 177
  Parliament:
    February 1366: 156 n. 154
    1409: 7
    January 1371: 59, 62
    June and October 1375: 51, 61, 213
Killincoole 10, 11, 18, 97, 99 n. 160, 148, 163 n.
    33, 199 n. 110, 216
Killineer 146
Kilmainhambeg 144, 145, 203
Kilmainham Wood 144
Kilmallock 46 n. 137
Kilmoon 148, 152, 153 n. 133, 199

Kilsaran 114 n. 53, 144, 145
Kiltallaght 157
Kinsale 167, 186
Kinton family 13
  David 13
  John 14
Knock, abbey of Sts Peter and Paul 77, 146, 205
  abbots of, see Broun, Geoffrey; Ledwich,
    Patrick; Locard (Lockhart), James;
    Mulchan, John; Richard; Simon

Labour, forced 125
Labourers, justices of 13
  migration of 124, 171 n. 91
Lacy family 25
  Hugh 5 n. 21, 148
  Margery 27
  Maud 27
  Walter 38
Lancashire 2, 3, 38, 67, 170
Lancaster, house of, see Henry, duke of
    Lancaster; Maud, countess of
    Lancaster; Maud of Lancaster;
    Thomas of Lancaster
Lannoy, Gilbert 135, 203
Laois 111
Latimer, Lord 69
Laurence, Edmund, escheator 56, 80
Leche, James 152
Ledwich, Patrick, abbot of Knock 146, 197
Leicestershire 2
Leinster 4, 43–4, 46, 48, 54, 71, 76, 85–6, 87,
    89–90, 185
Le Mans/Sens, bishop of 33
Leynagh, Thomas 179
Limerick 57–8, 60, 64 n. 83, 66, 88 n. 85, 174
Lionel of Antwerp, earl of Ulster, duke of
    Clarance (d.1368) 29, 31–3, 36, 39,
    41, 43, 45, 52–4, 56, 61, 80
  relations with settlers in Louth/Meath
    46–50, 65, 68, 72–3, 86, 142,
    161, 219
Liscartan 103
Lisgoole 195
Lisslanly 84
Llandaff, bishop of 88
Llanthony in Gloucester 5, 89, 146 n. 80, 160,
    163, 164 n. 41
Llanthony in Wales 5, 146, 159, 163–4
Locard (Lockhart), James, abbot of Knock 197
Loch Ryan (?Stranraer) 102
Logan, Henry 150
London 37, 61, 93, 111, 119, 142, 149,
    169–70, 199, 213, 219
  bishop of 88
London, Edmund 78, 79, 80 n. 32, 86, 87,
    95, 212
  William 34 n. 60, 49, 91, 148
Long Ashton, Somerset 53

Longford 82, 85
Lough Derg 43, 86 n. 77, 173
Lough Foyle 185, 188
Lough Swilly 185
Louth:
  abbey of, St Mary's 44
    prior of, *see* Magennis, Patrick; Sherbourne (Schorbrun), John; Staunton, Nicholas; William
  barony of 67, 97
  Irish of, *see* Irish
  liberty of 20, 25, 37, 62, 89–90, 92
  lordship of 80
  manor of 34, 194
  marches of, *see* Marches of
Lucy, Anthony, justiciar 26
Lucystown, *see* Castletowncooley

MacBrady (Mac Brádaig or Ó Brádaig)
  Nicholas, bishop of Kilmore (1398–1421) 195
  William 195
MacCabe [Mac Cába] family 84, 108–9
  Brian 82
Mac Cathasaigh, Matthew, bishop of Clogher (1362–?1369) 137 n. 9
Mac Cathmhaoil [MacCawell], Brian, bishop of Clogher (1356–1358) 40, 137 n. 9
MacCormack (Mac Carmaic), Matilda 195
Machaire Mucnamha 192; *see also* 'Maghery'
MacDonald [Mac Domnaill] family 31, 32, 53, 105, 121, 157
  Eoin Mael 83, 84
  Domnall, lord of the Isles 104
  Eoin Mór 104–5
  Eoin, son of Eoin Mór 105
  John, of the Isles 31, 76
  Somairle 52
MacGeoghegan [Mac Eochucáin] family 111
MacGilmore [Mac Gilla Muire] family 100
  Walter 193
MacGilroy (Mac Gilla Ruad), Richard 192–3
MacGowan (Mac Gabann/Smith), Philip 194
MacMahon [Mac Mathgamna] family 45, 51–2, 62, 95, 108, 117, 118 n. 81, 121–3, 146, 148, 185, 189, 196, 198, 202, 204, 206, 211–12, 220
  Aed (d.1344) 84, 194
  Aed Ruad, son of Rudraige (d.1453) 129, 217
  Ardgal (d.1416) 109, 111, 217
  Brian (d.1371) 32, 44, 45, 52, 184, 197 n. 95, 217
  Brian, son of Ardgal (d.1442) 8, 109, 117–19, 121–2, 126–8, 157, 185, 190, 205, 208, 210, 212, 217
  Cú Chonnacht, son of Philip (d.1411) 108
  Echaid, son of Philip, of Farney 95, 108–9
  Eimír 129 n. 154
  Feidlimid 'of the wine' 188
  John (d.1342) 30, 83, 217
  John (1390s) 215
  Magnus (d.1357) 44, 45, 208, 217
  Magnus (d.1443) 111, 118, 121, 126–8, 146, 212, 217
  Philip Ruad (d.1403) 45, 52, 217
  Rudraige (d.1446) 121, 124, 126, 128–9, 204, 206, 208, 217
MacMurrough [Mac Murchada] family 112
  Art 48, 215
  Domnall Riabach 48, 215
MacQuillin [Mac Uigilín] family 121, 186, 190, 212
  Janico 84
Maddan 82
Magennis [Mac Aengusa] family 53–4, 71–2, 79, 100, 108, 118, 120, 130, 202, 205–7, 213, 215, 217
  Aed (d.1424) 117
  Art (d.1449) 70
  Muirchertach (d.1399) 71, 83–4, 203
  Patrick, prior of St Mary's, Louth 197
  Philip 186 n. 23
'Maghery' [*machaire*] 191
Mág Oireachtaigh, David, archbishop of Armagh, *see* Armagh: archbishops of
Maguire [Mág Uidir] family 45, 119
  Thomas 122
Malt 167, 186, 188, 212
Man, Isle of 29, 104, 127, 168, 169
Mandeville, Henry 18
  Richard 26
Manning, Walter 170
Mansfieldstown [Maundevileston] 10, 28, 63, 100, 150, 156, 166 n. 57, 196, 198
March, earls of, *see* Mortimer family
March of Wales (Welsh March) 2, 90
March law/customs 187, 189, 191–2, 207–8
March warfare 30, 77–9, 92–3, 115, 120, 124, 126–7, 142, 190–1, 202, 204–7, 213
Marchers 66, 103, 202
  of Uriel/Louth 83, 189, 207, 209–10
Marches of:
  Ardee 202
  Dublin 189
  Dundalk 32, 83–4, 100, 178, 202–3
  Kells 203
  Louth 30, 44, 54–5, 62–3, 80, 103, 109, 115, 123, 125, 128, 148, 176, 183–210, 211, 219–20
  Meath 208
  Ulster 208
  Westmeath 51
Mareward, Thomas, baron of Skreen (d.1414) 111
Maryman:
  Adam 72
  John 70, 72

Maud, countess of Lancaster, wife of Henry, earl
    of Lancaster (d.1345) 180
Maud of Lancaster, countess of Ulster (d.1377),
    wife of William Burgh and Ralph
    Ufford 32, 35–6, 63, 72
Maurice fitz Thomas, earl of Kildare, *see* Kildare,
    earls of, Maurice fitz Thomas
Mcarcennaydy 206
McGonnes, Patrick, *see* Magennis, Patrick
McGylkaway, John 207
Mcheugh, Matthew 196
Mckasshyn, John 200
McKegan, William 189
McKewyn (?Mac Eoin), Philip 196
Meath:
    archdeacon/archdeaconry of 72, 148 n. 99
    bishop of 48, 56, 64 n. 83, 88, 143 n. 54,
        148 n. 97, 154, 203; *see also* Balscot,
        Alexander; Dantsey, Edward
    clergy of 160, 206
    diocese of 44, 48, 136, 138, 154, 160, 199
    liberty of, *see* Trim
Mellifont 6, 12, 88, 127, 146, 160 n. 8, 192,
        197, 200, 204, 217
    abbot of 17, 190
    Irish monks in 197
Merbury, Laurence 92 n. 117, 98
Mey:
    John, archbishop of Armagh, *see* Armagh:
        archbishops of
    William 154
Meynell, Elizabeth 39
Migrants/migration 31, 124, 170–1, 175, 177,
        186, 188, 192, 197, 203, 220
Milford 169
Mills, millstones, watermills, windmills 40, 72,
        76 n. 4, 98, 126, 131, 146, 175, 177,
        179, 193, 204–5
    millers 126, 193, 205
Minehead, Somerset 102
Modus Tenendi Parliamentum 114
Mole:
    Richard 13, 60, 153 174
    Simon 153, 172, 175
Montagu:
    Edward 33
    William, earl of Salisbury (d.1344) 33
More family 128
    John, sheriff 16, 100, 103–4
    Richard 153 n. 137
    Thomas 103–4
    William 216
Morgallion 79, 125
Morgan, Peter 153
Morice:
    John, escheator, justiciar 37–8, 148,
        163, 180
    William 153 n. 137
Mornington [Marinerstown] 38

Mortimer family 20, 71, 74, 87, 97, 119, 121,
        131, 219
    Edmund, earl of March and Ulster,
        lieutenant, (d.1381) 26, 36 n. 69,
        46, 54, 69–74, 76–7, 109, 138, 164,
        181, 219
    Edmund, earl of March and Ulster,
        lieutenant, (d.1425) 86, 96–7, 102,
        107 n. 2, 110, 119–21, 130, 173,
        184, 213, 216 n. 34
    Joan, *see* Geneville, Joan
    Matilda (d.1312) 25
    Roger, earl of March, lieutenant,
        (d.1330) 25–7, 30, 37, 70, 73, 131
    Roger, earl of March (d.1360) 26, 36
    Roger, earl of March and Ulster, lieutenant
        (d.1398) 73–4, 79, 81–7, 88 n. 82,
        89–92, 96, 103, 115, 152, 203, 212,
        215, 219
    Thomas 73
Mournes, lordship of the 112
Mowbray, Thomas, earl of Nottingham 87
Mowner, William 150
Moynagh, Nicholas 156
Mulchan, Mulghan, Omulchan
        (?Ó Maelcháine = Mulqueen)
    Bartholomew 196, 199
    John, abbot of Knock 196, 197, 199
    Richard 199
    Thomas 199
Mullanstown 69 n. 126
Munster 43–4, 54, 57, 71, 76, 85, 89, 90, 93,
        174, 175
Muriel, Nicholas 218

Naas 57, 112
    council at:
        1398: 152
        1416: 157
        1443: 213
    parliament 1447: 152
Nakanary, Moyre 206
Napton family 13, 18, 94, 113
    David, sheriff 12, 16
    Isabella 18 n. 86
    John 14, 19, 89, 218
Navan 33, 103, 120
    St Mary's abbey 145
Nenagh 40
Netterville family 94, 113, 127
    Elizabeth 89, 94, 113
    Laurence 189 n. 37
    Luke 11
    Nicholas, sheriff 15
    Richard 89
Neville:
    Maud, Lady Furnival 111
    Thomas, baron Furnival (d.1407) 111 n. 30
Newcastle 178 n. 139

Newry, abbey of 79 n. 28, 145, 147,
     202 n. 130, 209
Newtown 96
Newtown Cooley 145
Nithsdale, lord of, see Douglas, Sir William
Nobber 40, 122–3, 125, 127, 144, 148, 150,
     152–3, 182, 183, 191, 205
Normandy 38, 112, 164
Norris:
  Adam 188
  Philip 166
Northampton 177
Northamptonshire 170
Nottingham, earl of, see Mowbray, Thomas
Nottinghamshire 2
Novel disseisin, assizes of, see Assizes
Nugent family 127
Nysene, John 207, 209

O'Brien [Ó Briain], Brian 84
Obryn, Lavertagh 207
Ó Buge, David, O. Carm 199
O'Byrne [Ó Broin] family 86, 90, 115
Ó Calmáin, Thomas 77 n. 9
O'Carroll [Ó Cearbaill], Donnchad 52 n. 8
O'Connell family 127
O'Connor Faly [Ó Conchobair Failge]
     family 109–10, 111–12, 118, 121,
     125, 183, 216
O'Corkeran (Ó Corcráin)
  John, bishop of Clogher (1373–?1389) 195,
     214
  Thomas 195
O'Donnell [Ó Domnaill] family 86,
     122 n. 107, 125–7, 128
  Nechtain 121
  Niall Garb 119–20, 121, 127
O'Farrell [Ó Feargall] family 30, 85
Oferagaid, Christian 136
Offaly 39, 66, 110
Ofynan, Philip 186
O'Hamill (Ó hAdmaill), John 194, 195
O'Hanlon [Ó hAnluain] family 32, 52, 70, 79,
     81, 83, 85 n. 70, 100–1, 111, 121–2,
     127, 130, 157, 184, 186, 194,
     212, 220
  Ardgal 108
  Cú Ulad 84
  Domnall:
     1330s 29, 145
     1400s 108
  Malachy 52, 139, 155, 202 n. 130
  Magnus 78, 81 n. 43, 108
  Niall 84
  William 194
Ohannon, M. 207
O'Hanratty [Ó hAnrachtaig] family 118, 192
  Margaret 192
O'Higgins [Ó hUigin], Niall 110

O'Kane (Ó Catháin) family 126
  John 193–4
  Manus 84, 209 n. 177
O'Kelly family 127
  Ralph, O. Carm., archbishop of Cashel
     (d.1361) 199
  Thomas 187
  William 199
Okoyn (Ó Cadain)
  Gyllarevyth 195 n. 85
  Patrick 195
O'Loughran [Ó Lúchaireáin] family 192,
     194–5
  Christian 194
  Geffyn 192, 201
  Geoffrey 184 n. 73
  Thomas 194, 200
Olowan (Ó Luain), Simon 196
Omeghan (?Ó Mithidéin), William 196
O Molghallyn, Nicholas 187
O'More [Ó Morda] family 111
Omulchan, see Mulchan
O'Mulholland (Ó Maelchallainn) family 195
Omurry, Nicholas 196
O'Neill [Ó Néill] family of Ulster 50–1, 81,
     90, 92, 100, 108–9, 111, 139, 145,
     155, 179, 181, 183, 189–90, 192,
     205, 206, 208, 212, 219
  Aed Mór (d.1364) 32, 44, 45, 52, 138,
     214, 217
  Aed, son of Eógan of the Fews 127
  Brian, son of Niall Óc (d.1404) 81–2,
     107, 217
  Cú Ulad Ruad (d.1400), son of Niall
     Mór 109, 127
  Cú Ulad, son of Cú Ulad Ruad 93, 109
  Domnall, son of Aed Mór 45, 52
  Domnall (d.1432), son of Henry 86, 107–9,
     117, 119–23, 126, 217
  Eógan, son of Niall Óc (abd.1455) 107–9,
     117, 119–23, 125–30, 213, 217
  Feidlimid, son of Niall Óc 84
  Henry, son of Niall Mór (d.1392) 86
  Henry, son of Eógan 123 n. 111, 129,
     130–1
  Muirchertach, son of Cú Ulad Ruad 109
  Niall Mór (abd.1397) 52–4, 55, 70, 73–4,
     76–8, 80, 82, 84–5, 109, 152, 157,
     200, 203, 209–10, 212, 215,
     217, 220
  Niall Óc (d.1403) 8, 53, 74, 78–81, 82–6,
     91, 92, 95, 97, 107, 109 n. 17, 146,
     185, 191, 194, 202, 215, 216 n.
     38, 217
  Toirdelbach 53
  Úna, wife of Niall Óc 81
O'Neills of Clandeboy [Clann Aeda Buide] 45,
     78, 117–18, 121
  Brian 121

Concobar, son of Brian (d.1387) 78
Henry (dep. 1345) 31, 32, 217
John, son of Brian 78
O'Neills of the Fews 211
O'Reilly [Ó Raigillig] family 51, 78, 79, 82,
  85, 95, 103, 109, 117–8, 123,
  126–7, 139 n. 26, 144–5, 186, 208,
  214–15
  Eógan (1400s) 107
  Eógan (d.1449) 118–19, 125, 128–30, 136,
    212, 217
  Feidlimid 129
  Fergal (dep. 1450) 130, 217
  Fergal, son of John 108 n. 3
  Gilla Ísa (d.1330) 30
  Gilla Ísa (d.1400) 83
  John (d.1400) 82 n. 49, 217
  John, son of Eógan (d.1460) 130, 217
  John, abbot of Kells 119, 197
  Mael Morda (d.1411) 83, 107, 217
  Philip (d.1384) 51–2, 70, 203, 217
  Richard (d.1349) 30, 44, 205, 217
  Richard, bishop of Kilmore (1356–69) 51
  Thomas (d.1392) 206, 217
  Thomas Óc (d.1421?) 108, 109
Ormond, earls of, *see* Butler family
O'Rogan [Ó Rudacáin] family 127, 192
  Agnes 192, 194
  Auly and Petrus 32, 192, 203
  William 192
O'Toole [Ó Tuathail] family 157 n. 163
  Feidlimid 185
Our, Joan 170
  William 170
Outlaw, Roger, prior of Kilmainham,
  justiciar 145
Overton, John 208
Oxen 164, 167
Oxford, University of 42, 137, 149–50
Oyer et terminer, commissions of 13, 39,
  92 n. 115
Oweyn, Elena 191–2, 200
  Patrick 166
Oysters 154

Paris 42
Parliament, *see* Petitioning
  Irish, *see* Castledermot, parliament at;
    Drogheda; Dublin; Kilkenny; Naas
  English 99, 171–2
    Good Parliament (1376) 67, 91
    Merciless Parliament (1388) 89, 91
    Coventry (1404) 102
    York (1338) 28
Parsonstown 146
Parys, Peter 9
Patristow, John 168
Peacock, William 172
Pembroke, John, escheator 181
Pembrokeshire 91, 169
Penbroke, John 199
Penkiston, James 207
Pensions 71, 113, 148, 154, 166 n. 50
Pepper 9
Pepperstown 176
Percy family 20
  Thomas, earl of Worcester 88, 93
Perellós, Ramon 86 n. 77, 135, 157, 209, 215
Perrers, Edward 98, 103, 110, 177
Petit family 127
Petitioning:
  Chief governor and Irish council 32, 116,
    128–9, 145, 160
  presented to Irish parliament 124,
    191, 216
  king and English council 26, 46, 32–3, 63,
    90, 95, 104, 172, 185, 188, 189,
    201, 204
  presented to English parliament 102
Philippa, queen of England (d.1369) 36, 80
Philippa, countess of Ulster (d.1378), daughter
  of Lionel of Antwerp, wife of
  Edmund Mortimer 46, 69, 72
Philipstown 100, 146
Philipstown Nugent 142
Picardy 33, 80, 168
Pickering, James, chief justice 55–7, 60
Pigot, Bartholomew 73
Pigs 143, 164
Pilgrims/Pilgrimage to St Patrick's Purgatory 154,
  173, 203, 215; *see also* Holy Land;
  Rome; Santiago de Compostela
Pipard family 62
  Peter, sheriff 12, 16
Pisa, Council of 150
Plague, pestilence 40–2, 43, 50, 66, 70, 77,
  121, 130, 148, 164, 198, 215
Platin 34, 80, 100, 110, 174
Plunket family 10, 11, 12, 13, 19, 115, 127
  Barnabas 171
  Christopher 18–19, 87, 220
  Elizabeth 95
  John 9, 10, 68, 72, 197
  Richard 37, 49, 68, 69, 72–3
  Walter, sheriff, K.P. 10, 12, 14, 16, 17, 95, 108
Poer, Arnold 39 n. 90
  Eustace 35 n. 66, 39
Poitiers 33
Poley, Ralph 71
Port 144, 197, 198, 199
Porter, John 66 n. 100
Posswyk, John 200
Prene, John, archbishop of Armagh, *see* Armagh:
  archbishops of
  John, seneschal of Drogheda in Meath 154
  William 154 n. 140
Presentation, rights of 9–10, 143, 145–7, 157,
  164–6, 199 n. 110

Preston, Lancashire 39, 92, 170
Preston family 5, 6, 170, 177
  Sir Christopher 86–7, 91–2, 104,
    177 n. 131
    and John Talbot 113 n. 48, 114–15,
      116 n. 69, 117
  Richard, seneschal of Drogheda in Meath 28,
    38, 39
  Richard of Beybeg 164
  Sir Robert (d.1396) 13, 38 n. 85, 39, 47,
    48 n. 153, 49, 72, 91, 165, 168, 218
    and William Windsor 59, 65–9
  Roger (d. *c*.1350) 38
  William (d. *c*.1351) 38, 39
  William, sheriff of Drogheda 177
Primatestown 148
Prison/imprisonment 14, 56, 70, 84, 86, 94–5,
  98, 102, 111, 121, 126–7, 130, 164,
  169, 171, 189, 205–6, 207, 215–16
  of settlers by John Talbot 112, 114, 117, 179
  of settlers by William Windsor 57, 62, 63, 174
  see also Hostages/hostage-taking; Ransom
Pyrroun, William, archdeacon of Armagh 143

Ragg, Richard, archdeacon of Armagh 143
Ralph, count of Eu 34
Ransom 29, 59, 78, 94, 104, 111, 120, 122–3,
  205–7; *see also* Hostages/hostage-
  taking; Prison/imprisonment
Raphoe, bishop of 194, 195
Raskeagh 52, 100, 103, 108, 178, 202
Rath, Thomas 167
Rathbrist 14, 195
Rathcoul, John 186–7
Rathdrumin 63, 149, 151, 154, 170, 188,
  194, 198
Rathfeigh 27, 94
Rathmore 64, 220
Rathwire 27
Ratoath 35, 143
Rauf [Ralph, Fitz Ralph], John 35, 172
Rede:
  Michael 126
  Richard, chief baron of the exchequer 94–5
Repenteny family 5 n. 20, 12, 15
  John 9
  Peter, sheriff, K.P. 12, 17, 68 n. 119
Rice, Peter 73
Ricetown 174, 177, 205
Richard, abbot of Knock 196–7
Richard II (1377–99) 70, 71, 74, 98, 102, 113,
  137, 138, 148, 162, 171, 175–6,
  180, 191, 194, 200, 219
  in Ireland 82–95, 146, 157, 184–5, 202–3,
    209, 212, 215, 219
Richard, duke of York, earl of March and Ulster
  (d.1460) 121, 123, 129–31, 139,
  165, 181, 219
Robert I, king of Scotland (1306–29) 26

Robert III, king of Scotland (1390–1406) 102,
  104
Robes 156
Roche 8, 80, 100, 114, 117, 127, 130, 166,
  179, 202, 211
Roche, Pembrokeshire 91
Roche, John 40
  Laurence 200
Rochfort, John 87
Rogerstown 65
Rokeby, Thomas, justiciar 39, 44, 47, 61, 181
Rome 136–8, 143 n. 54, 150, 153
Ros, *see* Carrickmacross
Rose 9, 67
Ross, Richard 165
Roth, Roger, sheriff 15
  William 60
Rouen 110
Rowe, Walter 152
Ruffus, John 147
Rushbury, Geoffrey, sheriff 12, 15
Rushen, abbey of 169
Russell, Thomas 150
Rykard, John 208
Ryver, John 172

St Amand, Amaury 47, 65, 68
St Bernard of Clairvaux 43
St Leger, John 121
  William 121 n. 104
St Malachy 43
St Patrick's Purgatory, *see* Pilgrims/pilgrimage
Salisbury, bishop of 93
  earl of, *see* Montagu, William
Salt/salting 55, 60, 167, 177, 186
Sampford, Roger 151
Sander/Saundyr/Saunder, Henry 10, 199, 201
  Robert 208
Santiago de Compostela 136
Saunder/Saundyr *see* Sander/Saundyr/Saunder,
  Henry
Savage, Edmund, seneschal of Ulster 83,
  84, 203
Scargill, Thomas 96
Scotland/ Scots 135, 169
  kings of, *see* David II; Robert I; Robert III
  trade with 76, 101–2, 168–9, 185–6
  warfare against 11, 20, 26–7, 29–31, 37, 50,
    80, 94, 101, 104, 167, 175–6
  in Ireland 120, 125, 183–4; *see also*
    Galloglass
Scrope:
  Stephen, deputy lieutenant 93, 94, 95, 98,
    101, 103–4
  William, earl of Wiltshire (d.1399),
    justiciar 85, 88–90, 92, 93, 94,
    107 n. 1
Seal:
  of Aed Mór O'Neill 43 n. 131

Index 257

of Aed, son of Eógan O'Neill 129
of Brian MacMahon 122
of Drogheda guild of St Anne 160
of Domnall O'Hanlon 30
of Dundalk 114
Great Irish 91, 103, 122
of John Patristow 168
Privy, of England 99
'sealed charter' 119
of Thomas Wotton 169
Segrave, Stephen, archbishop of Armagh, see
    Armagh: archbishops of
Serle:
  Adam 169
  John 9
Serlestown 176
Sexton, Robert 60, 172, 176
Shannon, river 135
Sheep 164
Sherbourne (Schorbrun), John, prior of
    Louth 144, 197
Sheriff, office of 11–16, 216–18
Shrewsbury, earl of, see Talbot, John
Shropshire 2 n. 6, 111
Siddan 55, 56, 128, 189, 206
Siena, University of 137 n. 11
Simon, abbot of Knock 143
Singleton, John 185
Skinner, Thomas 60, 177
Skreen 92, 94
  baron of, see Mareward, Thomas
Skreen, Thomas 19
Skrene, Christine 171
  William 170
Slane 38, 46, 113 n. 48, 127
  baron of, see Fleming: Christopher, Simon,
    Thomas
  barony of 113, 125, 209
Sligo 117, 215 n. 27
Smarmore 145, 148, 201
Somerset 102
Somerwell, William 151, 152
Southampton 20
Spain/Spanish 38, 76, 102, 160, 167–8, 176
Spicer, Richard 170, 177
Stabannan 33, 68, 143, 149–50, 151–2, 192,
    195, 198
Staffordshire 2 n. 6, 28, 92 n. 115, 98,
    111 n. 30
Stameen 28, 38, 67
Stameen, John 174–5
Stanihurst, Henry, second chamberlain of the
    exchequer 103–4
Stanley:
  Alice 18
  John, burgess of Drogheda 9, 14
  John (d.1414), justiciar and lieutenant
    78–9, 92, 93, 94, 107, 110, 114,
    180, 181

Richard 9
Thomas, lieutenant 126–7, 139
Thomas, sheriff 15
Starkey, Matilda 67
  Nicholas 67, 69, 170
Staunton:
  James 149
  Nicholas, prior of St Mary's, Louth 143
Stokes family 18, 36
  Alice 189 n. 37
  Elizabeth 189 n. 37
  William 217
Stone, William 89
Stonehouse 188
Stonetown 211
Strange, Thomas, treasurer 126, 139
Strangford Lough 101
Stranraer 102
Strode, John 151
Stynt, Sir Thomas 121
Styward, John 165–6
Suerbeer, Albrecht, archbishop of Armagh, see
    Armagh: archbishops of
Suffolk 2, 36, 171
  earl of, see Ufford, Robert
Sugley, John 189
Surrey, duke of, see Holland, Thomas
Sussex 2, 3, 9 n. 49
Swayne, John, archbishop of Armagh, see
    Armagh: archbishops of
  Joneta 154
  Richard 154 n. 139
  Robert 154 n. 139
  Roger 154 n. 139
  Thomas 154 n. 139
  William 154
Sweteman, Maurice, archdeacon of
    Armagh 79, 153
  Milo, archbishop of Armagh, see Armagh:
    archbishops of
  Robert 153–4
Symcock, Agnes 160
  John 176
  William, seneschal of Drogheda in Meath,
    mayor of Drogheda 76, 160, 165,
    167, 175–6, 177, 188

Taaf family 11, 12, 18, 115, 128, 210
  Joan 93, 103
  John [several], sheriff, K.P.
    1370s 14, 15, 16, 17
    fifteenth century 9, 194, 211
    of Castlelumny, K.P 17
    rector of Castlerickard 200 n. 119
  Laurence 157 n. 158
  Sir Nicholas, serjeant of Meath, sheriff,
    K.P. 10, 14, 16, 17, 18, 116, 122–3,
    127, 190, 201, 214
  Patricia 18

Taaf family (*cont.*)
   Richard, sheriff 1270s–1310s 15, 17 n. 2
   of Braganstown, sheriff, K.P., 1330s–1360s
      10 n. 55, 14, 15, 17, 18, 218
   of Castlelumny 11
   of Liscartan 11
Talbot family 12
   John, Lord Furnival, earl of Shrewsbury and
      Waterford, lieutenant 21, 110– 23,
      129–30, 140, 179, 181, 206
   Richard, brother of John, archbishop of
      Dublin, justiciar 118–19, 120,
      127–9, 139, 181
   Thomas, brother of John, seneschal of Trim,
      deputy lieutenant 114, 119–20
   Thomas, sheriff, K.P. 16, 17, 18, 156–7, 209
   of Malahide
      1350s 169
      1460s 211
Tallaght 139, 157 n. 158
Tanner family of Dundalk 12
   John 89
   Matthew elder and younger, sheriffs 12, 14,
      16, 17, 165, 178
   Richard 162, 167
   Walter 89
Tany, William, prior of Kilmainham, chief
   governor 69, 145 n. 68
Tarragona 135
Taylor:
   John 166
   Margery 178
   Walter 177
'Tege of Trim' 127
Teeling family 12, 36, 127, 189
   George, sheriff, K.P. 16, 17, 55–6, 189, 206
   John, chaplain 33, 68, 151
   John 103, 219–20
   Philip 56 n. 26
   Stephen of Drogheda 171
   Thomas 56
   Walter, 'captain of his nation' 55–6, 189
Templars 114 n. 53, 144
Templetown 144
Terling, Essex 171
Termonfeckin 9, 70 n. 133, 96, 173, 208
   Irish inhabitants in 191–2, 194–5, 200–1
   manor of the archbishops of Armagh 9, 64,
      125, 130, 146–7, 150–5, 171,
      196–8
   convent of St Mary's at 146
   Dowdalls of, *see* Dowdall, John of Newtown
Testaments, *see* Wills
Thomas, duke of Gloucester (d.1397) 89
Thomas of Lancaster, duke of Clarence,
   lieutenant (d.1421) 7, 93–6, 98–9,
   101–3, 105, 107–8, 113, 152,
   180, 219
Thorleston, Stephen 206

Thorndon, Giles, treasurer 163
Tipperary 58
Tregury, Michael, archbishop of Dublin
   (1449–71) 141
Trent, river 29
Trim 4, 44, 46, 56, 57, 71, 78, 82, 86 n. 77,
   90–1, 94, 98–9, 110, 118, 129–30,
   140, 153, 188, 200 n. 199,
   219 n. 50
   meetings of king's Irish council at
      1382: 74 n. 164
      1391: 139
      1392 and 1393: 81
   castle of 26, 66, 70, 84, 86 n. 77, 108, 114,
      117, 121, 122 n. 107, 189, 209,
      215–16
   Dominican friary 108 n. 4
   liberty of 11, 20, 47, 51, 73, 83,
      93, 102–3
   lord of, *see* Mortimer: Edmund, Roger;
      Richard, duke of York
   officers of 12 n. 68, 33, 48, 49, 51,
      69–73, 119–20, 213
Troy, John, treasurer 56 n. 27
Tuarastal 190
Tutbury, Staffs 98
Tuyt family 127
   Joan 19; *see also* Cusack, Walter
Tyburn 25
Tynbegh, William, under-treasurer of the
   exchequer 113
Tynedale 178 n. 139

Ufford
   Ralph, justiciar (d.1346) 26, 32
   Robert, earl of Suffolk 32, 35–6
Uí Echach 70, 83
Ulster 32, 43, 46, 69–71, 73, 78, 83, 89, 91,
   100, 104, 107, 111, 117, 145,
   179, 219
   earls and countesses of , *see* Burgh: Elizabeth,
      Richard, William; Holland, Eleanor;
      Lionel of Antwerp; Maud of
      Lancaster; Mortimer: Edmund,
      Roger; Philippa; Richard, duke of
      York
   Irish of, 5, 8, 20, 31, 44–5, 50, 51, 53–4, 62,
      64, 76–7, 79, 82–6, 93, 95–6,
      108–9, 115, 119–22, 126–7, 130–1,
      152, 208, 211–14
      settled in Louth 192–5
   liberty/lordship of 20, 70, 92
   officers of, *see* Brugge, Walter; Hyde,
      James; Maryman, John; Savage,
      Edmund; White: Geoffrey, James
   trade with 76, 167–8, 169, 176, 188, 190
      see also Bonnacht
Urban IV, pope (d.1264) 140, 141
Usk 71

Index

Verdon family 8, 10–12, 20 n. 101, 34, 47, 48, 50, 61–2, 98, 111, 113–4, 166, 177, 184, 209
  Alice 19
  Anna, daughter of Thomas 18, 65
  Bartholomew (d.1427), son of Richard, K.P., M.P. 12, 14, 17, 65, 92, 94, 95, 122–3, 157
    role in murder of John Dowdall 96–101, 115
  Christopher, son of James Jr 18, 116
  Elizabeth (d.1360) 29, 34, 181
  Isabel (d.1349) 29, 47
  James (d.1383), son of Milo, K.P. 13, 17, 18, 53, 64
  James (d.1412), son of James 18, 65, 95
  James 212
  Joan (d.1335) 34–5
  John, of Staffordshire 92 n. 115
  Margaret (d.1377) 34, 61
  Matilda, daughter of Thomas 18, 65
  Milo, K.P. 11, 12, 17, 27, 29, 30, 33 n. 50, 38 n. 82
  Nicholas (d.1347), K.P. 11, 12, 17, 27–31, 33, 63, 97, 165, 178
  Nicholas of London 171
  Richard (d.1383), son of Milo, K.P. 12, 13, 14, 17, 18, 64, 144
  Robert 97
  Theobald (d.1316) 18, 25, 27, 28, 30, 35
  Thomas (d.1375) son on Nicholas 18, 35, 53, 92, 115–16
    confrontation with Archbishop Sweteman 9, 63–5, 155
  Thomas 214
  William 64
Verdon rebellion of 1312 26, 44 n. 123, 56 n. 26
'Verdonsgame' 96–7
Vere, Robert, earl of Oxford, marquis of Dublin, duke of Ireland 91, 175
Vernon, Richard 14, 57
Virley, John 50 n. 159

Wales/Welsh 25, 66, 71, 82, 85, 90, 98–9, 169
  March of, *see* March of Wales
  see also Llanthony in Wales
Waley, Thomas 18
Wallonia 135
Walsh:
  John 60, 216
  Milo 188
  Roger 188
  Thomas 187–8
Walton, Thomas 102
Walys, William 170
Wardship 34–6, 54, 66, 90, 92, 113
Ware, Sir James 5
Waring, Andrew 149
Warwickshire 2, 10 n. 61
Watermills, *see* Mills
Waterford 20, 41, 59, 82, 85, 167, 169
  and Lismore, bishop of 88
Wax 9, 163
Weirs 146; *see also* Fish, fishermen, fisheries, fishing
Westmeath 51, 82, 111
Westminster 5 n. 22, 37, 50, 56, 59, 61, 85, 88, 95, 114–15, 172
Weston, John 205
Wexford 112
White family 11, 12, 18, 112, 128, 209
  Alice, wife of Rudraige MacMahon 124, 128, 208
  Christopher 98–100
  Geoffrey (d.1392), sheriff, K.P. 13, 14, 17, 178
    dealings with the Irish of Ulster 45, 53, 77–8, 80, 91, 109
  Isabel 170
  James, sheriff, K.P. 8, 16, 17, 91, 109, 119, 122, 123, 125, 178, 208
    and the murder of John Dowdall 97–101
  Joan, wife of Peter Dowdall 112, 129, 131
  John, sheriff of Ulster, K.P. 17, 72
    burgess of Drogheda 11
    burgess of Dundalk 216
    of Dublin 154
    cleric 200 n. 112
    of Carlingford 206
  Nicholas, bailiff of Drogheda 172 n. 96
  Richard 156–7
    chief justice of the justiciar's bench 49, 69
    prior of Kilmainham, justiciar 145 n. 68
    of Kilmoon 152, 199
    mayor of Drogheda in Louth 172
  Robert, merchant of Drogheda 102
  Stephen, merchant of Drogheda 170
  Thomas 96, 136 n. 8
Whitehead, John 149–50
Wigmore 71
Wildegryce, Thomas 177
Wills, testaments and executors thereof 37 n. 77, 68 n. 117, 71, 73, 152, 159, 162, 165, 187, 200
William, prior of Louth 197
Wiltshire, earl of, *see* Scrope, William
Windmills, *see* Mills
Windsor, William, justiciar 21, 34, 89 n. 89, 91, 142, 149, 180, 195
  dealings with settlers of Louth and Meath 14, 50–69, 72, 74, 173–8, 218–19
Wine 76, 113, 129, 153, 163, 167–70, 176, 186, 188
Wogan, Elizabeth 19

Woodman, Simon 13
Worcester, earl of, *see* Percy, Thomas
Wotton
  Thomas 179, 189
  Walter 189

Yonge, James 118
York 72
  archbishop/archbishopric of 88, 142
  duke of, *see* Richard, duke of York
  see also Parliament